THE
Private Life
of
KIM PHILBY

THE
Private Life
of
KIM PHILBY
The Moscow Years

RUFINA PHILBY,
Mikhail Lyubimov
and
Hayden Peake

FROMM INTERNATIONAL
NEW YORK

Library
University of Texas
at San Antonio

First Fromm International hardcover, 2000

Library of Congress Cataloging-in-Publication Data
Philby, Rufina, 1932-
      The private life of Kim Philby : the Moscow years / Rufina Philby,
Mikhail Lyubimov, and Hayden Peake.
        p. cm.
      Includes bibliographical references and index.
      ISBN 0-88-064-219-X
      1. Philby, Kim, 1912- 2. Spies—Soviet Union—Biography. 3. Filbi,
Rufina, 1932-4. Espionage, Soviet—Great Britain—History—20th century.
I. Lyubimov, Mikhail. II. Peake, Hayden B., 1932- III. Title.
UB271.R92 P4324 2000
327.1247'041'092—dc21
[B]
                                                        00-025117

10 9 8 7 6 5 4 3 2 1
Manufactured in the United States of America

Contents

Contents

Illustrations

Illustrations

In the Memory Room, the name for the KGB/SVR museum of honour at the headquarters of the then Foreign Intelligence Directorate at Yasenevo, the day Philby delivered his speech to the assembled KGB officers, July 1977.

In Semenovo, near Sofia, Bulgaria, 1979.

On a rainy day in Dresden, East Germany, 1981.

Kim Philby addressing the HVA (Hauptverwaltung Aufklarung), the GDR foreign intelligence service, East Germany, 14 August 1981.

Philby with Markus Wolf during his August 1981 visit to East Germany.

At home with the family.

'Womaniser' Kim in Berlin, 1981.

The entrance to Philby's apartment building.

The view from a window in Philby's Moscow flat with one of Stalin's '7 sisters' in the background.

The inside view of the main entrance to Philby's flat.

The clock presented to Kim Philby by Yuri Kobaladze and Michael Bogdanov – members of the first class of KGB officer-students he tutored prior to their assignment to an English-speaking country.

The print that arrived in the mail unannounced and unattributed in the 1970s. Philby determined that it had come from Sir Anthony Blunt.

Philby's living-room with the Burgess wing-back chair to the left in which he sat when reading and entertaining.

The entrance hallway to Philby's flat taken from the main door.

Rufina in Kim's study.

Philby at his dacha near Moscow, c. 1985.

In Riga, during the filming of a documentary about the work of Soviet counter-intelligence in Latvia at the outbreak of the Second World War.

Grandpa Kim with granddaughter Charlotte, her father John, and Rufina's mother, Victoria Poukhova.

The table given to Philby by former wartime SIS colleague and antique dealer, Tommy Harris.

Genrikh Borovik, Kim, Rufina and Graham Greene at a party in Borovik's Moscow apartment, 1987 (*courtesy Genrikh Borovik*).

Illustrations

Rufina says goodbye to Kim at the memorial service held at Kuntsevo Cemetry, Moscow, 1988.

Philby is carried in the traditional Russian fashion to his grave at Kuntsevo Cemetery.

Rufina in her husband's favourite reading chair that once belonged to his Cambridge classmate and fellow KGB agent, Guy Burgess.

Introduction

by Hayden Peake

Kim Philby – Soviet hero and British traitor – has been the subject of numerous books, articles and television dramas over the last thirty years. What more, one might reasonably ask, is there left to say about this KGB agent – the notorious *Third* Man – who dedicated his adult life to the success of Communism?

A good deal, it turns out. His own memoirs, *My Silent War*, published in 1968 and written during his first four years in the Soviet Union, said little about his early life in Britain, almost nothing about his days in his adopted country, and were intriguingly imprecise on the details of his recruitment and defection. Only occasional brief glimpses of Philby's Moscow life surfaced from contacts with the few journalists and authors approved by his KGB masters.

Now that the restrictions of KGB security, Soviet politics and Philby's innate resolute insularity have been removed, his Russian wife of eighteen years reveals their life together behind the Iron Curtain. In this book, Rufina Philby provides an amazingly candid treatment of how she helped her husband fight his lifetime battle with the bottle and his struggle with depression resulting from the naive expectations he cherished about his future with the KGB. She tells us too of her

1

own all-too-typical life of struggle and survival during the Second World War, of her battle with cancer, and how she met and married the famous Cambridge spy. We learn about their domestic life, Philby's passion for cooking, the BBC and *The Times*, their travels, their friends, the visits by Graham Greene, and the constant often irritating but also helpful supervision of his KGB masters. In his Moscow years Kim Philby was no cheerleader for Communism and yet he stayed the course chosen on graduation from Cambridge. This is a chronicle of a husband's final years that only a devoted wife could write.

There are, of course, details of Philby's Moscow existence and his earlier experiences about which even Rufina was unaware. Several steps have been taken to at least partially fill these gaps with this book. To this end, four chapters of Philby's memoirs are published here in full for the first time. Drafted in part for *My Silent War*, Philby added more after he met Rufina, but never finished the intended second volume.

Although it is true that Philby did not discuss his work with the KGB, one document (untitled and undated) was found after his death that gives an indication of the contribution he made. Now titled 'Should Agents Confess?', it gives in some detail Philby's unequivocal views on the matter.

In July 1977, at Yasenevo, the headquarters of the First Chief Directorate (Foreign Intelligence), Philby gave what turned out to be his only presentation to an auditorium filled with his KGB colleagues. It was not without his characteristic subtle humour, though he did not forget to genuflect to the Communist Party, the founder of the KGB, Felix Dzerzhinsky, and even the fortieth anniversary of the Soviet football team. It is in this article, published here in English for the first time, that one gets closest to the reasons why he willingly joined the Communist movement and how he went about it.

Colonel Mikhail Lyubimov, KGB [ret.], was one of Philby's favourite colleagues. They met in 1975 and were in periodic contact thereafter. Now a successful novelist and an impish satirist when reminiscing about his service in London, Lyubimov has contributed his unique views on Philby in a piece titled 'A Martyr to Dogma'. It is here that the reader gains new insight into Philby – the old Bolshevik and latter-day dissident – and his Moscow years viewed from the KGB perspective: the hero, not the traitor.

The final section of the book contains an analysis of the Philby literature and a chronology. The latter provides a convenient summary of Philby's life and career. The former – based in part on interviews with several of the authors and some of Philby's former colleagues in Moscow, Britain and the United States – looks at what has been written about Philby the man – the myths, the outrageous claims and the realities – with attention to the early years in Moscow not covered elsewhere. Of particular interest is his role as teacher to young KGB officers bound for English-speaking countries. It was a task he enjoyed and for which he is fondly remembered by his former students.

The Private Life of Kim Philby: The Moscow Years is a story of betrayal and dedication, of an Englishman in Russia, of dreams unfulfilled, and of a Jurassic spook who earned a place in history and burial in the Kuntsevo cemetery.

Part 1

Kim Philby: The Moscow Years

by Rufina Philby

Translated by Geoffrey Elliott

Foreword

by Michael Bogdanov

They say that everyone has at least one book in them, if only an autobiography. Perhaps not an entire book, but at least some distinct and striking story taken directly from experience, something that will never be repeated, something that will therefore add materially to the sum total of human experience.

To my regret, I did not write the book you are about to read. But I was close to the story it tells, I was a part of it, and I wanted to make a contribution towards turning the idea into reality.

By any measure, Kim Philby was a remarkable man. In our country he was of course quite rightly renowned as a legendary intelligence officer. But strange as it may seem, he is also regarded as something of a folk hero in Britain as well. Certainly some people there regard him as despicable. Others condemn him. But it has been my impression that on the whole the British regard him with respect and even a touch of pride, reckoning that only an Englishman could demonstrate such exceptional talents.

Kim Philby has been the subject of reams of books, some investigative, some biographical, some works of fiction. But most of them deal with the middle period of his life, when he worked for Soviet

7

intelligence as an 'agent in place'. Ignoring the flights of fancy of Western fiction writers, very little is actually known about what the former Head of British Soviet counter-intelligence actually got up to after he had crossed the Soviet border for ever on 27 January 1963 on his way to Moscow.

It is worth reminding ourselves that he spent twenty-five years – a third of his life – in the USSR. He did not just sit back and rest on his laurels. Far from it. He fell in love. He had times of sadness, and times of great happiness. He travelled. He made and lost friends. He worked. He created. He even established his own training school.

In Kim's last years, the name that was dearest to him was Rufa, his wife Rufina Ivanovna. Kim was a shrewd reader of people, and had Rufina's measure the first time he met her. Just a few days later, he proposed. He did absolutely the right thing. They were unusually well suited to one another, and their relationship gave Philby much happiness in his later years.

He literally worshipped his Rufina and was absolutely lost when she wasn't around. She was his 'light in yonder window', his guide, one might say, through the awkward realities of Soviet life, without whom it would have been difficult – perhaps simply impossible – for him to preserve the dignity and 'legendary' image implied by his position.

I myself met Rufina Ivanovna towards the end of Kim's life, and in his last years we became really good friends.

She is a fragile, delicate and very bright woman who hesitated for a long time before finally resolving to commit her innermost thoughts to paper. But when, finally, after much persuasion, she forced herself to record several parts of her story, I realised that a book about 'her Kim' simply had to be written. And not by an outsider, but by Rufina herself. She set about it with inspiration and total concentration, producing vivid and graphic portraits which shed light on hitherto unknown facets of Philby as a person, and which conveyed very clearly the atmosphere in which he lived.

Going through his files long after she had handed over to his KGB case officers everything dealing with the professional side of her husband's life, Rufina Ivanovna came across unique documents, photographs and comments scribbled in the margins of books. Her most important 'find' though was the manuscript of four sections of a book Kim never got around to finishing.

When we first looked at the manuscript, it was hard to work out when it had actually been written. Kim had kept even Rufina in the dark about what he was writing. But when we read it closely, a key phrase struck us: 'Two years ago in Sukhumi . . .'. This dated the material to 1971, or just a little later.

The files also held much interesting material which might be described as Philby's conceptual musings on the problems of intelligence work.

What a pity, then, that so much of this invaluable material, the thoughts of one of the twentieth-century's best intelligence operatives, was never put to good use.

Instead of being utilised, as it should, as the cornerstone of a curriculum for the training of young officers, this treasure trove of professional and human experience was kept under wraps for many years. This has prompted me to suggest incorporating into this volume a section dealing with Philby's professional life in Moscow.

The book thus falls into three parts:

1   Kim on his own. Kim writing about and analysing his roots.*

2   Kim as remembered by the person closest to him. Kim at home with his family. Kim without embellishments, legends or myths.

3   Kim at work in the service of the KGB. Kim the professional.**

I don't want to try to prejudge for you which of the 'three Philbys' most closely reflects the real man. All three are probably equally close to the mark. Certainly a man portrayed in his own home, retired, with the woman he loves by his side, is a man behaving totally naturally, without any artifice. Nor do we have the slightest reason to suspect Philby of duplicity when he presents himself clad in his official mantle as the legendary intelligence officer and 'unyielding fighter for the cause of

---

* Published in this English edition in Part 2, pages 203–43.
** See Part 2, pages 244–68.

Communism' (not counting little evasions and economies with the truth in the interests of tradecraft). Any of his colleagues who were close to Kim during the final third of his life will readily vouch for this.

And this straightforwardness becomes even more evident when we come to his memoirs, which he obviously did not intend to be published during his lifetime.

In a nutshell, this book portrays a man of different faces. A man who was powerful, strong-willed, but at the same time someone of exceptional integrity.

To my mind, *integrity* is the key to the Philby puzzle. Though I make no claim to have the final word in the efforts which have been made for so many years to try to define his role in a historical context, let me try to explain what I mean.

'A cynical traitor or a man of conviction' is the question asked in bold type on the cover of the British edition of his book, *My Silent War*. The question reflects the two diametrically opposed views of him. The first description would be supported by a wounded British Establishment which even now cannot bring itself to understand how something like this could have happened, how 'one of us' (or 'several of us', if you take the whole of the famous Cambridge Ring of Five) could betray the Establishment's interests, their ties to it through school and university, by serving the 'bloody dictator', Stalin. This created yet another set of worries about whether there was also an 'Oxford Ring of Five', and led to an exaggerated view of the influence of Soviet Intelligence on British political life, and finally to the search for further 'skeletons in the cupboard' in the highest echelons of Whitehall, a search which continues even today.

The 'man of convictions' label has a slight tinge of cynicism about it. By diligently exploiting the unassailably positive image that the phrase conjures up, the Soviet propaganda machine sought to imply that Philby's sincere (and, we should add, extremely idealistic) Communist convictions meant an endorsement of everything that went on in those years – the crimes that were committed, the disgraceful acts so brazenly perpetrated 'in the name of a radiant future'. It would thus follow, by Soviet logic, that once Kim had adopted the USSR as his Motherland, he was duty bound to approve whatever policy its leaders – be they Stalin, Khrushchev, Brezhnev or Gorbachev – laid down.

The simple question of just 'who' and 'what' the 'cynical traitor'

Philby betrayed deserves close scrutiny. Even historians of British intelligence are compelled to concede that Philby put not a single British life at risk in what he did. To the end of his days, Philby himself remained an Englishman to his fingertips in his habits, his manners and his way of thinking, and in that sense was probably not all that different from his many fellow-countrymen who spent most of their lives, for example, in India or Africa.

What does 'treachery' really mean? Most people would say going over to the enemy camp, renouncing one's beliefs or convictions (one dictionary defines a traitor as 'someone who breaks their word', or 'a man who sells out').

But Philby did nothing of the sort! Once, and only once in his life, just a few months after his twentieth birthday, Philby swore to be true to the ideals of Communism, an oath he never betrayed.

These unpublished chapters of his life provide an opportunity to learn in Philby's own words how his view of the world was shaped from his early childhood. When and why he became an atheist, an anti-imperialist, a Socialist, then a committed Communist and finally a Soviet intelligence agent. The logic of this metamorphosis, especially the final stage, is laid out with exceptional clarity. It also emphasises clearly another of Kim's extraordinary qualities – he was always a *man of action*. Once he had chosen the path he wished to follow, he did everything in his power to make sure that path led to concrete results.

You might well ask at this point whether Philby was somehow blind to the 'flaws' – to use the mildest description – in the cause for which he fought. To this I would venture to comment that even the average Russian became aware of the criminal nature of the Stalinist regime only in the mid-1950s. And it wasn't until the early 1990s that an overall picture really emerged of what Communist doctrine had really meant – in practice rather than in theory, since there is nothing inherently reprehensible in the actual notions of equality, social justice and the like. They are, after all, noble and eternal. There were, of course, intellectuals in Britain and other Western countries (Orwell, D. Healey and others) who saw through the falsehood of Soviet Communism 'in good time' and renounced it. But what do you do, if you are 'deeply under cover', if you have no idea about the realities of Soviet life, and if you are bound by your word of honour, freely given a long time back, and if you are a man who has already made a major contribution to the cause of defending the USSR from Fascism? All the more if you are a man who sees day by day at first hand the techniques, just as dirty as the USSR's, employed by Western intelligence services in their bid to undermine the USSR and curtail Soviet influence in the world?

I apologise for this spirited monologue in Philby's defence. Maybe he didn't need it. Perhaps I have misread his motives. But I do want to highlight the *internal tragedy* of a man who was, I am utterly convinced, transparently honest and decent.

Behind a façade of bonhomie, Philby's relationships with the KGB's top brass were mixed, as the perceptive reader will sense. Yes, he was accorded the 'highest level' of official respect, culminating in the grandiose requiem ceremony at the KGB's Dzerzhinsky Central Club. True, he was on good terms with Andropov, then head of the KGB, he was in touch with Kryuchkov, then head of the intelligence division, and he was personally friendly with many KGB people at all levels, from senior directors to young field officers.

But there was another side to it. For example, even while Philby was still active, some sixth sense told him that practically all his Soviet case officers had been purged. When he finally reached Moscow, he had to come to terms with the fact that the KGB seemed not to have the slightest understanding of his real value as a unique source of information on the Western intelligence services. And there was a time in the 1980s when the young students of the 'Philby Seminar' were told not to have anything more to do with their Teacher. It was claimed that in the opinion of 'Senior Management', Philby had 'turned into a dissident', was criticising Soviet life and might even be seeking to leave for the West. To cap it all, there were some KGB people who treated Kim in ways that ranged from professionally illiterate to frankly unforgivable.

I do not need to dwell on the effects of day-to-day existence in the USSR on an Englishman used to a comfortable Western style of life. No one can describe that better than Rufina Ivanovna. I do no more than note that Kim faced this ordeal too with dignity, thanks in large part, I suggest, to the support of his devoted Rufina. The public, and even close friends, saw only the 'legendary', 'unyielding' Philby – his real problems were kept hidden from view.

As an observer of the Philby phenomenon for over thirteen years,

I used to ask myself why most of the Englishmen I met thought of the man with respect, and even with some pride, notwithstanding the facts. I came to the conclusion that in all likelihood the British saw in Philby the personification of everything they had been taught from their mother's knee to associate with the essential make-up of their national character, with whatever it is that makes a Brit a Brit. Perhaps at the heart of it is the integrity I referred to earlier, the innate sense of self-worth which prevents the British from compromising their beliefs, come what may. The pride that stops them turning traitor, resiling from a path they have deliberately chosen, a compulsion to finish whatever you start. Put another way, everything that is summed up in the famous British phrase, 'My word is my bond.'

We Russians have a phrase, 'From your earliest days, prize your honour above all else.' Although vilified by the British as 'once a traitor, always a traitor', Kim Philby always prized his honour above all else and never betrayed his beliefs. As we now know, it was not his beliefs which turned out to be false, but their practical manifestation, which is something completely different. When towards the end he came to realise this, Kim gradually faded away and departed this life.

'Regrets, I've had a few,
But then again, too few to mention,
I did what I had to do
And saw it through without exemption . . .'

From Frank Sinatra's 'My Way', Kim's favourite song

CHAPTER 1

Before Kim

I was born on 1 September 1932 in the heart of Moscow on Rozhdestvenka Street. That same year Kim, already committed to the cause that was to shape his life, became the treasurer of the Cambridge University Socialist Society. Or, as he used to say, 'By the time you were born, I had already started down the long road that would lead me to you.'

My father came from a farmer's family in Maloyaroslavets, the district centre of the Kaluga region. He had lived in Moscow since the age of ten, having been sent there by his parents to be an apprentice in the fur trade. He eventually became a leading expert in treating and dyeing furs.

My mother came from Sedlece in Poland, where her father had been a bank clerk. In 1914, when she was two, she moved with her family to Moscow. Her parents had tried to return when Poland regained its independence in the 1920s, but were denied permission to leave the Soviet Union. My grandfather died in 1933 and it was not until 1957 – a year before she died – that my grandmother finally managed to return to her home country.

I don't remember much about our first home. When I was just two, we moved to a flat in a new development of five-storey buildings on the outskirts of Moscow, rather aptly called, 'New Houses'. The old flat had been damp with only a wood stove. This one had steam central heating and even a bathroom, but no hot water.

My parents and I had a 12 square metre room in a flat shared with three other families. The room was dry and light, but not much wider than my school pencilbox. We used to amuse ourselves by rearranging the furniture, each time being convinced that we had carved out just a little more living space than before.

Each five-storey building was built around three sides of a large yard where there was plenty of room for children to play. Across the open end ran rows of washing lines on which fresh smelling sheets crackled in the frost.

I was eight when war broke out. At the time we happened to be staying in Tomilino, a little village outside Moscow, at a dacha belonging to one of my mother's friends. The 22nd of June is etched in my memory. The grown-ups were inside listening to the wireless and holding their breath. Suddenly they started to wail: 'It's war, we are at war . . .' I had no idea what it actually meant and could only think of those set-piece battles between heroes and villains so vividly pictured in my books of fairy stories. But one glimpse of the grown-ups' terrified, tear-streaked faces was enough to make me just as scared as they were.

My mother had been in Moscow running some errands. She obviously had no idea what the day was going to bring, and I ran to meet her at the train station. She seemed to take the awful news in her stride and, after calming me down, marched into the nearest grocers to buy flour, sugar, salt and matches.

My father dug a slit trench in the yard of the dacha, from which the trees had already been cleared, and fashioned seats out of narrow boards along each side. It served as a shelter for some ten people who lived in the dacha. I will always remember the smell of the damp clay earth and the whistle of the bombs. The big ones made a terrifying noise, just like a locomotive rumbling overhead.

That summer the air-raids were almost continuous. Night after cool night we scrambled into the dugout, packed tight along the uncomfortably angled benches. My parents would wrap me in blankets, which did little to keep out the bone-chilling damp.

16

The raids came in the day too, and I have vivid memories of one hot afternoon. The planes circled in the clear blue sky and the sirens wailed while my mother, seemingly oblivious, went on giving me a bath in a sun-warmed basin of water out in the yard. Then one night the anti-aircraft guns jolted me out of my sleep. Everyone else had managed to get to the shelter but my mother and I (Father was in Moscow) were trapped on the porch. Shrapnel rained down around us and it was too risky to run even the few yards to the shelter. Searchlight beams criss-crossed the sky and an anti-aircraft shell hit a plane trapped in their glare. Other shells burst like little stars. If it had not been so scary, it would have been almost beautiful. We had to spend the whole night out on the porch 'enjoying' the fireworks display.

Our family spent the whole war in Moscow as my parents did not want to be evacuated. The cellar of every apartment building was used as an air-raid shelter, but we never went down into ours, it just didn't seem safe. When the sirens split the night, my parents would get me dressed. Still half asleep, trembling with fright and teeth chattering, I always had time to dress my doll and never let go of her. All the neighbours used to sit in the hallways waiting for the all-clear. Our neighbourhood was bombed quite often as there were factories nearby.

I remember the general panic and the mass flight in mid-October 1941, when the Germans approached very close to Moscow. My parents did not lose their heads. My father even went to work that day only to find the place empty. The doors were wide open and not a sound came from the workshop, so he locked up and came home. My father spent his entire life working at the Rostokinsky fur complex. As an essential professional necessary for the trade, he was exempted from military service, though he had served in the Civil War in 1918–20. In time, the panic gradually ebbed and the people who had left the city returned to work.

Throughout the entire war I was only once in a Moscow shelter. It happened when my mother and I had gone to Gorky Street to get groceries on our ration cards (at the time everyone was allocated to a specific shop). The siren wailed. We began to rush across the street to the shop, but before we got halfway, a policeman grabbed us and dragged us to the nearest shelter, where we stayed until the all-clear sounded. When we emerged from the shelter, we saw only a huge bonfire where the grocer's shop had stood.

We had a large log stove in our kitchen. Since firewood was hard to come by, everyone in the apartment cooked on Primus and oil stoves. However, liquid fuel was also hard to come by. One day my father managed to get hold of some petrol. That night, by candle light, when everyone else was in bed, he and my mother began to decant the petrol into the Primus stove. Suddenly, my father's clothes caught fire, turning him into an instant fireball. Luckily he kept his head, ran out of the flat, down two flights of stairs, and rolled around in the snow outside to extinguish the flames. Fortunately, there was plenty of it and I do not think he was seriously burned.

My father set up a school at the complex to teach his trade secrets to younger workers. He dreamed of dressing me in a squirrel fur coat when I grew up, but things did not work out like that. He went through his entire career without managing to make a single fur for me or my mother. After he died in 1948, the complex gave furs to the whole family: sheepskin coats for mother and me, and a kidskin coat for my brother.

Before the war Mother had not worked, but once it started she had no choice. Her first job was making large nets out of thin cord. The nets were suspended from barrage balloons to snare low flying planes. In 1943, she was drafted to work in a military plant and she worked there as a welder until the end of the war. There was no public transportation in the city, no street lights, and all the windows were blacked out. Mother used to tell me how she would grope her way home in the pitch dark through the side streets and back alleys. It was a long walk that took about an hour and a half.

Food was a continual problem and Mother used to go to little villages outside Moscow, trudging through fields and woods, to barter household odds and ends for food. Looking back, I am surprised that even in those disturbed times, she was never attacked either out in the sticks or in night-time Moscow. Ironically, it was only well after the war, in 1949, that our flat was ransacked. And, in an unrelated incident, I was attacked in broad daylight while shopping. I had been at the bakery collecting our bread ration. Behind me in the queue was a plump girl who followed me out and began telling me a story while steering me up the street and into the entrance of her block of flats. As soon as we were inside, where it was dark, she ordered me to give her my bread and then grabbed my shopping bag. We struggled for what

18

seemed ages. She was bigger than me and looked stronger, but, in the end, I pulled the bag away and raced home. Even now I can remember her face and the dark birthmark on her cheek.

We never actually starved, but we were always hungry. Biscuits made of coarse bran were a rare treat. Looking back, I remember the sheer delight when our school served breakfast – a small piece of brown bread thinly spread with jam. Our teacher would bring the loaf into the classroom, cut it into paper-thin slices under our watchful eyes and then dole out half a piece to each.

Towards the end of the war the food situation improved and we started to get white rolls instead of brown bread. I used to swallow mine down in one gulp, but the girl who shared my desk would cut hers into small pieces, prolonging the pleasure by chewing each one slowly.

Early in 1946, my father was arrested and our room searched. I do not know the real reason for this, but I remember him saying that he had been denounced by someone at work mainly on the grounds that he was married to a Pole! He was lucky because he was released after three months without facing a trial. He came home from jail very thin, hunched over, and a broken man. He could not sleep, his ears always cocked for that ominous knock on the door. His personality changed beyond recognition; he was gloomy and introspective, and that is how I remember him. Still, in 1946, my brother Kostya was born, but two years later, in December 1948, my father died of lung cancer, aged forty-eight.

As the saying goes, misfortunes never come alone. Within six months, our room was robbed and everything stolen. The thieves even took linen and the hangers on which all our clothes had been. I remember opening the wardrobe and finding it completely bare.

In the autumn of 1949, I entered the Editorial and Publishing Trades School. My mother was very ill at the time and I also had to take complete responsibility for my little brother Kostya. Those were very difficult years for our family. Right after my seventeenth birthday, I got a job in a publishing house as a proofreader, while continuing my studies at night school. I would drop Kostya off at the kindergarten on my way to work and pick him up again in the evenings.

By the mid-1950s, my mother's health had improved a little and she went back to work. But she was often sick and earned much less than

I did, so I became the breadwinner, bearing a heavy load of family responsibilities. My years as a 'carefree youth' were actually pretty tough. This may be why the idea of getting married never crossed my mind. But I cannot claim that my life was all hard times. Somehow I did manage to get out to student parties and even have dates.

After my father died, we moved to another flat which we shared with three other families. It was less well equipped – smaller rooms, no bathroom, no hot water, we shared a toilet, and, perhaps most important, there was no telephone! – but it was in the centre of Moscow. Old and dilapidated, this three-storey building was said to have once been a monastery dormitory. This time our new room was not narrow, though it had the same number of square metres, but neither was it square. Being slightly out of kilter, it gave us even more scope for moving the furniture around, but the futility of that little diversion became evident when my maternal grandmother moved in with us after leaving her second husband and a twenty-year marriage. The room would hold a sofa and a bed. These now had to accommodate four people. Getting undressed and ready for bed was an experience best forgotten.

My grandmother and my mother never had an easy relationship. She could never forgive her daughter for marrying a '*kazap*', as the Poles and Ukrainians called the Russians, though she conceded that my father had his good points. When Kostya was born, she mellowed a bit and even allowed herself to be called 'Granny'. Up until then she insisted that I call her Aunt Martha.

Granny lived with us for three years before she left for Poland. In 1957, she managed to make contact with her large family in her homeland. All the brothers and sisters with whom she had lost touch when she emigrated to Russia in 1914 were still alive despite the war and occupation. She went to live with her younger sister in Warsaw, but it was too late for her dreams to come true. Warsaw, to her, was an unrecognisable foreign city and the grim reality of Poland bore no resemblance to the country whose images she had cherished for so many years.

In 1953, after graduating from the Technical School, I entered the Institute of Printing in the Editorial and Journalism Department. Unfortunately, in 1958, when I was in the final year and almost ready to graduate, I fell seriously ill. All the specialists agreed that I had lymphogranuloma, a form of cancer, and held out little hope of recovery. Radiotherapy was the main treatment: it nearly killed me. Only massive blood transfusions pulled me through. I was forced to take a year's sabbatical and did not graduate until 1960. Soon after I began to work as an editor.

The building we lived in had been in a very bad condition for years and we were afraid it would fall down around us. A heavy beam ran from the first-floor hall right through the stairwell to shore up the roof. We were hoping to be allocated a new flat, or more precisely a new room, since we did not qualify for a whole flat. In those years there was a quota for living space: 6 square metres per person. Families were allocated a flat or a room via the regional housing department or by authorities at work. In either case waiting lists were involved. Needless to say, it took many years for our turn to arrive, but when it did two of my colleagues from the trade union at work came to see me one day. Their job was to confirm that we were living in really bad conditions in order to justify my claim for a better flat. When they saw the beam, the broken staircase and the banisters leaning at an odd angle, one of them said to his colleague, 'You go ahead, I've got kids, you know.'

Despite these efforts, nothing came from the publishing house. We waited until 1968, and it was my illness that eventually entitled us to new living space. Even then it took three separate moves before we ended up in a two-room flat of some 28 square metres. This was the nicest thing that had ever happened to our family, something we had not dared to even dream of. When we moved in, I had my own room, though it was very small, about 9 square metres.

That same year also produced another happy event: my brother, who had been stationed in Czechoslovakia, made a 'hero's return' to Moscow after his military service. He had always been full of beans and a bit of a handful. As he grew up, he was known for his pranks, which gradually became rather dangerous, though mind you, compared with what the youngsters get up to these days, his games strike me as childishly innocent. Still one of his exploits could have ended badly.

One day as I was coming home late from work (my mother was in hospital), I noticed a man, clearly upset, waiting for me near the entrance to our building. It turned out that Kostya, who was ten at the time, had somehow got hold of an airgun with pellets and had been shooting at the building opposite from inside our porch. It turned out that he had hit and broken a window; luckily no one was hurt. These kinds of antics made it difficult for mother and me – mere women – to deal with him, and we were glad when, at eighteen, he was called up. We hoped that his army experiences would settle him down and provide him with a profession of some sort. He was posted to an armoured unit based in the Kaliningrad region and then, in 1968, he entered Prague on his tank. He was genuinely surprised when the Czech girls failed to toss flowers at the feet of the 'heroic liberators', as Soviet propaganda had led him to believe would happen.

My illness meant that I was always tired and I suffered frequent bouts of pleurisy and pneumonia. Despite these regular flare-ups, I continued my job and generally lived an ordinary, even normal life. I had friends and acquaintances, but only those who were exceptionally close knew I was ill. We would often go to the theatre, the cinema or an art exhibition. All this time the cancer specialists were urging me to give up work and have myself declared officially disabled, but I took no notice. The family was finding it hard enough to make ends meet as it was. Without my salary we would simply have been unable to cope.

It would be fair to say that I was not the most docile of patients, mainly because I would not believe I was really sick and refused to take the doctors' instructions seriously. I often missed appointments because, in their attempts to boost my morale, the doctors were fond of reminding me that a year, then two, had passed and I was still alive. While this was designed to make me feel better, it had the opposite effect. I remember one time I did allow myself a pang or two of self-pity. Back then Remarque's books were very popular in Russia, and I found myself envying the heroine of *Heaven Has No Favourites*. A young girl, facing imminent death from TB, decides she will spend whatever time she has left just having fun. She buys three smart frocks and sets about doing just that. I was in hospital when I read the book and could not help comparing myself to the heroine. The key difference was that while I too had little time left, or so I thought, unlike her I couldn't even buy one dress. But moods like that passed quickly and, as a rule, I refused to feel sorry for myself. In fact, the frivolous attitude to life that so annoyed my doctors was probably what helped pull me through.

My own battle with TB began during one of my regular bouts of pneumonia and I spent about two months under treatment in a special hospital. After I was released, though my health had improved significantly, I was just not able to cope with the workload at the publishing house and I started to look for a less demanding job. I found just what I had hoped for in mid-1969, when I became an editor at the Central Economic-Mathematical Institute (TsEMI). There, people did as much as they chose and few ripples ever disturbed the prevailing atmosphere of indolent tranquillity.

CHAPTER 2

The English Spy

Many of the economists who worked at TsEMI, for example N. Petrakov and S. Shatalin, later became quite well known. Conceivably, the relaxed atmosphere that persisted at the Institute brought out the best in them. It was the first time I had been in an office where most of the employees did not always turn up for work and where many of them did not have any specific job description. I was the 'odd girl out' on the staff since I actually had my hands full with some administrative assignments on top of my editorial responsibilities. Even then the workload was nothing compared to what it had been at the Higher School Publishing House. At that time, TsEMI did not have its own premises and its offices were housed in various buildings around Moscow. The head office and several other departments, including the one in which I worked, were located in what had once been a private house in the grounds of Neskuchny Gardens.

Among my new colleagues was a translator named Ida. One of her co-workers lost no time in telling me that she was having an affair with a foreigner, which, if true, was a serious offence at the time. Actually they were already married. Ida was often given work her bosses said was 'urgent', but since she had been at the Institute a long time and knew its ways, she was not above just shoving the papers in her drawer confident that their 'urgency' would soon be forgotten.

I, on the other hand, ploughed through my manuscripts conscientiously to the point where Ida would get cross with me for working so hard in an office where idleness ruled supreme. Sometimes she would snatch my work away, saying: 'You've done enough of that rubbish. Let's go for a walk,' and then drag me off into the nearby gardens. It was on one of these strolls that I first heard Kim Philby's name. Ida had already introduced me to her mysterious foreigner, George Blake. I asked no questions, but from one or two things she let drop I gathered George had been an intelligence agent. However, I hadn't the slightest idea of what he had actually been doing. I don't recall what caused her to mention Kim, but it was easy to guess that, like George, he too had been a secret agent working for the KGB. She told me he was an attractive man but with a weakness – a fondness for the bottle.

I recalled what Ida had said only when I actually met Kim after I had been with TsEMI for about a year. I got to know him by accident on a hot July day in 1970, when a touring American ice show was performing in Moscow. At the time, shows from abroad were rare and a big event. There were long queues for tickets, which were selling like hot cakes. Some had been allocated directly to arts groups and, as my mother worked at the House of Actors, Ida asked me to see if I could get hold of any tickets. I managed to buy four: one for myself, the others for Ida, George and his mother, or 'Mutter' as Ida called her, who was staying with them. The show was at the Luzhniki Sports Complex and I had agreed to meet Ida at the Sportivnaya metro station. Mutter was not too well and George had invited Kim in her place. Kim had his visiting son Tom with him on the off-chance of getting a spare seat at the door. So we all met at the station and it was there that I first laid eyes on Kim.

The sun was very bright and I was wearing dark glasses. 'Please take off your glasses. I'd like to see your eyes,' Kim said when we were introduced. I obligingly did so without thinking much of it. He made no special impression on me. I saw only an older man with a kind but rather flabby face. I never imagined at the time that this encounter was going to turn my life upside down!

Ida and I went ahead chatting. The men followed. Later Kim claimed that it had been right there, walking those few yards to the stadium, that he had decided to marry me. We often reminisced about that first meeting, and Kim always boasted about how prescient he had been. 'No flies on me,' he would say. When I tried to probe to discover just what he had seen in me, and from behind at that, he added with an enigmatic smile, 'If you could only see the way you walked.' He loved to tease me.

There were no tickets left, so Kim and Tom went home, inviting us to join them after the show for a glass of champagne. When it was over, Ida, George and I took the trolley bus into the centre of town. Before we got to the station near Kim's flat, I changed to the metro to go home, leaving them to drink the champagne without me, to their host's great disappointment, as I learned later.

Soon after that experience Ida invited me to spend the weekend at their dacha in Tomilino, the same village where, thirty years previously, I had been caught up by the war. I was surprised when Kim turned up with two large bags declaring that he was going to cook *coq au vin* for dinner. He had brought all the ingredients, including white mushrooms and vegetables, a saucepan and a frying pan. Needless to say, he had not forgotten the drink. Kim lorded it over the kitchen. Ida and I were not trusted to do anything more than wash and dry the mushrooms and vegetables. His *coq au vin* was a great success. We did not get up from the table until past midnight. By that time Ida, George and I were feeling sleepy. Kim and Mutter appeared unfazed and went on chatting as the rest of us went off to bed.

It was difficult to get to sleep with Kim and Mutter jabbering away non-stop just the other side of my bedroom wall. They were speaking English, which I could not understand very well at the time, but I did hear my name. Finally they called it a night.

As the house fell still, I heard a squeak and the door swung open slowly. In the pitch dark I could only make out a little red dot of light cautiously approaching my bed, like something out of a bad dream. The dot turned out to be the tip of Kim's cigarette. He lowered himself gingerly on to the edge of my bed and announced solemnly: 'I am an Englishman.'

'Yes, of course. You are a gentleman,' I replied.

'I am an *English* man,' he repeated stubbornly.

'That's wonderful,' I said, dredging the English words up from my sparse schoolgirl vocabulary. 'Tomorrow, tomorrow . . .'

That seemed to do the trick and he wandered slowly away, carefully closing the door behind him. He could hardly have had time to get back to his room before I heard the now familiar squeak of the door and the little red dot reappeared. We went through the same routine:

'I am an Englishman.'

'Tomorrow, tomorrow.'

Two seconds after he closed the door a second time, it swung open yet again.

Without waiting, I said 'tomorrow', doubling up with laughter. It reminded me of a loop of film replaying the same scene over and over. I thought it would never end and after the third or fourth apparition, I sat gazing apprehensively into the dark, but the Englishman had finally vanished. I fell asleep.

The next day after breakfast we went out for a drive through the forest. Sitting next to Kim in the car I looked at him out of the corner of my eye and noticed for the first time what an attractive man he was. He had a powerful, well-shaped head, a classic profile, thick silver-grey hair and bright blue eyes, with not a trace of a hangover on his freshly shaven cheeks. I was amazed at the transformation. Serious and smartly dressed, he bore no resemblance to the 'Englishman' of the night before, and even I found it hard to believe it had all really happened.

Kim did not say a word. I figured he was replaying the events of the previous evening in his mind and wondering what to say. When we stopped for a stroll, I picked a bluebell and gave it to him in an attempt to divert his attention from what I was sure were unpleasant memories. He was very touched. He held it carefully until we got back to the dacha and spent a long time looking for just the right vase to put it in. Sometime later when I reminded Kim of his nocturnal performance in Tomilino, he confessed that his only memory of the evening and the next morning was a nasty headache. So much for my feeling sorry for him.

Much of this second day of our visit was spent peacefully around the dacha. Kim tapped away briskly on a typewriter, editing the manuscript of George's memoirs, which were eventually published as *No Other Choice*. Later we went for a walk around the village, finding ourselves on the very same street where I had spent several childhood years. As Kim could understand some Russian and I some English, I told him how being there brought back vivid memories of the first day of the war. He was most impressed by the fact that my mother had not lost her head but quickly went to buy the essentials. Later on Kim liked to tell this story to other people, ticking off on his fingers, 'salt, sugar, matches . . .'

That evening Kim departed, explaining that he had been invited to go fishing on the Vologda river. He told me later that this turned out to be sheer torment rather than relaxation. He never even picked up a rod and had no opportunity to simply sit back and admire the scenery in peace. The normally glassy surface of the river had been whipped into a foam by motorboats roaring aimlessly about. (Kim could imitate the noise they made with uncanny precision.) And if he did manage to snatch a brief nap, some drunken fisherman would stumble into his tent hooting and hollering and waving the inevitable bottle. Kim claimed he did not get a moment's peace day or night. Since, for the English, fishing has been elevated almost to a sacred ritual, he could hardly be expected to know that in Russia the sport had become nothing more than an excuse for a booze-up. At that time, shops even sold vodka and brandy bottles specially packaged as 'sets for fishermen'.

Sometime after Tomilino, Ida invited me to her birthday party. There was only one other guest, a plump nice-looking woman. This was my first and last meeting with Melinda, Donald Maclean's wife. I had heard from Ida that Melinda had been having an affair with Kim, which was almost at an end, but I had not realised they had both been invited to the party. Kim, not wanting to find himself in an awkward position, failed to show up. In fact, neither his absence nor her presence made any impression on me.

A week or so later, Ida invited me to join her and George on a trip to Yaroslavl. Kim would also be coming, she added. Once again his participation was not the important factor in my accepting. I enjoyed travelling for its own sake and managed to get a week off from work. Much later Kim admitted he had actually arranged the trip so that he could see me again.

In the event, George drove his black Volga with Mutter sitting next to him. Kim, Ida and I sat in the back. It was a really nice trip. We spent time in some wonderful old towns: Pavlovskiy Posad, Yur'ev Polsky, Vladimir, Rostov, Velikly, Pereslavl Zalesskiy and Yaroslavl itself. Somewhere between Vladimir and Yaroslavl we went into a tiny abandoned church that, by the look of it, had been converted into some kind of club. I climbed up some wooden scaffolding to look at the frescoes when I lost my footing and went flying through the air. I remember being surprised that neither Englishman made any effort to catch me. They stood stock still, looking aghast. Kim said later that he was terrified that I was going to break my neck. But I managed a cat-like somersault in mid-air and hit the floor, damaging only my pride. That was the last time I was so lucky. Since then, whenever I have taken a tumble, even on the level ground, I have hurt myself badly.

Kim went on and on about my 'flight', as though it was some kind of miracle, though not in a religious sense. As a dyed-in-the-wool sceptic, he did not really believe in anything supernatural, but he did enjoy reminiscing about another miracle: his narrow escape during the Spanish Civil War. In that case, the car in which he was travelling with some journalist colleagues was hit by a Soviet artillery shell. Though during most of the trip Kim had sat in the right front seat, during a stop, something he could never explain made him go round to the opposite side of the car and get in the back. It was then that the shell exploded. When he told me the story, he drew a little sketch with arrows pointing out his movements. The shell struck near the front of the car on the side he had just left. All but Kim had been killed; he received a slight head wound.

In Yaroslavl, we stayed in a comfortable old hotel in the centre of town. In the middle of the night, I was wakened by someone knocking on the door and yelling, 'Open up!' At that time Soviet hotels had a concierge sitting sentry-like on each floor. I opened the door and our concierge rushed in, peered suspiciously around and looked in the bathroom, claiming that water was leaking into one of the rooms below. Then, finding no problem, she turned and left. I decided to take no notice and went back to sleep without wasting time trying to understand what had happened. But the next morning when I told the others about the incident, it turned out that Kim had been in the room directly below me. There had been no overflow. So what, or more likely whom, had the concierge been looking for? Most probably a man. These concierges worked for the KGB and operated as 'vigilantes', and this one obviously reckoned on catching me red-handed. In her eyes, a single woman, especially one who consorted with foreigners, had to be what she no doubt would have called 'a woman of easy virtue'.

The concierge was not the only person concerned about me. I was conscious from the start that Kim was rather single-minded on the subject. He was taut as a violin string, to the point where, instead of thinking myself lucky that here was a man who was in love with me, I found the whole thing rather hard to take. Though it was fun and interesting to be with him, I still did not feel the same way about him as he did about me. A middle-aged man with a puffy face was hardly the hero of my dreams. Kim accused the Blakes, quite unfairly, of trying not to leave us alone. Whereas I was trying to stay out of his way. Finally he lost patience. On our last day in Yaroslavl he grabbed my hand, sat me down on a bench in the park and said in Russian something like 'Cards on the table, I want to marry you.' I was too taken aback even to laugh at his broken Russian. He had obviously been rehearsing the phrases but could not cope with the Russian grammar or figure out which syllables to accentuate. (Later in our relationship he would do the same thing. Once he told me: 'I paying court at you because I love to you.' It sounded rather amusing in Russian and I did not always bother to correct him.)

Everything had happened so unexpectedly that I was speechless. Then Kim, having not grasped the reason for my confusion, decided that I had obviously not understood what he meant by 'cards on the table'. I lost my head completely and began to mutter something like 'impossible' and 'we hardly know each other'. But Kim's mind was already made up and he replied that he had had enough time to get to know me. He went on to say that he was in good shape physically and asked whether I wanted children. He was interested in my likes and dislikes, asking what kind of food I preferred. When I told him 'potatoes', he roared with laughter. He was delighted that I liked to travel and invited me to go with him to Siberia. It was very clear that he had thought the whole thing through and his mind was made up.

The situation struck me as laughable and I tried to turn it into a joke. But Kim remained serious and unshakeable. I then pled laziness, saying that I was a bad housekeeper and not in the best of health. But he remained supremely unaffected. Even a warning from Ida about my health had failed to deter him. Long before I met Kim I had told her in a moment of frankness that originally the doctors had diagnosed my case as terminal. That had been a long time ago and it was hard to decide whether they had been wrong or whether I had made a miraculous recovery. Years after we were married, Kim confessed that Ida had told him that I could drop dead at any moment. He had replied that this could happen to anyone.

Anyway, back in Yaroslavl, Kim said that he was not pressing for a quick answer. He said he wasn't a boy and could wait patiently for me to make up my mind. I decided to draw a line under this painful conversation and promised to think it over. When we returned to the hotel, he detained me for a second at the door to my room and asked, 'May I hope at least?' I nodded, not wanting to seem rude.

In bed, I tossed and turned until nearly daybreak, reliving other moments, half-remembered affairs, some fleeting, some that had drifted aimlessly along. Throughout my thirty-eight years of life I had always been pretty objective about myself and had long since concluded that my destiny was independence and solitude. But what if I were to decide to change my rather grey life? Could I, should I, just reject a proposal like this out of hand? But common sense still did not prevail and I finally dropped off to sleep convinced that to change the course of my life now was beyond my capacity. Moreover, as usual, I would probably make a hash of things, miss this last chance and then regret it for the rest of my life.

It was morning on the last day of the trip. I woke up in quite a good mood. Kim's proposal and my agonising over it had taken on an unreal dreamlike quality. Kim had got up very early and gone to the market to buy chrysanthemums for Ida, Mutter and me. On the way back to Moscow he asked me whether I had noticed anything special about the flowers. 'Of course,' I replied, 'they are very beautiful.' To his distress, I had missed the main point: my bouquet held eleven flowers, whereas the others only had ten. And me, the idiot, had not thought to count them. On top of this I had nearly left the flowers behind at the hotel. Ida reminded me at the last minute to take them.

Kim was very nervous during the journey, and when we stopped to stretch our legs, I saw him whispering to George – just like a schoolboy, though the day before he had insisted he was a grown-up. Kim told me later that George had reassured him that once I had let him pay my hotel bill, he could be sure of winning me over in the end. In Yaroslavl, Kim had insisted that I was his guest and said he would be deeply offended if I refused. George's analysis surprised him, but he was encouraged by the fact that George kept telling him, 'You're a lucky bloke.'

I sat next to Kim in the car and he took the opportunity to ask me to have lunch with him at the Metropole Hotel the following day. Then, as today, the Metropole boasted a fine restaurant; I accepted and closed my eyes feigning sleep. Afraid to wake me, he sat there hardly moving a muscle and shushed Ida when she started to read the guidebook aloud.

In Moscow, the car turned off the main road on to a street and stopped. 'George is tired,' said Ida. I said goodbye and dragged my suitcase over to the bus stop, thinking to myself, 'The ball is over, Cinderella.' At the bus stop I turned, waved and saw Kim looking puzzled. He did not realise that I lived two bus stops away, up the long street, from where they had dropped me.

While getting ready for our luncheon date I had the age-old problem: nothing to wear! I wasted a lot of time choosing between a suit and a dress, neither the least bit elegant.

I have always been late for dates, but this time my conscience pricked me just a little. He was, after all, an adult not a teenager. I was very late getting started and, convinced that he would not wait, briefly consoled myself with the thought that I could telephone and make my excuses. (Kim had given me his phone number on a scrap of paper in Yaroslavl.) But I thought better of it and though by now forty-five minutes late I rushed to the Metropole where I saw Kim in a light-weight navy suit and a snow-white shirt. The sun was hot and he was leaning against the wall, looking rather tired. When he spotted me, his face lit up in a happy smile and my heart melted. I think it was then that I began to feel about him as he did about me. I babbled something about having mixed up the time, but he just smiled.

Our table was in the famous dining-room with the fountain in the centre. During the meal Kim asked me if I had time to teach him Russian. I said that I did, and he promptly set about drawing up a timetable in a serious and businesslike way, but no lessons ensued.

I felt relaxed in his company and did not hesitate to accept when he asked me home for tea after lunch. His flat was only fifteen minutes' walk, and once there we sat in the kitchen, drinking tea and chatting. After tea, he brought out the brandy. I felt very much at home, as though I had been in his kitchen many times before. Kim even joked that he had only invited me to tea and here I was getting ready to stay for supper. We never got around to supper, even though we went on chatting until nightfall. Once again, Kim offered me his heart and his hand. By now his charm had me in its spell. I sensed his strength, self-assurance and reliability, coupled with an unusual delicacy of manner. This time his offer did not strike me as absurd, as it had in Yaroslavl, and I accepted. All this happened on 12 August 1970, a day which became very special for us both.

A few days later, Kim invited the Blakes and I to supper. There was another man there, his case officer Stanislav. (I shall deal with the subject of 'case officers' in a separate chapter below.) Kim solemnly presented me as 'mistress of the house' and then sat me down at the head of the table. My title was purely symbolic since he had cooked the entire meal, but I tried to live up to it by carrying the plates back to the kitchen after dinner.

I felt uncomfortable under Stanislav's piercing gaze as he inspected me in a cautious and unfriendly way befitting an 'outsider'. I had never had anything to do with the KGB and, as Stanislav later admitted, my turning up at Kim's was unexpected and undesirable. In contrast, Kim went out of his way the whole evening to underline the way he felt about me. At the end of the meal, I was greatly embarrassed when he presented me with a linen tablecloth which he had brought back from his trip to Vologda and a bottle of home-made blackcurrant juice.

From then on we began to see much more of each other, and soon Kim asked me to move in with him. But I was not ready to change the pattern of my life. Events were unfolding rather too quickly for my liking. So even though I had accepted Kim's proposal, I was determined to spend most of my time in my own flat. He did not pressure me and agreed to all my conditions. The agreement was short-lived; a month later I moved in with him. After that we paid only occasional visits to my old flat.

A few days after I had moved in, Kim phoned Stanislav and said he intended to marry me. Kim sounded tense but decisive, leaving no room for refusal. It was a *fait accompli*.

I took to my new life easily and naturally even though I still knew little English and Kim even less Russian. At the same time, the prospect of becoming even indirectly a member of the KGB 'family' was unappealing. As with so many people of my age, I had been terrified of the all-powerful NKVD/KGB almost from the day I was born, although

I had never come into contact with any of their people. Now, thanks to Kim, I got to know some of them – some high quality and interesting people. There were also some that were not so nice – all organisations are the same. And I have to admit that while joining the 'family' could hardly be said to have done me any harm, I could never forget that it was there in the background. At that stage of our relationship, the fact that Kim belonged in some way to the KGB made me a bit apprehensive. At the same time I was not in awe of him as a celebrity, partly because hero worship is not in my nature, but mainly because I simply had no idea who 'Philby' was. Until we met, I, like most of my fellow Russians, didn't know he even existed. From the time he arrived in the Soviet Union in 1963, he had always been surrounded by strict security. 'Philby' was as unknown in the Soviet Union as he was notorious in the West. It was not until 18 December 1967 that *Izvestiya* published an article under the heading, 'Hello, Comrade Philby,' the only article about him printed in the Soviet Union in his lifetime and one which I have never read. (In those days, it was very unusual for espionage matters to be written about.) When the article appeared, the paper received dozens of letters which they sent on to Kim. He had wanted to write via the paper to thank those who had written to him, but for some reason he could not get permission to do so.

Strictly speaking, the spy trade had no aura of romance for me. If anything, I was rather biased against it. When Kim proposed, I shared my hesitations with one of my girlfriends, who said, 'So what? We all like a good detective story.' As I got to know Kim better, my doubts faded. In my new home, sitting quietly by his side, I found it hard to imagine that this man had been a spy. Even as I learned more of his story, I was quite unable to reconcile the reality of this gentle, and sometimes helpless, person with the persistent myth of the legendary secret agent in so many histories and novels, most of them written by British authors. In addition to the books devoted entirely to Philby, which still take up a whole long shelf in his bookcase, the name of 'Kim Philby' often popped up in British newspapers and magazines, and he was often mentioned in thrillers which I later read in English.

The truth of the matter was that nothing at all was known about Kim's Moscow life and, consequently, wild and often contradictory stories sprang up about how he was being treated. At one moment Western commentators would claim that he was living in poverty, completely forgotten and rejected, while the next day they would allege that he was rolling in money and living in luxury.

On 26 November 1977, Kim wrote to his old friend, Erik de Mauny, for many years the BBC Moscow correspondent, describing what by then had become our routine of life in Moscow with annual trips to faraway sanatoriums:

> I understand that the [Alec] Guinness play is about my life in the SU [Soviet Union]. It is surprising that an actor of his standing should lend himself to an obvious fraud – obvious because nobody, not even my children, can know anything about it. Actually my year can be said to start somewhere around the middle of September, when all my colleagues are back from summer leave. I work steadily until mid-May, with a two-week break in Jan. or Feb. spent in a more southerly clime, in or out of the SU. Then, in mid-May we regularly spend the standard 24 days at a sanatorium in the Crimea. I'm afraid we occupy deluxe quarters (surely at my age that is permissible?), and the doctors now know that we are a couple of crazies who dislike medical attention. So they leave us alone to swan around in the gunboats of our Frontier Guard colleagues. Then back to Moscow for a few weeks of more sporadic work, depending on the presence or absence of colleagues. The late summer is spent in some friendly country, half by the waterside (sea, lake or river), half in the mountains. No nonsense about ropes and pitons; just gently putting one foot in front of another. Finally September when it starts all over again.
>
> . . . My personal feeling is that I have had enough exposure for the time being – not that I care much about that either way. More seriously, I resent the apparently unavoidable charge that everything I may say or write is dictated by my colleagues. Obviously there are things that I cannot, will not, discuss. But, leaded as I am with years, honour and embarrassing material wealth, I am quite experienced enough to decide for myself what can or cannot be discussed and, above all, how to discuss it. Whether you believe this is of course your own affair. But I have no reason to mislead old friends in whose integrity I trust. Misleading SOB's is another matter!

Kim himself, it need hardly be said, did not court publicity and refused most of the numerous approaches from Western journalists.

The one early instance when he was not upset by the attention he received concerned the publication of his book, My *Silent War*. Although written in Moscow in 1967, it appeared first in the West the next year. Ironically, it was published in ten other countries before the Russian edition finally appeared in 1980. Kim's KGB colleague and journalist, Stanislav Roschin, gave a detailed account of the trials and tribulations surrounding its publication in an article in *Soviet Youth Today*, a Russian-language newspaper in Riga. As he told his readers:

Philby took great pains writing his book. He did it entirely on his own, something that was very important to him. It was vital to him to tell the world about his mindset and his work. It should be noted that over six months or so before the book actually appeared [in the West] there were extensive press articles in the UK, as I recall in the *Observer* and the *Sunday Times*, representing the results of a whole year of journalistic digging into Philby, which yielded vast amounts of material on him.

Matters then took a rather dramatic turn. Britain has an unofficial Committee (the D Notice Committee) which does the same job as our censorship. The Committee Chairman simply called in the editors of the mass-circulation papers and told them in effect: 'Gentlemen, it would be undesirable if anything about [Philby's] book were to be published.' The Committee also banned publication of further serialisation articles. In an historic first, two papers rebelled and went ahead with their pieces. A little later, George Brown, then British Foreign Secretary, got himself into a lot of hot water over the book. When it became known that the book would be published in the US, but before it actually appeared, Brown spoke at a dinner for the newspaper proprietors where he told them officially that anyone who dared publish or distribute the book in the UK would be charged under the British Official Secrets Act.

In Moscow, long before Brown's speech, we had begun to think about a possible publisher in the UK as soon as the book was finished. I cannot recall whether it was the *Observer* or the *Sunday Times* which first offered to publish excerpts from it. We raised no objection. But a little while later, whoever it was, wrote to apologise that it would not, after all, be possible for them to publish. Via our own channels, we got in touch with a major French publishing house. Their representative came to Moscow, discussed terms and signed a contract with Kim. We sat back and waited . . . Suddenly, and to our complete surprise, the French told us that they had sold the rights to an American house.

But the most dramatic interference came from a totally unexpected quarter. When all our worries appeared to be behind us and there were only a few days to go before the book was to appear in the US bookstores, I was summoned to the bosses upstairs, quizzed about where things stood with the book, and then told abruptly: 'We've got to stop it.' This was a bolt from the blue, to put it mildly. They explained that at an international conference of Communist Party leaders in Budapest, the UK Party's General Secretary, John Gollan, had told Mikhail Suslov – then number two man in the USSR – that he had heard the book was about to appear in the US and that its publication would do serious damage to the UK Party. He asked for it to be stopped.

When he got back to Moscow, Suslov gave instructions to that effect, without bothering to look into the real reasons behind the book's publication. No one took the slightest notice of my arguments, which included the rather pertinent point that, had we cancelled, we would have been liable for sizeable damages for breach of contract.

After pondering the issue, I took a risky decision. I went back upstairs and told the powers that be that it was too late to do anything. The book had already been published. They all understood, of course only too well, that this was not true, but since in their heart of hearts they shared my feelings on the matter, I was told calmly, 'OK, that's what we'll tell Suslov.'

My Silent War was published as planned (in the West), even in the UK, in 1968 and was subsequently reprinted many times. In 1972,

Czechoslovakia also got ahead of the USSR. Preparing the introduction to this edition inspired Kim to start a new book. He told me one day, 'My second book will begin with your name.' Soon afterwards he showed me the first chapter. It covered his childhood memories and began, 'Rufina told me . . .'

But still the Russian edition of My Silent War was put off with various vague excuses. These delays damped Kim's creative ardour and the planned second book never got much beyond the first fifty pages. Only in 1978 was it decided to publish the book in Moscow. As usual, it suddenly became a rush job. I started editing the Russian translation, and we even postponed a trip we had planned to undertake. Then equally suddenly, the publishing process came to a grinding halt. We were told that the reason was the political situation, or, more precisely, the rather complicated relationship between the Soviet and British Communist Parties. This struck us as a little odd, given that the book had already been published in the UK and had by then been reprinted, not once, but many times. At the same time, objections began to be raised about the book's content. Philby was accused of what, under normal conditions, he might have reasonably been expected to be praised for: 'objectivism'. 'An objective point of view,' spluttered one of those involved in the decision whether or not to publish the book. The margins of the manuscript were sprinkled with similar comments. A Russian-language version of My Silent War finally saw the light of day in early 1980.*

---

* [For details of the Russian edition of My Silent War, see Lyubimov's comments on pp. 284–6.]

CHAPTER 3

Under the Microscope

From the beginning of our relationship, Kim's situation imposed changes on my life. The most difficult one was a consequence of the necessity for Kim to maintain a low profile which forced me to 'go underground' too. Before I moved to his flat, I had a big goodbye party for my old friends. I didn't tell Kim about it. (That was my first and only secret from him.) About fifteen people came on 1 September to celebrate my birthday in the traditional style, and no one suspected I was actually saying goodbye to them. I confided in only a handful of my closest friends, whom I later introduced to Kim and who became our regular visitors. I had to cut myself off completely from all the other people I knew who were left wondering why. I was not allowed to tell them my husband's name, nor give them our new address. Some went on trying to seek me out, others just felt hurt. Although this constraint changed as time went on, the only exceptions at first were a couple of my oldest friends.

Stretching a bit, I could draw a parallel between what happened to me and Kim's loss of his friends, which he describes in his biographical notes [see page 222]. When he was recruited by Soviet Intelligence in 1934, he was given a clearly defined part to play as someone with extremely right-wing views and his old friends dropped him. There are those in the West who believe that Kim secretly revelled in this duplicity, laughing up his sleeve at the friends he deceived. I can assure you, this is totally untrue. Kim often told me that the need to resort to deception was the most difficult aspect of his chosen profession. As someone who was fundamentally honourable and honest, he felt it acutely. He highly valued friendship and took the betrayal into which he was forced very hard.

Clearly, what happened to me was nothing compared to what Kim had to go through. I was totally engrossed in him, and this alone made me a happy woman. Unlike Kim, I didn't have to wear a mask. However, it still hurt me to know that I had upset people whom I was now compelled to drop.

I have already mentioned Stanislav's reaction to my 'invasion' of Kim's life. Kim himself never told me how the KGB had taken it when he had said that we were going to be married. I suspect they were displeased since I doubt very much they thought I was a suitable candidate for the role of Philby's wife. The main reason would have been my contacts with dissidents. Though these were entirely innocent and infrequent, and while I never took part in any political activity, they would certainly have come to the KGB's notice.

Nevertheless, certain friends and relatives of some close chums of mine, whom I often visited, became dissidents, and I got to know them. My friends were very hospitable, and there was always an interesting crowd around. But these were not political meetings, just friends sitting around a table chatting. Some of the evenings had a literary flavour, with guests reading their own poems or the works of their favourite poets. For example, it was a real treat for me to be invited to an unforgettable evening at their house when Aleksander Galich, a well-known writer, bard and poet, who had become a dissident, sang us some of his songs just before he had to go into exile. It was so sad to see the circle of friends shrink. Some emigrated, some vanished God knows where. Most of them had to leave their homeland when faced with the stark choice of 'The West' or 'The Gulag'.

My friends would often pass on to me illegal *samizdat* literature, which I used to read under Kim's nose, though he was very well aware that it could get me locked up. Despite that, he obtained for me from abroad the collected works of famous Russian poets of the 1920s and

1930s (Anna Akhmatova, Osip Mandelshtam and Marina Tsvetayeva at a time when all three were in disfavour) and even books by Nikolai Goumilev which were actually banned. Kim also ordered for himself a three-volume set of Alexander Solzhenitsyn (also on the forbidden list then) in English. He was most surprised when all the books arrived safely in the mail. 'Just don't show them to anyone,' he said, handing me my books. Whereas he kept Solzhenitsyn in full view in his bookcase.

It was impossible for me to be indifferent to what I knew – from the horse's mouth, as they say – about the persecutions and victimisation of dissidents, and I shared my views with Kim. While very sympathetic, Kim's responses were fairly measured and careful. He was not concerned for himself, but feared that his 'free-thinking attitudes' might tell on me, knowing the nasty minds of the organisation to which he had linked his destiny. 'I'm scared of making your life difficult, so I don't always behave the way I should,' he would say, trying to pacify me.

Once in 1974, Kim was driven home after a meeting and dinner with Yuri Andropov, then Chairman of the KGB. 'He asked me a lot of questions and actually listened to the answers,' Kim later wrote to Graham Greene. Some of the guests at the dinner also came to our place to make an evening of it. A little later two young KGB generals, Vitaly Boyarov and Oleg Kalugin, turned up. We soon understood that they had been taking part in the operation to expel Solzhenitsyn (this was in February 1974) and they had come straight to our flat from Sheremetyevo airport. They were cock-a-hoop and wanted us to join them in drinking to a job well done. I froze in horror with my glass already raised, and was just about to let them have a piece of my mind when Kim shot me a rather frightened warning look, and I refrained from speaking.

Oleg Kalugin first turned up at our flat in 1972. At the time he was Deputy Chief of Directorate K – the counter-intelligence directorate – for the foreign intelligence element of the KGB. He was different from the ordinary run of KGB officers, rather more relaxed and apt to make critical remarks about members of the Party Central Committee and the Politburo. Kalugin and other colleagues used to drop in to see us on the major public holidays. Among them the liberal-minded, erudite Mikhail Lyubimov, now a well-known writer, stood out. Kim really enjoyed seeing him. Later, when Lyubimov was posted to

Denmark, they corresponded frequently about everything under the sun.

Each year, the most significant day for Kim was 27 January, the anniversary of his arrival in the Soviet Union. On this day the visitors usually turned up uninvited, presenting us with a *fait accompli* by simply telephoning to tell us of their imminent arrival. Kim found it hard to get used to this, as he did with the fact that none of his colleagues, apart from the Kalugins, whom we visited twice, ever invited us to their homes.

The Kalugins' visits on major holidays continued until 1980, when he was 'exiled' to Leningrad. One of the by-products of these visits were his reminiscences regarding Kim in his book, *Spymaster*. I cannot judge the authenticity of the entire book because having looked at the chapter on Kim I knew that I didn't want to read another word.

Kalugin's description of his first visit to us is a complete fabrication. Yes, Kim's drinking was a problem and I will have something to say about that later, but he and I had coped with it before we got to know Kalugin. The Kim he describes bears no resemblance to the man I knew. Aside from the fact that Kalugin's account is complete twaddle, he makes copious use of what are claimed to be 'quotes' from me. Kalugin's story of how Kim allegedly bought some new furniture is so untrue that it makes me feel sick. Anyone with the slightest knowledge of Kim understands how little material things mattered to him by the way Kalugin himself stresses it.*

I must reiterate that 'my story,' as given in Kalugin's book, is a total invention. I cannot understand why he felt compelled to wrap the real facts he knew in a tissue of lies. That sort of embellishment might have been all right in a novel, but this book purports to be an authentic memoir. It surprised me even more because I believe that Kalugin felt a real sympathy for Kim. In fact, I must admit that he did

---

* [In *Spymaster*, former KGB Major General Oleg Kalugin claims that after Philby had persistently refused to take money for his services, Kalugin persuaded Rufina to visit a special store for the Kremlin elite, where she picked out some 'handsome contemporary furniture' for the Philby apartment. Kalugin quotes Rufina as telling him later that Philby had been 'amazed' and 'so happy' at the KGB's unexpected gift, even getting up in the night to fondle the new cushions in delight.]

play a positive role in Kim's life at that time (whether because his bosses had ordered him to do so, or on his own initiative, I don't know), reintroducing him to active work and seeing to it that his living conditions improved.

Another aspect of my new life dawned on me in 1974, when I met Boyarov for the first time. He looked me up and down with benign curiosity and said with a captivating smile: 'I'm fascinated to make your acquaintance at long last. Up till now I knew you only from your file!' For a long time I had supposed – though I tried to dismiss it from my mind – that the authorities knew all there was to know about me and had gone through my life with a fine tooth-comb. But to suppose is one thing, and quite another to hear it so frankly admitted: a chill ran down my spine.

Kim was half-expecting some sort of reaction on the part of the KGB, concerned that he would be hauled over the coals on account of my 'unreliable' friends. Every time his KGB contact or case officer telephoned to say he was on his way over, Kim would get depressed and await him pacing nervously from one corner of the living-room to the other, eyes fixed on the floor. After the case officer left, I would ask Kim nervously, 'Well, what was it about?' 'We discussed professional problems,' was his usual answer.

I can now see that for my peace of mind he may have concealed from me that, on occasions, his meetings with certain case officers had been unpleasant. Kim usually shut himself and his KGB colleagues away in his study, from which normally not a sound could be heard. But I did once hear Kim's voice raised sharply and angrily. He was not just shouting but banging his fist on the table. The office door was flung open and the case officer rushed out, face distorted with anger, ears all red. Slamming the door behind him, a furious Kim stormed around the flat shouting: 'They wanted me to sign this!' This was some sort of letter denouncing dissidents. It was the first time I'd seen Kim in such a state.

Though most Russians were critical of the regime, only a tiny per cent – a handful of courageous dissidents – went as far as open protest. Most confined themselves to political jokes and pouring out their fears to each other in what we call 'kitchen criticism'. Back then, few people believed real changes were possible.

Banging my head every day against what I saw as the shortcomings of Soviet life, I would vent my outrage to Kim. He didn't have the knack of using chats in the kitchen to let off steam and suffered in silence. A man of action, he saw no point in idle talk.

'What's the sense in just chatting about it? You have to act,' he would say.

Still, he knew that wasn't always possible and would get upset as if he were personally responsible for all that was wrong in the Soviet structure. He felt burdened by his inability to do anything, but at the same time was well aware that at his age he was just not up to new upheavals. 'I'm too old to begin everything again,' he would tell me. Seeing how badly Kim took all this, I reproached myself that the things I was saying were rubbing salt in his wounds. I decided to keep quiet and avoid this whole painful subject. In fact, there was no reason for arguing. Kim understood what was going on just as well as I did and would usually cut off my emotional outpourings by saying: 'I know everything!'

When talking to the KGB colleagues, on the other hand, he expressed his views frankly: 'You would do better to fight the real criminals instead of persecuting dissidents,' he told them. I particularly remember one evening with Lyubimov, talking heatedly about anti-Semitism, dissidents and Solzhenitsyn – the whole gamut of painful things that were going on. Kim and I attacked Lyubimov, who had trouble fighting back. While not wanting to appear hypocritical, he was simply unable, the times being what they were, to recognise the harsh reality of what was going on. Trying to strike a balance between the truth and his official duty, concepts that back then were pretty incompatible, he became seriously angry and jumped up from the table saying: 'Look, none of this is my fault.' Kim continued to press the point, not sparing himself in the process: 'You're guilty too. And so am I. We're both guilty.'

Kim expressed himself no less frankly in his letters. On 2 January 1980, he wrote to Graham Greene:

Lackaday, I am afraid we are in for a difficult year. I have no belief in doomsday, I don't believe in the Soviet threat to Europe, I don't believe in a NATO threat to the Soviet Union (though I do believe that renewed efforts will be made to detach our allies from the Warsaw Pact). But I think we shall spend most of the year saying and doing nasty things to one another until the various elections are over, thus diverting energy and skill from constructive purposes. Then, in 1981, with new leaders, or with old leaders relieved from re-election anxieties, we may get down to serious business again. In the meanwhile, a lot of innocent people will get hurt and die of hunger. So it goes.

. . . When you next buy *Pravda* at your local newsagent, you will see that I am expressing my views (if indeed they can be called views at all), not those of the government . . .

When Kim and I talked politics, I was usually the aggressor, while he, not wishing to add fuel to the fire, did his best to calm me down. He would try to justify a point, or find an explanation for something. While at a loss for arguments of substance, he would sometimes say: 'You know, over there,' (he meant in the West) 'we don't have it as good as you may think from here.' To which I retorted: 'You should now be saying: "Over there, *they* don't have it so good." Where we are is "here" and "we" is "you and me".' Smiling and lowering his head, Kim once said: 'You're right. I won't make that mistake again.' This failed to calm me down and I went on, ironically: 'You know, just because something is regarded as perfectly natural in terms of bourgeois morals, doesn't mean it can be reconciled with ours.'

Once, in the heat of argument, I retorted, 'What you are saying sounds just like a *Pravda* editorial.' He was very upset, the more so since playing on the fact that the word *Pravda*, title of the Party paper, means 'Truth', while *Izvestiya*, the name of the government daily, means 'News', he would trot out the old joke that there 'was no truth in *Izvestiya* and no news in *Pravda*'. It then struck me that Kim was not putting up a strong argument and I heard a false note in his replies. I couldn't stop myself saying something about which I had tried not to think: 'Perhaps they are bugging us?'

Kim didn't reply, but merely gave me a steady look. It seemed to me at the time that if he knew, or even suspected, that the KGB was bugging our flat, he should have warned me. Now I realise Kim was very wise not to let me in on whatever dirty little games were being played. He knew my volatile temper all too well and could picture my reaction to such a discovery. I simply could not have gone on living there if I'd known we were bugged round the clock. At the same time, it wasn't in me to weigh my every word, taking into account that some eager pair of ears was twitching to hear what I had to say. I just could not have stood the strain. I suspect that Kim, like me, simply preferred not to think about it.

But at the time I couldn't let it go, and a little later asked Kim again whether he knew if the flat was bugged. This time he told me: 'I don't know. But I really don't give a damn if they are listening or not.'

Another time, when I picked at this particular sore spot again, Kim told me: 'That whole bugging thing is so complicated and so costly that I really doubt it would be worth their while.'

Nonetheless, as I discovered years later, whether it made sense or not, the KGB did have taps in our flat. Kim's logic failed him. Not for nothing are there such words in our old very patriotic song: 'There is no price we will not pay.' This bugging was confirmed to me, informally, by Gennady, a KGB colleague who worked with Kim in the 1970s and 1980s. On a visit after the collapse of the Soviet system in 1991, he asked me: 'So, what do you reckon? Have they given up bugging your flat now?' I leaped to my feet, outraged. 'I should ask you that. Were we bugged before?' 'Of course you were. And Kim knew it.' My other friends also reminded me that when our conversation moved on to dangerous ground, Kim used to point meaningfully at the chandelier.

Any remaining doubts as to whether the flat was really bugged were dispelled by our former case officer Vladimir when we met after the collapse of the Soviet Union. He had looked after Kim much longer than the others and was removed only after General Kalugin was transferred to Leningrad. By the way, Kalugin in his book *Spymaster*, also takes as given that both Kim's telephone and flat were bugged. What if they have forgotten to disconnect the equipment?

Vladimir suggested we meet by the Monument to the Heroes of Plevna, not far from the KGB headquarters, the Lubyanka. It had been fourteen years since his assignment with Kim had finished, and he was now retired. We sat on a bench overlooking the broad street, warming ourselves in the last of the summer sun, and I was listening with great interest to what he had to say.

'He listened to me too at your flat,' he said angrily about his immediate boss. His boss, another case officer also called Vladimir, was on

46

friendly terms with Kim and often came round to see us with his wife. In fact, he and his daughter had joined me, Kim, Kim's son John and John's wife on a trip down the Volga. John had got to like him a lot and they became friends. It is hard to reconcile this apparent friendship with this man's decision to have Kim's apartment bugged.

Sitting on the bench, the first Vladimir told me how in the mid-1970s it was decided that Kim should be given the rank of lieutenant-general. Vladimir himself took the paperwork to Geny Ageev, who knew Kim personally. We had got to know him in Irkutsk in 1971 on our first visit to Siberia. At the time he had been Chairman of the Irkutsk Regional KGB and had been a gracious host. A year later he was transferred to Moscow, where he became Secretary of the KGB's Party Organisation and later Head of Personnel. He would call us up occasionally for old time's sake. According to Vladimir, Ageev should have forwarded the letter about Philby to Andropov (who, as Vladimir put it, 'worshipped' Kim) for signature. But for some reason our very good friend did not get around to doing so, and the letter went nowhere.

In 1993, the newspaper *Literaturnaya Gazeta* published excerpts from Kim's file, including the notation that he had a colonel's rank in the KGB. In fact, he never had any rank at all, a matter of supreme indifference to him.

Vladimir and I were still chatting on the bench when he interrupted himself and pointed to an elderly balding passer-by in a dark raincoat. 'Don't you recognise him?' he asked.

'No, I don't,' I said.

'That's Kryuchkov. He takes his morning walk along here every day.' Vladimir Kryuchkov, the former Head of the KGB, had been arrested in 1991 for his part in the abortive hard line coup against Mikhail Gorbachev and *Perestroika*; he was later pardoned. Now he continued his unhurried stroll along the avenue, at peace with the world, gazing benignly around him as if the coup had never happened and he had never been locked up in the Matrosskaya Tishina Prison.

Even though the democracy we achieved in 1991 has a somewhat transient feel to it, something did actually change in the minds of KGB officers as well. While Kryuchkov had reigned supreme in his KGB office, it would have been difficult to imagine hearing his people speak as frankly as now. Still, though Vladimir was retired and not putting himself at any obvious risk, he warned me, 'Please keep in mind that if the worst comes to the worst, I shall deny everything I just said to you and you will not be able to prove anything as you don't have a tape-recorder.' For that reason I haven't given Vladimir's full name and have quoted only a few of his comments.

CHAPTER 4

A New Life

We had tied the knot officially only in December 1971 because Kim had to renew his expired passport, and we also had to wait out the statutory three months 'trial period'. Stanislav and Valentin, two of Kim's case officers were witnesses at the Registry Office. We celebrated at home surrounded by my family, the Blakes and the case officers. The KGB gave us a Minton china dinner service as a wedding present.

Our married life began by Kim accompanying me right to the doors of my office every morning and picking me up there in the evenings. My colleagues were naturally rather intrigued by this, though I found it a bit embarrassing. Kim hated being alone. If I were gone too long, having nothing else to do he would resort to the bottle.

Trips were a problem. When I was sent to Leningrad on business, he jumped at the chance to come with me. He was very fond of the city and would have preferred to live there. As we went to my office, Kim said that he would show me the house to which he would like to move. As we approached it, he pointed out the windows, which looked out over the Summer Garden. We were both surprised to discover that the Leningrad Branch of TsEMI was in this very building which had so captivated Kim.

I didn't have that much to do during the five days assigned for my trip and we had a wonderful time seeing everything there was to see.

I realised then that Kim really needed me around all the time and back home always became concerned when I went off to work. My work itself gave no creative satisfaction and my salary of 140 roubles was of no great significance compared to the 500 (and later 800) roubles which Kim received, so I decided to leave TsEMI, to Kim's great joy. By that time, I had put in twenty-three continuous years of work and could look forward with a clear conscience to receiving my pension in 1987.

We celebrated my 'liberation' with a skiing holiday with the Blakes in Dubna, where there was a decent hotel (by our standards and those of the time) built for nuclear physicists. The restaurant was also OK, so we decided to have dinner there to recover from the journey. Kim hated noise and as usual chose a table as far away from the orchestra as possible. When he had to pop out briefly (to the telephone, he said), someone asked me to dance. Ida and George followed us on to the dance floor. As we were twisting and twirling, back to back, I came face to face with Kim, looking daggers at me. He grabbed me out of the circle, leaving my unsuspecting partner, who was facing the other way, still jiggling about. When it dawned on him that I had vanished, he came to our table to find out what had happened; Kim told him, politely but firmly in English, to get lost. Surprisingly enough, the chap got the message and slunk away. At the time I found Kim's adolescent behaviour simply a bit of a laugh.

Kim was a kind man and, in the eighteen years we were together, rebuked me only twice, criticisms I still remember word for word. It was in the first months of our marriage. He bought me a pretty quilted dressing-gown, which was smarter than any of my dresses, and I couldn't bring myself to take it off. Seeing me wearing it at midday, Kim remarked: 'Even a real lady like you can't wander about dressed like that in broad daylight.' The second incident occurred at about the same time. But while I felt I deserved the first rebuke, I thought the second was unfair and was deeply offended. It happened one evening at the Blakes: Valentin and his wife were there, as well as Stanislav. The two couples were dancing in the adjoining room, while Kim, Stanislav and I sat next door. There was an awkward silence, which I broke by asking Stanislav how he felt about dancing. He didn't have time to reply because Kim immediately piped up: 'It's rude to ask a man to dance.' That was not what I had meant at all. I rushed out like a skinned cat and ran home in tears. I was never far from tears in that first period of my life with Kim; it was probably just nerves.

Something similar happened in Prague about a year later. I was sitting in a restaurant with Kim, our Moscow escort, two drivers and two bodyguards. I was getting bored watching the chaps downing beer after beer and accepted an invitation to dance. The young Czech asked me for the next dance as well, first having politely asked Kim's permission. He danced in a very prim and proper way, not saying a word, other than to ask which of the men was my husband. Things got weirder when after the third dance my partner, without a word to me, asked Kim whether he would permit me to join him and his friends at their table. This was the last straw, and Kim, outwardly calm, launched into a long, albeit rather one-sided, dialogue with him changing languages. 'Do you speak English?' The Czech shrugged. 'German?' The young man shook his head. 'French? Spanish? Italian?' My erstwhile partner stood there blushing, like a schoolboy who hasn't done his homework. The interrogation ended with an English phrase, curt but delivered with sufficient emphasis to leave the young man in no doubt as to its meaning, just like that Russian in Dubna. At the time I didn't understand that there was a simple explanation for the way Kim behaved. He was very jealous and reacted badly even to something as harmless as dancing. It took quite a while before he became convinced that I wasn't about to stray, and then he calmed down.

When I was younger I adored dancing, but Kim gradually drummed that out of me. The last time I danced was at home with some old friends. I was dancing with my former permanent dancing partner when I was almost literally nailed to the floor by a sidelong reproachful look from Kim. I understood that my dancing days were over, but it was small price to pay for peace and quiet at home.

Ironically, once in Hungary I saw how well Kim could dance, when he was invited, or rather dragged, on to the floor by one rather determined lady. He never gave me the pleasure of partnering me though, since he reckoned that dancing was too frivolous.

One day, having read yet another UK newspaper piece about Kim, I teased him with the journalist's description of him being a 'womaniser'. Kim replied very seriously: 'I have only ever had one woman at a time.' Given that he had had four wives, this seemed at first blush somewhat paradoxical. But, unlike some of the 'model' husbands who go through life with just one wife, Kim, as far as I knew, never had more than one liaison at a time. Kim's first marriage was a subterfuge, which he referred to as 'political'. He had met Litzi, an Austrian girl of Polish origins, in Vienna – he had gone there at the suggestion of certain French Communists. They married at the Vienna City Hall in February 1934 and moved to London that May. Litzi was not only a member of the Austrian Communist Party but also an 'illegal', and the police were on her trail. Having married Kim, she then qualified for a British passport and so evaded arrest by leaving the country. The marriage didn't last long and came to a practical end when Kim went to Spain in 1937.

Kim met Aileen in London in 1939, when he was taking a short holiday before going to France as a *Times* correspondent. They married, and she gave him five children. Aileen died in London in 1957. Kim was then working in Beirut and married Eleanor soon afterwards. She had to go through the crisis of his disappearance from Beirut in 1963. She came twice to Moscow to see him, and in 1965 they parted company permanently. Eleanor went back to the USA and died there in 1968.

Kim put up stoically with most people, but there were a few, among them his maid Elena, of whom he found it hard to conceal his dislike. I met her when I moved in with him. He told me straightaway that not only was she idle, but she was simply not a nice person. He wanted to get rid of her, but didn't dare to do it himself. She was supposed to come three times a week for two hours at a time, but he couldn't stand her being there and would leave the flat, taking me with him as soon as she appeared. Kim used to tell me with great glee what he invented to get rid of her presence. Once, though he actually had no special preference for toothpaste, he asked her to go all the way to the Leipzig store, which was at the other end of the city, to get him a tube of Chlorodent. Elena loved the shop despite the long queues that the police had to control. Kim could then cunningly count on getting rid of Elena for the whole day. I myself visited the Leipzig store only once and came away empty-handed. As an alternative, he would simply tell Elena that there was nothing which needed doing and she just didn't turn up, even though she was still paid her full wage.

One day, sorting out Kim's shirts, I noticed that the collars were grubby. I set about scrubbing them. Elena found me at it and started to bluster that they were clean enough and that if they weren't 100 per cent it was because she had very poor eyesight.

'Why don't you wear glasses?' I exclaimed. Being short-sighted myself, I knew that washing shirts without glasses was about as effective as doing it with your eyes closed.

'I don't like glasses and won't wear them,' she said proudly, and added: 'Two women in one home get in each other's way.'

I decided this was my lucky break and agreed with her, saying that from now on I would do all the housework myself. Judging from the stunned look she gave me, she probably thought I should have been the one to go.

Kim was delighted. He told me to give her three months' salary as a bonus and to tell her she should leave the flat key in the mailbox downstairs on her way out in order not see her. To be absolutely sure to avoid this, he whisked me out for a stroll. Unlike Kim, Elena regretted her departure. She phoned me several times offering to help out, an offer which I could easily refuse since I literally had to scrape away the traces of her 'activity', or rather 'inactivity'. All of this goes to show just how patient Kim was. Elena was the widow of a former KGB man, and one of his colleagues had decided to do Kim a good service and recommend her to him!

My mother helped me with the housework until the arrival of Antonina, who was the exact opposite of Elena. She came to us not by recommendation but when I asked the Dawn domestic help agency to send someone over to wash the windows. Her opening shot was that the amount the agency had asked was too high and that she would take only what was due. From then on, I used to call her in from time to time to straighten the flat out.

And, although whenever she came she would tell me the place was spotless and we were wasting our money, she worked without a break for hours at a stretch. When I was settling up with her, she always tried to give me back the change, which to her was real money, and I had to argue with her. Kim couldn't help noticing how hard-working and honest she was, and grew very fond of her. Sadly, she had a weak heart and did not work for us for long.

CHAPTER 5

My Family and Friends

Kim accepted my family immediately and unreservedly. It was not just out of respect for me, but because he grew really attached to them and treated their problems as his own. He loved and respected my mother very much. 'It was worth marrying you just to get a mother-in-law like this,' he would say. He called her 'Mama' even though she was ten days younger than he was.

My mother had had a difficult life, like so many of her generation. She remembered the Revolution, the war, the purges and the air raids, the economic collapse and the famine. Kim much admired the courage and fortitude of our old people and was all too aware that they lived on the breadline. When he saw some decrepit, hunchbacked old lady, he said, 'And to think it was they who really won the war for us.' He could not resist helping old ladies cross the street, carrying their shopping bags or just seeing them safely home. Bravura speeches and slogans annoyed him. 'Our Glorious Youth,' he would parrot, exclaiming angrily: 'Why doesn't anyone talk about the old folks, their poverty? They are the ones who need help.' I wonder what he would say if he could see the swarms of beggars on our streets today.

Kim once received a rather modest royalty payment. He did not want to accept the money and asked for it to be given to a fund for widows. He was told that charitable organisations did not exist in the USSR, but that there was one real-life widow he might help, namely his own mother-in-law. He duly gave her the money and felt a lot better (in those days words like 'charity' and 'philanthropy', very much in vogue today, were not much used because they were thought to be demeaning). Mama, who often came to stay with us, was forever finding something to clean or do around the house. Kim found it hard to get used to it and would say: 'Why does Mama never take a break?' He also used to fret that she did not eat properly. Like most Russians she would eat bread as a substitute for other more nutritious foods, and he drew up a daily food chart for her. For the most part, he was singularly unsuccessful in persuading her to change the habits of a lifetime, though he did manage to get her used to champagne. Not only that, having once tried a champagne cocktail, the next time she was offered a glass she said: 'Put some brandy in, please.' When we had our evening drinks, Kim never forgot to bring Mama a glass of brandy or liqueur to her room. If he had a drink or two too many, he would become obsessive about Mama and would keep on asking me: 'Hey, Rufa, where's Mama?' When he was sober, he couldn't explain why he'd got so worked up the evening before on the problem of her whereabouts. I believe, realising that he was in a rather poor state, he wanted to avoid her seeing him.

Kim was also very good to my brother. Kostya, a jack of all trades, used to come over whenever we needed something fixed, as a carpenter, an electrician, a plumber or a general handyman. Kim used to call him our 'First Aid'. A few months after we got married, Kostya introduced us to his fiancée, Natasha. We offered them glasses of champagne, but Natasha didn't drink. She was so shy that she didn't smile once and didn't say a word, however hard we tried to get a conversation going. They got married soon afterwards and lived with my mother. Natasha gradually grew comfortable with us, and even with champagne! When their son Seryozha was born, Kim gave Natasha a monthly allowance, equal to her former salary, for three years so that she could stay at home to look after the baby. He was always helping Mama financially too, topping up her paltry salary and, later on, her pension.

Though there were now four of them, Mama still had the same 28 square metre flat. While she had her own room in ours, she spent most of the time at Kostya's with the baby, with whom she shared a 9 square metre room. The other room served simultaneously as a dining-room, a sitting-room, and Kostya and Natasha's bedroom. In fact, the room at Kim's was the first that Mama ever had (and still has) to herself. Seryozha was very attached to his Granny and moped when she went out. Often, she would just have arrived at our flat when the phone would ring and Seryozha would be asking plaintively: 'Where's Granny?'

Kim couldn't do enough for my family. For instance, he didn't think it was beneath him to call the appropriate person to get Seryozha on a trip to a Young Pioneers Camp for the children of KGB staff, although he didn't usually care to bother his colleagues with personal matters.

It was only natural that during his first and most lonely years in Moscow, Kim became friends with George Blake, of whom he grew rather fond. Aside from meetings with a very small group of colleagues, his only other choice was forced seclusion. In the first years of our marriage, we and the Blakes saw a lot of each other and would spend the public holidays together. One might have thought Kim and George had much in common, but though superficially close, they were very different. The more one saw of them, the more obvious this difference became. The final break came in 1975, over the appearance in the UK of photographs taken by Kim's eldest son, John. John took shots of us all at the Blakes' dacha. I was there when Kim asked George point blank: 'Do you mind if John tries to make something out of our photos?' 'Of course not,' George replied. Two or three days later, just before John was due to leave, Ida called to say that she and George didn't want the photos published and had never agreed to it. Kim felt it was a matter of principle, having always abided by the rule that 'your word is your bond'. I thought we should abandon the project, but neither Kim nor John agreed with me. On hearing this, George immediately reported it 'to the appropriate quarters'. After that our relationship cooled, although I will always be grateful to them for introducing me to Kim. John went home and published the photos in the *Observer*, getting quite well paid for his work.

At the beginning of our married life, the Blakes were the only people with whom we socialised, but later I introduced Kim to my friends. He liked them a lot, and we began to see quite a bit of them. One of them, a nuclear physicist, spoke fluent English, and it gave Kim a great deal of pleasure to chat with him. 'I like his dry humour,' he used to say. The others spoke much less English, but made up for it by being obviously on the same wavelength as Kim, and he easily found a way of communicating with them.

Kim took hospitality seriously. We worked on the menu together. I usually did the hors d'oeuvres and Kim cooked the main dish. When we laid the table, he gave a lot of thought to the 'placement' so that everyone would feel comfortable.

While Kim liked entertaining, he usually declined invitations. Big noisy groups where, in the usual Russian style of entertaining, everyone spoke at once, interrupted each other and did not listen to anyone else, tired him out. He would get confused and stressed, trying in vain to pick up the thread of the conversation.

Kim became very attached to our new Moscow friends and was upset when one couple decided to emigrate to the USA. They were not dissidents but motivated by sheer economic reasons. It was the husband's decision, his wife (a friend of mine and, like me, an editor) didn't want to leave and was very upset, but she had no alternative. As someone who worked on what was called the 'ideological front', even if she divorced her husband she would automatically lose her job as soon as he emigrated and would be left with her two children without any way of earning a living. Kim tried to persuade them not to go, warning them finally of the difficulties they would encounter, even though he had no doubt that they would achieve some success in the end. He was unable to stop them. All he could do was promise that if they ever decided to return, he would use all his influence to help them. Our friends left in 1972. At the time, we never expected to see them again. For all his sympathy, Kim did not quite understand the Russians' turmoil over emigration. He did not regard it as a big deal in itself and could not understand why we thought of it as such a tragedy. In his view everyone was free to live wherever he wanted. He was never troubled by feelings of nostalgia and described himself as a cosmopolitan. As it happened, Kim turned out to be quite right about our friends. They had a hard time in the US, with many setbacks, but they are now firmly established, have their own business, and don't give a thought to coming back, having got over their homesickness.

Kim and I always invited friends on such days as anniversaries and birthdays. I remember celebrating my fortieth birthday. Since 1 September was a Monday, we decided to have the party the day before. The usual group came, except Lena, one of my friends who was at her dacha with her children. Her husband Slava came on his own, and as usual Kim remembered to get some gin, which Slava liked.

It was well after midnight when everyone left, except for Slava, who had missed the last train and who we persuaded to spend the night on the sofa. But the next morning, when Kim came out of the bedroom, he rushed back in terror and shook me awake. 'Rufa, there's someone lying down out there and breathing.' For some strange reason he seemed especially scared by the fact that whoever it was, was breathing! 'It's Slava,' I muttered, only half awake, and turned over.

Then I remembered it was 1 September, the start of the school year, and Slava was teaching at the Institute. I scurried out to the sofa, on which Slava was still breathing peacefully, and asked him: 'Aren't you going to be late for work?' 'No,' he murmured, his eyes still closed. 'It's the 1st of September,' I pointed out. 'What did you say?' he yelled. He leaped off the sofa, swallowed a cup of coffee and rushed off to his students.

Later on, Mama rang. 'Happy thirty-ninth birthday,' she said. 'It's my fortieth,' I corrected her. Kim settled the argument after working out with pencil and paper that I was really thirty-nine, however hard it was to believe that a woman in such advanced age would be daft enough to add an extra year. I hurriedly telephoned my friends to set the record straight and to tell them how young I actually was.

CHAPTER 6

Kim's First Encounters with Moscow Life

By the time we met, Kim had been living in the USSR for seven years. From the occasional things he said, I realised just how difficult a period it had been for him. By and large he wasn't like those soldiers who loved to reminisce about days gone by, and he rarely talked about what he had been through. But on the odd occasion he would let something slip along the lines of: 'You can't imagine how unhappy I was.' Later on, he told me that in those first Moscow years he had suffered greatly from having nothing to do and feeling unwanted. 'I was full of information that I was keen to hand over, I wrote countless memos, until I realised that no one wanted them, and no one even read them.' It is therefore understandable that in the 1960s he tried to commit suicide by slashing his wrist. One day, quite by accident, I felt hard scars on his left wrist and blurted out: 'How did you get these?' Kim, who was just downing his third whisky, declared: 'We Communists have to be able to withstand pain, be strong and not surrender to weakness.' Then, fuddled as he was, he stopped, pulled away his hand, clenched his fist and snapped: 'Never ask me about that.' And I never did.

Horrified by the decrepit state into which the USSR had sunk,

Kim used to say: 'I'm a first-rate manager and could run pretty well any business, such as a freight handling agency, but I would insist that no one else meddled in what I was doing and that I could select my own staff.' That was around the time the Western press was claiming that Kim Philby was chauffeured every day to the Lubyanka, where he had an important job and his own private office. In fact, he did not set foot inside the KGB headquarters until 1977, and even then only as a visitor, when he addressed a group of KGB intelligence officers.

Kim usually preferred to recall the funnier side of life. He was fond of telling me about his first impressions of Moscow. One day, on his first stroll about the city, he decided to pop into a large delicatessen. He opened the door, then stood politely aside to let a woman go ahead of him. Suddenly a crowd of people flooded in, pushing both him and the woman to one side. Kim was left standing jammed against the door for quite a few minutes looking like a professional doorman.

There was some magnetic force about him which made him stand out in a crowd. Old ladies loved to chat with him and children were drawn to play. He was often pestered on the streets by people asking him directions. At first, since he spoke no Russian, he would only answer, 'That way,' accompanied by a pointing finger. Kim got to know Moscow very thoroughly and even drew a little town plan on which he marked all the public toilets. However, once he had learned to speak some Russian and thought he could give detailed answers to those who asked him the way to wherever, they tended to look at him rather askance and usually set off in the opposite direction.

When he wanted to visit someplace, he was often being warned about the risk of an attempt on his life and at times was advised not to go out. One day though, before he learned any Russian, he decided to risk going to the barber's, which was just around the corner. There were two men waiting their turn. He sat down beside them. The door opened and a man came in, saying something in a loud voice. The other two men looked at Kim. A little while later another man came in and yelled something that Kim completely failed to catch. Again, everyone fixed their eyes on Kim. He began to feel uneasy and, pretending he was concerned about being late, he shot a worried look at his watch and scurried out. It turned out that the men were simply asking who was the last person in the queue.

Soon after he got to Moscow, Kim began to furnish his flat. It was not easy to do so the way he wanted since, like with many other things, there was a marked shortage of furniture available, compounded by the fact that Kim didn't like the varnished finish that was then in vogue. However, he was told that the Likhobory Furniture Works outside Moscow produced custom-made furniture and Kim ordered, to his own design, several wall units with bookshelves and drawers, a chest of drawers, a coffee table, two side tables and a divan. Soon afterwards he had a stroke of luck when a suite of upholstered furniture came his way and he found he didn't need the divan. A few days after he placed the order, Kim went back to the factory to cancel the divan. They were nowhere near even starting on his order, but they still insisted they could not cancel anything without a valid reason. The clerk simply refused to accept his explanation and Kim was stuck. He could not think of any other answer to the question: 'Why do you need to cancel?', when it dawned on him that a stupid question called for a stupid answer. He told the clerk: 'Because my Dad died,' and then watched in surprise as the clerk carefully wrote his answer on the form. The fact that his father had by then been dead for five years was immaterial.

Kim lived under an assumed name. His Soviet passport gave his name as Andrei Fedorovich Fyodorov, though another official document, his Moscow Residence Permit, did give his real name. Why 'Fyodorov' is difficult to guess – most likely, because it was a fairly common name that would not attract any attention. But the first time Kim had to use it, it caused something of a to-do. He went to the dentist with a sore tooth. 'What's your name?' the dentist asked. 'F-Fyodorov,' Kim stuttered with much effort. The woman burst out laughing. 'Fyodorov?' she demanded, her plump body shaking with laughter. 'Just look at you! Who would take you for a Russian? Fyodorov indeed.' And she poked at Kim with her finger. After this, Kim chose for himself another name, 'Martins', as something both more appropriate and at the same time natural. It was a perfectly Western name. He was issued with a new passport in the name of Andrei Fyodorovich Martins, Latvian, born in New York. But Kim had trouble getting used to this name too. Sometimes, walking a little way behind him, I would call out, 'Andrei Fyodorovich', but he wouldn't even turn his head.

The new passport also put Kim in a difficult situation in Tbilisi, the last place a Latvian might expect to run into someone from home. The woman in charge of our floor at the hotel, who had kept our passports when we checked in, exclaimed gleefully: 'I'm Latvian too. From Riga.' Kim lost his head and, terrified of having to answer more questions, vanished into our suite without a word. Not only did he not speak a word of Latvian, but he had never been to Latvia. (We eventually went there the year before Kim died.) We did our best to avoid the concierge, who probably dismissed us as arrogant and rude.

One evening in Moscow, when Kim was having supper with his son John, a man who was sitting at their table, and who had been listening to them talk, asked: 'What language are you speaking? Who are you?' 'I'm a Chuvash,'* Kim replied. 'You're a Chuvash?' the man asked in amazement. 'But I'm a Chuvash too.'

Kim's comment that he 'never saw Guy Burgess melt into any background', could easily apply to Kim during the Soviet period of his life. He always stood out in a crowd and would virtually be rejected by a crowd as some sort of foreign body. He never managed to go with the flow of people. Getting on to a bus, people would shove him and he would move aside, letting them go first. I was always losing him in the metro. Even if we were walking down some broad street and came up behind a cripple, Kim would waddle slowly and patiently in his wake, too shy to overtake somebody handicapped. Once, at the Policlinic, his doctor took him up to consult a specialist. As usual with someone important, there was no question of an appointment. When Kim reached the consultant's door, he saw several other patients waiting their turn. He turned tail and fled rather than be seen to jump the queue, and I managed to catch up with him only on the next floor down. Needless to say, he didn't see the specialist that day.

---

* A minority people within Russia who numbered about one million.

CHAPTER 7

Battling the Bottle

From the moment we began living together, I came face to face with the 'weakness' Ida had told me about when she first mentioned Kim – his excessive fondness for the bottle.

The ritual began, as these things do, in quite a harmless way. At six sharp every evening, Kim liked to mix me a cocktail he called 'orange blossom', brandy mixed with orange juice. He then poured himself a whisky or brandy and water. We would sip our drinks slowly while we chatted or listened to music.

Kim would give himself a refill, which should have been enough as he got drunk very quickly. However, when he went to pour himself a third drink, which he clearly did not need, I would try to stop him. But he just could not understand why I wanted to stop him enjoying himself.

He would refill his glass, then offer me another too, though by that point just the smell of the 'orange blossom' would be making me queasy. Kim would completely lose control of himself, a stupid look emerging over his face and his eyes glazing over. It was unbearable to see a clever man turn into a complete cretin as the evening wore on. The only thing I could do was to wait for him to fall asleep.

But there was no peace at night either. Kim would yell in his sleep, or he would wake up the moment I dropped off, leap noisily out of bed, switch on the light and begin chain-smoking. The night would become a complete nightmare. If I went into the other bedroom, I could not sleep, worrying that he might set the place on fire. The sheets and the mattress were already covered with cigarette burns. And if he fell quiet, I got even more worried, tiptoeing in to make sure he was still breathing. Only when I heard him snoring noisily could I relax and collapse into sleep, by then absolutely worn out.

A quiet murmur in the sitting-room would wake me up early, in a foul mood, with a splitting headache, as though I was the one who had drunk too much. There was Kim serenely sipping his tea, his ear glued to the BBC World Service on the wireless, with an innocent look on his face, remembering nothing of his drunken stupor the night before, except for a headache which three glasses of tea and aspirins would soon fix.

'Tea's better for you,' he used to say. I was hardly going to disagree. My own anger at him soon dissipated. It was hard to believe that the whole episode would soon be replayed.

Unfortunately, another of Kim's favourite wisdoms was, 'The hair of the dog that bit you.' He would pronounce it at noon and down a 'restorative' tumbler of vodka. And off he went again.

Once in a fit of impotent rage I ran off and hid. He rushed around the flat looking for me, yelling my name. I saw him for what he really was – a helpless old man. My heart ached with pity and I realised I would never be able to leave him.

Kim did not know that and, I understood later, he was scared that I might leave him, though I had never tried to do so and never even threatened it. But I could not just sit there and watch him killing himself. Once he started on the drink, there was nothing I could do to stop him. When he sobered up and was back to normal, I would do my best to make him see sense. I actually think it was my nagging that helped to keep him alive.

I wondered why he punished himself like this. As if to answer my unspoken question, he once remarked that drunkenness was the least painful method of suicide. He would listen to my reproaches in silence, head bowed, but never made any promises.

One winter morning when we were getting ready to go out for a walk, I could not find one of my boots. We looked at each other questioningly and rummaged all over the flat. This was very odd, we both said. Suddenly Kim slapped his forehead as though he had just remembered something, went into his study and brought out the missing boot. In his cups the previous evening he had hidden it there to stop me from running away. It was funny and it was sad.

Drunk, he became unintelligible, and I never knew what weird trick he would pull next. Once in the middle of the night he almost choked to death trying to swallow a heavy metal cigarette lighter in a velvet cover, about the size of a box of matches. Luckily I managed to pull it out of his mouth.

After one of his especially difficult nights, I could not even bring myself to speak to him and met his playful attempts to start a conversation with gloomy silence. But then I could not help laughing when, inside a saucepan, I found a note saying: 'I love you, though it may not always seem that way.'

The only consolation was that when Kim was plastered, he never left the house. Kim used to tell me that when Donald Maclean was in the middle of one of his bouts of drunkenness, this usually calm and even-tempered man would get into fights and make the most awful public rows. He would, for example, feel compelled to 'straighten things out' at the House of Journalists. Maclean's alcoholism was eventually cured and he didn't touch another drop.

Kim never raised his voice. Far from fighting, even when drunk, he usually remained kind and tender. He would only become enraged to the point of becoming uncontrollable if I took his bottle away. The only way to calm him down was to beat a hasty retreat. But he sometimes became a completely different person, cruel even.

Once, when I had a bout of appendicitis, Kim sat by my bed and downed a bottle of whisky to show that he was sympathising with me. At that stage in our lives, heavy drinking was his standard reaction to any difficulty or unpleasantness. Suddenly, I developed such a pain that I could not bear it any longer and needed an ambulance. I begged Kim to stop drinking, saying that I was feeling very ill. This failed to sober him up and he sat muttering to himself about 'crafty women's tricks'. He would not have noticed if I had dropped dead. I managed to hang on until the morning, when Kim woke up and took me to the hospital.

The first time I invited a couple of my friends over for dinner Kim proclaimed that he would cook a curry, his favourite meal. Working away in the kitchen he started on a bottle of dry red wine and was well away before the guests even arrived. 'A good cook is always a little bit drunk,' was another of his favourite sayings.

He had no idea why I was so cross. 'After all,' he said, 'I've done the entire meal for you.' It pained me to have to introduce my friends to him as he swayed unsteadily, but they were old chums so, although they were rather dumbstruck, it was not too much of an embarrassment.

Kim's bouts of drinking usually exacerbated his bronchitis and sometimes brought on pneumonia, but that did nothing to quench his thirst for the hard stuff.

One night he fell off the bed. I managed to pull him up and tucked him in. He fell off again and yet again I hauled him back. The third time I pulled off one of my fingernails. It began to bleed. I had no more strength and left Kim where he lay, putting a blanket over him and a pillow under his head.

Of course, it caught up with him. By the next evening, he was running a temperature and during the night he got worse, breathing with difficulty, his face beet red. I called an ambulance, which came quite quickly. But the lift in our building was switched off at night and the doctor – an elderly, heavy set woman – had such difficulty climbing the stairs that she needed first aid herself. It took the paramedics longer to get up the six flights of stairs to our flat than it had taken them to get from the hospital to our building.

For some time Kim was seriously ill, but no sooner was he back on his feet than he was back on the bottle. I wonder where I got the strength to cope with it all. I tried the usual tricks, hiding the bottle, putting a lot of water into his glass, diluting the whisky in the bottle, and so on. But as time went on it took less and less to get Kim drunk and three shots were usually enough to put him to sleep.

Luckily, I avoided the fate of other boozers' wives who find themselves turning into lushes as well. I went completely the other way. Though I was never that fond of alcohol, I used to have a glass or two in friendly company. But at the sight of Kim in his cups, my mood turned and all desire to have a drink disappeared. 'It's a miserable soul that doesn't know how to have fun,' he would complain. And I wanted to cry.

Only after his death did I realise that Kim actually knew full well how difficult it was for me to put up with him. On the cover of a file containing the manuscript of a book he never got around to finishing, I found a weird inscription in Russian: 'If Rufina Ivanovna has killed me, I testify that she had good and sufficient reason to do so. KP.' This must have been written in 1970–1 in our first, very difficult year together.

It is difficult to remember exactly when the breakthrough came. One day, in 1971, Kim said to me: 'I'm frightened of losing you and I have to make a choice.' He chose me and began to co-operate.

After pouring himself a drink, he would hand me the bottle, saying with a smile: 'Put it away.' But it wasn't that easy. Quipping that, 'A chap can't fly on one wing,' he would repeat the performance with glass number 2. But that, he realised, was the limit. Sometimes he would ask for a third glass, but without a hint of his earlier aggressiveness. Though I didn't like what the third glass did to him, I tried not to be too strict, in order to reinforce his evident resolve to fight his own nature. It was through this constant balancing that in the end I succeeded in helping Kim pull himself back from the brink of self-destruction.

Things gradually got better, to the point where I not only stopped hiding the bottles, but on special occasions even gave Kim a glass of the whisky he liked so much. Once I was sure he had coped with the drink problem, I felt that I had no other care in the world; he didn't have any serious 'weaknesses' at all. A phrase which he often used about me, 'Too good to be true,' was equally applicable to Kim. His illness behind him, Kim was a different man. His eyes looked younger, his face became smoother and lost its puffiness. He put himself on a diet. The doctor who looked after both of us noticed that he had lost weight and was rather concerned at first. She then saw that it was for the good. Indeed, he fell sick less often. Now when I looked at him I thought, all I want in life is for him to stay alive and well, a phrase I kept repeating to myself almost like an incantation. But alongside my love for Kim, I was scared by the difference in our ages, which made it very likely he would go before me. I felt a bit more relaxed for a while when our doctor told Kim, after giving us a physical, that I was in a much worse state than he. In fact, at that time he had almost no health problems other than the chronic bronchitis which had plagued him from early childhood.

CHAPTER 8

Every Day a Holiday

With his drinking under new-found control life was more relaxed, but not for long. From 1978, Kim's health gradually but noticeably deteriorated, and I was in a near constant state of anxiety. I did my best not to show my concern and simply treasured every day, every minute, of our life together. It is difficult to find words to express the enduring sense of happiness I felt. Throughout the eighteen years we were together, he always expressed surprise at the 'treasure' that had come his way. One evening when I was busy in the kitchen, he asked my friend why I hadn't been married before. Since she didn't know the answer, she came to ask me. 'Tell him no one asked me,' I advised her. Kim never asked me about that sort of thing directly. On the contrary, he didn't want to know anything about my personal life. It was as if he was scared to come in contact with my past (which, if the truth be told, was pretty unexciting). Sometimes, when I was harking back to something perfectly harmless that had happened before we met, I noticed him grimace, as if in pain. Kim obviously thought that I was just as jealous as he was about his past. This is no doubt why he was shocked when, on Ida's advice, I said I wanted to read Eleanor Philby's memoirs (a copy of which was standing on his bookshelf). A sharp change came over his face and he left the room in silence. After that, I never saw the book again.

Though we did a lot of travelling, Kim was really only happy at home, and when I mentioned some new trip, a look of stress would cloud his face. If he had his own way he never would have left the flat, which he called our 'island'. It was not so much the travelling that he did not enjoy, as having to meet new people. As he wrote to Mikhail Lyubimov on 17 January 1978:

There are three slots in our schedule when we are due to be away from Moscow; i.e., around the end of February, the end of May and the end of July. I am sure you are thinking my life is one long holiday; in fact, I get far more holidays when I am working away peacefully at home than I do travelling around various foreign parts – people, people all the time.

When he first came to Moscow, Kim lived near the Sokol metro station. Later on he was shown the flat we finally lived in and fell in love with it straightaway, especially because it had a view to the west, east and south. The building was right in the heart of Moscow, near Pushkin Square, down a quiet side street. Kim loved the view, a typical urban landscape of roofs all at different levels – 'They are like little lids on the houses,' he would say sentimentally – with the spire of a Stalin skyscraper dominating the horizon. From our kitchen we used to watch the sun set in a blaze of colour, sliding slowly down the spire.

Kim always wanted me to be where he could see me. Even when I was doing housework he would complain quite seriously, 'I never see you.' It was difficult for me to know what to say as I scurried busily backwards and forwards between the bathroom and the kitchen. 'Where are you going now?' he grumbled. He wanted to know so that he could come and sit nearby, and he would follow hard on my heels, repeating: 'It's boring being on my own.' I understood Kim better than anyone else and got used to him being with me all the time to the point that when on rare occasions he went to official meetings, I found it difficult to relax without him. These meetings were virtually the only time he went out without me with the exception of going to the kiosk for cigarettes. Actually, there was one instance when I was in bed with a high temperature and Kim had to go out to meet my friend Yuri to return a book I had borrowed. Since they had never met before, I told each of them how to spot the other: Yuri had a curly beard; Kim would be holding the book and the *Literaturnaya Gazetta* in his left hand. Yuri acted as a spy approaching a clandestine rendezvous and had much fun telling people about it afterwards. Operation 'Book' went off successfully. The 'spies' took to each other and Yuri became our frequent guest.

Every time I left the building I would see Kim at the window watching me intently and waving. I waved back before turning the corner. I loved spending time at my friends' homes. There was often a large and interesting group of people, who dropped in at random from 6 to 10 p.m. But just when everybody gathered and the liveliest and most fascinating conversations were really getting under way, it was time for me to rush off home. But whatever pleasure I got from seeing my friends, going to the theatre, the cinema or anything like that, could hardly compare to the pleasure that awaited me when I returned home. As I turned into the little side street, I could see the lighted window on the top floor. I flew home on wings, but my joy was always tempered by a nagging sense of sadness, and I couldn't banish the thought that there would come a day when the light would be switched off and Kim would not be there to meet me.

Among all his other virtues, Kim was an unusually easy man to have around the house. There was seldom any friction – his common sense told him that it was better to agree on small things. For instance, to avoid criticism he used to ask me which shirt or tie he should put on. Though Kim readily admitted he was sensitive and easily hurt, he was never riled by anything I said. If I criticised him or when I gave him 'lessons' (like reminding him to wash his hands before a meal), he would take it patiently without getting annoyed. But sometimes he seemed genuinely surprised, showing me his hands and asking: 'Are they really dirty?'

As time went on I even succeeded in teaching him to wash his face and hands under running water, rather than in the basin. I couldn't bear to see him splashing about in a washbasin full of dirty water and winced every time I heard the gurgling that indicated that Kim had finished his morning wash and had pulled the plug. He found it hard to shake the habits of a lifetime, for during most of it mixer taps were unknown. He would answer my hints with a little joke, and often asked ahead of me: 'Have you washed your hands?'

I wasn't always very good at keeping my temper under control, and when I exploded, Kim would exclaim gleefully: 'What a temperament!' stressing the last syllable. As he wrote to Erik de Mauny on 27 November 1977:

> I have also re-married, also a tempestuous red-head, although in the seven years (no less!) of our married life, the tempests have been rare and very, very short. She is not, as always reported, a former interpreter, she was an editor at the Academy of Science. Her English is now passable, but still far short of interpreter standard. However, she has, on impromptu occasions, translated *my* Russian into Russian for the benefit of somewhat bemused audiences. Am I boasting or abasing myself when I say that her mother is ten days younger than I am? Anyway I can attest – as I hope you can – that the evening of my life is golden!

Contrary to what I said before, Kim could not stand me complaining about his smoking and barely concealed his irritation when I said anything. He even boasted about his half-century of 'service' in the smokers' ranks. In his later years he gave up pipes and cigars, but he smoked cigarettes up to the end of his life, and only the strongest brands, without filters, would do. He was very fond of Gauloises and Gitanes, which his students sometimes gave him, but usually made do with the cheap Soviet brands, Dymok or Prima. 'That's natural tobacco,' he would say, and he scorned American cigarettes like Marlboro and Camel, which he reckoned were 'synthetic'. If he couldn't get his favourite brands and had to make do with filter tips, he would make a big thing of tearing off the filter. As it happened, recent research has proved him right in that the material in filter tips is apparently more dangerous for your health than pure tobacco. His day began and ended with a cigarette. He would reach for one the moment he woke up and stub the last one out as he switched off the bedside light. His instant remedy when he felt unwell or had a coughing fit was to reach for a cigarette and when insomnia kept him awake, he would just sit and chain-smoke. I, of course, had no hope of persuading him to give up smoking. In fact, I reckoned that, after so many years, giving up might even be harmful. I would only ask, when I saw him reach for another cigarette, having barely stubbed out the last one, that he make an effort to keep it under control. Kim assured me that he was on no more than a pack a day, but I was far from convinced, all the more when I lost count of the number of opened packets lying around the flat.

Since I was the one who was sent out to buy the cartons for him, it wasn't hard for me to see that in truth he was going though his cigarettes at an alarming rate. One day he began to write down on a sheet of paper the time he smoked each cigarette and showed it to me proudly. His aim was to taper off gradually to no more than one an hour. On day 3 he got down to a record low of seven, but then got fed up with the game and reverted to his old ways. It was not until the last years of his life that Kim made any concessions by switching to filter-tipped Yavas. He also finally agreed not to smoke in the bedroom, but I eventually lifted that ban myself when I saw how difficult it was for him to get out of bed to go for a smoke.

In many stories in the press, Kim was depicted as a deeply unhappy man. The Kim I knew was completely different. I knew him as a man full of *joie de vivre*. He literally glowed with happiness and loved to sing 'Every day is a holiday because I am married to you.' I can see his face now and his bright, sparkling eyes. I can hear the floods of laughter with which, his head thrown back, he would react to my little jokes. He wrote to Graham Greene on 6 June 1980:

So you don't like being 75. I am still seven years short of that goal, so can offer nothing but sympathy. My own sixties have been more satisfactory than any period I can remember. Work proceeds reasonably satisfactorily within the restraints imposed by my chosen profession (not that I chose it myself, but I cannot think that those who chose it for me did wrong) and my private life is as rich a mixture as I can take; no tedious social obligations and enough travel to make me appreciate lares et penates that await my return home. My upbringing taught me that it is bad form to praise one's wife (our tenth anniversary in September – good gracious me!), so I will simply say that I have a wonderful mother-in-law too.

'I'm so happy with you,' he would tell me time after time, shaking his head in amazement. 'I've never had a woman like you.' I found it hard to understand why he was so delighted, since I reckoned I was nothing out of the ordinary. 'You may find this hard to understand,' he would try to explain to me. 'No one ever gave me anything. They only took.' But it seemed to me that it was simply impossible for any woman not to love him and thus want to make him happy. 'You do so much for me,' he would say, as if surprised. My perfectly natural concern for him, every tiny thing, he took as if I had given him a big present. Quite possibly I would not have done for someone else what I did with such pleasure for Kim, who himself radiated a kindness that was palpable.

CHAPTER 9

Day by Day

Kim suffered from insomnia. He was constantly taking sleeping pills, but even then he slept badly. However little sleep he had, he always got up early. He would put on his dressing-gown, light up a cigarette and go into the kitchen to make tea. On the dot of 7 a.m. he would listen to the BBC, sitting by his old 'Festival' radio in the living-room, a traditional Russian glass of tea at his side. Kim was very attached to his old-fashioned set, preferring it to a new transistor his colleagues had given him for some anniversary or other. My brother worked hard to keep the 'Festival' going, filing down and soldering its various worn-out components. Kim called his morning tea 'Russian', taking it with lemon in a glass with a metal holder. At 5 p.m. he brewed himself 'English' tea, which was very strong. He drank it with milk from an old china cup. In his later years, he abandoned 'English' tea, and drank only 'Russian'. In the morning, as he swigged his second or third glass of tea, he would make himself a piece of toast, which he ate with butter and jam; his favourite was Oxford Coarse Cut Orange Marmalade, which his children and later his students used to bring him from the UK. After the toast and the news, he would take out the special Italian pot and brew himself some Espresso coffee. Later on, when he developed glaucoma, he had to give up coffee. He said that it was less of a hardship than giving up tea, something he would not have been able to do.

Kim would sometimes make himself bacon and eggs for breakfast. He would fry the thin slices and put them on a sheet of paper to soak up the grease (he used to save thick wrapping paper for this job). Then he would fry two slices of bread in the same pan, followed by two eggs. He would put the whole lot on one plate, the fried bread with an egg on top of each slice on one side and the bacon on the other. When Mama saw him doing his conjuring tricks one day, it looked so tasty that she asked him to fry up the same for her. Ever after, Kim would offer her bacon and eggs whenever she came to see us. After breakfast we would go for a walk. Our favourite route took us along Tverskoy boulevard, ending up at the supermarket from which we always returned with heavy bags loaded with fruit juice, mineral water, dry wine and a variety of groceries. Kim, once accustomed to life in Moscow, had educated me in how to buy in bulk.

One day when we were on our way back, even though he was concentrating on coping with his heavy load, Kim still managed to spot a tiny bug on the pavement and snapped at me to stop so that I wouldn't step on it. 'Watch out! Look at the tiny little creature,' his fond term for insects. Another time he sprang to the defence of a cat which had unfortunately run across the path of a hulking big drunk, who booted her out of the way. Kim rushed to the man yelling: 'You fool.' I managed to restrain my gallant cat defender by literally holding on to his coat – the young thug could have beaten Kim to pulp.

Getting accustomed to always coping with shortages, Kim often talked about his 'stores', by which he meant the stacks of tins tucked away on the kitchen shelves. Many people stored food, Kim just did it differently. Despite my protests, he once opened a tin of fish in tomato sauce, which had already begun to bulge ominously, and scoffed the whole lot. For the next two hours I trailed him around the flat terrified that he would be struck by food poisoning. He just laughed and told me the fish had been very appetising. He claimed that he could digest anything, even nails. After that, I stealthily used to throw out a couple of tins at a time from his 'stores'. Kim thought it amusing that I had been so scared and often used to tease me about the fish in tomato sauce.

But even when he was increasing his 'stores', Kim acted as no one else. Once when we were in the supermarket and had loaded our basket with a few cans of juice, I left him with the basket while I went to look for other things. When I got back, there was only one can in the basket. 'There weren't enough left on the shelf, so I put the rest back,' he explained.

Kim was well used to the rudeness of sales assistants, but was surprised when we came up against it even in the KGB's pharmacy, whose staff were taught to be polite. We had gone there on the advice of our neuropathologist to buy Valeriana roots. She told us we should both drink an infusion of them as part of our daily diet. 'Buy more than you need, while we still have it in stock at the pharmacy,' she counselled. Following the routine, I paid for ten packs, but it proved a mistake to have taken her advice literally. I handed over my cheque, but the assistant threw it back at me saying, 'Are you mad?' I let it drop to the floor and hid in the corner of the pharmacy, unable to stop crying – proof in itself that ten packs weren't enough to calm me down. Poor Kim just couldn't understand why the chemist had become so angry and embarrassingly fussed around me.

It was difficult to find answers to the many 'whys' that Kim used to pose about Soviet life. I remember when he spotted a handbag in the window of the GUM Department Store and wanted to buy it for me. He didn't believe me when I told him it wasn't for sale. He plodded around various departments trying to find it. To pacify him, I telephoned the Enquiry Desk and let him listen to their resounding confirmation that it definitely was not available! He still couldn't understand how GUM could display something that wasn't for sale. The same thing happened in the shop near our flat where we always bought grapefruit juice. It seems we were the only people who drank it, since most Russians found it rather bitter. Kim told me once that when he was buying some orange juice, which he found too sweet, the shop assistant advised him to add some extra sugar! On this occasion, the girl in the shop told us that there was no grapefruit juice left, even though a whole pile of cans of it were stacked behind her in the window. 'Things in the window aren't for sale,' she snapped.

But even though one might miss the grapefruit juice in one shop, there was always the chance of getting lucky with 'real' fruit in another. Strolling down quiet side streets, we used to pop into little shops which were pleasant and useful at the same time for buying something to put away. Maybe next time when we went shopping we could avoid at least one queue. Kim loved to go to the market despite the torments he went through in the apple season. He was allergic to apples and couldn't stand their smell. Even drawings of apples made him sick! He would rush down the rows of stalls with a handkerchief clapped to his nose. One day I saw him wandering around the flat with a worried look on his face, sniffing like a bloodhound and muttering, 'What a horrible smell.' It turned out that Mama had left a little bag of apples in her room and Kim couldn't settle until she had thrown them out. Apples became a forbidden fruit for me too. Kim told me how a romantic country stroll with a girl had ended ungloriously for him when they came across a pile of apples. His girlfriend oohed and aahed over their ripe colours, while Kim ran from her, his hand over his nose. That was the end of the affair. He couldn't stand the smell of pears and bananas either, though he did allow me to eat them if I shut myself in the bathroom and immediately flushed away all traces of my crime. On one occasion I remember how the people who were escorting us on a trip to Bulgaria were taken aback when we entered our deluxe suite, where every room smelled delightfully of roses. Sniffing nervously, Kim rushed to the room at the end of the suite, where, in a bowl of fruit among peaches and grapes, nestled his deadliest enemy, one single apple.

Though he was not otherwise faddy when it came to food, Kim had to have vegetables, which he always bought in the market. Once I watched the Georgians (the name we usually applied to the traders from down South, who are now for some reason referred to as 'people of Caucasian nationality', most often in the crime reports in the newspapers) literally and liberally applying spit and polish to their tomatoes before stocking them in a neat pile, which gleamed temptingly in the sun. Kim was, of course, immediately drawn to these most attractive vegetables. Later, when we were laying the table for lunch, I noticed that he was slicing the tomatoes he had just bought without having washed them. I had already noticed that he had put vegetables on the table straight from the fridge. It then occurred to me that the English washed their vegetables before putting them in the fridge. It never crossed my mind that Kim wouldn't think he needed to wash them. 'Don't you ever wash vegetables?' I asked. 'Only if they're dirty. Why wash them if they're clean!' replied Kim innocently. He reckoned that if something looked clean, it was, and I had a vision of those spitting Georgians. 'How could you?' I spluttered. Kim then explained that if the British had been squeamish, Britain could never have become a great empire. It had been this lack of squeamishness, plus a strong stomach, that had enabled him to survive in the East. 'If only you had seen the Eastern bazaars, with the meat, fish and fruit all buried under a thick layer of flies. I remember being given a bowl of delicious soup once in Turkey, but before I could start on it I had to use my spoon to haul out several flies that were swimming in it.'

After lunch, which was usually some cold cuts, vegetables and dry wine, Kim liked to take a nap. At 5 he had a cup of tea and at 6 his apéritif. In the evenings Kim would read poetry to me (he was specially fond of Edgar Allen Poe), or we might listen to classical music – Beethoven, Mozart, Vivaldi, Liszt, Mahler, Tschaikovsky and others. But Kim's preference was for Wagner. When he listened to *Tannhauser* or *Das Reingold*, he would start conducting himself, so emotionally that he seemed to be about to levitate from his armchair. At 9 p.m. Kim invariably watched *Vremya* (*Time*), the main Russian TV news programme. We had just one TV set and I would yield to Kim when the football, ice hockey or boxing were on. We usually watched the figure-skating competitions together. Kim knew the names of all the football and ice hockey players and, as he watched, he was just like an ardent fan in the stands, yelling 'Goal' at the same moment as the commentator Nikolai Ozerov. As a 'company man', he was a supporter of the Dynamo team, which was backed by the KGB. He also cheered the Soviet team whenever it appeared. He was twice invited to speak to our ice hockey team at their training camp near Moscow when they were getting ready for a world championship game. He wrote to Lyubimov about this on 2 May 1978:

Another reason for our having a long holiday was another nerve-racking experience I was recently induced to undergo: a vystuplenie to the Soviet hockey team on the eve of their departure for the world championships in Prague. My last one, to the Dynamo team, was disastrous; they promptly lost four matches in a row. And I am not too happy with the early performances of the national team in Prague. Four wins sound all right, but they were all against pretty weak opposition, and not too convincing at that!

Kim's other favourite TV programmes were *The World of Animals* and *Travellers Movie Club*. He rarely watched films. One exception was *The Irony of Fate*, which was shown every New Year's Eve and which Kim never missed. He greatly enjoyed watching the leading Soviet actors, like Innokenty Smoktunovsky, Inna Churikova, Lia Akhedzhakova and Ludmilla Gurchenko. Kim liked to listen to BBC programmes besides the news, such as political commentaries, sports and music. He had been a fan of Arsenal, the British football team, since he was a boy and remained its supporter.

Kim had a sweet tooth and never ceased to amaze me with the strange concoctions he would make himself for dessert. He would crumble shortbread in a bowl, smother it in sour cream or yoghurt, plop some jam on top and call the result 'pudding'. He had to give up shortbread when he started to watch his weight. After that I began to give him my home-made cottage cheese (he called it 'your cottage cheese' and wouldn't touch the store-bought variety) for pudding. He would add dried apricots or figs and mix it all up with yoghurt or sour cream. Kim liked to grind currants or cranberries himself and then add them to his pudding.

But most of Kim's time was spent reading while sitting in his favourite wingback armchair, which Guy Burgess had left to him. To his right, on a little table decorated with a Russian folk painting, was an ashtray, and next to it was usually a box of chocolates, which emptied at the same rapid rate that the ashtray was filled. Kim would stick one chocolate after another into his mouth without taking his eye off the page and was soon astonished to find that his hand was rummaging at the bottom of an empty box. And I hadn't been able to eat even one chocolate from a box that had usually been intended for me!

Chocolate also helped Kim to get through sleepless nights. After sitting up in bed with a book for several hours waiting for sleep to overtake him, he would set off for the kitchen in search of a bar of chocolate. He usually took a piece of matzoh (which a woman I knew used to buy for us at the synagogue during Passover) as a substitute for English water biscuits. He would break the matzoh into small pieces, put a chunk of chocolate on each and arrange the little 'sandwiches' on a big plate. I would drift back to sleep to the accompaniment of his reassuring 'crunch crunch'.

Every morning Kim would ask me exactly the same question: 'What are your plans?' I was rarely able to give him a specific answer. Unlike me, Kim did not like to change his plans. Unexpected changes, even of the most insignificant kind, upset him. For example, we might decide to roast a chicken for dinner one day and to have steak on the next. I would then get lucky and manage to buy some fresh fish, but when I suggested to Kim that we put the chicken off to tomorrow, he would object: 'But we agreed.'

'The kitchen is *my* patch,' Kim told me when I moved in with him. Though this rather surprised me, I was actually pleased since cooking was never one of my favourite pastimes and I gladly ceded the culinary honours to him. But once when I had bought a live carp, I decided to cook it myself. Kim didn't object. While the fish was cooking, I went to the bathroom to do some washing and, as was bound to happen, while I was away the fish got burned. I was very upset that this demonstration of my culinary prowess had ended dismally. 'Black carp,' Kim said in surprise, but he still ate the poor fish and said he had enjoyed it. At that, I burst into tears. He was puzzled at my reaction and insisted that it really had been very good. I was offended because I thought he was simply humouring me. In fact, though one side was burned, I hadn't managed to ruin it completely. But Kim didn't forget 'the black carp' and often teased me about it.

When he cooked, nothing ever went wrong. If he was cooking, he stayed in the kitchen sometimes for hours, firmly planted at the oven. The only distraction he would allow himself was a paper with a crossword. That meant when he was in charge nothing ever overcooked or boiled over. Everything came out absolutely ideal. Gradually, of necessity, I did manage to win back the chef's hat and took over the kitchen almost completely near the end, though my victory didn't exactly thrill me. In time, Kim began to get a little lazy and less and less inclined to mess about in the kitchen. Even so, when it came to cooking something where precise timing was essential, I was no match for Kim and gladly handed over to him when it came to roasting meat or poultry.

Kim was an inspired chef, but nevertheless followed recipes to the letter, surrounding himself with cookbooks in the process. He was very fond of spicy dishes, especially curries. Wiping his forehead for dramatic effect, Kim used to tell me that his father reckoned a curry wasn't a proper curry unless you broke out into a sweat after the first spoonful. Kim used a lot of strong spices. Whenever he asked his children or his colleagues to bring him items from abroad, it was always things like sauces and condiments, as well, of course, as marmalade. One day, Kim decided to make Peking duck for dinner. He followed his Chinese cookbook slavishly. It prescribed that before cooking the duck had to be hung overnight in a draught to let it dry out thoroughly, this being the key to making the meat tender and the skin crisp. He spent a long time looking for just the right place to hang it before finally hammering a nail in the frame of the kitchen door. After that little episode I managed to convince him that duck could be roasted just as well without sending it to the gallows first, and we both agreed that, taste-wise, hanging made not the slightest difference.

Kim liked his flat a lot, but used to complain that the kitchen was rather small. He didn't have enough room to rise to his full culinary heights, and even I got in his way. So I would quickly wash and peel all the food and leave the kitchen before he launched into the cooking. He cooked with single-minded concentration and couldn't bear anyone intruding. Even behind the desk in his office dealing with KGB work he didn't look quite as serious as he did in the kitchen. It was as if when he was in there, peering into a saucepan, he was solving the problems of the world! While he was conjuring up the food, the pile of dirty crockery and cutlery would grow, and I used to wash up surreptitiously so as to leave the field clear for the master chef. While he was cooking, Kim had a habit of wiping his hands on his trousers, and I used to rush to tie an apron around his waist. The apron notwithstanding, his hands would still stubbornly find their way to the trousers, and I had to run up a special wrap which went right round his waist like a skirt cutting off access to the trousers completely.

The state of Kim's trousers was something with which I fought a long and unsuccessful battle. He liked flannel trousers, but I could never find any in Moscow. Once, when we were in Hungary, I managed to buy several lengths of flannel, which were made into five pairs of trousers by a Moscow tailor. But I never managed to teach Kim how to hang them up properly and they soon began to look scruffy. On the other hand, he swore that flannels always had to be old, crumpled and slightly dirty, otherwise a man didn't feel wholly comfortable in them. Kim's laughing answer to my complaints was: 'It's stylish. That journalist was right when he described me as "carelessly elegant".' It was difficult to argue with that.

Once a week we would go to the main Post Office, where Kim rented a box and where he picked up his *Times*, *Sunday Times* and *Herald Tribune*. Unlike our home address, which was carefully concealed, the box number was known abroad, and letters arrived from all over the world even with such addresses as: 'Kim Philby, The Kremlin, Moscow' and 'General Philby, The Lubyanka, Red Square'. Kim also received numerous religious letters and even proposals of marriage. I recall a letter from a lady in London offering Kim her heart and her hand. She said she had sent a copy of the letter to Kurt Waldheim at the UN. In a follow-up letter, Kim's new 'fiancée' told him, among other things, that she had named him in her will as her heir. There was also enclosed a photo of herself. When I saw it, I ceased to be gnawed by jealousy! That was the last time we heard from her. In a pile of similar letters I found a note from Kim saying: 'For curiosity only: this letter, which is addressed to Mr Kim Philby, Kremlin, Moscow, Russia, arrived during my absence, bearing a Canadian postmark. It is odd that half the letters I have received from religious maniacs are sent from Canada, while the proposals of marriage come chiefly from England and France.'

We usually walked to the Post Office along the Petrovsky, Strastnoy and Sretensky boulevards and I had a hard job keeping up with Kim, who was tireless. Going up the hill from Trubny Square to Sretenka, I used to drop way behind, vainly chirruping: 'Don't run.' On the way back we would take the same route, or, if we had a lot to carry, we would take a taxi. When we got home and Kim began to sort through the newspapers, it always irritated him that they seemed to arrive out of sequence so that on 1 February, for instance, he would get the newspapers for the 15th, 16th, 19th and 20th of January, while those for the 5th, 7th, 10th and 18th of January would turn up on 8 February. The case officers assured him that that was how the papers were dispatched from abroad, a story they had apparently been sold by the Post Office! Newspapers were either rolled up tightly or folded like an accordion. Thorough in everything he did, Kim would flatten them out by putting them between two heavy atlases with an old iron on top. The next day he would extract one copy of *The Times* from his makeshift press and set impatiently about the crossword, which he called 'mental gymnastics'. These crosswords were very complicated and nothing like we have in Russia. Someone once gave Kim a book of English crosswords composed in the same rather simple style as ours, but he threw it away because it was too easy and boring. On one occasion our case officer Vladimir asked Kim for a few newspapers he had finished with so that he could give them to some unidentified Englishman. According to Vladimir the latter asked: 'Who's the genius who does all the crosswords? I've lived in Britain all my life and still can't figure out the basic principles.' I was delighted to hear that and felt somewhat less of an idiot since I too had never been able to understand the system and logic behind the crosswords, even after careful explanations from Kim. And he could finish off any crossword, leaving no blanks unfilled.

CHAPTER 10

Back to Work

A year or two after we were married, Kim began to be asked to do an occasional job for the KGB. A case officer would bring him the relevant papers and Kim would immediately set to work. On the surface nothing changed, and he went about his usual daily routine, but I could easily tell that his thoughts were far away. He would go on like that for days, sometimes as much as a week, pondering the problem, without making a single note. Then, when he was ready, he would sit down at his typewriter and tap out his conclusions without making a single mistake. When he had finished, he would telephone the case officer to say so. If the case officer told him the assignment was urgent, Kim would take him literally. As with everything he was asked to do, he would take the KGB's request and would get down to work immediately, finishing the job at lightning speed. He used to be rather amazed when the case officer took his time in coming to pick up an 'urgent' job. I, of course, didn't have the slightest idea of what Kim was actually doing. In the first place, it didn't interest me in the least and, secondly, I reckoned the less I knew about espionage secrets the better off I was. When an assignment arrived, Kim would usually comment briefly: 'This is quite interesting' or 'Very boring'. I heard the latter more often than the former. As far as I could gather from his rather neutral comments, what was happening was that he would be given ideas, or half-developed plans that someone or other in the KGB had produced, and his job was to brush them up and give a finished version. He would often lose his temper, saying that some plan he was revising wasn't worth the paper it was written on and was just a senseless waste of time. Sometimes though he got very enthusiastic, saying he had been given a difficult – which meant interesting – assignment. He once told me with real pride that something he had done had been widely circulated and talked about.

A little later the nature of Kim's work changed and became rather more methodical and systematic. Instead of a case officer doubling as courier, Kim was given a permanent supervisor, Gennady, who came to the flat regularly once a week. The two of them would shut themselves up in Kim's office with me bringing them tea from time to time to sustain their creativity! Their work finished, they would move to the sitting-room and let themselves go over a bottle of brandy, with a feeling of a job well done. As Kim wrote to Lyubimov on 27 January 1980:

Somewhat frenzied bouts of professional activity have been punctuated by my flopping into my old armchair to 'catch up with my newspaper reading'. In cruder language, this means that between the frenzied etc. etc., I have been lazy. When your age approximates to mine, you may sometimes feel the same.

Gennady told me later that it had been his idea to involve Kim in active work. He suggested it to Oleg Kalugin, then Head of Counter-Intelligence, who gave it his blessing. In 1980, Gennady began to have differences with his immediate superior to the point that later he was transferred to another division. His visits to Kim ceased abruptly. He simply vanished, as our couriers had done before him. Anatoly appeared on the scene as his replacement, and the work went on. Several months after he disappeared, Gennady turned up at the flat out of the blue, without, as he usually did, telephoning in advance. He told us he had been ordered without any explanation to break off all contacts with Kim. He nevertheless thought he should tell us what had happened. Gennady spoke in a whisper and looked excited. He was the first of those who 'vanished without trace' and who eventually reappeared. When Kim was told that he could not see Gennady socially, he reacted sharply. He considered it a violation of his human rights. As a form of 'silent' protest, he stopped receiving as guests those people who had forbidden Gennady to see him. However, after a while, Kim continued to meet Gennady. Anatoly didn't work long with Kim before he was posted elsewhere. He had warned Kim in advance and sent us rather nice little notes from abroad. Yuri, who replaced him, worked with Kim up to the end. Kim had a high regard for their professionalism and found it easy and interesting to work with them.

That said, however, the KGB simply did not listen to much of the really valuable advice Kim gave them. I remember Kalugin coming to see us once and telling Kim with delight that the Islamic revolution had triumphed in Iran. Kim was not at all pleased, envisaging the dangers that the spreading of Islam would bring. He was surprised at the short-sightedness and incompetence of Soviet politicians, who seemed unable to recognise the new danger. Writing to Graham Greene on 2 January 1980, Kim gave his views of the Ayatollah:

> I don't think that being my father's son qualifies me to speak of the Ayatullah. I have never had any religious experience, and probably find it more difficult than most to understand irrational behaviour, even when it is my own. I tend to the view that the Ayatullah is a hateful old fraud, and that his precious Islamic republic is meaningless.

Kim went on to express his concern about the hostages taken when the fundamentalists stormed the US Embassy in Tehran.

> There seem to be two problems: the hostages and the future of Iran. On the hostages, I think we are all agreed, if only because Allah alone knows whose Embassy is not next on the list for sacking, looting, burning or occupation. But how best to free them? By action or inaction? I have no insight into the mind of the A. or the holiday-making students, so I just don't know. On the bigger question, your idea of joint action culminating

perhaps in spheres of influence may look attractive (I have passed it on to the competent authorities). But surely such an operation, in such an area as Iran, presupposes mutual trust and goodwill – commodities in distressingly short supply these days, and getting shorter (it seems to me) by the hour.

When he heard that Soviet troops had been sent into Afghanistan in 1979, Kim almost tore his hair out in despair, since he felt that this act of criminal stupidity would end with heavy loss of life. Although the war had just begun, he foresaw this risky adventure ending in tragedy, or, more likely, continuing without end. Kim shared his thoughts on this too in the letter to Greene quoted above:

And now this infernal Afghan business. I need hardly tell you that I am very unhappy about it; what may surprise you is that I have met no one here who *is* happy about it. It was apparently very necessary to get rid of Hafizullah Amin, who was literally making a bloody mess of things, calling himself the Stalin of Afghanistan and behaving as if to prove it. But was it essential to take up the military option, as it is called nowadays? Wouldn't a quiet kinjal-thrust from behind an arras have done just as well? These, of course, are simple gut-reactions. I don't know the facts behind the decision to intervene. What seems certain is that the decision has stung [US President] Carter badly; my guess is that for some months to come he will prefer pepper to salt.

I did in fact hear Kim giving his KGB colleagues his views on the invasion in no uncertain terms, but sadly his advice was unheeded.

Alongside his written 'homework', the KGB gave Kim a new responsibility as a mentor for young officers. It was Lyubimov who first had the idea in 1974, when he became Deputy Head of the Third Department of the First Chief Directorate. According to Lyubimov, he suggested to Kalugin that Kim should be used to 'put some life into work on the British target'. At the time it was a pressing need since, in 1971, 105 Soviet diplomats had been expelled from the UK. The KGB London Residency had been virtually destroyed, its sole survivor a Latvian named Janis Lukashevich (who, by coincidence, we actually met several years later in Latvia during the shooting of a doc-umentary film on soviet counter-intelligence). Kim was brought in to help prepare the young trainees for duty in English-speaking countries and to share with them his professional experience.

He held his classes in a safe-house, a ten-minute walk from our flat. There were usually three or four men in the class, but the line-up changed from time to time as some were posted abroad and their places were taken by new recruits. Kim worked on his new assignment with great interest. He enjoyed mixing with young men, who, as he saw it, were thinking along his own lines, and was extremely outspo-ken with them. I was delighted that Kim had finally found something to do which really suited him and I did my best to encourage him, if only to get him out of the house. Kim used to tell me what he thought of his students, whom he described as intelligent and capable. He was particularly impressed by one of them, Michael (as he called him), whom he rated very highly and who he felt showed great promise. 'He's simply brilliant,' Kim told me, and he very much wanted me to meet him. But a long time passed by before I actually got to know him.

I saw Michael only once while Kim was alive. The second time I met him was when he called to pay his respects on the day of Kim's funeral. Later, we became good friends and his family and I began to meet rather frequently.

Kim and his pupils wrote to each other even when they were posted abroad. For example, on 16 April 1982, Kim sympathised with Michael when he was working in the UK:

> Yes, I can imagine that your path these days is strewn with
> more mines than roses. For the first time, I am beginning to get
> really afraid of what those lunatics in Washington are up to;
> and, of course, Reagan's poodle (Mrs T.) will not be far behind.
> However, British politics seem to be getting really interesting
> for once. Not that I feel any enthusiasm for the Lib/SDP; they
> are just members of the old gang who have seen fit to change
> their clothes. You must know more about this than I do, so I
> will say no more.

Kim planned his lessons as discussions or plays like at a drama school. The atmosphere was relaxed, with plenty of brandy or tea. Kim would teach his students how to make a good impression, how to behave, how to socialise, what to say and how to say it. His advice, even in simple details such as what to wear, or even how to carry things, was extremely useful. No one else had the background to teach this sort of thing. In this way, Kim helped his students to create a certain image, to adapt to a different environment, to merge with their targets, to really be English. At the same time, Kim regretted that he hadn't been utilised earlier when he really had a great deal of valuable information. He reckoned that his experience was now hopelessly outdated, that he had withdrawn from real life and wasn't able to be of sufficient value to his pupils. But they had no doubt that his experience was unique and greatly valued their seminars with him. Kim wrote to Lyubimov on 14 April 1977:

> We are off to Leningrad next week (on business) and the week after that to the Crimea for a holiday which I hope I have deserved. Meanwhile I continue to talk nonsense to the boys, but as they seem keen to continue, perhaps they are getting something out of it all!

Kim used to prepare meticulously for these sessions. You could tell it from the concentrated, even distracted, look that came over him the day before each seminar. But I never actually saw him sit down at his desk to write up a synopsis or an outline of what he planned to say. He would just improvise. As he wrote to Lyubimov on 31 October 1983:

> We have started the old round again, with two new boys this year, with one or two old ones thrown in. I am seeing them for the second time this afternoon, and am beating my poor old brains to think of what to say that they don't already know.
> I wish you all professional success, and if any chance remarks of mine will prove to have contributed towards it, I shall feel proud and happy.

In the latter years of his life Kim was often ill, and just leaving the flat was a problem. Once en route to the seminar, he had to walk up to the ninth floor, as the lift had broken down, and he came home totally exhausted. After that Kim suggested to his case officer that the students should come to our flat. This was agreed, albeit reluctantly, since the KGB thought it undesirable to multiply the number of visitors calling on us. But even when the venue had been shifted Kim found it increasingly difficult to cope. As he wrote to Michael:

> I am now out and about, taking very seriously my doctor's recommendation to 'take it easy'. A gentle walk or two, morning and evening, and an afternoon's sleep – sounds like the recipe for a perfect life! When I am supposed to do any work is another matter altogether. Actually, I start my third seminar next Friday, and no doubt our dear colleagues will soon forget about my afternoon nap.

Kim complained to me that talking without interruption for two hours left him exhausted. At one point the interval between seminars started to get longer, and I found myself calling the case officer more and more often asking for the next session to be put off for a week or for an indefinite period. Nevertheless, these sessions continued, albeit with long gaps between them, until Kim's final year.

Writing to Michael on 4 November 1979, Kim told him: 'Immediately after the holidays I shall be starting my fourth course [of lectures to] the younger generation. It seems incredible that I should already have three. Whoever first said "Time flies" sure spilt a mouthful.'

Kim kept quite closely in touch with his students even when they were stationed abroad. Writing again to Michael on 8 January 1983, Kim told him:

> I had just got into the clear again [after a bout of double pneumonia] when my eldest daughter arrived on a long planned Christmas visit with her husband and my eldest grandson (now 20!), and we have only now begun to settle down to a normal life . . . I was very interested in your interview with Peter Ustinov. I met him several times in 1944–46, at the start of his career, but it was his father whom I really knew. Klop, as he was known, was a very interesting character. After emigration, his family first took German nationality, and Klop was inducted into the German foreign service. While serving in the German Embassy in London, he

was recruited by MI5. He 'defected' when, under the Nazis, the going got too hot for him, but continued to work among German circles and did a lot of good work. When, in 1944, his usefulness to MI5 declined, they offered him to me, and I was mostly instrumental in getting him sent to Lisbon where there were a lot of Germans who by then were thinking mainly of saving their own skins. That was when I got to know him quite well.

Of course, I saw the smiling face of our old friend looking out at me from the front page of The Times last year.* As you say, he behaved very well indeed, and I feel very proud of him. After all, he served his full term *and* got an extension, which was perhaps more than we expected. And, as far as I know, nobody got into trouble on his account. Well, Michael, you are still carrying the torch, and I can well believe that you must have some anxious moments to say the least. It is difficult to see many gleams of light these days or indeed as long as such ignorant clowns as that Ronald Reagan can find the backing to become President of the US. We just have to pin our hopes on the longer term, and meanwhile work patiently to strengthen the cause of sanity wherever we can find it. I feel for you strongly working in that hostile atmosphere, but hope that your personal qualities will have found you at least some people whom you can meet at a human level.

---

* [A reference to the expulsion from the UK of a KGB officer who had studied at a 'Philby seminar'.]

CHAPTER 11

Meeting the Children

At various times all five of Kim's children, three sons and two daughters, as well as four grandchildren, came to see us in Moscow and brought a pleasant variety to our lives. Tom was the first one I met; in fact, as I've already recounted, I met him and Kim simultaneously. After that he came to Moscow two years running. He was a carefree chap, full of life, if slightly eccentric. As a jockey, he had to watch his weight carefully and most seriously assured me that he needed a diet of caviar and champagne. One evening four of us went to a restaurant. Tom and my brother were walking in front of us, chattering away twelve to the dozen and giving every impression that they understood each other completely. Following them, Kim and I tried to guess what exactly they were talking about and, more to the point, in which language. We concluded that each was talking in his own, since Tom spoke not one word of Russian and Kostya not one of English.

Later, I got to know Josephine, Kim's eldest daughter, who visited first in 1973 and almost every year thereafter. At first she came on her own, then with her second husband and sometimes with her children. (She and her first husband had come to see Kim before I arrived on the scene.)

Miranda, Kim's younger daughter, was the only one I didn't meet in Moscow. I got to know her in London only after Kim's death. She visited Kim only once, in the summer of 1969, the year before Kim and I met. She came with Josephine and her three little children, each one tinier than the next. Kim took the whole family to Sukhumi on the Black Sea, where he had asked his case officer Valentin to rent a house for them, which he did. The only problem was that it wasn't vacant but came complete with its entire household and their guests. Everybody swarmed around the English visitors with great curiosity, but they got only two rooms for the six of them.

Over the years I have had accounts of how it was from each of them. The one common theme was how truly awful it was. The landlords were a gregarious bunch and the house was always full of people having a good time and knocking back the local triple-distilled brandy, 70 per cent proof, known as 'Chacha'. They were always very generous to Kim in the process, with the result that when he got to bed at night after another bout of boozy toasts, he had nightmares and frightened the children by shouting in his sleep. They had left one room for him, while the rest had to share the other, until Miranda chose the lesser of the two evils and moved in with her father. The landlord allowed Josephine's children to eat whatever they could lay their hands on and, as a result, they permanently suffered from stomachaches. The other visitors, who may well actually have been lodgers, slept all over the house, in the corridor and on the floor, with Kim's family doing their best not to trip over them. Kim didn't get much pleasure from the warm sea either. Spoiled by years and years of sandy beaches, he couldn't get used to the pebbles. (He couldn't even wear shoes with thin soles, because his sensitive feet felt the tiniest rough patch on the pavement.) Before he went into the water, he would put on as many pairs of socks as he could, swimming around in them to the amazement of everyone on the beach. Their trip left an indelible impression on Miranda. She never came to see Kim again.

Ten years later, Josephine returned with her children. We racked our brains where to take them. What could we offer people spoiled by years of European resorts except the 'Sukhumi Version', which Kim did not want to repeat. Then he thought of Bulgaria. Kim got the OK from the Bulgarian Deputy Minister of Internal Affairs when we were in Sofia on holiday, and the next year we went there to meet the justifiably worried family, who were arriving direct from London. On 18 July 1979, the day before this trip, Kim wrote to Lyubimov:

The delay in answering has been partly due to renewed misbehaviour on my part – a savage attack of bronchitis which laid me low for a couple of weeks. It is all over now, and we are leaving early next week to meet my eldest daughter and three grandchildren in 'another socialist country'. The eldest boy is said to be a strapping sixteen, several inches taller than I am, so I shall have to watch my step. Perhaps my control of the purse-strings will enable me to exercise a little grandfatherly control, but I doubt it. I am afraid we are in for a strenuous 'holiday'. It is ten years since I last saw them, so it will be an interesting reunion.

. . . I am afraid we are having a lousy summer, with alternating weeks of too hot and too cold, plus a lot of rain in July – just when we don't need it. I hope we find kindlier conditions in Bulg. (I mean another socialist country); otherwise entertaining the kids will be quite a problem. We are keeping our fingers crossed.

We drove to the Sunshine Shore, a resort area, from Sofia in two Russian-made cars, a Volga and a Chaika, a large government limousine. The oldest grandchild, Julian, generously ceded the Chaika to his younger sister and brother, Lucy and Jeremy, who squabbled constantly over which of them got to sit next to the driver. We were put up in a Rest Home belonging to the Ministry of Internal Affairs, near the ancient city of Cozopolis surrounded by the Black Sea. The day we arrived Lucy and Jeremy shocked the guests in the garden by starting a fight in the fountain, bashing away at each other in a frenzy and taking no notice of the dirty looks they were getting from the silent spectators, until a loud yell from Kim brought them to their senses. We never had such glorious weather as we saw in that fortnight. We spent every day at the beach. Instead of having two cars at our disposal, we were given a minibus, but the children were disappointed at being deprived of their Chaika.

Kim's son John (two years younger than Josephine) was also a frequent visitor, either on his own, with his first wife or later with his second wife and their daughter, who was less than a year old when she paid her first visit to Moscow. When John and his first wife Nishiya ('a pretty Israeli girl!' as John described her in the telegram in which he told us they had been married) were due to visit us in 1973, Kim booked as a surprise for all of us a steamer trip down the Volga from Moscow to Astrakhan and back. He was sure that they would enjoy it, but this proved only partly the case. Though John had a lot of fun on the trip, Nishiya was bored and was constantly complaining: it was either too hot or too cold.

Through no fault of ours, her visit to Moscow got off to a bad start. The trouble began in London when they were transferred to another flight only minutes before they had been scheduled to leave. Kim had gone to Sheremetyevo to meet them (I stayed at home getting the food ready for their 'welcome' party). No one could tell him anything about the incoming London flight. He searched the airport high and low and finally went outside with no idea of what to do next. He then spotted a girl slumped despondently on the pavement. 'Are you Nishiya?' he asked. 'Yes,' she replied in surprise. Meanwhile, John had been rushing all over the place looking for Kim and was at his wits' end, since he didn't have our address or telephone number. Fortunately, it all ended up happily.

The Volga cruise lasted sixteen days. Our case officer Vladimir acted as our escort and brought his teenage daughter with him. Vladimir and John got on very well, even though they had some bitter battles across the chessboard. We had barely settled into our cabins when the stewardess dropped in for a 'chat'. She was a chemical blonde with restless eyes, metal teeth and a wonderful figure. She spotted us straightaway as people of substance and offered us personal service in supplying the drinks. While making her sales pitch, she gave each of the men bold, appraising glances as if trying to decide who would be a target for her favours. She was as good as her word when it came to refreshments and we were well supplied with beer and mineral water throughout the entire trip.

We stopped off at all the main towns along the Volga. At the larger ports, we usually had several hours on shore and were always met by two black 'Volgas'; needless to say, this did not escape the attention of our fellow passengers. We were always given a warm welcome by the local KGB representatives, and after some sightseeing our visit would be rounded off with a rather good meal in our honour. We were used to this sort of reception, which we regarded as something we just could not avoid, much as we might have liked to. John enjoyed Russian hospitality, but Nishiya found it so excruciatingly painful that she often chose to remain on board. Her dissatisfied look, and her lack of appetite, melted the heart of the rather grim waitress in the dining-room, who asked her sympathetically what she would like for breakfast. 'Marmalade,' Nishiya replied dolefully. But she had to laugh despite herself when the waitress, for whom as a Russian the English word meant something rather different, proudly produced a little box of fruit candies wrapped in chocolate.

At an official dinner in the old merchant town of Kostroma, John, who had no idea of how extravagant such functions could be, was taken aback when the waiter removed a half empty bottle of vodka from the table only to replace it with a full one. Kim had to explain Russian VIP hospitality to him.

In Astrakhan, a big city in the Volga estuary, we went to the fortress, whose beauty, like the profusion of products at the market, is difficult to describe. We were particularly struck by the tomatoes, which came in all shapes, sizes and colours, from lemon yellow through bright orange to blood red. We spent most of the day there exploring the backwaters in a launch, swimming and casting a fishing line over the side. Though we caught nothing, we were fortunate that before we arrived someone had landed a large sturgeon, which was sliced up for cooking as we watched. We were treated to fresh caviar, which we ate with our tablespoons, followed by fish soup. The river people became very fond of John. They were amazed to see anyone drink so much vodka without losing self control. They even let him take the wheel of the launch, which he drove with aplomb and rather fast. The lights of the city rushed towards us, and I closed my eyes in fright, thinking we were just about to smash into a multi-storey building on the bank. But John brought the launch smoothly up to the jetty, to applause from the crew.

Judging by the number of times John and Josephine came to see us, they enjoyed their visits. John said as much, but he once surprised me when, peering into my kitchen, he remarked: 'It's all so primitive, but I really do feel at home here!' Whereas I thought our kitchen was rather smart. So did my friends, who had to make do with something much more modest. It was only when I visited Kim's children in the UK that I understood the huge differences in our living standards.

Harry, Kim's youngest son, came only once (he had been in Moscow before I met Kim and they had travelled together to Estonia). This time he came in December. It was an unusually frosty and snowy winter, and we took him skiing in the Ismailovsky Park (having specially bought him a pair of skis and boots), after which we went to Mama's for dinner, where she served Russian pancakes as a special treat. Harry enjoyed the meal but didn't seem to want to go skiing again. Nor did he fancy a second visit to the Moscow pool. We did our best to show Harry all the sights, but neither Moscow life nor the city itself seemed to spark any interest in him. I was rather upset that I couldn't seem to find anything that would appeal to him, but he assured me that, given the extreme cold, he preferred to stay at home and lie in bed late in the mornings, like a hibernating bear.

The children usually stayed for a fortnight and we stocked up with fancy foods before they came so that they began to believe that caviar was a regular feature of our diet. In their turn they delighted us with nice presents from the UK. We obviously wanted to show them the attractive features of Moscow life, and I think we did. Judging by their reaction, the children had an exaggerated impression of Kim's standard of living and he did little to dissuade them. Though they were surprised at the very limited choice available in the ordinary shops, they assumed that was not relevant to us as we lived at a different level. What were readily available in that era were all sorts of souvenirs – stone, metal and wooden artefacts from Khohloma, Palekh ware and lots of other things. We would invite our visitors to make their own selection and buy them presents.

When family visited, Kim usually asked his case officer for an office car, which we used to pick up or drop off the children at the airport and also for longer trips like to the ancient Russian towns such as Zagorsk and Suzdal. The KGB never said 'No' when Kim asked for something, but for day-to-day living we made only limited use of such favours.

Though he was delighted to see the children, Kim was not really upset to see them go. He had grown accustomed to a solitary life, and no matter who they were, he found having visitors tiring. I went to great lengths to get everything ready before the visitors arrived and loved to go to the airport to meet them; Kim usually stayed at home. And I was always sad to see them leave. It did cross my mind that these visits actually gave me more pleasure than they did Kim.

Surprisingly, people often asked Kim about the persecution his children must have undergone. Soviet Russians were all too well aware that in the USSR, in a case like this, the whole family would inevitably have suffered. They couldn't believe that his spying career had had no consequence for the children, though there might have been distant echoes just once, when John wanted to cover the Vietnam War as a photo-journalist. His visa application was held up at the Passport Office, and he thought the reason might have been that his name was 'Philby'. But in the end he got the visa and duly went to Vietnam. It is worth noting that none of the children ever encountered any problem with their trips to the USSR.

In my view the youngest children, Miranda and Harry, had the most difficult time; just a few years after their mother died in December 1957, they lost their father too. None of the five children looked like each other, and even less like Kim. It was difficult to see any common features between them and their father, though sometimes you could catch a glimpse of him in a feature of the face, or in the way they walked or moved. John, a very warm and sincere person, was closest to Kim and shared his political views. Once at midnight during the May Day holiday in Moscow, John liberated two red Soviet flags off the street flagstaffs (it was amazing he was able to carry them across town without being stopped) and stretched them over the bed in Kim's room, evidently as a sign of respect for his father's ideals.

Kim's younger sister Patricia had another way of showing that she too understood him. She sent him a Frank Sinatra record with a very warm letter. She highlighted My Way on the cover and next to it wrote, 'To Kim from Pat!' Kim was very fond of Patricia and was touched by her gesture, all the more since the words of the song were amazingly close to the way he thought about his life.

I doubt that any of the children really understood why their father did what he did, and they preferred to avoid the subject. So it was all the more surprising for me that the children, otherwise so different from each other, unanimously told me the same phrase: 'He was a great father.'

CHAPTER 12

Pleasures and Enjoyments

When we started to live together, I tried to introduce Kim to our entertainments until I realised he just didn't enjoy that sort of thing. I was delighted – prematurely, it turned out – when I managed to get tickets for the premiere of a British film. I don't recall the title, but it was some literary classic, and I thought that, since Kim would know the book, he would enjoy the film. But he couldn't understand a word and was irritated by the way the Russian translation swamped the English dialogue. He left the cinema rather rapidly a short time after the beginning. Another time I managed to twist his arm into going to the famous Maly Theatre to see *Tsar Fyodor Ioannovich*. He usually avoided the theatre like the plague since he didn't understand much Russian, but on this occasion I hoped he would enjoy the play, since he knew a lot about Russian history and was a fan of our celebrity Innokenty Smoktunovsky, who was playing the Tsar. (Earlier, Kim had enjoyed his performance in the film *Hamlet*.) My hopes didn't come true. Halfway through Act One, Kim was obviously bored and fidgeted in his seat. In the interval, he announced that he wanted to go home. I went into a sulk and let him go. I watched the rest of the play in solitary splendour, but without quite the same enjoyment. For several days after this little outing Kim seemed thoughtful and distracted. Finally, he asked me: 'Who is Shurin? Why haven't I heard his name before?' What had happened was that in the play, whenever Tsar Fyodor speaks to Godunov, he calls him 'Shurin'. Kim thought it was a Russian surname, like Shuisky or Godunov, unaware that Godunov was the Tsar's brother-in-law and that the Russian for 'brother-in-law' is '*shurin*'! He was upset that he didn't know the name of the main characters in the play and in Russian history, and he couldn't find peace until he finally plucked up the courage to speak to me and fill this gap in his knowledge.

Though it sounds strange Kim did like the Hungarian comedy *Wake-up and Sing* at the Satire Theatre starring the wonderful Tatyana Peltser. He had no trouble in making out what was going on in this light-hearted comedy, whereas usually at the cinema or the theatre he would be bored to death and distract me badly in the process. We eventually reached a compromise: he stayed at home and I went out with my friends. On the other hand I didn't say 'No' when he asked me to go with him to ice hockey or football matches, but after a time I was thankfully able to get my brother, like Kim a passionate sports fan, to take my place.

Kim *did* enjoy the circus because he could follow everything that went on. He also liked the symphony concerts at the Conservatoire and performances at the Bolshoi Theatre, and we seldom missed the exhibitions at the Museum of Fine Arts.

We especially enjoyed a concert of the London Symphony Orchestra conducted by Benjamin Britten at the Conservatoire. He made even our ponderous National Anthem sound unusually light and cheerful. Mstislav Rostropovich, the cellist, was already under a cloud and this was to be his last concert in his Motherland. The front rows were reserved for distinguished visitors, foreigners and celebrities. Our seats were there too, but we had given our tickets to some friends, who sat proudly alongside Dmitry Shostakovich, while we perched modestly in the back row in order to avoid bumping into people Kim might not want to meet.

Kim always dreaded the thought of running into foreign journalists when he was out in public. This actually happened once at the Bolshoi, when we bumped into Dick Beeston, the *Daily Telegraph*'s Moscow correspondent, and his wife Moyra, both of whom were friends of Kim's from his Lebanon days. Moyra asked if we went to the Bolshoi very often. I said not as often as we would like to because getting tickets wasn't easy. 'And what is easy here?' she asked with a hint of irritation. That was a rhetorical question Kim and I had often asked ourselves. At that period in our lives, if we wanted tickets or indeed anything else, we had to ask our case officer, but I tried to ask for as few favours as possible.

The Beestons complained that they had been staying with friends for more than a year, having been unable to find a flat. Kim promised to see what he could do and was delighted when in due course he was able to help them. They used to send him affectionate letters and invitations to spend Christmas with them, but sadly we were never able to do it. When Kim's book finally came out in Russia in 1980, the Beestons had already moved to America and I went to the Post Office to mail them a copy autographed by Kim. But no luck – a ban had just been introduced on sending books abroad.

Kim was very jealous even of my friends. In truth, he had absolutely no reason to be jealous; it was simply that he wanted me to be with him all the time. From the very beginning he had doubts about how I felt and even told me: 'Obviously you are in love with me, but I'm always astonished that you are.' Kim was my life. But even so, I didn't want to be out of touch with my friends, and I still wanted to go to the theatre or the movies. Kim always sulked when I went out, though he did his best not to show it. At first, he really took it hard when I went out. I realised this only when, with Kim's permission, I went with my friend to a matinee at the cinema. We went for a stroll afterwards. We were chatting away and I did not notice the time. I was out for longer than Kim had anticipated. Apparently, he had spent hours by the window looking out for me. When I eventually got in, he was trembling and looked so disconsolate that I expected he would take his rather justifiable anger out on me directly. But I heard not a word of reproach. From then on, I always felt guilty when I went out and tried never to stay out too long. As time went by my friends started to tell me that when I was out he would ring round trying to find out where I was, and later I actually came across a confused and anxious note which he had written to me on the day I had been so late.

I had no sense of time and was always running late until Kim re-educated me. When I was getting ready to go somewhere, he would always ask me what time I had to leave. For me, being expected at 7 p.m. didn't mean I had to be there on time, but Kim would be pacing the hall long before it was time to go. I would be affected by his anxiety but, despite that, would find myself slowing down rather than hurrying. Kim himself was exceptionally punctual. Whether he was going out or expecting visitors, he was always 'on parade' well ahead of time. If someone told him: 'I'll drop over in a little while,' he took it literally and was completely undone when, as usual, 'in a little while', in typical Russian fashion, stretched out to several hours. He was amazed that I would then go to the trouble of preparing something to eat for the unscheduled visitor.

Kim hated the phone. He always expected that it would play some mean trick on him, like someone calling to take me out. But he never stopped me and I never abused my freedom. Kim hated being on his own and if I wanted to go somewhere, I knew I had to prepare him for the 'blow' gradually. His face would cloud over whenever he heard that I had been invited somewhere, but he would soon control himself and always told me: 'But of course you should go if you want to.' Obviously I would have liked to have Kim with me when I was out 'socialising', but he preferred to be on his own than being with other people, however nice they were. He was taken aback when a lady we knew told him how she and her husband had gone on a trip and taken a rather disagreeable man along with them, on the grounds that even his company was preferable to being on their own. 'When it is just the two of you, it's boring,' she explained. Kim couldn't conceive of that being the case with us and often asked me, knowing what I would reply: 'Is it boring, just the two of us?' And after he had said good bye to visitors, he would come back saying: 'I only want to be with you. Just you.'

At the beginning I knew very little English and Kim and I spoke to each other in Russian. The fact that he was far from fluent didn't mean we couldn't understand one another and there were only the occasional misunderstandings. 'What does *Istumutsa* mean?' he asked me. 'There isn't such a word,' I told him in some surprise. 'But you just used it,' he insisted. I tried to remember my exact words and it turned out that when I had said, 'I'm going to put the rubbish out,' Kim had heard the Russian phrase, '*Idu vynesti musor*' as one word, '*istumutsa*', which we used from then on whenever I was putting the rubbish out.

My English gradually improved, at least on a day-to-day level, and I began to use it when talking to Kim. He then complained that I was depriving him of the opportunity of learning Russian. Actually, he was rather lazy and never made a real effort to master the language; with me as an interpreter he didn't need to. We gradually developed our own language, a rather awkward blend of Russian and English, which only we could understand.

Kim often simply could not make out a word when other people spoke to him in Russian, and many of them were surprised when they heard me explaining to him in Russian what they had just said. When he and I were talking, I used words he could understand, and I had an instinctive sense when he couldn't grasp what particular words meant. Kim and Mama didn't understand each other either and it was fun hearing them trying to chat. They would both look at me enquiringly, waiting for me to translate what they had said into a form of Russian that each of them could understand. Though Kim now pronounced Russian words clearly and correctly, his foreign accent sometimes had a hypnotic effect on those he was talking to. I remember once in a dairy I asked him to pay an extra 47 kopecks to the lady at the cash desk. I was queuing on the other side of the shop and heard Kim say clearly: 'Forty-seven.' 'Fifty?' the cashier asked. 'Forty-seven,' he repeated. 'Fifty?' she asked again. 'Forty-seven,' he insisted, and I had to hurry over to give him a hand.

Once when Tom was staying with us, we were going to Mama's for dinner, and I ordered a taxi. As was the custom, the dispatcher usually called to say that the taxi driver had left for our home. But sometimes the driver would just appear and ring the bell, while other drivers simply used to park outside and wait. This time I was still in the bedroom getting ready when the doorbell of the flat rang. I heard Kim open the door and say something. When we went down, the taxi was waiting outside, a lady driver at the wheel. She gave us a dirty look when we got in and growled under her breath: 'First they say they don't want a cab, then they just walk down and get in!' I looked enquiringly at Kim, but he put his finger to his lips, telling me to keep quiet. He later explained that when he opened the door, there was a woman outside who asked, 'Did you order rusks?' 'No, I didn't,' he replied and closed the door. At that time you often found private traders cruising in the hallways offering potatoes, fish and so on. True,

I'd never seen anyone selling rusks, but Kim had never come across a lady taxi driver before, especially one in a brightly coloured summer dress and every inch a housewife. When she said 'taxi', he had misunderstood and thought she said, '*sukhari*', the Russian for rusks.

One summer's day we went on a steamer trip round the Bay of Joy near Moscow, which Kim later renamed the Bay of Rage. We sat on the deck in the sun, listening to the birds singing and to the quiet splashing of water, when we were suddenly assailed by a terrible noise from the loudspeaker bearing not even the remotest resemblance to music. I went to switch it off, only to find a large lady bearing down on me threateningly. 'It's all right for you, just warming your old bones in the sun, but we want to enjoy ourselves.' No one else seemed to share my view that listening to the birds was preferable and, given that she outweighed me by a considerable margin, I had little hope of winning the argument. But though the loudspeaker continued to emit its crackling and wheezing, there was nothing else to suggest that anyone was actually having fun. Also, along the shore, every little group was making its own music, and the overall noise was unbearable. As Kim wrote to Graham Greene on 5 April 1980:

> The only quiet place I have found in the SU is my flat – a
> backwater bang in the middle of Moscow, where all I can hear
> is the tapping of my typewriter and the soft, gentle and low
> voice of my wife. Everywhere else, I am infuriated by
> transistors, stereos, outboard motors, cars, trucks, aircraft – all
> those bloody decibels.

So, finding that the outside world irritated him rather than giving him pleasure, Kim immersed himself again in the quiet of his 'island' on the sixth floor. For a long time we stuck to the habit of going out to eat on Saturdays. Kim thought there were fewer people around, and in any case we got to the restaurant at a time when most people hadn't even begun to think about eating. We used to like the Metropole, which had an attractive decor and good service. We took Josephine there on one of her visits. Most of the items on the menu had been crossed out, and even though it was high summer and the streets of Moscow were lined with people selling cucumbers and tomatoes, the only fresh vegetable in the restaurant was 'Russian salad' – potatoes in salad cream. When we expressed surprise, the elderly waiter confided in us: 'I'm now ashamed to work here. Everyone is interested only in banquets. When you're serving 50–100 people at a time, it's easier to fiddle.' In fact, the waiters did so well on the side that Kim's generous tip left them unmoved. So we lost interest in the Metropole Hotel. The waiters' blatant attempts to swindle us ruined the evening for us at the Razdan, while at the Tsentral'ni they were downright rude.

There were pleasant exceptions, but most of our experiences were bad, and after a while we gradually lost our appetite for eating out, all the more since Kim could cook any dish we ordered better. The famous Georgian restaurant Aragvi tried our patience for a long time. It was there that, having ordered the Georgian dish 'Chicken tabaka', we got half of an old, cold, roasted rooster. Instead of a well-grilled carefully flattened bird, they brought a plate with a lump of 'chicken that died of shame'. Looking crestfallen at this colourless and unappetising offering, I asked for the garlic sauce, which always came with it. 'We're out of garlic,' I was told.

Another time when Josephine was with us, we arranged a big reception at the Aragvi with some of Kim's colleagues. We had good and attentive service, but for some strange reason there were fish bones in the chicken pilau. But despite our bad experiences, the Aragvi was the most interesting place we could think of to entertain Graham Greene when he came to Moscow. Afterwards, Kim apologised to him for the poor food. We had a better time there, admittedly, when we took Phillip Knightley and his wife to lunch. They seemed to enjoy it and Phillip, as if inspired, took photo after photo of us at the table. Sadly, when he got back to London, he discovered that there had been no film in his camera. Kim wrote to Greene on 27 January 1988: 'We had some non-Soviet friends here the other day and we took them to the Aragvi, fearing the worst. Actually, they gave us a wholly acceptable meal, with plenty of greenery and four bottles of Georgian wine in addition to the usual snake-bite.'

Our case officer Vladimir I had sung the praises of an out-of-town restaurant called Rus, and we took Josephine there. While Vladimir was booking the table, we strolled around a lake and came across a little tower-like building that turned out to be a bar, which was completely devoid of customers. I ordered a glass of vodka for each of us. The barman, evidently bored, went on cleaning his fingernails but muttered: 'Can't serve neat vodka.' 'Well, how can you serve it?' 'In a cocktail.' 'Then we'll have brandy.' 'You can't have that either.' 'And what's in a cocktail?' 'Vodka, brandy, champagne and synthetic lemon juice.' Recoiling from the recipe alone, we left this 'hospitable little nook'. In the meantime, they had our table ready, covered with appetisers and opened bottles of sweet fortified wine. Kim was taken aback to see what they had decided to choose for us. He never touched fortified wine, but the restaurant said they had neither dry wine nor vodka and we had to make do with brandy before, during and after the meal.

There were two types of customers in the restaurant – foreign tourists and Soviet tradesmen (who, at that time of total deficit, still managed to have a very high standard of living). You could spot the latter straightaway (nowadays, leaving aside the 'new' Russians, 'class' distinctions aren't quite so obvious). They had all the hallmarks of men whom life had treated generously: bulging bellies straining at Crimplene suits, heavy gold jewellery and briefcases stuffed with bottles of vodka nestling under the table. They ordered music (in the literal meaning of the phrase, as well as its Russian sense of lording it over in a restaurant) and were having a hell of a time. They started to dance, flinging their arms round each other, and sat on each other's knees. For some reason the women danced together leaving their affronted men to follow their example. The foreigners watched all this as if it was a fairground show, thinking they were watching something authentically Russian.

One cold winter's day I took Kim to the Uzbekistan restaurant. I had fond memories of it from the first time I used to go there with my friends from the editorial department when I worked at the publishing house. You could eat well there without spending too much money. It had mainly a Central Asian clientele, and every time I had been there I saw the same thing – while the men feasted, their wives sat outside in the corridor chewing bread and rolls; for them, that was dinner. But when I went there with Kim, the Uzbekistan had changed. It was crowded, smoky and not very appealing. We did not enjoy the meal and were getting ready to leave when all of a sudden we found we couldn't get out. The restaurant was bursting at the seams and outside an excited crowd of angry men in astrakhan caps was swirling around the door trying to get in. The doorman was frightened to let us out in case they came piling in. Finally, he managed to open the door just a crack. Kim and I squeezed out and he slammed it shut behind us. It crossed my mind that going hungry might do these fellows good when I found myself staring at close range into a shiny red face. His furious look left me in no doubt that he was about to swallow me whole and that if he somehow didn't manage it the others would trample us underfoot. With a threatening look I said: 'You should make way for a lady,' flicked him on the forehead and took a step forward. He started and moved backwards. The crowd grew quiet and began to make way for us. We proceeded with dignity through the human corridor. It was yet another confirmation that Kim was right when he maintained that 'home is best'. He was delighted at my quick-witted reaction and loved to retell this incident.

CHAPTER 13

Travels in the USSR

Most of our travels were, of course, without the children. Each year we went on holiday to a different part of Russia or one of the Soviet-bloc countries. In the summer of 1971, we set off on our long-awaited trip around Siberia. Kim had been there before we met, with John, and had fallen in love with it. Irkutsk was hardly a quick trip – it was four days on the train – but Kim didn't mind travelling with me under these conditions. He sat staring out of the window, checking in his guidebook every time a town flashed by. We had brought along our own food and relied on the train only for tea. The tea was a bit on the watery side, but scalding. Kim was understanding and valued the little pleasures of life.

A car was waiting at Irkutsk station to take us to the sanatorium. When Kim first arrived in the USSR, he had asked for advice on where to go for holidays. He was a bit surprised to find that for Russians 'holidays' were usually synonymous with taking some sort of medical cure. People told him: for your liver you go to Kislovodsk, Zheleznovodsk is good for digestive problems, you go to Yalta for your lungs, and so on. But in any event, in Siberia we had to stay at a sanatorium since it was the only civilised place around Lake Baikal. It nestled on a hill overlooking Listvyanka Bay. Curiously, it owed its existence to President Eisenhower. On a state visit to the USA, Khrushchev had invited Eisenhower to the USSR. Eisenhower had said that if he did, Baikal was a place he would really like to visit, but it turned out that all the Baikal area could offer as accommodation were little village huts. There was not one decent building, let alone anything where such a distinguished visitor might stay. So a road was hurriedly laid from Irkutsk to Listvyanka, where a two-storey wooden cottage was specially built.

But despite all this bustle Eisenhower never actually made it. So as not to waste all the effort and use the natural beauty, two large two-storey structures were built across from the cottage, creating the sanatorium where we stayed. The original cottage, incidentally, was the venue for a magnificent dinner in our honour given by the local KGB boss, Geny Ageev, and the Regional First Secretary.

Kim was surprised when we were met in the dining-room by a white-coated doctor with a stethoscope round her neck. 'What about a drink?' Kim asked me, looking round in some trepidation. 'This is a sanatorium,' I replied patiently. 'No alcoholic drinks allowed!' The merest mention of the word 'doctor' was enough to get Kim into a state. This was a family trait. His father, St John, also did his best to steer clear of any form of medical attention. When he had a heart attack, Kim, braced for an angry rebuff, suggested tentatively that he should see a doctor. To his surprise his father agreed, at which point Kim realised that he really was in a bad state. The doctor gave St John an injection and he fell asleep. He awoke only once and said to Kim, 'I am bored.' He died late in the afternoon, on 30 September 1960.

Most of the people in the sanatorium were carrying, shall we say, more than the average amount of weight. Kim decided that they were all patients suffering from obesity and would be on a strict diet. He was greatly surprised when he saw them tucking into macaroni and bread, taking any leftovers back to their rooms even though they had been well fed. Although the sanatorium specialised in cardiac troubles, the doctors seemed as indifferent to the weight problems as the fat patients themselves. 'For some reason, you people from Moscow never seem to want to put on weight,' the doctor said in surprise, looking at our far from emaciated frames. Most of the people there were from Siberia. There were only two other couples from Moscow and both, like us, were interested in the unusual and exotic things the Siberian landscape had to offer.

Kim decided he wanted to lose weight and went for walks every day, even when it poured. (I couldn't indulge in such heroics.) Wrapped in a raincoat and striding briskly, he would always cover at least five kilometres. He would be back in an hour, tired, soaked through, but looking much better for it. Nonetheless, when he saw that after ten days his weight hadn't budged, he got very annoyed. However much I tried to convince him that his body fat had been converted into muscle, I couldn't reassure him. He bundled up his clothes and asked me to put them on the scales separately, so he could figure out what he really weighed. He drew no comfort from the result and abandoned his exercise.

The sanatorium's grounds, though not that large, were well maintained. One broad walkway had been cut through the woods up to a cliff from which there was a far-reaching view of the lake. There was nowhere else to walk. Lorries rumbled along the dusty road which ran along the shoreline past the sanatorium, making it a dangerous and unappealing place to stroll. But even right by the busy road, the water was still clear and clean enough to drink. The lake was a real wonder of nature, with the unique capability of cleansing itself. The Baikal salmon, called omul or grayling, are the tastiest fish I have ever eaten. At one picnic we had a whole freshly caught omul stuck on a spit and roasted on a bonfire. Omul can also be frozen and later eaten raw. We tasted grayling at a dinner given by new friends met on the trip, the Novokshenovs, in the city of Angarsk. They wrapped it in leaves and then broiled it over charcoal like a barbecue.

Our favourite way of passing the time (there actually wasn't anything else to do) was to take a rowing boat out on the Angara river. There were not that many people in the sanatorium who liked to go for a row, and even fewer boats, so any break in the weather produced an edgy queue on the quayside. Though the boats were actually the property of the sanatorium, they were looked after by a malevolent little dwarf who behaved as if he were the real owner. 'I'll give you a boat if I feel like it,' he would say.

Once when we were down there the local KGB man, Valery, who used to drop in from time to time, decided we needed his special clout and whispered something into the boatman's ear. 'What's your precious KGB got to do with me?' he snarled, deliberately raising his voice. In the end, I figured that the best way to get him on our side was to slip him a bottle of vodka, after which we had no more problems. Having emerged victorious from the battle of the queue, I took the oars and we surrendered to the beauty surrounding us along both banks of the Angara. There was not a living thing in sight except for a wonderful crested bird pacing along the sandy shore. He was always at the same spot and never failed to keep level with us as we rowed along. It was easy to row with the current and I was totally absorbed, but with his unerring sense of timing Kim brought me back to earth telling me it was time to head back. We changed places, and I saw how right he was. Rowing against the current on the way back took us twice as long.

The next year we went to the same sanatorium and then took a cruise on the lake. The minute we went on board it dawned on us just why Siberians had given us funny looks when we told them about the trip. The tiny little steamer with a high funnel looked a bit like my great-grandmother's smoothing iron. Ironically, the ship was called the *Komsomolets*, which means 'the Young Communist'. It was in fact a river fishing trawler rebuilt to carry passengers. It was the only way of travelling around the lake. Built to carry 100 people, the *Komsomolets* actually had some 400 on board. Kim and I had two berths in a cramped four-passenger cabin, with a porthole about the size of a saucer, which seemed better suited to be the crew's quarters. The other cabins were taken by our escort Valery, two couples, and several mathematicians on their way back from a symposium in Novosibirsk. The run-of-the-mill tourists had no roof over their heads, only a tarpaulin which was unrolled at night to cover the rows of sleeping bodies which occupied the entire deck. When we saw them, we felt ashamed at our 'comfort', but consoled ourselves with the thought that our two berths would not have solved their problems. The toilet or, more precisely, the 'head' consisted of two holes modestly concealed behind green curtains adorned with brown stains of assorted vintage. You had to hold your breath and sidle up to the appointed aperture, taking care not to touch anything. Anyone who has been lucky enough to visit similar facilities in Soviet railway stations can imagine the level of 'hygiene'. In the mornings men and women formed two gloomy lines outside. To minimise the need for such visits, we put a jam jar into service as a chamber pot, emptying it out of the porthole.

There was no shortage of those little adventures which are an essential part of any journey. Already on Day One, the fridge broke down, and all the meals had to be jettisoned. The dining-room was closed. That same night someone smashed the padlock and looted the food store. We were saved from starvation only by the cucumbers and tomatoes we had had the foresight to buy in the market in Irkutsk, as well as the raspberry jam (whose jar came in so handy!) which the Novokshenovs had given us. When the restaurant eventually reopened, we were taken in by the service door as a 'perk'. But seeing a long queue, Kim hurried round the table to take his place at the end. When our turn came, Kim exclaimed, breathless with delight: 'Fried eggs!' I had never seen such a pleased expression on his face. I was all the more surprised because at home he wouldn't trust even me to make them – cooking them himself and timing the operation with exquisite precision. God forbid they should either be underdone or overdone!

Despite these minor inconveniences, Kim didn't regret the trip, though he did decide he would not do it again. We were able to see Lake Baikal in all its grandiose beauty and to enjoy the fantastic colourful flashes of the sunset. The weather was sunny, if cool, and once the sun had gone down the temperature dropped sharply, with a hint of frost in the air. The captain was a Buryat, who came from one of the little villages around the lake. He reigned supreme not only on the boat, but over the entire lake. In love with the sound of his own voice, he would hold forth on anything and everything, getting on our nerves by shattering the blissful silence with periodic monologues. But one of his statements attracted our attention. 'You know,' he said, 'those so-called scientists got blind drunk and ended up in a dreadful state.' As we discovered later, the one who had been in the worst state had been dumped in a dinghy at 4 a.m. and put ashore at some almost uninhabited spot – there were only three huts there – so that he could sober up on dry land and in the fresh air. Since there was no other means of transportation, the poor guy was condemned to stay there for six days and nights waiting for the *Komsomolets*'s return trip, with the same captain, this time though in the role of rescuer. Once they had sobered up, the other mathematicians worked themselves into quite a lather, sent an official complaint to the captain and collected signatures from passengers who had seen what happened. Meanwhile, the boat cruised steadily ahead, its funnel puffing briskly and making its scheduled stops.

The crew of the *Komsomolets* blended in well with the decor. Stripped to the waist, burned almost black by the sun, they looked half-wild, more like pirates. Other than at Listvyanka, there were no piers on the lake. Instead, the ship either tied up at tumbled-down wooden jetties or simply moored offshore, landing its passengers in a small boat. When we were approaching the next stop, Kim beckoned me into the cabin. We needed to hide from the captain, who had got into the habit of pushing aside other passengers while pressing us to get into the boat. Having done this twice, we decided not to risk it again, not wanting to end up in the icy water, as the penalty for admiring the scenic splendour of the dense Siberian forest which fringed the lake. Getting the passengers into the boat was an unforgettable sight. Herded like sheep by the loud voices of the crew, the passengers would leap into the boat and huddle in terror on one side. The sailors never managed to get them more or less evenly on each side. We were always expecting the boat to capsize and someone to fall out, though, as luck would have it, this never happened.

After the Baikal trip we made a long tour of Siberia, beginning with a journey from Irkutsk to Bratsk on a double-decker steamer, which, compared to the *Komsomolets*, was the height of perfection. At one point I had left Kim for a moment, only to find him surrounded by a group of young people pressing him with questions. 'We saw *Dead Season*, the movie was about you?' 'No, no,' said Kim, 'that was about Lonsdale.' 'So you're Lonsdale?' 'He's dead.' 'How do you know?' At a loss Kim called me to his rescue and I liberated him. What had happened was that Valery, our KGB escort from Irkutsk, had confided in the captain who Kim was. Following the principle that secrets are meant to be shared, the captain told his crew. In due course, one of them invited Kim to say a few words to them in their mess. After a certain amount of toing and froing (Kim always avoided speaking in public), we agreed that we would meet with a small group, say not more than five. The small group expanded to twenty, among them the inquisitive young people. In fact, though Kim had trouble expressing himself in Russian, and at the time I knew little English, it turned into

113

a sort of ad hoc press conference, with Kim at first answering in English, then he whispered to me in Russian: 'You know what to say,' and I carried on from there. Everybody seemed pleased and the crew, being thankful, treated us to their own fish soup.

Though you could count the customers in the restaurant on the fingers of one hand, we usually had to wait well over half an hour to be served. The waitress, her mind obviously far more on sex than on her job, wandered between the tables like a sleepwalker, unable to tear her lovelorn eyes from a sailor who sat in the corner taking not the slightest notice of her. When she did finally bring the appetisers, she would forget the fork; she would bring the soup without spoons, or only remember the bread when we had finished eating. This time she plonked empty soup bowls in front of us and disappeared for a long time. 'Waitress, waitress,' the customers called imploringly. Finally, she re-emerged with a huge saucepan and headed for our table. She filled our bowls with fragrant fish soup, pouring a generous amount over Kim's lap in the process. The soup was delicious even to the point that we couldn't feel sorry about his trousers.

Our cruise finished at Bratsk, where we spent two days. This little town of four- and five-storey buildings was created in 1953 alongside the reservoir when the hydroelectric station was being constructed. People were kind enough to give us a tour of the station, which was hugely impressive. One of the other sights in Bratsk was a lovely little bear (in a cage). He looked quite good-natured and harmless, but when some stupid man had decided to stroke him gently, the bear had bitten off his fingers. Vitaly, the KGB escort, took us home for coffee and brandy so that we could meet his wife Valentina. She was a leader of the local Young Communists League. She had a powerful voice and vast bosom, and only had to snap, 'Vitaly,' for him to shrink visibly and shut up. It was obvious who was the boss. Two years later Vitaly, who happened to be in Moscow, came to see us.

In Kranoyarsk, we stayed at the Central Hotel. When we went to the restaurant for dinner, the waitress warned us that the fish was inedible and recommended the house special, steak. This, however, turned out to be difficult to cut and impossible to chew. The next day we tried a restaurant which someone had recommended as top-class, apparently because it had an orchestra. The orchestra played so unbelievably loudly that when the waiter came to take our order, we couldn't hear each other and were reduced to scribbling down what we wanted on a paper napkin. Learning from our bitter experience we ordered *Boeuf Stroganoff*, but like the steak, it was difficult to get your teeth into. Kim had compared the steak to eating the sole of a shoe and the *Boeuf Stroganoff* was like eating shoelaces. In those years, Krasnoyarsk was closed to foreign tourists, so everything was in pretty short supply. Meanwhile, the decibel level had reached maximum, and in the end we left the restaurant not only hungry but reeling from the noise. On the other hand, the outskirts, surrounded by a forest with a wide variety of different trees, were very picturesque. We took some lengthy strolls there along the tourist paths, and on one of them came across a small private zoo, whose owner collected strays, sick birds and some small wild animals, and took care of them.

In Divnogorsk (near Krasnoyarsk), despite our reluctance and the 'NO ENTRY' signs all around, we had to climb up to see the hydro-electric power station. Still under construction, it was reckoned to be one of the most powerful in the world. We scrambled perilously along the girders with Kim saying over and over again: 'This is very danger-ous.' We weren't able to wriggle out of a nocturnal fishing trip either. Our host's idea of entertaining us was to do what he liked doing, with-out a thought as to what his guests might like. Five of us had to spend the night huddled on one bench in the stuffy hold of a small launch. I got seasick. Kim reckoned that as a guest one had an obligation to go along with your host's whims. 'Everything has to be paid for one way or another,' he was fond or repeating.

It was terribly hot – 36 degrees C. – when we set off on a two-day cruise along the Yenisei river, one of the longest on the continent, that runs south to north across Russia. It was just as hot on the river, and the air was motionless. We landed on an island and immediately rushed to the water. Here it was completely the opposite. The water was icy; it numbed your feet, and even the children couldn't pluck up the courage to get in. It turned out that because of the power station, the river water at this point was constantly being recycled and did not have time to warm up even in the hottest weather. The heat was something I had never encountered before, and I could barely stand it. It seemed that the blood was boiling in my veins and I felt my head was close to bursting. Kim was very frightened to see me in such a state. I, plus our escort from Krasnoyarsk, Andrei and his wife, planted ourselves in the shade of a tree, though this did nothing to protect us from the heat. Despite the hot air, Kim decided to explore. Hatless, and looking like a torch in his yellow T-shirt, he eventually circled the island. He didn't mind the heat. Only the mosquito bites bothered him, even though he slapped on a special ointment which he had had the foresight to bring with him.

In contrast, we much enjoyed the River Ob; the temperature there was more moderate and the water warm. The wide, deserted beaches were covered in clean, fine sand as white and crunchy as snow. The water in the shallows was so warm that even Kim, who didn't like cold water, risked a dip. Akademgorodok, the town of scientists and the location of many research institutes, on the riverbank downstream from Novosibirsk, was a mass of greenery and thus swarming with mosquitoes. When Kim had asked me to come with him to Siberia, I had warned him that the mosquitoes there ate one alive. 'They are real brutes.' 'There aren't any mosquitoes there,' Kim assured me. In fact, the first time he went to Siberia, there weren't any mosquitoes. They had all been wiped out with the help of DDT; birds, squirrels and similar creatures had also perished. But by the time Kim and I got there, the blood-suckers had multiplied again. Siberian mosquitoes are of terrifying size and very aggressive. Watching people strolling under their dive-bombing attacks, you see the walkers going into a sort of ritual fan dance, flapping little branches around to try to ward the wretched things off. It was funny to watch a sheepdog puppy with paws too big for his little body shaking his heavy head and snapping his teeth angrily to shoo the pests away.

Our Siberian friends suggested we go back to Moscow by plane. It seemed sensible after such a lengthy trip, though it was against our rules! The six-hour flight seemed endless compared to ninety hours in the train, which had flown by without our noticing. We were met in Moscow literally by 'the smoke of the Fatherland', in the words of the classical Russian writer, Aleksander Griboedov. There had been a terrible drought that summer and brush fires had broken out in the Moscow area. They had been extinguished by the time we got back, but the air was still full of dense smoke and the smell of cinders.

Kim suffered from chronic bronchitis and in 1973 I persuaded him to go to Yalta in the Crimea, because it was considered to be the best place to cure it. (The famous Russian writer Anton Chekhov, who had had TB, had spent several years there.) We decided that May, when everything came into full bloom, would be the best time and were given vouchers for the Russia Sanatorium of the Council of Ministers. We arrived in Simferopol by train, where we were met by the local KGB official who drove us to Yalta.

Our holiday started inauspiciously: there was thick fog and snow all the way from Simferopol and the sun began to break through only when we reached Yalta itself. The weather was miserable almost the entire month we were there. After sunset, even when it had been sunny in the daytime, a cold fog descended in the evenings. The locals said that we were unlucky and that they had never had such bad weather before. They reckoned the construction of the Simferopol Reservoir had altered the weather pattern for the worse. We were rarely lucky with the weather when we travelled, and the phrase, 'We've never had weather like this before,' became a familiar refrain.

The sanatorium was built in typical Stalin-era style, ponderous and grandiose, though one had to admit that it was built solidly and to high standards. Deep loggias and thick stone walls shielded the rooms from the sun, not that we saw much of that. Our deluxe suite comprised a bedroom, a sitting-room and a bathroom, with the added bonus of an electric samovar, which Kim was delighted to see. He couldn't manage without his hot, strong tea. The central heating was set to be shut down on the 15th of April, which is when the warm dry season (at least hitherto) started. Unfortunately, it went off automatically, without regard to what the weather outside was actually doing, and it was colder inside than out. We slept under two blankets, and in the daytime warmed ourselves with tea and from the steam of the samovar. As a result, Kim's bronchitis persisted throughout the holiday.

Whenever we arrived at a sanatorium, it was my job to persuade the doctor in charge to ignore us, and to make clear that we would not be undergoing any cures or subjecting ourselves to any remedial treatment, even massage, of which everyone was allegedly fond. Kim did not care to be touched by anyone else's hands. I did manage to persuade him to come with me to the swimming-pool. He swam very well and had even won medals at school and university, but he was soon regrettably compelled to give it up. What happened was that every first-time visitor to the pool had to listen to a lecture on the rules, the most important of which was that you had to wash yourself thoroughly with soap and a loofah before swimming. Kim found himself listening to this homily along with three other men. They looked like guilty boys, quite an accurate description, as it turned out, since Kim told me later, with a laugh, that none of them, apart from him, had gone anywhere near the shower. The tone at the pool was set by the cleaning lady, a rude, loud-mouthed woman who regarded the people coming in to swim as no better than carriers of dirt whom she would have to clean up after, and she made it clear that she detested them. She would rummage in the bags in which people had their swimming gear looking for 'clues'. If she didn't like the look of your loofah, or your piece of soap (too small), or if she caught you without a spare swimming suit (it was forbidden to swim in the same suit you used for sunbathing), public disgrace was inevitable. She was immediately suspicious of Kim, viewing him as an unknown, alien being, and assailed him on his second visit to the pool. Kim, who was as clean in body as he was pure in spirit, felt her attitude to be both insulting and unfair and never darkened her doorstep again. The cleaning lady was a sad exception; the rest of the sanatorium staff were polite and welcoming. Kim generally won over people attending to him by being undemanding and kind-hearted.

On our first visit to the Russia we weren't able to escape a brush with the doctors. Kim – I went with him to keep him company – underwent a cardio-vascular examination with paradoxical results. According to what they showed, my tests were typical of someone sixty years old, while Kim's were characteristic of someone aged forty.

Despite his bronchitis Kim was strong, with a lot of stamina, whereas I got out of breath quickly, especially going uphill. Kim walked at a steady, level pace and would have to stop to let me catch up. Kim's colleagues from the KGB in Simferopol would take us out from time to time, and I remember one sunny day out on a launch when I was fishing for the first time in my life and caught more than anyone else. We had an unforgettable trip into the mountains to see the 'croaking' Lake Karagol nestled among the pines. The frogs sang in spring chorus at deafening volume, each desperately trying to outcroak the other. Kim took great delight in their happy dissonance, which drove a black spaniel nearby to hysterics, as he rushed along the bank, his wet fur sticking to his thin shivering body as he tried in vain to catch the frogs. He lost his bark and could only howl plaintively.

Having decided that we could not possibly be unlucky with the weather every year, we went to Yalta again the following May, but a week later. Once again, we heard the refrain that, 'We've never had weather like this before,' even though, to be fair, there were more sunny days. We did a lot of walking and were especially fond of the Tsar's path, a picturesque shady path which winds above the sea through the park of the former Tsar's estate Lyvadiya and comes out at Miskhor. Kim did not care to sunbathe, and it was too cold to swim. He preferred returning to familiar places and to people he knew. It was important for him not so much to get used to them, but for them to get comfortable with him and not to see him as a 'white crow'. It was easier for me too. We didn't have to begin all over again to persuade the doctors to leave us alone and explain just why we needed a table to ourselves. One reason was Kim's allergy to apples, which I mentioned earlier. Just the sight of them made him sick. He could not bring himself even to enter the dining-room if he saw apples laid out ready on plates, and often went without dinner as a result.

But the principal reason we needed to be on our own was that Kim found it agonising to mix with unfamiliar people, not only because of the language barrier but because of the inevitable questions which we would simply be unable to answer. Since the initial stay in the Crimea had brought no perceptible improvement in Kim's health, the doctors decided that next time he should stay at least twice as long. As he wrote to Mikhail Lyubimov on 2 May 1978,

> We are off to the Crimea in a couple of days and propose to
> stay there 6–7 weeks, enough to recuperate from a poorish
> winter and stoke up energies for the coming year. In our case,
> we will both be fishing, which is too bad because Rufa always
> catches much more than I do, and boasts for weeks afterwards.
> I think she could catch a whale with a bent pin.

After 'serving a third stretch' at the Russia, we moved to the Chernomoriye Sanatorium, a little further from Yalta but nearer to the Tsar's path. It was June. The weather improved and I went swimming though the water was still too cold for Kim. The Chernomoriye was less expensive and slightly more modest, though the people there seemed nicer than those at the Russia, whose clientele was mainly provincial big shots giving themselves airs. We were soon on good terms with our new doctor. She said that it was already a bit late to be able to count on good weather, there was a lot of rain and the air was humid and cool. Years ago the weather had been predominantly sunny and dry, which had helped clear up lung problems, but the Crimea now seemed to be losing its unique healing powers, she told us, confirming our own doubts. That was our last visit there.

A trip to Tbilisi was Kim's brilliant idea of a way to outwit nature, to escape from the winter and get a slightly longer spring. So at the beginning of March 1975 we left for Tbilisi, where spring had already arrived. Ten days later we would be back in time for the start of our second spring in Moscow. As usual we went by train. It was Kim's second visit there, and my first. But the weather played us a dirty trick. It was cold with fog and wet snow, and an unwelcome gloomy pall hung over this astonishingly unique city. On the one sunny day we had, it underwent a complete transformation, and I could see just how it would sparkle when all the trees and flowers were in bloom.

We stayed at the Central Hotel. The little breakfast buffet downstairs had a small assortment of milk, cheese, curd and sausages. It turned out that this was not all the Georgians ate for breakfast. We saw four of them set off for the buffet leaving behind under their table half-a-dozen empty champagne bottles. That evening, when we went down to dinner in the restaurant, we couldn't help noticing at the long table facing us a large group of rather quiet men tucking in to a sizeable meal. A European with film-star looks stood out from the swarthy crowds of Southerners. We noticed that they drank nothing but champagne, which they would uncork and pour into large pitchers. The waitress kept bringing them armfuls of new bottles. A nice young couple sat at our table. They ordered champagne to celebrate their wedding anniversary. We couldn't believe our ears when the waitress told them there wasn't any, all the more when we looked at the lines of bottles ranged on the table across the room. But the young people didn't seem surprised, just looked a little disconsolate and made do with the wine. We started a conversation, and it turned out they were musicians. They told us how difficult life was for intellectuals in a corrupt society. Suddenly, the waitress appeared and put a bottle of champagne in front of me. I was very pleased for the young couple and pushed the champagne towards them telling the waitress they had ordered it. But she grabbed it back, saying, 'It's for you,' and nodding over at the large group. The 'European' gave me a beaming smile. We had finished our dinner by then and persuaded the young couple to drink 'my' champagne. The 'film-star' suddenly swept up and asked me to dance, embracing Kim in the process. I told him that unfortunately I could not dance as I had a wooden leg. Without losing face and very dignified, he went back to his group; the party atmosphere gradually tapered off and the crowd there began to thin out. Remembering the Georgian custom that one should avoid being in anyone's debt, I ordered a bottle of champagne for the 'film-star'. This time the waitress didn't refuse and the bottle reached his table without mishap. But my admirer brought it back to us and said goodbye, yet again, embracing Kim. We left soon afterwards, without touching the champagne, so our young friends managed in the end to get two bottles. As we left, they looked apprehensively at my legs trying to decide which one was wooden.

Volodya, the KGB contact who escorted us, was a nice, bright Georgian. Kim wanted to show me the town of Telavi, which had left an indelible impression on him when he first came to Georgia. On the day we were supposed to go there, the weather took a very decided turn for the worse, making the trip a complete waste of time, but Volodya said there was no way it could be postponed and, as usual, we gave in. The fog was so thick that you could not see your hand in front of your face. The car could do no more than inch forward, which was just as well, otherwise we would have run over a man walking along the edge of the road; as it was, we stopped just short of hitting him. We got out to 'admire' the valley, which the fog had filled like a bowl of milk. Chilled to the bone and hungry, we finally reached Telavi, where we were taken to a house which looked like a barn someone had nailed together in a hurry. There was a long table with benches and a pot-bellied stove. It was colder inside than out. Kim glanced at the stove, but the owner, a friend of Volodya's, nudged him aside and called for someone. A man came in, opened the door and stared at the cold ashes. Then he carefully closed the door and departed. Twenty minutes passed. Kim grabbed the matches and an old newspaper and rushed towards the stove. The landlord again stopped him. 'I can't possibly let you,' he said and summoned someone else. A second chap appeared and stared at the stove thoughtfully for a long time, as if looks alone could get it going, but he had no luck and left. Another hour went by before a third stoker appeared and managed to light the fire.

Meanwhile, the table was laid and, shivering from cold and hunger, we could not wait to sample the food and wine. We had our glasses halfway to our lips when Volodya stopped us. First, there had to be a toast. The landlord delivered the first toast – to parents – explaining at some length that without parents we wouldn't have been there. Imagine! Apologising for our ignorance, we reached for our glasses. Not so fast. '*Allaverdi*,' Volodya proclaimed, announcing the general purpose toast which allowed him to hold forth on anything under the sun. He took full advantage! Finally, we got to drink our first glass, had a bit to eat and gradually warmed up. The next toast was to 'Peace'. We heard that peace was better than war, came to understand the blessings of peace and the misfortunes that war brought in its wake. And we couldn't even take another sip of wine until all the ramifications had been thoroughly explored.

I was surprised at the change in Volodya. Up to that point, he had seemed to be on the same wavelength as us, but once here he had become ultra-orthodox, taking his cue from his friend. It struck me as odd that such a sophisticated man, who was far from stupid, lacked the tact and sense of humour to turn the evening into a far less formal occasion. He must have seen that Kim wasn't enjoying the proceedings; indeed, found them painful. All the formalities might have been fine for a group of distinguished old fogies, but apart from Kim and me, there were only two other people there, both young: Volodya and his friend.

We gradually warmed up and made inroads into the excellent dry wine, the appetisers and copious quantities of vegetables. We were very tired and wanted nothing more than to get back to the hotel as soon as we could, but Volodya's pal had another idea. He wanted to show us an ancient church and, ignoring our protests, drove us there. We stumbled through dark alleyways towards a tumbled-down church, whose silhouette was almost indistinguishable in the dark. The friend hammered on the window of the house next door to it. There was a dreadful noise, the light went on inside, but the door stayed firmly shut. So we never got to see this particular local attraction. We finally got to bed well after midnight.

Kim and I spent most of the time strolling around the town. Before we left for Moscow, Volodya arranged a picnic in the snow. He treated us to a nice home-made wine, which we drank with bread and cheese; this time, thankfully, there were no toasts.

Back in Moscow, we found exactly the same weather. Here too spring had decided to come late.

CHAPTER 14

An Invitation We
Couldn't Refuse

In November 1971, the KGB told us that, 'according to information received', Kim was in danger and that attempts were being made to track him down. They told us we had to leave town for a month and go as far away from Moscow as possible. Kim was disinclined to believe the 'information', but we went along with it and, after asking around, decided to go to Armenia, which we had not visited before. We were put up in a private house deep in the mountains near Yerevan. There was only one road up to the house, which ended at the gates, flanked by a sentry box with a watchman. Along the front of the house was a small yard and an iron fence encircled the property. Our bedroom windows looked out on an empty plot. Around the house, as far as the eye could see, bare boulders lay scattered at random in a grim and depressing landscape. We felt we were living in an impenetrable fortress. I realised it wasn't quite impregnable when, sunbathing on the balcony one day, completely relaxed, I heard someone hiss. I looked down and saw a teenage boy standing in the garden. 'Come here,' he called. I rushed to find the bodyguard.

In fact, there were two bodyguards, Volodya and George, who alternated. One of them was always around. One day, when we were strolling along the one and only path, Kim asked Volodya: 'Assume someone were to rush at me with a knife or pistol. What could you do?' 'Nothing,' Volodya admitted. In addition to the bodyguards, the house came with a cook, a young guy with a somewhat louche air about him, and an elderly lady who doubled as a waitress and a housekeeper. At breakfast we were offered the most expensive brandy. Though we said we didn't want any, George would open the bottle in a way that brooked no argument and pour us each a glass. We left it untouched. A fresh bottle appeared at lunch and a third at dinner. But we drank only dry wine, which, unlike the Georgians, the Armenians do not drink at all. Over lunch one day the Head of the Armenian KGB remarked in some surprise: 'Why isn't Kim drinking brandy today?' I understood what was behind his question only a bit later when Kim asked for some dry wine with dinner and was told there was none left. Volodya went to the kitchen to be told that it looked as though we had drunk everything in the house. Then it dawned on me: George's conjuring tricks with the brandy, and the cook waving a bottle at one of his chums, inviting him in for a drink! It was easy to figure out what had been going on. Three bottles of the most expensive brandy, of which we had not touched a drop, had been charged to Kim's account, whereas the dry Armenian wine for 70 kopecks a bottle, of which he was so fond, could not be found for the 'distinguished guest'.

I decided to have a word with Volodya while we were out for our evening walk. He seemed a decent young man, and I wanted him to know the truth. He said he had seen George taking bottles of brandy home and was planning to report on him. Whether he did or not, I don't know. George was older and more senior. Even as a bodyguard George was not up to much. Once when we were walking along our now familiar path, we met a large ram and said, 'Hello,' to him. Instead of greeting us with a smile, he dropped into an aggressive crouch and rushed headlong at Kim. Kim punched him between the eyes (luckily he had no horns), at which the ram scurried backwards, took another run and rushed at Kim again. Kim managed to fend him off. I ran around in circles trying to draw the ram away. George meanwhile stood to one side watching the duel with a condescending look on his face. He clearly thought Kim was enjoying playing the toreador. The ram was taking a longer and longer run-up before each assault, and I finally succeeded in dragging Kim away. Kim bore the scars of the encounter for quite a while. 'His skull was as hard as rock,' Kim said. 'I didn't know you were not supposed to say "Good morning" to an Armenian ram.' His hands were swollen and bruised, he could barely hold his knife and fork, and he grimaced in pain when he had to shake hands. By contrast the two dogs that came with the house were very friendly and always accompanied us on our walks.

At the beginning, our enforced isolation was no hardship. The weather was dry and sunny, and we toured around a lot by car, with one bodyguard next to the driver and two more in a following car. On one trip we had with us the top man of the Armenian KGB and were heading off to see an ancient temple. It was a long and tiring journey. When we set off it was warm and sunny, but two hours later we ran into a snowstorm. We had to drive very slowly, so we did not get to the temple for another four hours. It stood, solitary, huge, half in ruins and obviously neglected, but it had retained its majestic beauty. We had hardly wandered in under the archway and started to look around when someone declared, 'Time to go. There's nothing to see here. They're waiting for us.' We made a vain attempt to stay a bit longer, but were hustled away unceremoniously. The KGB people were fretting that we were two hours late for lunch. The sun had come out again. As we drove up to the crowd waiting rather impatiently to greet us, we saw to our great surprise that instead of a meal which we had expected to be rapidly getting cold, there was a bonfire laid with a large log across it. When the log burned through into the glowing charcoal, they would grill shashlik over it. Meanwhile, we had to sit, dying of boredom, in the middle of a crowd of macho men. Then we were invited inside, where a flock of women were fussing around a long table, laying out appetisers in vast profusion. We sat at the side, mouths watering. The nice English tradition of offering a visitor a drink the minute he arrives was much in my mind. It was another hour or more before we sat down to eat. Then everything came in a rush. We had no time to try the appetisers because they started serving soup. And before we had time for more than a spoonful, the boiled meat was brought in, followed by the shashlik, and so on. All had to be washed down with brandy, alternating with vodka. The people around kept a sharp eye for any glass that wasn't emptied, regarding it as a personal slight.

We spent most of the time in our 'fortress' and were getting thoroughly bored, but cheered up when we learned that they planned to take us to Lake Sevan. Accompanied again by the local KGB top brass, we set off early in the morning so as to arrive in time for lunch. On the way, we stopped in a little village. 'They make the most delicious lavash, flat bread, here,' we were told. An old lady stood by the roadside wearing little more than rags, holding some long, flat strips of bread. Our delighted host bought some and invited us to go in and see how it was baked. We climbed up some steps into a dark, stuffy room, where a pile of clothes and old quilted jackets kept the Lavash dough warm. Our high-ranking official escort looked so out of place in his elegant suit and snow-white shirt against the background of such stark poverty, but he obviously didn't notice it and was totally relaxed, acting as if he owned the place and pulling apart the grey rags to prod the warm dough. We finished our journey in silence. I felt ashamed of the way we had swept out of the village like grandees. When we sampled the lavash, which was actually very tasty, it stuck in my throat.

Our KGB hosts took their privileged position for granted. One of them told us proudly how his wife had gone to Moscow to buy some trimmings for their dacha. She had had no problem buying the material that was unavailable to local people in Moscow. As he explained, 'Once they knew she was Armenian, then they knew she wasn't short of readies.'

As can be imagined, when we travelled, we were only shown the better side of Soviet life. Kim was later shaken to see a documentary during the *Perestroika* which showed real life slums almost in the heart of Yerevan, slums where generations had lived and died in one room.

But as we approached Lake Sevan (the seventh largest lake in Europe), our destination, our KGB escort – alas! – had something different in mind. To them any excursion was a reason for another big feast. They wouldn't even give us time to stop and look down at the lake from the road. 'Lunch is waiting,' they said and surrounded Kim. Mule-headed, I decided to clamber up the hillside to look at the lake, but the men scrambled after me. Since by then my mood had been completely spoiled, I rejoined the group who were already sitting around chewing voraciously. They served us their renowned local dish – boiled Sevan trout. Its thick skin had been left on. We did not appreciate this 'tastiest part' of the fish and mightily offended our hosts by leaving it untouched on our plates. We came home well after dark – so much for seeing Sevan.

We covered the length and breadth of Armenia, but when I try to conjure up in my mind memories of its architectural and artistic treasures, which we loved so much, all I can see is those mouths, chewing away.

Let me tell you what happened in ancient Leninakan (now Kumayri) in Western Armenia, near the Turkish border. After yet another feast, we ended up at the home of some young couple. They had a bar in the basement, where we languished until 2 a.m. Nevertheless, shortly before 10 the next morning, we were hauled out of bed, tired and sleepy, and taken to a God-forsaken little eating house to be fed khash, the Armenian national dish made from pigs' trotters. The traditional way to cook the dish is to let it simmer through the night and serve it at dawn. Originally it was served as a hot, filling breakfast for shepherds and peasants setting off for the fields. But a dish created way back for the poor has now become a delicacy, and the KGB bosses were proud they had been able to give us such a treat. We were served a piping hot consommé, rich and fatty, accompanied on a separate dish by the trotters, the meat coming off them after being boiled for so long. The technique was to use one's hands rather than a spoon, scooping it up with lavash, and then gnawing off the meat and sucking the bones. Taking off their black jackets and rolling up their sleeves, the KGB bosses gave us an expert lesson in how to do it. The whole meal was lubricated by brandy. Fending off our nausea, we took a few spoonfuls, but, to the disappointment of our hosts, left the trotters alone. After a heavy dinner and a sleepless night, it would have been hard to think of a less suitable breakfast, all the more having to cope with the brandy as well. We were still reeling from the effects of the first glass when someone's fun-loving friend popped up with a bottle of vodka, which had to be finished off so as not to insult him.

Our month's exile was coming to an end, and we were already getting ready to return home, when news came from Moscow that the threat was still there and that we had to stay for another month at least. We were fed up to the back teeth with Armenia and decided to travel around Central Asia. Had we known how it would turn out, we would have stayed in Armenia.

We were on the point of leaving, when I went upstairs to collect my things and say goodbye to the housekeeper. To my astonishment, this kindly old granny suddenly turned into a malevolent fury, pacing around the room and shoving me. But when she suddenly saw on the table the tip which I had been too embarrassed to give her personally, her rage vanished and she rushed forward to kiss me goodbye.

Our first stop was Baku in Azerbaijan. Our escort was Sasha, a rather boring man who talked non-stop about his mother-in-law. We were met in Baku by the Head of the Azerbaijan KGB. Time and again he would hug Sasha, making a big thing of how Armenians and Azerbaijanees could still be friends. It only proved that the 'friendly, united family' of the USSR still had a few problems. In Baku we stayed in a hotel, in a deluxe suite the size of a dance hall. There was a long sideboard along one wall, which was completely bare – no glasses, no spoons, no nothing. A grand piano graced the middle of the room. Sasha told us with great reverence that Lev Yashin, the famous Soviet goalkeeper, lived here. But whether he played the piano and what he had done with the china and cutlery remained a mystery.

On the very first evening, all our money disappeared. I found it the next morning in the little toilet paper holder. Kim always kept both money and toilet paper in the back pocket of his trousers and had simply got two wads of paper mixed up.

The next day we went to Sumgait, originally a suburb of Baku. It seemed an odd place to choose, but as usual nobody was interested in what we wanted, and no one explained why we were going there. We passed through a surprisingly verdant industrial town and came to a deserted sea shore, where an endless grey and unwelcome beach merged into a grey and unwelcome sea. It was windy and uncomfortable. We still had no idea why we were there. Everyone seemed to be waiting for something. In the end, an excited man appeared and reported to the KGB boss with obvious disappointment: 'They can't catch a sturgeon today.' So we were taken to a manmade cave, with low arched ceilings and an earth floor, into which were dug tables and stools made from single pieces of wood. The feasting began with huge dishes of spit-roasted lamb, chicken and finally sturgeon.

'We thought they hadn't caught any sturgeon today,' we remarked in mild surprise. 'That's not proper sturgeon,' we were told. 'Just small fry.' And the dishes continued to come. We had never before had spit-roasted shashlik like this; it was so good. Everywhere else the meat had been tough, either because they didn't know how to cook it or because the sheep were too long in the tooth.

Since we were in Azerbaijan, we took the opportunity to pay a quick visit to the Museum of Fire Worshippers. Kim could not stand guides. He felt that they were interfering with his appreciation. He preferred to see everything for himself. 'Any information they give you goes in one ear and out the other,' he would say. I warned the guide to keep her comments brief, since Kim did not understand much Russian and we were in a great rush. Her response was to spew out, without taking a break, every scrap of information that was in the visitors' booklet, like a record being played at high speed. Kim listened attentively and smiled. I asked him if he had understood everything she said. 'Not a word,' he told me, 'but she's a very nice girl.' Sometime later in Samarkand we had a very pushy guide, who kept saying: 'Look here. And now look here.' Kim made an attempt to slip away, but the guide grabbed his sleeve, admonishing him: 'You have to look at this, not over there.' Kim told me how in Istanbul he had dealt once with an intrusive guide by striking a deal with him: the guide would get paid only if he said not a word during the visit. After a few minutes the guide could not resist making a restrained brief comment. Kim warned him: 'One more word and you won't get paid.' The guide kept his mouth shut.

Our visit to Azerbaijan was brief and on the whole enjoyable. Everything went off smoothly with the exception of an amusing episode when we were driving back from a trip out of town. Both cars ran out of petrol at the same time and all of us – including the KGB's top man – had to walk several kilometres along the highway. But we were still able to complete the second half of our scheduled visit and go to the circus.

We then took the ferry from Azerbaijan to Turkmenistan. Our hotel in Ashkhabad was big and ultra-modern. Unfortunately, there was no running water, though the manager insisted that there was and I just didn't know how to use the taps properly. No sooner had we breathed a sigh of relief that there would be no more official dinners than our escort Sasha appeared to say that his aunt had invited us to dinner. I was feeling unwell – I must have eaten something that disagreed with me – and we declined. Sasha protested that 'Aunty will be upset,' so Kim sacrificed himself to Aunty's *amour propre* though he had never met her in his life and would never meet her again. I stayed in the hotel. There then followed an endless series of dinners with an assortment of uncles and aunts who would have taken offence if we did not appear.

One good thing about Armenia was that the same faces showed up at practically every function. Whereas in other republics, each time we were in a different place, we had to meet different people, a constantly shifting kaleidoscope of new faces, discharging their pent-up energy on the exhausted Philbys! The most difficult thing for us was that once we had said all the right things about how grateful we were and our delight at the kind way they were receiving us, we ran out of things to talk about. I reckoned the people we were meeting had no idea who Kim was and weren't the slightest bit interested in him. They were simply doing what they felt was their duty towards any visitor.

The proceedings always began with a ceremonial bowl of tea, which was then topped up with brandy. Kim called it 'Armenian tea'. The food was always good, and there was plenty of it, while the brandy flowed like water. Indeed, on one picnic they used it to rinse the glasses. We would then launch into the appetisers and just when we thought we could not manage another mouthful, they would bring in the shashlik, to which it was just impossible to say 'No.' At the point when we felt we had eaten enough to last us for the rest of our lives, the *pièce de resistance*, a giant *plov*, would arrive, which again had to be eaten at the risk of giving the host deep personal offence. We were thoroughly exhausted by the constant exhortations to 'Have some of this, have some of that.' And it was clear that our ever welcoming hosts would feel seriously insulted if we didn't eat every last mouthful and drink every last drop.

From Turkmenistan we travelled to Uzbekistan. In Tashkent, Sasha was replaced by Sunnat, a pleasant chap. When we were finally allowed to return to Moscow, he escorted us all the way. He understood how we felt about socialising and did his best to look after us, but there was little he could do when the people involved were his senior officers. Though Kim had found the other escorts hard to take, he got on well with Sunnat. We often refused to go on sightseeing trips, simply to get away from the 'courtiers' who were constantly dancing attendance on us. One day Kim ran out of patience and, short of stamping his feet, snapped: 'I want to go for a walk just with my wife.' We broke away from the group and headed towards the hills, where Kim relaxed and basked in the sun. But there was no peace. Someone scrambled up alongside and, trying to be helpful, started to explain to Kim what he could in fact see for himself. 'There's, pray, the sun. There are, pray, the mountains.' Ever after, when Kim was showing me something, he would say: 'Here is, pray, the sea. Here is, pray, a fish.'

There was an unpleasant incident in Tashkent. We were deadbeat and when the local KGB representative turned up with yet another invitation, we refused point-blank. Kim said he was going for a walk in the hills taking just me and the faithful Sunnat. But the KGB man – a Russian, by the way – alerted someone and, as we were driving along, we were stopped on the road to be told that we were expected for lunch. They had been cooking up the meat-filled little rolls known as '*manty*' since early morning. We declined and drove further into the hills. We walked for a couple of hours. Driving back we saw a crowd of the local bigwigs at the spot where we had been flagged down initially. Black Volgas were parked everywhere. We were ready to bow to the inevitable, but Sunnat told the driver: 'Put your foot down,' and we swept past the bewildered crowd. A sense of guilt at having hurt these people's feelings lingered for a long time.

As on all these trips we combined a packed official programme with visits to collective farms. The boss of one of them was very proud that he was related to the well-known author Rasul Gamzatov. In his effusion, he embraced Kim so tightly that the poor man could hardly breathe and almost fainted; for a long time after his ribs hurt. We were taken to the wealthiest collective farms and each time were proudly shown very costly gilded monuments to their leaders and heroes of Soviet Labour. All the farms also boasted luxurious cultural centres, whose 'facilities' were rather less 'cultural' holes in the ground. Kim could not understand how they could spend huge amounts of money (they always boasted how much it had cost) on pompous monuments instead of using it to put in proper drains.

I have terribly depressing memories of our two days in Bukhara, a wonderful city with unique architecture. Our hosts made Kim drink too much and he couldn't comprehend why I wasn't having a good time. We rounded off our trip to Middle Asia with two days in Urgench, its beautiful minaret towering above the surrounding desert.

It was a depressing, grey undulating terrain, made iron-hard by frost and broken only by an occasional drainage ditch. It was very cold and windy, but the local children, hardened to it, invariably went barefoot despite the frost. Just to look at them made me shiver.

We had been put up in a small barrack-like house – were told it was a general's dacha (though we never saw him) – and looked after by two soldiers and a maid. The house may have had more comfortable rooms, but ours had only two metal bunks and side tables. I decided to take a shower after the journey, but had no idea I was starting a flood. We hadn't been told that the bathroom drainpipes were broken and the water poured into the corridor, where some unfortunate soldier had a tough job mopping it up with a cloth. After a great deal of fussing, we went to sleep. No one tried to entertain us, to get us drunk or stuff us with food. The food was in fact simple but good, and we had only Sunnat for company. Though it was a pretty modest set-up, we enjoyed the unexpected break.

From Urgench we went to Fergana, where we picked up the train for Moscow, though not without one final farewell dinner. The local KGB representative came up to me and asked very seriously: 'Will Kim be upset if we serve brandy with the meal?' On the one hand, I could be justifiably pleased that my two months of hard work to stop brandy appearing automatically had finally paid off. On the other, I was a little frightened that having no brandy might be going too far, since without even one glass of something the whole affair might prove too hard to take. So I assured the man that it would be just fine, and that Kim would not take offence.

Finally, we took the train back to Moscow, but the loyal Sunnat let me down when he enticed Kim off for drinks to the restaurant car and then to a friend's compartment. I was in something of a state waiting for him to get back.

CHAPTER 15

Home Again

We had been travelling for more than two days. When we reached home at last in the evening and dropped our suitcases in the hall, Kim said: 'Let's keep a low profile. I don't want to speak to anyone, or answer the phone.'

As he spoke, the phone shrilled: 'Hi, it's me, Vitaly from Bratsk.'

I went cold. It was not Vitaly's fault – I remembered him and he was a decent enough chap – but I just didn't feel like seeing anyone at all that evening. I asked him: 'Where are you?' 'Pekin Hotel.' 'Are you staying here long?' I asked, trying to play for time, but well aware that one could not turn away a visitor who had come from so far away. 'I'm flying off to Sochi tomorrow morning, I'd really like to see you.' 'We've just got in. We're very tired,' I said. 'Then I'll drop by tomorrow,' he replied. I breathed a sigh of relief – at least we were spared for that evening – and plucked up my courage to get Kim to accept the idea. He had just reconciled himself to it when the phone rang again. 'It's me again. I can't wait until tomorrow. I'll come over now.' I gave in and started to explain how to find us, but Vitaly would not listen. 'Don't bother, I'll take a taxi,' he said and hung up. From the Pekin Hotel to where we lived was a fifteen-minute walk and a 50 kopeck taxi ride. Forty minutes later he arrived. 'I gave the taxi driver 10 roubles and your address,' he told us proudly. The taxi driver had punctiliously driven around until the meter showed 10 roubles – hard to believe nowadays that we once had honest taxi drivers.

Vitaly was a sight. His face was chalk white, even though it was minus 20 degrees outside, and he looked dishevelled with his tie slung over one shoulder and his scarf over the other. He produced from the recesses of his coat an open bottle of Hungarian red wine. Hardly surprisingly, the wine had spilled and stained his pullover. When he saw it, he tugged the pullover off and handed it to me, saying in the sort of tone one would use to a maid: 'Here, take this away and wash it.'

Kim was very taken aback and did not know how to react. I went meekly away to wash the pullover, after serving them some simple appetisers. Kim opened a bottle of brandy. Vitaly downed glass after glass, without eating a thing. Both didn't know how to start the conversation. Here was a chap who had popped in to have a good time, and there we were, tired and stone cold sober. He comforted us by saying that when he headed home in a month's time, his wife Valechka would be going to the same sanatorium in Sochi and would certainly drop in to see us on the way. 'Why don't you go on holiday together?' Kim asked in surprise. 'We always take it in turns,' Vitaly replied, adding in a confiding tone: 'While you're still young you know . . . and, anyway, you need to trust one another. It's a bit boring here. There isn't even any music,' our guest said, looking gloomily around the room. 'Make me some coffee . . .' I brought coffee, but he pushed the cup away and reached yet again for his glass. Things were taking a dangerous turn. He couldn't stand up. I offered him sandwiches and more coffee. Vitaly sniffed at the cup and pronounced: 'It's cold. Make some more.' I trotted out meekly to make a fresh cup. He left that to get cold too and then barked: 'Make another.'

Kim could not restrain himself any longer. 'We're out of coffee,' he pronounced despondently and gripped my hand. There was a painful pause. 'Well, time for me to go,' Vitaly declared. The words were barely out of his mouth when we jumped to our feet in joy. But as I was parcelling up his wet pullover, I heard him say from the depths of his armchair: 'Perhaps I'll spend the night here. I feel faint.'

Kim, without raising his head, started to lace his shoes in silence. Working as a team we managed to get Vitaly up and dressed. I found a melted bar of ice cream in his coat pocket, but there was no way I was going to clean up his coat. We grabbed him under the arms and took him back to the Pekin through the invigorating frosty night air. The next day, sober, after a good night's sleep, he phoned to apologise and say goodbye.

Kim was very surprised to learn that Soviet couples took separate holidays. I explained that most of the time this wasn't a matter of choice. Either their holiday periods didn't coincide or they couldn't get two places in a sanatorium at the same time; it was also that sanatoriums and holiday homes didn't take children at that period. Vitaly's remark struck a chord with Kim, and he loved to repeat: 'While you're young you need to trust one another.'

CHAPTER 16

Security

Even after our return from Central Asia at the end of 1971, the KGB believed that Kim was still at risk and maintained his protection for about a year. It worked like this: before we went out, I had to dial a certain number to say 'We're leaving.' Two or three bodyguards, who were probably located in the building next door, would follow a few steps behind us down the street. Once, when we went to the Beryozka foreign currency store (Kim had foreign currency left from his book royalties) to buy me a birthday present, one of our bodyguards asked me: 'Does Kim have a foreign currency account as well?' They didn't ask about the roubles account – they were sure he had an unlimited account, like all the *nomenklatura* at the time – whereas actually during his stay in Moscow Kim hadn't managed to put away any money. It was only in Kim's last two years, when he was often ill and we gave up travelling, that I was able to cut down on our expenses and put a bit of money away in the savings bank. In fact, the people around Kim had no idea of what money he really had, even though they thought themselves to be very well informed. To them, Kim seemed to be very rich. They were convinced that such a legendary personality as Philby had plenty of earthly goods.

Kim almost never went out on his own. But when I went shopping, he would come with me for the sake of the walk and would wait for me outside the shop or the pharmacy or wherever I was going. Since I thought it was Kim, not me, who needed protection, I failed to call the bodyguard one day when I decided to go to a swimming-pool. I walked fast, jumped on a trolley bus and then realised I had been 'intercepted' by a young man who was rapidly following me. He got so carried away with trailing me that he even stuck his head in the ladies' changing-room. He was probably stopped by a sign outside the shower exhorting: 'Citizen Visitors: Check That Your Neighbour Washes Thoroughly.' I took my regular forty-minute swim, while up on the balcony my faithful sentry's bright blue windcheater stood out like a beacon.

Whenever we went anywhere by taxi, the bodyguards used to follow us in their car. It did, however, look more than odd when we took the trolley bus and the entire team would duly trail behind us in a car. One night I had an attack of appendicitis (I have described that nightmare evening earlier on). In the morning, Kim took me down to the taxi, which, as often happened, had not yet arrived. Our bodyguards watched me for a while writhing in pain and then offered to give us a lift.

Another time they did us a similar favour when we were coming home from an evening with the Blakes and couldn't get a taxi. On another occasion Kim and I took a crammed trolley bus to a watch and clock repair shop. There was a long queue there, so I told Kim that I would stay and he should go home, hoping that, as he was on his own, the bodyguards would run him back in their car. They didn't. He went all the way back by trolley bus without any of the passengers suspecting that he had a guard of honour in a car behind. I wondered whether the protection given to Kim was of any value if he were riding in a trolley bus and a threat to his life occurred. I told our case officer Stanislav about the casual way in which it seemed to be organised. He got rather excited and told me that the trolley bus rides had been another cock-up by his mate who ran the 'bodyguard operation'. After our talk, we began to get use of the car from time to time.

Finally, we were told that the threat was over and that we were free to live a normal life. We decided to celebrate by taking a stroll through the Kremlin. Just as we drew level with the Intourist Hotel, I noticed a thick-set man approaching us with a rather frightening look on his face. For a brief moment I froze in terror, but was relieved when he suddenly broke into a broad smile and gave Kim a warm hug. The 'assailant' was Petukhov, who had helped Kim to escape from Beirut. It was the first time they had met in Moscow. We subsequently got to know him quite well.

When Kim was under protection, we were indoctrinated into the rules of the 'game'. Whatever we thought about it, we had to go along with it, like it or not. But to learn that we had been under surveillance and had not spotted it was even more unpleasant.

The Exhibition of Agricultural Achievements (VDNH) (now the All Russia Exhibition Centre) was one of the sights we usually took our visitors to see. When we took Kim's daughter Josephine there with her husband, she asked Kim if he realised he was being followed. He expressed surprise and denied it, but she was convinced. While we were sitting by the Friendship of the Peoples Fountain, I tried to check for myself. The square in front of us was vast and open on all sides. It was deserted and, try as I might, I couldn't spot any sign of someone watching us. After a stroll along the tree-lined walks and working up an appetite, we went into a fish restaurant on the lakeside. I had quite a surprise in the toilet: there was a whole roll of toilet paper. I couldn't believe my eyes! This was so improbable that I checked the next stall and the one after it. In each one was an unopened roll of paper. That had to have been specially organised. Soviet loos usually had no paper whatsoever. I went back to our table in some confusion. Then I saw him: our benefactor was sitting on his own at a table way over in the corner.

In the days ahead, our escorts became even more obvious. One day I almost felt sympathy for the 'boys'. We had barely managed to squeeze into an overcrowded trolley bus when I lost sight of them. But I was relieved when I saw that they had managed to grab on to the outside handrails. Another time we were on our way to Mama's for dinner when the taxi driver pointed out a trailing car. 'Do you know you're being followed?' 'Why on earth should anyone do that?' I protested. 'You have a vivid imagination.' 'I've got a nose for these things, and I spotted the Volga on my tail,' he said and went on to explain the difference between a KGB Volga and the ordinary model. Later, when Kim told our case officer Andrey about Josephine's suspicions, he was clearly at a loss what to say. Judging by his reaction, we were not supposed to be able to spot the surveillance. In fact, we hadn't spotted it ourselves until the observant Josephine had pointed it out. Who knows what else we failed to spot?

This reminded me of another episode before we were married when I had been as observant as Josephine. Kim and I had gone to Yaroslavl with the Blakes and while we were walking around the park, I noticed we were being diligently followed by a dark-haired young man in a short-sleeved shirt, carrying a newspaper. I didn't think the others had noticed and I didn't say anything to them. When we came to the end of the deserted tree-lined pathway, we stood around lost in thought before heading back. The man who I thought was watching us also hung back, then crossed to the other pathway and strolled along, keeping level with us, back to the other end. I'd still recognise him today.

CHAPTER 17

The Case Officers

The case officers from the KGB played a significant part in Kim's Moscow life. What their titles were, or their job description, or indeed whether they may have had certain additional responsibilities, I have no idea. Talking to them and to each other, we used only the first names by which they originally introduced themselves. Kim usually had two case officers, one dealing with professional problems, the other, who was one level junior, with day-to-day issues. Their jobs were not precisely defined, and what they actually did rather depended on the sort of qualities each of them brought to the assignment. One would be easy to deal with. Another might answer any request by saying, 'That's not so easy.' Kim was fond of quoting that phrase frequently when various problems cropped up. The case officers helped Kim enormously, saving him from a great deal of aggravation. The down-side of this was that he couldn't move an inch – for example, he was not allowed to leave the Moscow region – without telling them first. It was a combination of police supervision and keeping a friendly eye on him.

The case officers kept Kim clear of any contacts they regarded as undesirable, especially with foreigners. They told him this was out of concern for his safety, because foreign intelligence services might try to assassinate him. Kim dismissed the notion as utter rubbish, but by and large a solitary way of life suited him. He didn't want to end up like Donald Maclean, who often had a crowd of foreign journalists camped on his staircase. Though the KGB shrouded Kim in secrecy, they didn't create a proper 'legend' for him, and we were frequently stumped, not knowing quite how to answer the questions that might be asked by a caretaker, a doctor in a sanatorium or even just a neighbour. Though it was readily apparent that Kim was a foreigner, we were supposed not to let anyone know it, but we lived in a very run-of-the-mill block of flats and it just was not possible to avoid all contact. I kept on asking the case officer to create a legend for Kim, and he eventually did so: Andrei Fyodorovich Martins (which, as I noted earlier, was Kim's cover name in the USSR) worked at the Omega Scientific Research Institute as a consultant, and there was even a specific telephone number to be used in case anyone wanted to confirm this.

At one point the KGB recommended that for security reasons Kim should change flats and suggested we should go and inspect our future home. We went to the address we had been given but simply could not find the building. We asked a passer-by for help. 'Oh, that's the building where Louis Corvalan* lives,' he told us, with evident delight at knowing something about the life of the Secretary of the Chilean Communist Party. A little later I went to see another flat in the building, so as to get some idea of how ours might look. The building was only half occupied. I was shown one of the empty flats and told, again with pride, 'Louis Corvalan lives on the floor below.' Clearly Kim would not be able to live there incognito for very long, and in the event, since we were not at all keen to give up our flat, of which we were very fond, we flatly refused to move.

On the surface Kim was not frightened of anything. He let his guard down so much in Moscow that he didn't notice (or perhaps did not want to notice) the obvious surveillance that the KGB maintained on him. But there was an element of fear still lurking in his

---

* Louis Corvalan was the former Secretary of the Chilean Communist Party who had come to Russia in 1976 in exchange for the dissident Vladimir Bukovsky.

subconscious, going back to his years as an active spy – the fear of exposure. He had nightmares and would yell in his sleep. One night a powerful kick almost jolted me out of bed. It turned out that Kim had dreamed that as President of France (at that time the President was Pompidou), he had taken a nap on his office sofa after a tiring day, when the door opened and Pompidou walked in, claiming that he was the real President. 'Then I got ready to defend myself. I pulled my legs up to my stomach and kicked out as hard as I could . . .', but he kicked me, not Pompidou!

From time to time the case officers would advise Kim to be careful. Once they suggested he hold off going to the main Post Office, where we used regularly to pick up our mail, since some foreigner had been spotted lying in wait there and asking officials from the mailbox department lots of questions about Kim. From then on, I went there myself. But there were also instances when the case officers, without telling Kim, who found out about it only too late and by accident, denied him access to people whom he would have liked to see. Kim felt bitter that the case officers had concealed from him Guy Burgess's desire to see him before his death. They gave Burgess the excuse that Kim had left Moscow. In truth, he had not gone anywhere and heard about it only after Burgess's death. 'He probably wanted to tell me something important. Why are they so cruel?' Kim asked in bewilderment. One 'solicitous' case officer Leo also deceived our Bulgarian friend Todor. When he came to Moscow and wanted to see Kim, he was told we were away on vacation. He told us about it two years later when we met him again in Bulgaria.

The case officers were usually changed every two years, though some stayed with us longer, and others left earlier. Kim would barely have time to get used to one when a new man would appear on the scene. Some of them he was relieved to lose, some he was sorry. The first ones I met were Stanislav and Valentin. In Moscow, I did not have much to do with Valentin, but he was later with us for a whole month in Czechoslovakia – an episode I will come to shortly. Stanislav simply vanished. By then Kim was already used to his professional friends' disappearance from his life without warning or even a 'goodbye', but was still taken aback and upset when it happened. He did not blame them, since he felt they were simply obeying orders, though quite what the sense of the order was, he failed to understand.

Sometimes, though, this sort of thing did rouse him to anger. For instance, writing to Mikhail Lyubimov on 27 January 1980, Kim said:

> Oleg has left us for a point further north; there are rumours that Victor Panteleyevich may be moving away from us; and even Gennady is showing signs of anxiety. I think, though I should not say it, that his boss is an SOB, who would be better placed in some minor clerk's job in a village three hours' bumpy truck drive from Verkhoyansk. However, every big organisation must have its share of bloody fools. C'est la vie!

Unlike the others, Stanislav did give us warning that he was about to disappear. He said he was leaving for a long-term assignment and even arranged a farewell lunch at the Metropole. Quite by chance, we discovered a little while later that he had not actually gone anywhere, though we never saw or heard from him again. Stanislav was still working with Kim when his mate Valentin was replaced by Leo. As with Valentin, Leo once went on a trip with us and then 'took care' of us for a long time in Moscow. Kim tried to have as little to do with Leo as possible and did not ask him for favours. Leo was a man who seemed to do everything reluctantly and took forever to respond to any request without saying 'Yes' or 'No.'

Whatever Kim felt about his case officers, he complained to their superiors only once. On the contrary, he did his utmost to say how much he valued their services. As a rule we knew only the case officers' first names; they were rarely as open as to tell us their surnames. Once Kim needed to get hold of Leo urgently. I dialled the number he had given us, and a very polite woman's voice answered with a typical Russian sense of humour: 'We've got a tiger here' (i.e. Leo meaning 'lion'). Since I had no idea of Leo's surname, I couldn't reach him, and when finally he appeared I was ready to turn into a tigress myself and went for him: 'Would it really be a breach of official secrets if we knew your surname?' But Leo stood his ground and kept the secret. We discovered it by accident long afterwards, when a doctor in the hospital opened Kim's file and read out the surname and telephone of our mystery man Leo, telling us: 'That's your case officer!'

After Leo we had a string of Vladimirs, with all of whom we were on good terms. Josephine, who as a frequent visitor met several of them, decided that Vladimir was a code name shared by all KGB officers. I recall one in particular, who stayed with Kim for quite a long while. He looked after the household side of things and was a big, imposing and impressive fellow with a larger-than-life personality. He loved to tell stories that he thought had some sort of point, which always started with, 'I, for example . . .' One of these examples was how he spent time with a friend at his country dacha. He described with relish how the pair of them got into the cellar and had a whale of a time in the cooler, eating and drinking everything in sight. 'Now that was a real holiday,' he concluded, holding his thumb up in the air triumphantly. 'Yes indeed.' He was a colourful personality. Kim was particularly tolerant of his minor weaknesses. He got much amusement from his remarks and often quoted them.

Kim hated and feared any changes, and was very put out when this Vladimir was replaced by another. But this time we were in for a pleasant surprise. The latest – and, as it turned out, the last – of the household case officers was a real Godsend. He helped us whenever he possibly could and out of kindness would often offer to do such favours I would never have dared to ask for. Kim used to tell me that Guy Burgess used his case officers like errand boys, sending them out almost with a snap of his fingers to buy bread or cabbage. We rarely asked for favours and if we did it was for minor things like train tickets or the use of a car when we couldn't get a taxi. But when problems did arise, then the case officers' assistance proved essential. For instance, Mama was going to Poland and taking a television with her as a present for her elderly relatives. At the time this was entirely legal, since there was a glut of televisions on the market due to over-production and every effort was being made to encourage people to export them. Kim, my brother Kostya and I took Mama to the station. When we reached her carriage, right at the end of the platform, it turned out that she should have had a receipt allowing her to ship the television. Only Kostya's nimbleness saved us. He sprinted back down the platform, found the right cash desk, stood in the line and got back to see Mama safely on board just as the conductor was blowing his whistle for the departure. But it wasn't by any means the end of this unfortunate tale. In the middle of the night Mama telephoned from Brest and told us that she had been put off the train at the border with all her luggage, TV included, on the grounds that she couldn't produce an invitation from her relatives in Poland. In fact, she did have one which she had used to obtain her passport for foreign travel and visa, but she had left the letter at home. While I was racking my brains wondering how to help her, Kim telephoned our ever attentive Vladimir II. Kim rarely used the telephone himself, and I usually did all the talking for him, like a sort of personal secretary. This time, however, he didn't want to risk using me, remembering that Vladimir had given me a rather abrupt answer when I had recently asked him for something. Vladimir immediately called Brest and sorted it all out. The people who had turned Mama off the train said they didn't need to see the invitation, but the Polish immigration people might have demanded it. As it turned out, the Poles were not the slightest bit interested in seeing any invitation. Nonetheless, thanks to our vigilant border guards, Mama was forced to sit in the station for hours waiting for the next train. God knows how long she might have sat there without Vladimir's intervention.

On another occasion, the same Vladimir rescued me from the police station where I had ended up on the day before my birthday. Kim wanted to buy me a present, but as he didn't like shopping he gave me some cheques and left it for me to decide what to buy. A girl-friend and I went to the Beryozka shop on Kropotkinskaya Street, where we were the only customers. I chose some knitting wool for a sweater. When I was at the cash desk paying in rouble cheques, my girlfriend rushed up looking terrified and told me: 'They're going to arrest us.' She had seen the salesgirl press a button while making rather desultory efforts to wrap my wool. Sure enough, as we got to the exit, we were stopped by two young men. 'You go with us,' they barked, and we meekly followed them into the courtyard and then into the militia station housed in the same building as the shop. We were taken to separate rooms and the questioning began. 'Where did you get the cheques?' 'My husband gave them to me.' 'Have your got any more left on you?' 'Yes.' 'And do you have more at home?' 'Yes, I do.' 'How did your husband get them?' 'He has a foreign currency account at the bank.' 'That can't be.' 'Why don't you check?' I said and gave him the account number. The officer did not believe me and made no attempt to check. I was allowed to phone home, but I knew before I did so that Kim wouldn't pick up the phone; he never went near the phone if I wasn't there. We had reached an impasse and reluctantly I gave my husband's name. But that was no help either – they refused to believe me. I had no choice but to ask for Vladimir's help. I said he worked for the KGB and gave them his phone number. The militia officer who was questioning me dialled it and asked: 'What organisation have I reached?' 'The one you need,' they told him. He handed me the phone and I explained to Vladimir what had happened. 'You're going to have to let her go,' Vladimir told the man. He and I agreed to meet in a short while on the Gogolevsky boulevard, not far from the shop to get the details.

Meanwhile, my friend was being questioned in the other room. 'My' young interrogator kept going out, presumably to compare notes with his partner. The latter had already searched my friend's handbag, telling her in the process that he was Kalinin's grandson (Kalinin was once a member of the Politburo). Despite the fact that she had no cheques, they would not let her go either. When I played the 'Kim Philby' card, both interrogators, who didn't believe me, asked my friend what my husband's name was. When she told the same thing, they still refused to believe her. Finally, after a full two hours, Vladimir's intercession, by phone, prevailed and we were released.

My friend was very keen to flaunt herself in front of the malevolent assistant who had turned us in, and we marched victoriously though the shop, somewhat assuaging our wounded self-esteem.

I said goodbye to my friend and went to meet Vladimir. He obviously thought I had been up to some sort of fiddle and generously suggested: 'We won't tell Kim about this.' As it turned out, he did not know that Kim had a foreign currency account. Vladimir took me home to find Kim rather overwrought at my absence. I, of course, told him about our 'adventure'.

In that era it was illegal for Soviet citizens to have foreign currency. If they earned it while working abroad, it was paid over to them in the form of cheques, which could be used in the Beryozka shops. Not many people remember the cheques of the 1970s and 1980s now, though they were very much sought after at the time. The Beryozka hard-currency shops were the only places you could buy the imported goods which were totally unavailable elsewhere. It was also against the law to buy and sell cheques, but people nevertheless traded them openly outside the shops.

Vladimir II, who had been best at coping with professional issues, was replaced by Nikolai. Kim used to complain that it was very difficult to deal with him. At the outset he thought this was because Nikolai spoke little English. Kim switched to German, which Nikolai spoke well, or even Russian, but it dawned on him that language was not the problem. 'He's thick as two short planks,' was Kim's final assessment. Around that time we often gave large parties. After one of them, Kim was amused when two generals were stuck in the lift for more than an hour while the rest of us were enjoying the celebrations. Kim particularly liked to celebrate 27 January, the day of his arrival in the USSR. Nikolai would be there, along with other KGB people, but he stood out from the rest because of his worried look, his eyes flicking from one visitor to the next, his face screwed up as he made agonising efforts to concentrate. We didn't realise that at this time he was trying mentally to compose his report; we found this out only later from Gennady, who worked with Kim regularly. Nikolai used to complain to their boss that Gennady did not write reports on Kim. In one of the reports that Nikolai wrote after every meeting with Kim, he included the especially 'valuable' information that Gennady was courting me, which came as news to me, let alone to my supposed 'suitor'.

Kim finally lost patience and demanded that Nikolai be replaced. I do not remember him ever asking so firmly for anything, but the answer was, 'It isn't that simple,' as Vladimir would have said, and the struggle went on for a whole year. Nikolai's boss told Kim he just could not find a replacement of Nikolai's calibre. It was depressing to think that someone like this man was irreplaceable. Kim was amazed to learn that someone as low grade as Nikolai had worked successfully for the KGB for several years in the USA and elsewhere. Nikolai was eventually replaced by Andrey, who was less than bright and often got on Kim's nerves, but he was a nice fellow and that made up for a lot. Kim often spoke of the high level of professionalism of the KGB officers with whom he had worked abroad, but at the same time he was disappointed at the incompetence of some of those whom he encountered in the Soviet Union.

Though he tried very hard to be independent, Kim understood the limitations under which he lived; even something as simple as a visit to Dubna or Leningrad needed the KGB's help, because any hotel we tried on our own would tell us categorically: 'We're fully booked.' Kim often ran into insoluble day-to-day problems and greatly valued the help his colleagues gave him to sort them out. We had a clear demonstration of the price of independence when Kim and I went to Suzdal, an ancient town not far from Moscow. The KGB kindly provided a car and a driver and booked us a motel room for three nights. We explored the town and enjoyed the sights, but when we decided to get something to eat, we could not get into a single restaurant. Though they were all virtually empty, we were told that they served only foreign tourists. We ended up whiling away the evenings in our motel room nibbling dry sandwiches. By contrast, when we went there again with the children, accompanied by a KGB escort, we were warmly welcomed at the restaurants.

At the same time Kim never believed his position entitled him to privileges and was grateful for even the smallest favour. For example, when we travelled abroad by train the case officer would advise the local KGB people where we were headed of the time we were due to arrive at the frontier and we would be met and entertained for the long hours it took to change the carriage wheels – an inevitable part of all rail trips abroad since the Russian railway operates on a different track width. They would also see to it that we were waved through customs formalities. I remember once, en route to Bulgaria, we arrived at Ungeny, a Moldavian town on the Soviet-Romanian border through which the trains pass at 5 a.m. and Kim was stunned to see a table groaning with appetisers and drinks in a private room. 'Could be a whole lot worse,' he muttered, offending our hosts mightily, until I explained that his comment really meant, 'I've never seen anything better.' He was even more surprised to discover that at such an early hour a glass of vodka worked wonders and was even enjoyable to drink.

It didn't always work out as grandly as that, though. There were sometimes misunderstandings and miscommunications with the result that people were there to meet Kim either the day before he actually arrived, or after he had left. The next time we arrived at Ungeny, we were looking forward to a big 'do', but no one was there! It was very cold and damp, and we stood on the open windswept platform wondering what on earth to do during the two or three hours' wait. Luckily, the station restaurant was open. We didn't have to bother about deciding what to eat. All they had were pancakes. Kim fell on them with gusto as he had on the fried eggs at Lake Baikal. We warmed up with the help of some brandy and were feeling in seventh heaven when a nice young man, whom we recognised from our previous visit, came up to our table explaining that, based on what Moscow had told him, we had been expected yesterday, but he had decided to check. He took us off again to the private room, where the table had been hastily but tastily laid.

We went to Bulgaria more often than to any other country, and each time we had to wait at Ungeny we always met the same people, Kim's KGB colleagues. They used to invite us to visit Moldavia, and we went once en route from Sofia to Moscow. The Moldavian friends who accompanied us gave Kim a present of some dry wine and a box of cherries, which we in turn gave to the two girls in charge of our carriage. We were jolted out of our beds in the middle of the night when we heard the girls scream. Opening our door, we saw them leap into the corridor from their booth in a desperate attempt to get away from some hairy caterpillars which had crawled out of the cherries. Kim split his sides laughing.

CHAPTER 18

Exploring Foreign Countries

Our first trip together outside the USSR came about when Kim's book, *My Silent War*, was published in Czechoslovakia in 1971. He decided that rather than have the royalties remitted to him in Moscow, they should remain in Czechoslovakia and he could spend time there, giving himself a good excuse for a trip. We spent a most enjoyable month, seeing Prague, Karlovy Vary and the Tatras. Kim got VIP treatment and had a Czech bodyguard, Vladek, as well as a Czech escort, Viktor. We also had two chauffeur-driven Tatra saloons at our disposal.

The Minister of the Interior gave a dinner in Kim's honour. He struck a bizarre note when proposing a toast: 'We are so proud to be the first socialist country – after the USSR, of course – to have published your book.' No one in Czechoslovakia could have imagined that in fact it would take no less than nine more years for the book to be published in the Soviet Union, the country where it was written and to which Kim had dedicated his life.

Our case officer Valentin, who had accompanied us from Moscow, was no adornment to our trip. He was a big hit with the Tatra drivers and, imagining himself the life and soul of the party, went on incessantly, usually telling the same stories over and over again, while Kim, forced to listen to him, almost died of boredom. Valentin was particularly fond of recounting how, while he was working in London, he had pretended to be a millionaire shopping for presents for his wife. According to him, he had sat sprawled in an armchair, a cigar clamped between his teeth, and lined up the sales girls before deciding which one was closest to his wife's size. Our drivers naturally got a huge kick out of stories like this, but the problem was that Kim had no option but to listen to Valentin's ravings too. When I tried to get him to be quiet, he sneered that obviously not everyone appreciated his IQ. The Minister singularly failed to appreciate it also when Valentin took him aback by bursting into a Russian folk song during a banquet in Kim's honour. His contribution to the trip was, however, evidently highly regarded in Moscow, since on his return he was promoted and left us. He was replaced by Leo, who was not exactly a gift either. Later on, when we compared the exuberant, conceited Valentin with the rather dreary Leo, we could not decide which we preferred: each had his 'good' qualities.

Although we had some fascinating trips and excursions in Czechoslovakian cities, Kim always preferred our walks, especially in the mountains. However, not all of these were easy. Kim found going up into the High Tatras on a ski-lift a hair-raising experience. I too held my breath in terror as we flew over the bottomless chasms and jagged cliffs, bouncing uncomfortably in our lightweight seats every time the cable ran over one of the junction wheels. But little by little I began to enjoy the wonderful panorama and plucked up enough courage to turn to Kim and wave 'Hello'. His face, on the other hand, was strained; in reply, he did not dare to move a muscle and he was clearly not sharing my enjoyment.

The next day we were supposed to take a funicular up to the mountains. Not surprisingly, Kim was unenthusiastic at the prospect. We had already set off when it began to rain, and the view which we were supposed to be admiring was covered in clouds. We persuaded our hosts to put the trip off, though they really did not like changing the programme (even the word 'programme' itself used to annoy Kim; he would always protest when someone used it). When we came back from a walk we had taken instead, we heard the tragic news: the funicular had collapsed and its passengers had been seriously injured.

Among them was a pilot who had miraculously escaped death after crashing his plane in the mountains shortly beforehand. Search parties had found him, put him on a stretcher and loaded him into the ill-starred funicular, where disaster had struck again.

Viktor, our faithful escort, once played a dirty trick on us when we were in the Low Tatras. He suggested we take what he called a 'fascinating' trip to the 'Slovene Paradise', which involved no more than an easy stroll, though there were one or two ladders to climb en route. As he said this he cast a critical eye at my shoes and advised me to buy some sneakers. It all sounded vaguely intriguing. He gave us no more details and we set off in good spirits. The ever-sensible Valentin claimed to have something else to do and didn't come with us.

We clambered with difficulty down a steep slope, clutching at bushes and trees to avoid falling head over heels. Our legs began to hurt from the strain, but we were only at the beginning. Climbing towards us came a group of haggard young people, groaning and barely able to stand. We finally reached level ground and were sure we had now reached 'Paradise'. It turned out to be the gateway to hell: ahead of us was a little mountain stream. Giving us no time for second thoughts, Viktor ploughed ahead, leaping from one stone to another – I could barely keep up with him. Kim scrambled along behind me with Vladek bringing up the rear. The little stream turned into a rushing brook, and moving ahead became really dangerous. We had to clamber along a slippery log laid across the water. My head was spinning, and I could just imagine how Kim was feeling, since he was more afraid of heights than I. We then found ourselves in a ravine. There was no turning back. We had to go on. Every time we got over some new obstacle, we hoped it would be the last. Turning back would have meant retracing the route that had presented so many difficulties, and at the end of it we would have a steep uphill climb. So on we went. The three of us stuck together, but we could not keep up with Viktor, who had vanished around the next bend, without even looking back or offering a hand to help us.

We were now jammed between a rock and a waterfall. Ahead of me was a thin tree that had been dropped across the fast-moving water. I was not cut out to be a tight-rope walker and stopped dead, saying: 'Enough is enough. I can't go on.' But when I looked back, I saw Kim balance on one leg with Vladek hanging on to him. There wasn't even room for turning around and going back. So I crawled along the tree trunk on all fours, like a monkey, my two valiant companions trailing behind me. With a worried look and a wet handkerchief wrapped around his head, Vladek did not look much like a bodyguard. There was no trace of Viktor.

Then we came to the much-heralded ladder made of thick wire and chains and fastened to the cliff-face at an angle which meant that when climbing up, you had to lean backwards. Compared to the tree trunk it was, of course, a more reliable way to get from A to B, especially since you could hold on to it properly. But we were at the end of our tether, and the green ladders seemed endless.

After a steep downhill stretch, we came to the place from which we had started out, having successfully coped with all the obstacles. Several hours later we emerged from 'Paradise'. There was no doubt the route was intended only for experienced walkers and had been really dangerous for us. Up at the top we met our excited driver, who was in a panic, having heard an account of their trip from the young tourists we had run into when we set out. Viktor was sitting calmly in a nearby cafe nursing a glass of Borovicka, the local juniper vodka. Vladek rushed at him angrily, but we were too exhausted to show any emotions. We were puzzled by Viktor's behaviour. He had been generally a little odd, possibly because of some trouble at home that he had mentioned to me earlier, but was this a good reason to put our lives at risk?

In contrast to Viktor, Kim could always be relied upon to be a navigator. He was quick to get his bearings, knew his limits and had an unerring instinct for danger. We had no Moscow escorts on our subsequent visits to Czechoslovakia. When we next went to the High Tatras, Kim appointed himself as tour guide and we set off into the mountains under a bright, cloudless midday sun. He walked at a steady even pace and never let the tempo flag. I was hard put to trudge along in his wake, and even young Pavel (our Czech escort) found it difficult to keep up. A barely discernible pathway wound through a rocky landscape, broken by mountain streams. We were heading towards a wall of high cliffs which towered ahead of us, but the higher we scrambled, the further away they seemed to be; it was as if they were teasing us. Then a small cloud appeared in the clear sky. The sun faded and the clouds began to descend to ground level. It became chilly. Kim turned back immediately, urging us to get a move on. Almost the very minute we scrambled clear of the last tricky sections of the route, fog blanketed the mountains and when we reached level ground and looked back, everything was pitch black, shrouded in thick fog.

The 'dangerous curves' notwithstanding, our trip to Czechoslovakia gave us a taste for foreign travel and Kim enthusiastically accepted an invitation to visit Bulgaria. We had first visited the country in 1973 and then, in 1981, Kim's book was published there following its appearance in Russia. When it had been published in Czechoslovakia, his contract had given him the choice of taking his royalties in crowns or roubles, but, as he only found out after the Bulgarian edition appeared, he had no say in how he was to be paid. We fantasised about what we would do with all the money. The first thing would be to buy a new fridge (our early model ZIL was disintegrating and the service people said it was beyond repair), but the 700 roubles left after Mezhdunarodnaya Kniga, the Soviet go-between organisation, had taken its 70 per cent were not even enough for a fridge. Nevertheless, the publication of the book did lead to Kim being invited to visit Bulgaria, where he was given the same VIP treatment as in Czechoslovakia. Leo came with us, along with Todor from the Bulgarian service (mentioned earlier), who had a good command of both Russian and English. Leo knew no Bulgarian and little English, and we could never quite understand why he had been sent along.

We had become very friendly with Todor and it was largely due to him that Kim became so fond of Bulgaria, to which we returned many times. On 6 January 1975 Kim had written to Todor: 'If our plans come to fruition, the main thing, please, is that you should try to be there when we arrive. We would not like to have some Bulgarian Leo telling us that you are "out of town". In fact I don't believe there could be a Bulgarian Leo – he really is one of a kind.'

On our second visit, Todor met us but said that he was unable to accompany us because he had to go to Moscow to take a special course. Kim was disappointed and when he met the Minister of the Interior, Stoyanov, he told him: 'If Todor stays with us, I promise that I will give him better lessons and for a shorter time than he can get in Moscow, and it won't cost you anything.' Stoyanov agreed, and Todor took special leave so that he and his wife Radka could spend some time with us. We also became friends with another young couple, Konstantin and Donka, who gave us a great deal of care and attention, especially when Kim fell ill.

Bulgaria is rich in natural beauty. It has everything – a warm sea, sandy beaches, inaccessible mountains and verdant valleys. On our first visit, after we had toured the country, we stopped for a seaside break at Golden Sands, near Varna, a resort on the Black Sea. Towards the end of our stay we spent a short time at Sunny Shore, a seaside place we liked a lot. Kim, always inclined to avoid change, thereafter preferred to take his holiday there. Every time we went to Bulgaria we spent 2–3 weeks in the same holiday home and the Director treated us like old friends. The beach had a wonderful view of Nesebr, a small town with the remains of buildings dating from the ninth to the twelfth centuries. The town was on a peninsula joined to the mainland by a narrow strip of land, and it looked fairytaleish, as though it were floating in the water.

Kim and I loved strolling around its narrow curving alleys looking at the tiny open-air tavernas. Kim fell in love with Bulgarian food and was delighted by the profusion of vegetables, which were in such short supply everywhere else we went. Even Leo, sitting opposite him with a sour look on his face, did not spoil his appetite. Unlike Valentin, who knew how to enjoy life and who took every opportunity when we were in Czechoslovakia to slip away from us and to have a good time (something that we encouraged), Leo always gave the impression that it was all a bit too much for him. He was constantly complaining that the sun was burning his head, or blinding him, and I was on the point of buying him some sunglasses when he said: 'I can't stand glasses. They weigh on your nose.' Kim could not fathom how he had been able to work in Arab countries from which he had just returned. In Bulgaria, it was late autumn and the sun wasn't actually too much of a bother.

At that time Kim was healthy and full of energy. He even liked going shopping and choosing presents for relatives and friends. Everywhere he went Leo was close at his heels, making clear by the look on his face that he was above it all. He bought nothing in the shops. Once when Kim was taking a nap after lunch, I decided to go for a walk and suggested that Todor accompany me. Leo insisted on joining us, though there was no need for him to do so, and Todor joked: 'Perhaps Kim has told Leo to follow you.' While Todor and I were strolling around and popping into the shops, Leo waited in the car. When we came back, he asked irritably, 'Where've you been all this time?' I decided the reason for Leo's bad mood was that he had no spending money. I then began to feel sorry for him and even asked Todor how we might help him. Todor just laughed. I understood why when we were ready to go home and I saw all of Leo's luggage.

After this trip with Leo, Kim raised strenuous objections to having a KGB escort when travelling and declared that unless the rules were changed he would simply not go anywhere. His protest had the desired effect and other than on our trip to Cuba, we saw no more of these 'fellow-travellers'.

We first visited Hungary in 1977. Kim had warm memories of it from his student days, when he had toured Europe on an old motorbike. In every country we visited, Kim was treated with dignity and respect, like a VIP, but in Hungary no one tormented us with food and drink, and there were no endless toasts. In Hungary, we even managed to visit some wine cellars without any fuss and bother. However, we did have to put up with a certain amount of formality and as a rule, the smaller the town, the larger our 'entourage', to the point when some of the walks we took began to remind me of our experiences in Central Asia. The weather wasn't that kind to us in Hungary either. On one of the few nice days we arrived at the beautiful town of Eger. Sitting in a stuffy room surrounded by the town's official representatives, we watched despondently as the sun set slowly in the sky while we endured a lecture about how many metres of gas and water pipes they had laid, how many hectares were under cultivation and the excellent alfalfa crop, something of which the locals were very proud.

Finally, when the speaker paused for breath, I seized the opportunity to translate the sense of what he had said and, declaring: 'It's better to see something once than to listen to it seven times,' jumped to my feet pulling Kim along. Everyone else followed us out with evident delight.

Afterwards, because I could not bear uncertainty, I asked what an alfalfa crop was. The very charming lady who was interpreting for us was meticulous to a fault, and her translation into Russian was twice as long as the original Hungarian. She was terrified of omitting the slightest detail and chose every word with exquisite care. I do not speak Hungarian but even I was able to grasp in the first few words the essence of what was being said. Kim was desperately bored, but stayed his usual patient self.

Kim remembered Hungarian quite well and surprised everybody with how good he was. Even I had an opportunity to demonstrate my language 'skills' when, in answer to the Hungarian greeting, '*Kezet csokolom*,' I repeated the same phrase – much to the amusement of the men; I did not know that it meant: 'I kiss your hand.'

In Myskovec, I 'conveniently' hurt my knee, which saved Kim a climb up the local television tower. Another noteworthy feature of the place was the manufacture of artificial flowers. I was given a huge bouquet of artificial carnations in every conceivable shade. They were laid out on my bed and I shivered as if I had seen a grave.

We visited Hungary two years in a row, each time vainly hoping for good weather while we sat for a fortnight on the shores of Lake Balaton. I was able to swim only once. On the other hand, we did strike it lucky in Silvashvarod, an unusually pretty mountain spa whose remoteness particularly appealed to Kim. We were housed in a small villa in a quiet spot on high ground with a marvellous view. We could walk for hours without seeing a soul. There was just one woman looking after the house, doubling as a cook and a housekeeper. Our Hungarian escort, the delightful Gaidosh, went everywhere with us. Having got used to the Soviet refrain that, 'It isn't that simple,' we were much taken by Gaidosh's 'No problem!'

Gaidosh was noticeably on edge when we first arrived at Silvashvarod. He relaxed only after dinner. It turned out that he was worried that he might have to go through a repetition of what had happened when he had been escorting a German delegation. They had had a very full day and had sat down to dinner tired and very hungry. They were given one small trout each, which they swallowed in a flash and sat waiting for the next course. Only there was no next course, and the only thing left to do was to go off to bed. Gaidosh was so hungry that he couldn't sleep, and crept stealthily down to the kitchen to raid the fridge. The Germans, likewise unable to sleep, were ahead of him and they all bumped into each other in the dark! But the fridge turned out to be completely empty. I too used to steal down to the kitchen, but in the mornings and with something else in mind, namely to get in ahead of the housekeeper and make Kim's tea. She had her own technique, which involved putting the tea leaves into a large cast-iron teapot, filling it with cold water and then bringing it to the boil as though it were soup. On the other hand, she made great coffee!

One evening we were taken to a nature reserve and promised a surprise – we would not only hear, but also see the deer calling to each other. We went up an observation tower which stood in an empty field exposed on all sides to the wind. We sat shivering but saw and heard nothing while the stars twinkled mockingly down on us. We clambered down from the tower and sat beneath a tree, tenderly wrapped by our hosts in a checked rug. Kim sat there glumly, his teeth chattering from cold and fatigue, and could just not conceive why he was being subjected to such an ordeal. In the end, our hosts apologised and we were left in peace.

Our little house seemed even more comfortable and welcoming when we returned. We had supper and began to warm up. Before we went to bed, we decided to go out on to the balcony to breathe the fresh air and enjoy the stars. Suddenly, we heard a trumpeting 'Oooohhh'. Then everything went quiet again. Though the deer were evidently on the taciturn side, we still felt the day had not been entirely wasted and took to our beds with a clear conscience.

CHAPTER 19

Cuba

In the autumn of 1978, we received an unexpected invitation to visit Cuba, which turned out to be the most exciting and exotic place we had ever seen. Much thought had to be given about how to get there, planes and passenger ships being ruled out for security reasons. In the end, it was decided that we should use a freighter which sailed to Havana directly, without calling at any ports on the way. Armed, on Vladimir's advice, with a supply of tinned food and smoked sausage, we arrived in Leningrad on 1 October to board the *Sculptor Golubkina*. It was loaded with containers for Cuba – God knows what was in them! We were housed in one of the three well-appointed cabins.

Before we left Moscow, we had been introduced to Gennady II, who was to escort us and with whom we got on very well. Unfortunately, after Cuba, we never saw him again. The infamous Nikolai, who had taken Vladimir's place, forbade Gennady to visit us in Moscow for reasons never learned.

During the whole trip, we stayed on the deserted deck, rain or shine. We made the most of not having an 'entourage' – no one fussing around. Kim had finally got what he loved best and what he never got when we were travelling before, namely solitude. It was just us and the ocean. We hardly saw Gennady. We would meet up with him and the captain at meal times when we ate with the crew. They made us feel completely at home. The food was simple home-cooking, tasty and rich. The supplies we had brought from Moscow remained untouched.

When we sailed through the Straits of Dover, Kim pointed out to me his old prep school, Eastbourne, but sadly the visibility was poor and I couldn't make anything out. We saw no other ships at all. It seemed as if we were alone in the universe. The only things we saw from time to time were playful dolphins swimming alongside, and a flock of birds which one day appeared on the deck from nowhere. They looked like sparrows, but Kim, ever observant, noticed straight-away that, unlike sparrows, they didn't hop, but ran, putting one foot in front of the other. On the next day, the birds vanished as unexpectedly as they had arrived. Once we were circled by a small plane, which came down so low that we could see the pilot. Just in case, we left the deck.

Suddenly, a storm hit us. We felt it during dinner, when our soup plates started to tip over. Kim was completely unaffected by the tossing and claimed that it merely helped him to drop off to sleep. Rolling from side to side like a little baby in a cradle, he slept more soundly than ever. In contrast, I could not settle and finally moved on to a small sofa which lay at right angles to our wide bed. I tried to wedge myself in place, digging my head and feet into the armrests.

After three days, calm returned and the sun shone once more. Two weeks went by without our even noticing. We were sorry the voyage had come to an end. On 15 October the ship entered Havana harbour. We said goodbye to the crew, who had been so nice to us, and a few minutes later a small launch landed us on Cuban soil.

We received a very warm welcome. The Cubans put us up in a two-storey house, a legacy of 'damned imperialism', where we stayed for several days touring the city and the area around it. Kim and I ate our fill of seafood, but poor Gennady pined for meat and bread (crackers were a poor substitute). We flew from Havana to Santiago de Cuba, where, to use the Cuban newspaper cliché, we visited 'sites of military and revolutionary glory'. We explored every inch of the Island of Freedom. It would have been wonderful were it not for Kim's health. Although the weather did not bother him, the high humidity and abrupt changes in temperature had a devastating effect. It might be 35–40 degrees C. outside but inside the buildings, with the air conditioning going, it was only 15 degrees C. When he came in hot and sweaty and was hit by the cold blast from the air conditioner, his bronchitis flared up immediately and later developed into pneumonia.

The hours of travelling, the heat and sweaty clothes sticking to your body, were very exhausting. Even downpours of rain brought no relief since the water evaporated in an instant, only boosting the humidity and having no cooling effect whatever. We were also tired by the incessant meeting and greeting of a kaleidoscope of unknown faces and were overjoyed when we got to Baradero, where we were able to take a fortnight's rest.

We arrived there late one evening. It was pitch black and our bodyguards spent ages wandering up and down the streets, banging on doors while trying to find out the house. It was right on the water's edge. Sitting there with yet another group of unknown people, I could hear the sound of the surf and was bursting with impatience to 'feel' the sea. 'What's the water's temperature?' I asked. 'Fifteen degrees, it's very cold,' they told me.

The bright rays of the sun woke me up in the morning and the gentle hissing of the surf pulled me out of the house. A few steps across a green lawn and I was on a beach as endless and as deserted as the sea itself. The white sand burned my feet. The water was as warm as a bath. So much for their 15 degrees; it was a good 30, if not more. In any event, I hadn't been in water as warm as this even at the height of summer on the Black Sea. I sat in the water for hours on end, thus avoiding the need to talk to anyone. I literally sat and splashed since a strong current, eddies and sharks all combined to make swimming dangerous. Kim did not even go near the water and hid himself away in the shade. I was the only one bathing. For the Cubans, it was winter and the water was too cold. They looked at me and shivered, as if I was splashing in one of those holes we cut in the ice in Russia for winter fishing.

We were not left alone for long. We were told to expect visitors for lunch, though the precise time was left rather vague. They appeared, without explanations or apologies, for dinner. Being a stickler for punctuality, Kim was very annoyed at this, though he did not show it. He hated being taken by surprise. We usually were not told who our visitors were, and why they had come. They would drink, eat and make desultory conversation, but it seemed to have nothing to do with Kim.

We were close to the vast and splendid Dupont Villa near Baradero which was open to tourists. Kim was contemptuous of wealth and refused to visit this 'palace'. Nor did he want to see Hemingway's house. On the other hand, when we were in Havana we did spend one evening in Hemingway's favourite restaurant, the Floridita, where we tried a Daiquiri of which he had been so fond. The most important ingredient, along with rum and lemon juice, is the crushed ice, which gives it that special 'something' after the barman has worked his dextrous magic with the shaker. The Cubans told us that that was the only place where we could taste a real Daiquiri. They also told us how dangerous it was. 'It slips down easily, like water, and you don't notice its effects,' one of them said and did a mock karate chop to the back of his neck. Our hosts ordered another round but only for themselves. I said rather pointedly that we would like to check for ourselves just how dangerous it was, but they were unmoved by sarcasm and simply repeated their warning with the same chopping gestures. We left the bar and went into the restaurant, where we were offered crocodile on a spit. I could not overcome my prejudice and didn't have any. Kim didn't like the dish: it was dry and a bit tough.

The city hadn't been able to preserve much of its fading beauty. The plaster was peeling off the splendid buildings. We were struck by the poverty, though the people seemed cheerful and happy-go-lucky. We had the sense that no one was actually at work, an impression that was false, but which was reinforced when we saw on television people dancing from dawn to dusk. Everything in the shops – food, household goods – was rationed. Only ice-cream was freely available. We spent most of the time travelling, having to attend formal meetings and listen to stories of victories and the achievements of socialism. Faces, faces . . .

We spent several days in Santa Clara. There was always a crowd of visitors around the table in the beautiful little private villa where we were staying. In the evening, the owner took on the role of barman, but only served himself. And when we sat down to eat, he had a bottle in front of him from which he filled only his own glass. This struck us as odd, but bothered us far less than the insistence of our hosts on food and drink in Central Asia. We seemed to have gone from one extreme to the other.

We had heard a lot about the beautiful Cuban women, but we didn't see one worthy of such a description. Perhaps all the really pretty ones came out only at night, we thought, but when one evening we went to a night-club, the girls there were such grotesque caricatures that they reminded us of dolls from the Moscow puppet theatre.

I remember a nice stroll by the lake, followed by a barbecue with shashlik on the lakeside. Our host had spent several years training in Moscow. While mastering his main profession as an intelligence officer, he had also learned to cook shashlik, a skill of which he was especially proud. Threading the pieces of meat on to the skewers, he smiled and turned to Kim muttering just one word: 'Mookoo, Mookoo, Mookoo'. We hadn't got a clue what he meant. It turned out he was trying to say 'Moscow'. I don't know how successful he was in his job, but the shashlik was as tough as the steak in Krasnoyarsk.

We had a wonderful time out on a launch. Divers hauled huge crabs and lobsters from the sea bottom. They had been cultivated by a brilliantly simple technique: used car tyres were sunk a little way off shore and lobsters would nest in them. The divers could then catch them bare-handed. So easy!

A month passed. We returned to Havana and began to get ready to go back to Moscow, but all of a sudden we ran into delays and inexplicable vagueness. Someone or other had made a mistake, and the ship we were meant to take had left. It would be a fortnight before the next one. We finally left Cuba at the end of November on the freighter *Yanis Lentsmanis*, which was a little smaller than the *Golubkina* but just as comfortable. Oranges and grapefruit, as well as the Philbys, were loaded on board and we could once again enjoy being alone and watching the water stretching to the horizon. This time the change in the weather was much more marked. One month we were in tropical heat, the next in the cold of winter. The weather got worse at a very inopportune moment, just as we were approaching Istanbul. A snow storm started and all the mosques disappeared in the fog.

As we passed through the narrow straits, we could see cars moving on the road and lights in the house windows, including the house where Kim had once lived. They say that there is now a plaque on the house: 'Kim Philby, outstanding intelligence officer, lived here 1941–48'.

We didn't manage to escape without a real storm. The ship rolled so much that a heavy box with bottles of water slid around the cabin as if on wheels. Trying to get out of its way, I just failed to catch a carafe of grapefruit juice as it tipped over, sending the assiduous efforts of the captain, who had squeezed the fruit for us, literally down the drain.

The *Yanis Lentsmanis* followed a different route and our voyage back took two days longer than the outward run. But on 8 December we sailed into a snow-covered Odessa and took the train to Moscow. Though we had had a wonderful time in Cuba, the sea voyage was incomparably more enjoyable. Unfortunately, it adversely affected Kim's health. After we returned, he became ill more often and grew perceptibly weaker. He reckoned that the Cuban climate had had a disastrous effect on him. Though he was ill, Kim wasn't given to whining. He was always in good spirits and, however poorly he felt, he never showed it. Writing to Mikhail Lyubimov on 26 January 1979, Kim said:

Today, you are missing a colleaguely party to celebrate the 16th anniversary of my arrival in the SU, and two busy females, Rufa and her mother, are sweeping the flat from under my feet. So I will give you our news as briefly as I can . . . We had two wonderful sea-trips: Leningrad-Havana-Odessa, with three days of only slight motion in the Atlantic outward bound and another three in the Mediterranean coming home. Otherwise, glassy seas and a bright sun all the way (almost). The reception in the 'island of freedom' was more than overwhelming, with [crowds] of people wherever we went. Very flattering, of course, but not quite our cup of tea. And the climatic conditions were tailor-made to ravage my bronchial tubes, *very* damp warmth outside, cold dry air-conditioning inside. So I got back in poorish shape to face a grozny combination of our colleagues, doctors and Rufa, who pitchforked me into hospital for observation and general workover. Result: nothing whatever wrong! Lungs as clean as a whistle and a liver that made a beautiful picture under radio-isotopic examination. So you see what can be achieved by an (almost) fifty-year-old diet of alcohol and tobacco! Never despair!

CHAPTER 20

Kim's Last Trip Abroad

For a long time Kim refused invitations to visit the GDR. He still had his deep-seated prejudice and hostility towards the Germans dating back to the war. We went there only in 1981 and, contrary to all our expectations, the visit turned out to be a success. We were made very welcome without the obtrusive attention we disliked so much. As elsewhere, we had a Russian-speaking interpreter at our disposal, which was handy for me, but Kim preferred to speak German. He got so used to it that he would sometimes drop into German when talking to me.

We met the famous Markus Wolf, head of their foreign intelligence service. He spoke to me in Russian, without the trace of a foreign accent. When I expressed surprise, he explained that he had spent his childhood and teenage years in Moscow and gone to school there. We also got to know Eric Mielke, the Security Minister, who invited us to dinner at his villa in the suburbs, where there was a large group of senior officials from his Ministry.

We stayed in a Berlin suburb and travelled widely around the country, spending two days in Dresden in the pouring rain, but we enjoyed seeing the masterpieces in the Dresden Gallery. The people who were with us noticed that Kim stopped for quite a while to look at a Canaletto, and when we got back to the villa there was a surprise waiting for us – a wonderful copy of Canaletto's view of Dresden.

We also spent several days by the sea at Rostock. The days were sunny, though there was a cool breeze. The water was bracing, as it usually is in the Baltic. Kim, of course, did not want to bathe, so I had to swim for two. One cold evening we were taken to see a large-scale open-air spectacle, a huge show by the sea. There was not an empty seat. Our hosts put Kim and me right at the front, having taken the trouble to supply us with rugs, and passed us a little glass of brandy while the show was on to ward off the cold.

The action took place both on land and at sea. It was a wonderful sight. Two sailing ships appeared as twilight was fading and launched into a fight at close quarters. Cannons roared, the water foamed. The sea and the sky were lit up by the flashes of exploding shells and the leaping flames of a bonfire. The knights in armour on the shore swung at each other with swords.

Unfortunately, our visit to the GDR turned out to be Kim's last trip abroad.

CHAPTER 21

The Dacha

Over the years Moscow became a home town to Kim. He knew the central part of it like the back of his hand and loved strolling with me through its quiet streets any time of the year; he even liked the Moscow climate. He could take any sort of weather and any season, but he was especially fond of the real Russian winter, with its snow and frost. He loved to walk in the coldest frost, taking deep breaths of icy air. The frost didn't bother me either, but I could not stand the heat, especially in the city. Warned that it might also affect Kim, I used to ask him: 'How are you feeling? Is it too hot or stuffy for you?' He would be surprised at my question and reply: 'Not at all, it's nice and warm.'

It didn't take Kim long to notice that hot weather made me bad-tempered and irritable. This upset him and he used to sit glued in fright to the weather forecast of the *Vremya* evening news programme. If they said the temperature was going to be over 25 degrees C., he would bring me the sad news with a downcast look. On hot days I literally felt like a fish out of water and could survive only under the bathroom shower. That was where Kim discovered me one day, doing something a little unusual, namely sitting in a tub of cold water peeling potatoes. I can still remember the expression on his face. Perhaps it was this event which helped me convince Kim that we should spend the summers in a dacha or country house. Up till then he had maintained that though he would like to have his own dacha, he had seen nothing that suited him, especially since they all lacked even the basic amenities.

It was only after I had been in England that I understood what Kim was after, and what he couldn't find in the Soviet Union, namely, something more like an English country cottage. Then in the summer of 1972 – a little before we broke up with the Blakes – George and Ida invited us to share their dacha in the KGB compound in Tomilino. They occupied half a large house with 'all mod cons' except hot water. The other half, at the back of the house, was available. Kim finally agreed to move in though without much enthusiasm. Behind the house was a large neglected garden, surrounded by a solid fence. My needs were modest – fresh air and a shady tree. I was 100 per cent happy and asked Kim: 'Why don't you sit in the garden?' He frowned and stubbornly refused to leave the house. 'The earth here is acid,' he insisted. His English eye, used to well-tended gardens and lawns, was offended by the sight of a plot of upturned soil. Later, I too noticed that the trees were dying, eaten alive by forest bugs which flowed in red rivers up their trunks.

Another feature of the landscape were the rabbits bred by the watchman who lived next door. He used to let them run loose in search of food, and they would scamper under our feet, making a good job of fertilising the soil and covering the grass with their little black pellets. Kim wasn't enjoying it. He would sit inside with a scowl on his face, his nose buried in his books and newspapers. At night he was bothered by the sound of aeroplanes (there was an airfield nearby at Bykovo). He used to stuff cotton wool in his ears, but slept poorly all the same. The days went by, and Kim would not say what was bothering him and suffered in silence. I couldn't bear his 'silent victim' look and we soon returned to Moscow.

But towards the end of the 1970s, as Kim's health deteriorated, we were compelled to raise the dacha issue with our case officer. He gave us the by now painfully familiar: 'It's not that simple.' We had no idea what difficulties had to be resolved, but several months later Kim was asked to go and have a look at a dacha. This KGB dacha compound was about 20 kilometres from the centre of Moscow. There were about a hundred houses all the same, without fences, scattered around the compound at some 40 or 50 yards apart. When we went there, I was worried that Kim would react in the same way he had in Tomilino, but happily he liked it all. We spent the next summer there (1981) and returned every year thereafter. By that time Kim had already abandoned his fantasy about building an English cottage and was perfectly happy with our little Finnish house. We had two bedrooms, a sitting-room, a terrace, a bathroom and a kitchen, and all the conveniences including hot water. The house was not winterised, so the dacha season was restricted to the five months from May to September.

Kim wrote to Erik de Mauny on 25 March 1983:

. . . I have acquired a very nice dacha with all mod. con. within easy reach of Moscow, half-an-hour's drive. The road stops at the edge of a forest, so we have no through traffic nor even a serf with a tractor. Our only real noise comes from our friendly woodpecker, which sounds off in five-second bursts like a Bren [gun]: astonishing that so small and frail a creature should have such neck muscles – and such an immunity from headaches (presumably). There is a bi-weekly delivery of spring chickens, eggs, milk, smetana, etc. which I took to be one of the advantages of living in the country. What innocence! On further enquiry I was told that it all came from Moscow.

Kim set enthusiastically about cultivating his 'garden' though the soil – a dense clay – was better suited for pottery than planting. He spent a long time digging it over thoroughly to make a flower-bed and then spent the next day forking over the solidified clods of earth yet again, until the compound commandant came by, explained that Kim was wasting his time and sent over a barrow of fresh soil. Sometime later, our ever-willing Vladimir brought some more.

Kim knocked together some bird feeders. He loved to watch their little ways, enjoying the peace and quiet; he was only disappointed that there were no butterflies. The birds responded very well to our hospitality. The first to arrive was a large woodpecker, who reckoned he was in charge and chased the other birds away. He had a fondness for little bits of bread. He would pick them up clumsily with a sideways

170

peck and scurry back up the tree with the bread in his beak, until he came to a hole in the bark, into which he would push his booty. He soon began to appear with a fledgling, who was not much smaller – a bright red spot on the fledgling's breast was the only sure way to tell them apart. The young one would squawk demandingly while the daddy (or mummy?) woodpecker dropped pieces of bread one after another into its insatiable beak.

The yellow and green tomtits flew around in noisy flocks. They chirped cheerfully as they flitted to and fro, picking restlessly at the food, chasing each other and carelessly dropping the crumbs which flew around in all directions like spray. In contrast, the meek little chaffinches had much better manners. They would sit for a long time on a lump of bread, each on its own piece, relishing the profusion of food at their disposal and giving it only the occasional peck. The nuthatch was smoky-blue with a pink breast. It would come down the tree to the feeder head first and rush back up with a piece of bread for its young ones. The little wagtails, elegant and haughty, would prom-enade along the path picking up the leftover crumbs. There were sometimes sad accidents when the birds flew straight into the win-dowpane of the terrace and dropped dead. I once picked up a tiny motionless bundle. It was a nightingale. While I tried to revive it, a persistent mosquito buzzed around my nose. The bird's claws, which had folded in on themselves, slowly straightened out and into my fin-gers, but its eyes were still glazed. Suddenly the glaze vanished and I saw its little beady eyes looking up at me. At that moment the nightin-gale struck the mosquito, thanked me with a cheerful trill and flew off like lightning. Kim guarded the peace of his little birds jealously and chased away cats, who became his worst enemies. Squirrels used the feeders too. Once, when I was sitting under a tree, I heard a strange noise. I looked up. On a branch there sat a squirrel, tut-tutting at me reprovingly, its bushy tail quivering in annoyance. I had invaded her space. Having chased me away, she started to eat her meal.

CHAPTER 22

Meeting
Graham Greene

For Kim and Graham, old MI6 colleagues and friends, seeing each other again in September 1986, after thirty-five years, was as happy an event as it was unexpected, or even – for those times – improbable, although they used to write to each other.

Greene was making his first trip to the USSR in twenty-five years at the invitation of the Writers' Union. One of his first comments when he landed at Sheremetyevo was that he was looking forward to seeing old friends. But when a journalist asked whether this meant he would actually be seeing Kim Philby, he replied tersely: 'I don't know.' His hesitation was justified. Back then, in those pre-*Glasnost* days, there would have been no meeting unless some high-up official had decided that it would serve some purpose.

For almost twenty years the works of Graham Greene were not published in the USSR and even his name wasn't mentioned after he had defended the dissident writers Daniel and Sinyavsky, jailed in 1965 for publishing their work in the West. In protest, Greene had refused to visit the USSR and to allow his books to be published there. He had also publicly condemned the sending of Soviet troops to Czechoslovakia in 1968.

Genrikh Borovik, the well-known Soviet journalist and then President of the Soviet Peace Committee, told us that Greene was in the country and, afterwards, that it was he who had arranged for the two old friends to meet.

Through Borovik, Kim invited Greene to dinner at our flat, and we spent the whole day preparing to receive our distinguished guest. It was a specially happy occasion for me since I had always had a high regard for Greene as a writer and had read his books in Russian. And when I had started learning English, I had turned to *The Heart of the Matter*, one of my text books and the first of his works I read in English.

It was an evening I will never forget. I went downstairs to meet Greene in a state of anxious excitement. I was nervous since I gathered he had a rather sarcastic tongue. I remembered the first time Kim and I had talked about him that summer in Tomilino in 1970 just after we had met. I had spotted a copy of *The Times* with a picture of Greene on the front page and, as if in answer to a question, I pointed to it and said to Kim: 'He's a fantastic writer.' 'He's a friend of mine,' Kim replied.

I remembered the face in the photo: unsmiling, even a touch angry. We had no idea then that Greene would be a guest in our home. Greene had never thought a meeting would be feasible, nor, as he once wrote to Kim, had he ever thought there was any point in trying to telephone.

A Chaika limousine turned the corner and slid silently to a halt alongside me. The driver switched off the headlights. When the real-life Greene popped out in front of me, with a smile on his face, I just could not believe it. He was tall, so tall that the only thing I could think of was that he must have had to bend practically double even to fit into such a big car.

He got out and said in a low voice: 'I am feeling *so* shy.'

I was touched. Being shy myself, I was surprised to hear him say this about himself, but before I could think of anything to say he repeated: 'I am so *shy*.' We walked across the pavement into the darkness of the rundown hallway of our building and went up in the lift, heavy with unpleasant odours.

Kim met us at the door. They hugged, clapping each other on the back in embarrassment and pleasure.

Sitting Greene down in our living-room on the couch, Kim said: 'Just don't ask me any questions.'

'Actually,' Greene said, 'I've only one thing to ask. How is your Russian?'

Looking at the two of them, it was hard to believe that they had not seen each other for thirty-five years. They chatted like close friends after only a brief time apart, remembering mutual acquaintances, laughing as they shared old memories.

They had become friends in the 1940s when they both worked in British Intelligence. In Kim's book *My Silent War* (Grafton edition, pp. 125–6), he recalls Greene's short stay in his Section:

Graham Greene was brought back to reinforce Section V from Freetown, where he had been supposedly watching the intrigues of the Vichy French. He will forgive me for confessing that I cannot recall any startling achievements of his in West Africa; perhaps the French were not intriguing? I do remember, however, a meeting held to discuss a proposal of his to use a roving brothel to frustrate the French . . . The proposal was discussed quite seriously, and was turned down only because it seemed unlikely to be productive of hard intelligence. Happily, Greene was posted, where I put him in charge of Portugal. He had a good time sniping at OSS, and his tart comments on incoming correspondence were a daily refreshment.

The Greene sitting opposite me was nothing like the Greene I had imagined. I was captivated straightaway. He was nice, delicate, soft-spoken, with the clear, naive eyes of a child. As we chatted he was attentive, interested in what I had to say, reacting to my little jokes in an unforced way, with a pleasant chuckle.

He and Kim had several subtle characteristics in common: inquisitive, piercing blue eyes, and a directness and sincerity combined with a British reserve. But the similarities were not just skin-deep. They had a lot else in common, notably a strong sense of fair play; their sympathies were always on the side of those who were striving for freedom.

Kim remembered a long chat with Greene when he joined Section V: 'Of course I couldn't talk to him as a Communist but I did talk to him as a man with left-wing views and he was Catholic. But at once there was human contact between us.' They would often take their meals together and soon became close friends. Greene later admitted that one element of Kim's character he found hard to take was his personal ambition. When *My Silent War* came out, Greene wrote in the preface to the book: 'I am glad I was wrong. He served a cause, rather than putting himself first, and as a result my earlier affection for him was rekindled.'

'I think you are one of the few people in England who really understand,' Kim wrote to him in April 1968 after reading Greene's concerned letter to *The Times* about the trial of Sinyavsky and Daniel. That was the start of their correspondence. They exchanged views and discussed political events, neither of them in any doubt that their letters were being read by the authorities at both ends. Greene was one of the few friends with whom Kim stayed in contact until the end of his life. Kim approved of Greene's reaction as 'honourable, fair and decent. Like you, I hope things will change soon and for another reason as well, because change might allow us to get back together again, sitting around a table, chatting like we used to in the good old days.' Twenty years later his hopes were fulfilled, the two of them sitting around a table in a Moscow flat knocking back vodka, Greene's favourite drink.

'Funny how vodka never makes you drunk,' Greene pronounced, slowly sipping his drink.

Kim was surprised but not convinced.

'Can you believe what he said?' he turned to me in surprise after Greene had left our house. 'Obviously it makes you drunk.' Greene hardly touched the appetisers, explaining that the older he got, the less hungry he felt.

That meeting with Greene left Kim not just happy but also relieved. It was the first time they had been able to be completely frank with one another. They were no longer separated by Kim's secret.

'He is burdened by doubt as well,' Kim said after he had come back from showing Greene out at the end of the evening.

As Greene said, citing his hero Monsignor Quixote, 'Sharing a sense of doubt can bring men together perhaps even more than sharing a faith.' Perhaps for that reason Kim rated *Monsignor Quixote* as one of Greene's best books.

The day after this visit, we went with Greene, Yvonne (Greene's companion) and the Boroviks to the dacha of the painter Vukolov. The weather was gorgeous, dry and sunny, a real golden autumn. We drove into a dense virgin forest, weaving for ages along a dirt road with not a soul about. Suddenly, the road ended at a solid fence, gates opened and there stood a very pretty house, in the building of which obviously no expense had been spared. The owner, alert and full of energy, came out to greet us with his tall, well-built, very good-looking wife.

Inside was a spacious well-lit studio. Greene's favourite among the pictures the artist showed us was one of helmeted astronauts about to set off into nothingness. It gave off a sad feeling: two tiny figures lost in infinite space. After viewing the pictures, we sat talking around a table groaning in the usual Russian way with food and drink.

Sergo Mikoyan (the scientist son of Anastas Mikoyan, Stalin's first deputy) and his wife, who had the dacha next door, came to eat with us and afterwards we went to their place for coffee. We sat around the fireplace in a comfortable living-room eating a delicious pineapple ice-cream with our coffee. Graham asked for a second helping, but before he could get his spoon to his mouth Artem Borovik, Genrikh's son, and Sergo Mikoyan were all over him with questions, pushing tape-recorders in his face. 'How do you like our *Perestroika*?' 'What do you think of Gorbachev's policies?' 'What is your attitude towards the Pope?' 'What are your views on religion?'

Graham answered in a patient monotone. Asked again about his views on religion, he responded without any change in intonation: 'I want to pee.'

I almost choked with laughter. His inquisitors, looking serious and concentrating hard on trying to understand what he was saying, were unfazed. They waited for him to go on.

'I want to pee.'

Suddenly, it dawned on them and they escorted him to the loo. He never answered the question. On 24 September 1986 Kim wrote to Greene:

> While the memory of your visit is still fresh in our minds, I am writing to tell you how much we appreciated it. Rufa said, without any prompting from me, that the three days we spent on and off together were among the happiest in her life. As for myself, I find myself suffering from an acute attack of the esprit d'escalier: so many questions I wanted to ask, but didn't, so

many things I wanted to say, but didn't. Well, you can't bridge a gap of thirty-five years in a few hours. Zut alors!

Five months later, in the snows of February, Greene came back to Moscow, this time without Yvonne, to participate in a Forum styled 'For a Nuclear Free World and the Survival of Mankind'.

He came to dinner. I stood waiting for him at the curb-side watching the passing cars. Greene stepped straight out of his Chaika into a pile of snow on an uncleared patch of pavement. We picked our way carefully along a narrow path which had been trampled in the snow, me in the lead, Greene following, gingerly attempting to walk right in my footsteps and gripping my hand hard as his city shoes slipped and slid. In the end, I delivered him safe and sound into Kim's embrace.

When Greene went into the sitting-room, one particular picture caught his eye. Kim told him the story behind it. At the end of 1979, his case officer brought him a parcel which he said had been handed in at the Soviet Embassy in London by a man who had asked that it be forwarded to Kim Philby. Inside was an engraving of the Column in Rome consecrated to the Emperor Marcus Aurelius, a member of the Antonine dynasty.

A little while earlier, on 15 November 1979, Kim had heard on the BBC the news of Prime Minister Margaret Thatcher's announcement that Anthony Blunt had been a Soviet agent. Kim had been stunned since after he confessed in 1964, Blunt had been promised immunity from prosecution and that his role would never see the light of day. When he read the inscription on the engraving, 'Piranesi's Antonine Column', Kim guessed that the parcel had come from his old friend Blunt, art scholar and Keeper of The Queen's Pictures. It was obviously a secret sign, a very special way of saying 'Hello' and a reminder of their fight together against Fascism.

'It was so like Anthony,' Kim said. 'I had no doubt whatever.' At the time, Kim couldn't make up his mind whether to let Blunt know that his message had been received, but when he heard of his death, on 26 March 1983, he regretted not having done so.

Meantime, warming up with his favourite vodka, Greene mused to Kim: 'You and I are suffering from the same incurable disease – old age.' He complained that it was so difficult to take a shower that he had grown scared even to attempt it. Kim shot me a meaningful look.

177

He appreciated better than most what Greene was saying; as he said afterwards, 'I was dying to admit to him that it's ages since I was able to take a bath without you there to help.'

Greene visited the USSR four times in two years, so we saw quite a lot of him despite his heavy schedule of official engagements. In September 1987, when he again came with Yvonne, we took them to dinner at the Aragvi, the Georgian restaurant, where Vladimir had booked us a private room. While the service was all right, the food left a lot to be desired (a feature of Moscow life to which, sadly, we had become accustomed). Still we had a good time and a nice chat.

Kim later wrote to Greene: 'I am afraid that during our rather tumultuous goodbyes I forgot to apologise for the disgusting meal we gave you at Aragvi's. Rather more than a little disappointing. The previous year we had taken guests there with quite good results.'

When Greene came to the Forum, he was put up at the Cosmos Hotel, of which he said in a tone of loathing: 'Terrible cockroaches scuttling in all directions and full of very dodgy characters.' The Sovyetskaya, where he stayed on subsequent trips, was rather grander but also had its share of petty crooks. After a reception one evening, Greene lost his way in the corridors and could not find his room. He asked the concierge for help, and she had rustled up from nowhere a gloomy-looking oddball to show him the way. As Graham told the story:

> He looked just like a tramp, unshaven and wearing a filthy suit. When we got to my room he jabbered something, looking furtively up and down the corridor. I thought he was asking for a tip and reached in my pocket to pull out some money. Then I realised it was an English banknote so I began rummaging for something else. But the guy grabbed it. I tried to hang on to it but he went on tugging away until he had finally snatched it from me, pushed something into my hand and was gone in a flash. I saw he had left me holding a bundle of roubles. When I counted them they added up to more than I would have got if I'd changed my sterling at the official rate.

Kim's last meetings with Greene in February 1988 cost him a lot. His health had deteriorated badly, his heart was playing up and it was difficult for him even to leave the house. But we did meet at a dinner given by Genrikh Borovik in Greene's honour at the House of Writers. The poet Andrei Dementyev and the ophthalmologist Svyatoslav Fyodorov were also there with their wives. Fyodorov was not only an eminent surgeon but also an entrepreneur on quite a large scale. Greene asked him: 'How can you obtain independence from state control when no one else can?' 'Because I'm pushy,' Fyodorov said with a smile. 'If I can't get in the door, I'll climb through the window.'

I still have a photo of Kim's final meeting with Greene when they said goodbye for the last time. It shows the pitiful state Kim was in by then. In marked contrast to Greene, he looked tense and unnatural, compounded by the fact that the day before the barber had mutilated his hair. It looked as though he had used an axe instead of scissors.

I met Graham for the last time five months after Kim's death. He had decided to celebrate his birthday in Moscow. The Institute of World Literature had wanted to mark his eighty-fifth birthday with a special ceremony, but Greene, then coming up to eighty-four, was reluctant to wait that long: 'At my age a year ahead might be too late.' His birthday was on 4 October and Greene invited me to a reception given by the Writers' Union in the restaurant of the Sovyetskaya Hotel. Kim's daughter Josephine and her husband were staying with me, and they were invited too.

Greene sat me next to him and gave me his undivided attention. The other guests and the organisers were not surprisingly disappointed and a little put out to see the guest of honour concentrating on me, all the more since I was a complete outsider. I sensed what they were feeling, but it wasn't my fault. I was just answering one of Greene's questions when someone stood up to propose a toast to the guest of honour. Greene cut him short with a wave of hand and said: 'I want to drink to the wife of my close friend who died not long ago and to whom I was bound by warm memories.'

He went on about Kim at such length that it seemed for a while that the ceremony was in Kim's honour, not Greene's. I had to mobilise all my willpower not to cry.

When I left the hotel with my guests, we saw a long line of taxis for hire. We were delighted since it was usually impossible to find them. The drivers stood draped over the bonnets of their cars, taking not the slightest notice of us. It was actually not that unusual – they were waiting for some special clients, the tarts who worked at the hotel. I had to take my surprised guests home by trolley bus.

During the dinner, the music critic Svyatoslav Belza had told me how he too had once tried to get a taxi after he and Greene had been to the Bolshoi Theatre. In the end, a moonlighting private driver had stopped for them and Belza told him his passenger would be the famous writer Graham Greene. The delighted driver asked for an auto-graphed playbill instead of the fare, something no regular driver would dream of doing. 'My wife will never believe I had the famous Graham Greene sitting right here next to me,' he had said.

After Greene's eighty-fourth birthday celebrations, he, Yvonne and I had spent another evening together at the House of Writers. They gave me a lift home. Greene got out of the car behind me. We said goodbye on that same stretch of pavement where we had first met. I remember, as though he had just spoken, Greene's last words to me: 'Talk to Kim before you go to sleep. You'll feel better. I don't know if there is anyone up there,' he said, pointing to the sky, 'but if there is, he will hear you. And tell Kim I love him.'

I had a premonition that we had said goodbye forever.

CHAPTER 23

Our Final Travels

After our trip to Cuba, Kim's health took a marked turn for the worse. As he admitted to Graham Greene:

What really got me was the damp warmth outside and air-conditioned cool indoors. I coughed all the way from Havana to Santiago de Cuba and back, with the contrast between temperatures and humidity playing merry Hell with my bronx. I wouldn't have missed the trip for the world, but I doubt if I would go again. The climate and the general ebullience made me feel my age for the first time.

But as always, Kim was quite unconcerned about his health and was surprised that other people took it seriously. 'The Russians are such hypochondriacs,' he used to say; 'they talk too much about their health.' When he heard the phrase: 'To your health,' which was traditionally used when proposing a toast or wishing someone well, he would always interrupt and say, 'To love. What good would health be to me if I didn't have Rufa?' Even in the first year of our life together Kim had had a bad bout of pneumonia. At the time, the doctor who was looking after him had urged him to go to hospital, but Kim had refused point-blank. The doctor brought in the professor in charge to try to persuade him, but after he and I talked, the professor agreed that Kim would be better left at home. Kim always thought of 'the hospital' as something uniquely dreadful and furiously resisted any attempt to send him there.

For the first ten years we were together, Kim was full of strength and generally healthy. His blood pressure, according to doctors, was the same as the cosmonauts. The only thing which plagued him was bronchitis, which he treated like an old if unwelcome companion. 'As far as I can recall, I've been living with it ever since I was so high,' he said, trying to get me not to worry. But I could not accept this and persisted in my efforts to cure him. Over time it flared up less and less often, and his cough almost disappeared. Kim needed looking after as if he were a child. He was quite oblivious to things that might affect his health. Even a mere cold put him at serious risk, and the slightest little breeze could bring one on. Walking along the boulevard on a warm spring day, Kim's quick pace would make him hot, but it never crossed his mind to take off his raincoat or jacket. And when the sweat was pouring off him, he would do all his buttons, wrap himself in his scarf and proclaim: 'See what a good boy I am!' Later, I would be beside myself with frustration. I had seen the problem, but hadn't done anything about it. And lo and behold, he was in for another bout of bronchitis.

After Cuba, these attacks began to be more frequent and Kim became visibly weaker. Writing to Mikhail Lyubimov on 6 March 1978 he admitted:

I am afraid that I have been behaving very badly this winter;
all the worse because it has been our best for several years with
lots of snow and sunshine. In all I have spent more than ten
weeks cooped up in my flat, with bronchitis in December, a
severe grippe in January, then more bronchitis in February. As
you see, it's now March, and I am only just getting over the
third onslaught. It has played hell with all my plans. I have had
to postpone repeatedly my meetings with our young men, but
hope to begin again next week. We also cancelled a proposed
trip abroad, because it would have been absurd to have turned
up in uncertain health. Rufa's health has also been slightly

suspect, off and on; and her mother has crowned it all by falling on the ice and breaking her right arm.

In the autumn of 1981, we visited Bulgaria for the last time. Kim spent the entire three weeks there in his bed in the holiday home at Sunny Shore. On the first night he did not get a minute's sleep. He sat propped up on his pillows since lying down made him short of breath and brought on endless coughing. The next day our Bulgarian friends took us to the Out-Patients Department for Kim to get a chest X-ray. The doctor rattled off something in quickfire Bulgarian. I didn't understand a word and asked her to stick to two phrases – 'Breathe in,' and 'Breathe out.' She nodded as if she understood, though, as it turned out, she had the phrases the wrong way round. She yelled from behind the screen: 'Breathe out.' Kim stood there, his arms raised, and his trousers slid inexorably towards the floor. I realised that he had done what he should have done, namely, breathe in, though she was telling him the opposite. They diagnosed pneumonia, as well as pulmonary and cardiac insufficiency. But Kim still set his face against going to a hospital and stayed in the holiday home under intensive care. The doctors came every day and Kim used to joke: 'I've got doctoritis, not bronchitis.' The cardiologist who came to see Kim could not believe he had never complained about his heart and never had a treatment. The doctor recommended quite firmly – along with several other things – that Kim should drink a glass of whisky every day, but by that time Kim had lost his taste for strong drink and did not follow the advice.

Once we were back in Moscow, Kim quickly got back to normal; being in his own home always worked wonders for him. But though I had begun to rejoice at his recovery, problems flared up again. He began to find walking difficult and was troubled by shortness of breath. Up until recently when we were walking, I could barely keep up with him. Now, he could manage only a few steps before he had to stop to catch his breath. Even a mention of 'the doctor' was enough to upset him, though he had a high regard for our doctor, who was extremely competent and attentive. Ironically her surname was 'Quack', which amused Kim no end. About the only way to get Kim to the clinic was to lasso him and drag him there by brute force. So I had to tell him that if he did not go, the doctor would get into trouble, since she had to report to her superiors on each of her patients (this was actually true to some extent). So for my sake, and the doctor's, he agreed to go. The doctor called me her 'assistant' and trusted me completely, to the point where, when I came to get prescriptions for Kim, she would ask: 'What does he need?' This was in complete contrast to the previous doctor, a nice woman in all respects but one who pathologically disliked drugs. For Kim's chronic insomnia she used to prescribe evening walks and warm milk, which made him feel sick.

The next time I went to get a prescription, the doctor stunned me by saying: 'You must prepare yourself for the worst. The fact that he's alive at all is due to the good care he is getting. He can last only another two or at most three years.' How on earth could I prepare myself for that? I sat there for several hours to get myself under control and then went home as if nothing had happened. The doctor's opinion turned out to be close to the truth. Kim lived for another four years.

At home I was doctor, matron and nurse all rolled into one. When someone is ill in the house, you quickly acquire basic medical skills almost despite yourself. I kept a full medicine chest, with everything from antibiotics to mustard plasters. Kim would swallow uncomplainingly whatever I gave him so long as he could stay at home. 'Just don't send me to a hospital,' he would say.

But it wasn't reasonable to treat the cardiac and pulmonary insufficiency at home, and in 1988 Kim was taken to the Kremlin hospital in Kuntsevo. Though he was promised a separate room, there was another patient in there, coughing and hawking. As if that wasn't enough, there was a bowl of the detested apples on the side table. They didn't have another ward to offer us, so we sat in the corridor. I could achieve nothing by myself and decided to call the case officer, who told me: 'Wait there.' As usual Kim sat patiently, not saying a word. Nobody decided anything in the hospital without first consulting the Director, and he was either out or hiding from insistent visitors. I finally caught up with him towards evening, when he assured me the hospital had no single rooms, an answer I had to wait several hours to hear. We went in the reception office and waited another hour and a half for a car to take us home. A day later Kim was taken to the KGB hospital and put in a room of his own. They 'consoled' him that from now on he would be their regular client.

Unfortunately, that turned out to be true. Kim spent two or three weeks in the hospital every year and sometimes twice a year. He always had his own room and I was given a permanent pass so that I could visit him at any time. I was there almost every day and stayed with Kim from morning till evening. The staff was amazed that I was there so much and I heard one nurse say: 'What a fuss she makes of him.'

The main treatment in the hospital was drip-feeding, in addition to the array of pills that he took all the time at home. The hospital timetable dictated that each patient was given a thermometer at 7 a.m. and 4 p.m. every day. Kim usually fell asleep only just before daybreak, so this was a needless interruption, all the more since his temperature was always normal. I managed to convince the doctor not to wake Kim in the morning. I brought a thermometer from home and Kim recorded his temperature with great care. Needless to say, no one was the slightest bit interested in his little chart.

Having a room of his own was a real boon for Kim, especially at night when he couldn't sleep and would pass the time reading. But one evening the sister on duty interrupted this harmless activity with a loud yell: 'Lights out at 10,' and flicked off the switch. It was then about 11 p.m. Kim lay there sleepless in the dark for the rest of the night, and when I saw him in the morning he was exhausted and upset. We were surprised that the nurse had spoken so sharply; she had no reason to be irritated. In fact, even the doctors and other nurses said that Kim was an ideal patient who caused no trouble, being neither faddy nor demanding. I know better than anyone just how patient and undemanding he was. After this incident, I had a word with the doctor and Kim was not bothered at night again.

The nurse who put his drip in would often forget to take it out at the proper time. Usually I would go and look for her, but if I wasn't around to fetch her, Kim would pull the needle out himself. Another time I was there Kim asked me: 'Do you know where Tanya is?' 'Who's Tanya?' I asked. 'I don't know either. It's just that the cleaning woman woke me up this morning asking, "Where's Tanya? Where's Tanya?"'

I dealt with the little problems as they arose. For example, the bathroom door had no lock, which was probably a sensible precaution. The door was wide open all the time and it remained like that. I had to tie a string to the handle so that Kim could hold the door shut when he needed to be in there on his own. The hospital food was, in Kim's words, 'boring', but much better than in an ordinary hospital. Kim wasn't fussy about his food and would swallow a little of whatever was put in front of him, without really caring what it was. I tried to cook something more appetising, but the hospital atmosphere did not improve Kim's appetite, and he was even beyond enjoying home-made food. All he wanted was hot, freshly brewed tea, so I brought in a little immersion boiler with which I could boil water in the tea glass itself.

The bathroom, which was unusually large, also contained a cot and a big ZIL fridge, which was plugged into the only electric outlet in the room, on the floor. To make the tea I used to put the glass of water on top of the fridge, disconnect it and plug in the immersion boiler. One day, when I went to pull out the heater plug by its cord, the glass tipped over on to my head. The heater was still in it and got trapped in my hair, hissing away as it was doing its job. My head, cheek and shoulder were scalded. Only the thick collar of my sweater saved my neck. Kim was terrified and called the nurse. My only fear was that after this they would stop me brewing him tea, but everything worked out all right. They gave me first aid and allowed me to stay the night, which I spent on the cot in the bathroom. Our irreplaceable Vladimir brought me a bottle of salve, which I smeared on my scalded cheek. The thick brown scab, which looked like the sole of a shoe, came off after a few days without leaving a scar, though my shoulder showed traces of the scald for quite a while. Putting on such an extravagant diversion for Kim was not, of course, a good thing. Though it momentarily relieved his humdrum hospital day, it might have had a bad effect on his health.

In an attempt to put Kim in a better mood and improve his appetite, I sometimes brought in a miniature bottle of brandy, but it failed to cheer him up. 'I can't enjoy a drink in circumstances like these,' he said. 'There's a time and a place for everything.' During Kim's last spell in hospital, Oleg Kalugin brought over to the flat two bottles of Cahor red wine, long regarded as a tonic for pretty well any illness. 'These came from the Church cellars, thanks to the KGB's close ties with the Orthodox church,' he told me proudly. Kim drank the Cahor with the same 'enjoyment' as he did his medicine, since he did not care for sweet wine and was sceptical about its curative properties.

Kim ticked off the days and minutes of his allotted time in hospital and was bursting to return home, irrespective of how he actually felt. He was convinced that the hospital treatment was of little use, even though his bouts of illness were more and more frequent and the threat of going back into hospital was ever present.

Kim was still unable to face up to the fact that going back in was inevitable and did his utmost to hide that he was unwell, deceiving both me and himself. But I could see how difficult it was for him to breathe, how his back shook and shoulders heaved, and I understood the danger he was in. He was tormented by insomnia and believed that if only he could get a good night's sleep, he'd be quite all right again. He never complained and never expressed the slightest concern about his health, except to admit from time to time that he was tired. The minute he switched off the light, he would switch it on again and sit there for a long time, his legs over the edge of the bed. Unlike him, I reckoned his insomnia was the result of his sickness, not the cause.

One sleepless night Kim sat on the bed with his back to me and without turning his head, said sadly: 'Rufa, I'm going to die soon.' My heart sank in terror and through my tears I yelled at him: 'You mustn't allow yourself to think that way. Don't even dare think about it. Right now you're ill and you can't sleep, but it will soon be all right; you'll get better and everything will be OK.' I did my best to put these terrifying notions out of my head, but I couldn't stop thinking. Kim was silent, sitting head bowed. I was in despair; there was nothing I could do to comfort him. As long as I live, I will regret that I did not have the courage to hear him out. I cannot forgive myself for lacking the self-control and the common sense to let him speak and to talk to him calmly. I should have. Even now I cannot bring myself to speak and write about it calmly.

Despite all this, in October 1987, Kim accepted an invitation to visit Riga to be interviewed for a TV documentary on the work of Soviet counter-intelligence in Latvia at the outbreak of the war. I was surprised when he agreed, because up to then he always refused to meet journalists. It was around this period that the foreign press came out with all sorts of stupid comments and fantasies about him, including reports that he was dead. He agreed to give the interview in order to put an end to all these rumours, and we set off for Riga. When we arrived at the station, it was pouring with rain; as our carriage was at the other end of the platform, we got wet through. We were walking rather quickly, and Kim became totally worn out. He wasn't fully himself again even by the time we got to Riga. At the station he was met by a crowd of journalists with microphones and TV cameras. He was not prepared for it, was panting and looked very tense.

The next day we were taken to the well-known health resorts of Sigulda and Yurmala, where they were filming. Kim's knees were buckling under him from weakness, and he was ready to drop. By the end of the day he could barely stand, and I said we had to get back to Riga fast as Kim needed a doctor. But I was told that a meeting had been arranged with Raymond Pauls, the famous composer, and we couldn't possibly decline such an honour. We declined nonetheless, whereupon Lukashevich (the retired KGB general who had written the documentary) said that we must not offend his wife and took us back to his house. No one understood how seriously ill Kim was.

We finally made it back to our hotel. The doctor came and was alarmed by Kim's condition. The next day a professor examined him and prescribed injections and confinement to bed. Soon after this a journalist turned up to talk about the TV interview scheduled for the next day. I said that it was out of the question, though Kim's unhealthy appearance spoke more loudly than words. The interviewer got very cross and almost slammed the door when he left. A little later Lukashevich appeared and tried to soft-soap Kim into accepting. I came up with a compromise, namely, that the filming would take place in the hotel lobby and would last no more than twenty minutes. They agreed and made no more demands on Kim. Since he would have to spend a whole day on the train home without access to a doctor, I decided that we would stay on for several more days to give Kim time to get a bit better. He spent most of the time in bed, but we went down to the bar once or twice to cheer ourselves up. When he felt stronger, we returned home having spent all of a week in Riga.

CHAPTER 24

The Beginning of the End

By November 1987, Kim's health had deteriorated further. I had exhausted my knowledge and possibilities, but he still stubbornly refused to let me call the doctor. Sometimes I would spend several days trying to persuade him. In the end, I called the ambulance and the doctor warned me: 'Next time you won't be able to get him to a hospital alive.' This happened again and again. Kim was in such poor shape that he twice ended up in the resuscitation unit. Visitors were not allowed in there, and I could only telephone to hear the routine answer: 'He's in a satisfactory condition.'

Once I was allowed to see him briefly, and I had time to change his pyjamas. He had wires fixed to his chest with suckers, as if he were having an electrocardiogram. He told me that if he needed to get up, he could take them off. He was in a large room with another patient at the other end, but apart from his loud snoring he did not bother Kim at all.

When Kim was back home a little while later, he admitted that the thing that had depressed him most while he was in the unit had been the minor irritants, such as the absence of a proper toilet. He had had to use a chair with a hole in the seat and an ordinary bucket underneath. It surprised me that these 'little things' hadn't been thought about in a hospital that was still quite new – it was built in the late 1970s – and in most other respects fitted out with the most up-to-date equipment.

Though Kim had come round to the idea of going back into hospital at the end of 1987, he took a rapid turn for the better and looked quite healthy in the television film on Graham Greene. Through the entire winter, right up to March, Kim felt fine and was in good spirits.

At the end of January 1988, he met the British journalist Phillip Knightley. His interview was published at the end of March that year. Shortly before that, at the beginning of March, Kim's health deteriorated and as usual he was afflicted by insomnia as well. He sat up in bed night after night, reading one book after another. When I saw him holding a medical encyclopaedia, he admitted he was 'seeing double'. 'How long has this been going on?' I asked in alarm. 'Three days,' Kim replied, though he wouldn't allow me to call the doctor, even though I read in the encyclopaedia that this was the most dangerous symptom of heart disease.

The next day Kim fell over in the bathroom. He couldn't get up, but was still conscious. 'Lift me up,' he begged. He was a dead weight and I could not shift him. While I was calling the ambulance, he tried to crawl. I warned him that it was dangerous to move and strain himself. I put a pillow under his head, but despite my protests he crawled a few inches, pushing the pillow in front of him. By the time the ambulance arrived, he was lying in the hallway.

A general doctor and a neurologist stuck him in bed and examined him. They did not find anything dangerous and even thought he did not need to be taken to hospital. Though I told them about the 'seeing double', they did not seem concerned. Kim improved a little and the next day was uneventful. Then he deteriorated again and had great trouble breathing. His GP came and insisted he go to the KGB hospital. Kim put up no resistance. I was promised that a car would come to collect him the next morning. When none came, I called the Out-Patients department, which told me that they had no car available, but would call me as soon as one turned up. They finally rang to say the car had left, so it would reach us in fifteen or twenty minutes. We got Kim dressed and waited. Kim was sitting on a chair by the door. An hour passed. Then another. I tried to find out by phone what the problem was. They told me the car had indeed left, but for where, they had no idea. It finally turned up and we were told they had had to make an urgent diversion along the way.

We got Kim to the KGB hospital in the evening and he was left outside an empty consulting room, no one taking the slightest notice of him. As we sat in the corridor, a man in a white coat went past, but when I tried to stop him he waved me away. I grabbed at the sleeve of the next white coat and got the same answer: 'Just wait here. This isn't my area. I know nothing about it.' A woman appeared from one of the other rooms. I could not tell whether she was a nurse or a doctor. I explained that there was a seriously ill man here who had been waiting for over an hour. She professed surprise, but also said she knew nothing about it and told me: 'Just wait.' Kim's patience was infinite! Finally, someone took a serious look at him and said: 'Just a minute.' It was 'just' about two hours before Kim was finally examined by a doctor. The doctor asked him routine questions, examined him rapidly and wrote something down. I got Kim into his pyjamas and he was wheeled away to the ward.

This time he was put in the heart unit. As before the principal treatment consisted of various intravenous drips, combined with the pills he had been taking at home. I would come in the morning and stay till after having given Kim his supper. I couldn't stay longer because the hospital cloakroom closed at 7 p.m. Kim's doctor wanted to make an intestinal examination. Kim refused since he had never had any problem in that area or in his stomach. It was a waste of time, he assured the doctor. But I decided it would be sensible to have it done while he was in the hospital anyway, and I persuaded Kim. He agreed reluctantly. By that time he had been having his basic treatment for two weeks, but there were few signs of progress. Contrary to the doctor's assurances, the examination was very hard to bear. It weakened Kim considerably, and he went right back to his initial state. They found a polyp in his intestines and we were told that Kim needed an operation. He and I set off in a car to the surgical wing, which was in the hospital's old building. Soon after we arrived, a nurse came to take him up to the theatre. Kim could barely put one foot in front of the other and was very short of breath. The nurse walked quickly ahead of us looking back at us impatiently. From time to time I tried to make her stop and asked if we could get a trolley. 'It's not that far now,' she snapped and forged ahead.

Rather than get into a row, I decided to believe her 'not too far'. Kim trudged along, stopping from time to time and leaning against the wall. We went down a long corridor, turned into another one, then went down in a lift. By the time we reached the theatre, Kim could barely breathe. They brought him back on a trolley. He reckoned the operation was less hard and painful than the examination. He was left in a room. No one told us anything. As usual we waited and yet again everyone brushed my inquiries aside. I ran to find the doctor and hated my impotence. Kim, however, thought I was a magician to be able to get anything accomplished at all in this mad world. 'Where would I be without you?' he asked sadly. I finally found a doctor, who as usual knew nothing, but told us that if we got a move on we could get a lift back to our building in a van which was due to leave in fifteen minutes; we made it.

I usually got to the hospital on the metro, from which I would walk along a road that ran through a wooded park, a walk which (there was no other way to get there) took twenty minutes. I walked gingerly along a slippery winding little path which had been trampled in the snow, terrified that I might fall. 'What would happen to Kim if I broke my leg?' was a constant worry. The thaw came, and by the beginning of April the road was a muddy swamp. In the centre of Moscow, the streets were already dry, and once there I could walk at my usual pace.

In the evening of 11 April, I was on my way back home. As I approached our building and turned the corner, my leg twisted under me and I only just managed to make it to the flat. By morning my leg was swollen and I had to ask the case officer Aleksey for a car to take me to the Policlinic. It turned out that I had broken my ankle and I had to have a cast put on right up to the knee. I asked if I could walk on it. The doctor burst out laughing: 'You can walk if you can.' He told me the cast would be removed in exactly one month's time, and not a day earlier. I put a thick black cross on my calendar against 11 May and began to count the days. If only I had known what that cross would mean to me. I could walk only on an absolutely flat surface, so in order to visit Kim I asked Aleksey for a car, which was provided every other day.

Kim's stays in hospital usually lasted three weeks, but this time it went on forever. He lost his patience and wanted very much to be home for the May Day holiday. But seeing the state he was in, I had little confidence that that would happen. Some of his KGB colleagues came to see him on 7 May, to mark the eve of Victory Day. They cheered him up no end by bringing him fresh honey in the comb. Up till then I had been Kim's only visitor. He had not wanted anyone else to come. After a second official visit he was lively and excited. 'I asked about your pension and they assured me you would get it. I must admit I couldn't bring myself to find out exactly how much.'

Kim had a phone in his room, and when I was stuck at home I would be waiting from the morning onwards for him to call me. I did not bother him by telephoning myself since, as he didn't sleep much at night, he would sometimes doze in the mornings. And if he was plugged on to the drip feed, he could not reach the phone anyway. So we agreed that Kim would phone me when he eventually woke up. I spent the whole day with him on 9 May and, kissing him goodbye, I said that I would see him again on the 11th. On the morning of the 10th, I was cooking Kim's meal for the next day and was looking impatiently at the clock as I expected his call. Though it was still early, I was getting more and more worried and decided to phone myself. The doctor picked up the phone and told me that Kim had been found lying on the bathroom floor and was being examined by the neurologist.

I asked for a car urgently. It came an hour later than I was told. Up to that point all the drivers had been very punctual. The one who came this time was a man I had not seen before. I explained to him how to get to the hospital. Being very worked up, I failed to spot at first that he had taken the Leningradskoye highway instead of the Volokolamskoye, and it dawned on me only as we were approaching Sheremetyevo airport. The road was deserted and I begged him to make a U-turn and head back. The drivers were pretty quick-witted and, if they needed to, were quite prepared to break the traffic rules. But this one ploughed stubbornly on, heading away from the hospital and then, though it made absolutely no sense, detoured back along the Ring Road. We finally reached the hospital an hour and a half later, instead of the usual twenty minutes. I asked the driver to come back for me at 9 p.m., as agreed with the case officer. If I had to change my plans, the case officer would be in touch with him. The driver said that he was on a late shift and would simply come back on the dot of 9 p.m. and would wait right there for me.

When I entered Kim's room, he broke into a happy smile. He hadn't been expecting me until the next day. I spoke to the doctor. He was not alarmed at Kim's condition and the neurologist had not found anything serious. But just in case, they would do an ECG test the next morning. Kim dozed; occasionally he woke up and we chatted. He was weak, but I had already seen him like that for a year. He went to the bathroom several times to have a smoke. Then came a time when I heard a steady tapping. Kim hadn't been able to get up off the seat and was calling me by tapping with the soap dish. I got him back to bed. He lay there for a while, then sat up. I spoon-fed him cottage cheese with blackcurrants – his pudding. He laughed and told me: 'That's what love does: I can eat this only when you feed me yourself.' While Kim was in the bathroom, I telephoned Aleksey. We agreed that I would decide by 6 p.m. whether or not to stay overnight. I thought at first I should, but I was afraid to alarm Kim. After watching him for a while and talking to the doctor, I became a little reassured. It never crossed my mind that the worst might happen. On the other hand, since I had a premonition that he might deteriorate and that I would need to be with him all the time, I decided to go home and bring a few necessary things for myself and, most important, have the plaster taken off so that I would no longer have to depend on the car.

Kim cheered up, and when I rang Aleksey I told him I would leave at 9 p.m. as agreed. I went out a little before 9 after promising Kim that I would be back as soon as I had had the plaster removed at the Policlinic. As I was leaving, I looked back and was struck that he had not turned his head. That was the image that stuck in my mind – his pyjama-clad back, head sunk on his chest. I hobbled down to where the car was supposed to be waiting, but it wasn't there. That had never happened before. I waited for twenty minutes, then went back inside to call Aleksey. Everything was dark except for the night duty office. I asked if I might use the phone and the nurse reluctantly agreed. There was no answer from Aleksey's phone even though he had told me he would be at home, and in any case he had a small boy whom he would not leave on his own. I decided to check with Kim whether I had copied down the number correctly – he had it on the table by his bed. He read it over to me – I had it right. I noticed his voice sounded cheerful. At point another lady in white appeared and gave me a lecture about using an official phone.

I went out again to the spot we had agreed on. Still no car. It was pitch black and there was a cold wind. I tucked myself into the space between the inner and outer doors. One of the minivans they used as ambulances drew up; a blanket-wrapped body on a stretcher was carried past almost touching me and was loaded into the van. I was terrified. Should I go back to Kim? Why hadn't I stayed? It was 10 p.m. I went down the passage. 'May I use the phone?' I asked. 'It's out of order,' I was told. They looked at me as if I were a burglar. I picked up the telephone. It was working fine. But none of our case officers answered. (It later turned out that one of their phones really was out of order.) There was no alternative but to try to get back to the main road and pick up a taxi. A private car with a passenger stopped and picked me up. I got home after 11 p.m. I rang Kim straightaway and was once again delighted to hear how strong he sounded (with him, a weak voice was a sure sign he wasn't feeling well). I took a sleeping pill and lay down with a book. I looked at my watch. It was exactly 2 a.m. I switched off the light.

Aleksey had promised, at my request, to send a car for me at 9 a.m., to take me first to the Policlinic and then to the hospital. As 10 a.m. approached, there was still no car. So as not to disturb Kim, I telephoned the nurses' station and asked the sister on duty how the patient was. 'You'd better ask the doctor,' she replied. There was no answer on the doctor's phone. I rang Kim. No answer. I rang the nurse back. I was now panicking and yelled down the phone, 'Is he alive?'

'He died at 2 a.m.,' was the reply.

CHAPTER 25

The Last Journey

Despite what the doctor had said, I was totally unprepared for the blow. From that point on, my actions were those of a robot.

I rang Aleksey and told him what had happened. I asked him to send another car and waited for an hour and a half for it to arrive. We drove to the hospital. I went into the ward. Everything was just as it had been, except for the empty bed.

I went to find the doctor and asked, 'Why didn't you suggest I stayed the night?'

'It never crossed my mind that this might happen,' he replied. 'Even the neurologist wasn't worried – he had arranged for Kim to have a routine check-up.'

The duty sister told me: 'I popped in at about 11 p.m. He smiled and said he felt fine. I went back about 2 a.m. He was still warm, but there was nothing we could do.'

I collected his things together, every last scrap. In the bathroom, I found his pyjamas slashed across the chest, presumably when they had tried heart massage.

Back home later in the evening I called Josephine. It was the first time I had rung London; we had not been able to telephone before.

She was crying: she had just heard the news on the television. In the Soviet Union, Kim's death went unpublicised until 14 May, when the army newspaper *Red Star* ran a brief obituary, official and dry in tone, signed by an anonymous 'Group of Comrades'.

There was a requiem at the KGB Club. A huge crowd – all of them from the KGB – were there to say goodbye to Kim. The street outside the Lubyanka was closed to traffic – probably the first time anyone who happened to be passing would have heard the name 'Kim Philby'.

Josephine and her husband, and her brother John, flew out from London for the funeral. I sat facing Kim's coffin, my family on either side. In the second row were Josephine and her husband, John, a couple of my friends, and Kim's doctor and nurse. Outsiders were barred – Kim's death was as shrouded in secrecy as his life – so I had only been allowed to have two friends with me to bid him farewell. I remember Vladimir Kryuchkov, Geny Ageev and George Blake, accompanied by a tearful Ida, coming up to offer their condolences. The Blakes stayed for the requiem and sat in the second row. A seemingly endless line of people filed past the coffin to say goodbye.

The burial ceremony at the Kuntsevo cemetry was quite official, with soldiers standing to attention and military honours although Kim never had a military rank. According to Russian tradition, the coffin was brought uncovered and placed on a dais near the grave.

There were foreign journalists and cameramen as well as a couple of my relatives, who had been stopped by the KGB and had had to explain who they were before being allowed to approach me and express their sympathy. The foreign press descended on them as they made their way out. Vladimir Kirpichenko, first Deputy Head of Intelligence, delivered the eulogy. Volleys were fired as the coffin was lowered into the grave.

The 'wake' was held at the Ukraina Restaurant, with a large crowd – perhaps a hundred people – from the KGB as well as my family. For some reason Kim's children were not invited and a KGB officer took them to eat at another restaurant. In the foyer of the Ukraina, I was introduced to Yuri Modin. This was the first time I had set eyes on him, even though he claims in his book that, in Kim's later years, he often came to see us at home. Inside, a single row of tables lined the four walls of a huge room, leaving the space in the middle totally empty. The gaping void meant that people simply sat peering at each other across the room and I couldn't make out who was actually there. There were official speeches. Thinking back, I recall the event as being cold and protocol-laden, and it wasn't until the first anniversary of Kim's death, when about twenty of the KGB people who were closest to him, got together in our apartment, that I heard words that were really warm and sincere.

I don't recall any of the people who were around Kim while he was alive coming to see me on the day of the funeral or in the time that followed. I was astonished that none of them even bothered to telephone. But the younger people, Kim's students as well as Gennady, did come, and they have remained true friends on whose support I know I can always rely.

I did in fact receive a visit from the case officer and his immediate boss, who came to tell me about my pension and to say that the dacha remained at my disposal; also, that the case officer's services would continue to be available. Before they came, I had rummaged quickly through Kim's papers. In the safe, there were two quite thick, black files. Apprehensively opening one of them, I realised straightaway that they contained professional material and I read no further, not wanting to stick my nose into secrets of that kind. I handed the files to my visitors. With hindsight, I realise that I was a bit too quick off the mark; I should have given the situation more thought and asked friends for advice. I believe the files contained Kim's 'memoranda', which no one ever read and which I very much doubt were of any interest to his colleagues later on.

Looking back now, my concerns seem laughably naive. But at the time I was frightened that they would get all of Kim's papers off me by claiming that they had to take away all secret material. I reckoned that by giving them the black files, I was to some extent protecting myself, since I had kept a lot of material in Kim's own hand about which no one yet knew. This included chapters of his second, unfinished book, his correspondence and various notes – all things of great value to me. My fears were nevertheless not entirely groundless. Soon after this, the KGB asked me to hand over all of Kim's books on intelligence subjects. I selected twenty, but held back all of those in which Kim was mentioned. I also had to hand back his decorations.

One day about a year after Kim's death, when my case officer – by now a new man – came to see me, he went into Kim's office and, with a broad sweep towards the bookcase, asked: 'Shouldn't we take all this to the KGB Museum?' I was lost for words and, seeing my crestfallen look, the case officer didn't pursue the point. We lapsed into silence.

I was very upset, but this time I was in no rush to surrender anything. I asked Gennady for advice. As he recalls, I looked terrified – we had swapped roles. He calmed me down.

From then on, the KGB never bothered me with any further demands and the case officer turned out to be a nice man, who was quite decent and a reliable source of support.

Epilogue

Very few people in Russia had heard of Kim while he was alive. Genrikh Borovik's television film on Graham Greene contained a brief interview with Kim and, as I have already described, he was filmed a short while later in Latvia. There are no other 'live' shots of him. Regrettably, the KGB never got around to making a film about him, if only for internal use.

The first documentary on Kim, *The Man from Cambridge*, was shown a year after he died. Over time the odd piece appeared in newspapers or magazines, but it was not until ten years after his death that Kim became famous in Russia as well following the publication of the anthology, *I Did It My Way: Kim Philby in Intelligence and in Real Life*, which incorporated *My Silent War* and some previously unpublished material, as well as my own book, *Island on the Sixth Floor*.* The anthology was also well received when it was published in Bulgaria in 1998.

There have been innumerable publications about Philby in the West, depicting him as a legendary spy, and often portraying him in a

---

* The Russian title of this book.

rather sinister light. I had read so many concocted stories and downright lies about Kim's life in Moscow that, in the end, I decided to write about him myself. My book retells our everyday life, showing what Kim was really like and how he reacted to particular events. I refrained from any speculation about him. After all, no one ever really knows what another person is thinking.

The main point is that nothing reliable was known about this significant and lengthy (1963–88) chunk of Kim's life, the Moscow years. The closest was Eleanor Philby's *Kim Philby: The Spy I Loved*, which described a fifteen-month period in Moscow spanning 1963 and 1964. Kim hardly ever met journalists, so they had nothing to go on, filling the vacuum as they saw fit. Paradoxically, at the time when Kim had absolutely no work to do (which brought about his depression), it was thought in the West that he was running the KGB's British Section.

Kim and I spent most of his eighteen years in Moscow at each other's side. We never spent a day apart. In telling his story, I wanted to show the real man, the flesh-and-blood person I knew so well rather than the 'legendary intelligence officer'.

I regret very much today that I never asked Kim questions I wanted to ask, but thinking back I realise that my restraint was deliberate. What Kim wrote in the dedication to the Russian edition of his book goes some way to explain why. He said: 'Most wives of *razvedchiks* [intelligence officers] labour under a special disadvantage: they are unable to participate in or even know about their husbands' working activities. To all such wives I dedicate this book, and in particular to my own: Rufa.'

I also had the feeling in my bones that certain subjects would be unpleasant or even painful for him. He was a man racked by doubt. In his interview with Phillip Knightley, he said: 'Doubt is a terrible thing. In fact one of the most rewarding aspects of my relationship with Graham Greene has been our meetings in the past several years. For the first time in our long friendship we were able to speak frankly with each other. We were able to discuss this matter of great importance to both of us – doubt. The nagging doubt we both had. Him as a Roman Catholic and me as a Communist.'

As a man of strong conscience, Kim could not help but think of the sacrifices he had been forced to make. He also regretted the loss of contacts with friends. But, in summing up his life, he would say: 'The right I've done is greater than the wrong I've done.'

In the last years of his life Kim was a happy man. He was honoured and respected and had been awarded many state decorations – The Order of Lenin, The Order of the Military Red Star, The Order of the Friendship of the Peoples, The Order of the Patriotic (Second World) War First Class, as well as Hungarian, Bulgarian and Cuban awards. The pupils of whom he was so fond came to see him. And he even realised his great wish: 'to have Graham Greene opposite me and a bottle of wine on a table between us'.

Ten years have passed since he died. The pain of my loss has eased a little and my memories bring me joy rather than grief. These memories help me to cope with being alone. I live surrounded by Kim's things and the eyes in the picture of him on the wall follow me around the room.

Kim brought me happiness of the kind that dreams are made of and I am infinitely grateful to destiny for the years I spent with him. It comforts me to know that I was able to do something to make the last years of his life easier, and it makes me happy that he felt able to say: 'The evening of my life is golden.'

Part 2

Kim Philby's Unpublished Memoirs and Articles

In her late husband's study, Rufina Philby found nearly one hundred pages of his unpublished writings. They included reminiscences of his early life in India and England, the story of his recruitment by Soviet intelligence, the only lecture he ever gave to the KGB, and an article on whether an agent should confess when caught. Each is reproduced here, in full, for the first time. Some passages were crossed out on the original pages and, because there is no indication of what Philby's ultimate intentions were, they have been included and are shown here in brackets in italics. H.P.

1

Autobiographical
Reminiscences

*T*here are two chapters in this typescript (originally forty-eight pages), each with corrections in Philby's hand. The first is merely titled Chapter 1 and was written, the context reveals, after his marriage to Rufina. It was apparently intended to begin the promised sequel to My Silent War. Here Philby recalls hazy memories of India and his father and mother, his more vivid memories of life in England with his grandmother, and his days in kindergarten. We learn too of his reading at the age of five, his early encounters with religion, and his years at school in Eastbourne, where he developed his lifelong affinity for cricket and earned a 'public school scholarship' to Westminster.

The second chapter is titled Decision. It was written before he met Rufina and the context suggests, in this case, that it was probably intended to be part of My Silent War, although he makes no direct reference to that circumstance or why it was excluded. At the start he is on the train to London returning from Vienna in 1934 with his first wife, whom he calls Lizy. His years at Westminster and Cambridge are mentioned only in passing and he adds little to the parsimonious account found in My Silent War. In these pages, Philby tells of his intention to join the Communist Party of Great Britain, his introduction by a 'friend from Vienna' to Otto, and his *recruitment into the Soviet intelligence services. He tells too how he helped his new masters recruit his Cambridge colleagues, Donald Maclean and Guy Burgess, and he relates his first espionage assignment – spying on a former Westminster classmate, who is now in the Government. Philby then writes at some length about his early journalistic efforts, his putative Fascist period, the long-term NKVD decision to have him penetrate British intelligence, and the decision to go to Spain as a Soviet agent. After describing his training for espionage in Spain, including his first encounter with codes, Philby ends the chapter by commenting on the harsh demands of secret work. H.P.*

CHAPTER 1

Rufina told me early on that I must always wash my hands after touching money. Her gentle command took me back some fifty-five years in time, and sideways some fifteen hundred miles in space, to Camberley, in Surrey, where my grandmother had principal charge of me between the ages of three and twelve.

'Never put pennies or halfpennies in your mouth, Kim,' my grandmother used to say. 'You never know what horrid poor people may have touched them. You might fall very ill.'

There is a difference, of course. For my grandmother, silver coins, sixpences, shillings, florins and half-crowns, passed muster. Only coppers, the coins of the poor, were suspect. For Rufina, all money is dirty; though she likes some of the things that money can buy. Rufina, although half-Polish by blood, was born in Moscow, some fifteen years after the Revolution, and has lived there all her life.

I must not give the impression that my grandmother lacked compassion for the poor or unfortunate. She would cross a busy street to press a few coppers into the hand of a beggar whom she considered particularly deserving – one, that is, who looked conspicuously hungry or sick. But between my soft-hearted grandmother and the poor there lay an impassable gulf. None knew this better than Kate, the cook-general, who served her devotedly for more than forty years, and to whom she was herself devoted. Kate's place, throughout the decades of her service, was the kitchen and the backyard. Never once did I see her in the flower-garden, and vegetables from the kitchen-garden were delivered at the scullery door by Mr Bishop, the gardener. Occasionally a noise like the tearing of many sheets would penetrate the house, at which my grandmother would prick up her ears and look at the clock. 'Kim,' she would say, 'that must be Darracott's man with the cakes. Run through to the backyard and ask Kate not to laugh quite so loudly.'

When I first went to Camberley, my grandmother ran the household, but was not its head. Her own mother, Granny Duncan to me, was still alive. She was a pale, frail, white-haired old lady of about seventy. She spent the mornings in her bedroom, the afternoons in the drawing-room, and the evenings, when it was fine, mucking about in the herbaceous border, shredding pair after pair of mittens. (*I saw her only at meals, during which her rare comments persuaded me, for a long time, that she had eyes in the back of her head. She used to sit at the head of the table with her back to the French windows, and pass remarks about the doings of the birds on the garden path behind her. Many months passed before I realised that the source of her information was a huge framed engraving of the meeting at Lucknow of Havelock, Outram and Sir Colin Campbell, the glass of which reflected the garden in detail. Beside the engraving hung a brilliant tapestry which, I was proudly informed, was loot brought home by a great-uncle from the Summer Palace at Peking.*)

As befitted the home of one old and one elderly lady in those days, the regime, though not harsh, was well-defined. Just as Kate's place was the kitchen and the backyard, mine was the nursery and the garden, with strict injunctions against treading on the flower-beds. I was kept in order by a succession of young nursemaids who shared my bedroom and gave me a vague awareness of sex, presumably because they were sexually aware themselves. Unfortunately, when I search my memory for something concrete that might have contributed to that very fuzzy awakening, I can remember nothing. The drawing-room was forbidden territory. I was allowed into it only when one or other of Granny Duncan's cronies, dropping in for tea, expressed a probably insincere wish to see 'the dear little boy'. My nurse would then take me, loudly protesting, to the bathroom for a good scrub-and-brush before ushering me into the presence. There, my resentment would be fanned by cooing voices, exclaiming, 'Oh! What a lovely *clean* little boy!' Prominent among the cooers was Aunt Ada, a sister of Granny Duncan's, whom I held in awe. It was not her fault but my grandmother's. 'You must be a good boy today, Kim,' my grandmother would say at breakfast. 'Aunt Ada's coming to tea.' So from four o'clock onwards, I would peep through a crack in the garden fence and run for cover as soon as I saw poor Aunt Ada's black veils flapping down the road.

Apart from understandable anger at being scrubbed, brushed and produced as an exhibit, I can remember no stirrings of rebellion against the social taboos of 'The Crossways' – our house stood near the point where Park Street crossed Gordon Road. They seemed to be as fixed as the stars in their courses. I had no wish to enter the drawing-room, and would probably have been dismayed if Granny Duncan had visited the nursery, a possibility that never crossed my mind, or hers, although the drawing-room and nursery doors were scarcely three paces apart. (*I am inclined to think that the regime had much to recommend it over the free-for-all of modern family life.*) In Camberley, it was recognised that both children and adults had an equal right to their own (*very*) different ways of life.

It was not the sort of household to encourage an influx of little boys, so I had few acquaintances of my own age. Yet I have no recollection of regretting the circumstance at the time. My most frequent companion was my cousin Frank, whose parents, like mine, spent most of their active lives in Asia. But I was the established grandson, and so clearly my grandmother's favourite that I earned the undying hostility of Frank's mother, my Aunt Kitty, who never tired of telling me that, whereas I was eight months older than Frank, his father was a year older than mine, and that Frank was therefore my senior. At first, this argument was quite unintelligible to me, and when, at a later date, it acquired meaning, it simultaneously lost all relevance to our situation. For what it might have meant in terms of inheritance fell to the ground in a situation where there was nothing to inherit.

It was probably the lack of friends of my own age which drove me to books at an early age. Before my fifth birthday, I was struggling through a children's edition of Sinbad the Sailor, and soon went on to Arthur Mee's Children's Encyclopaedia. (*I devoured the chapters on natural history and geography.*) Then there was another book of short stories, the title of which I have forgotten. The story that remains clearest in memory, oddly enough in view of later events, concerned an attack by a pack of wolves on a sledge in Siberia. The wolves announced their presence by 'a long, low, melancholy howl'; the traces of several horses were cut to delay the pursuit; and the story ended happily with the twinkling lights of a village. But that phrase about the howl stuck in my mind, and caused me many a nightmare. With other stories, illustrated by pictures of snakes and sea-monsters, it gave me a fear of the dark that lasted two or three years. (*When walking back from school in the dusk, I avoided overhanging branches for fear of the leopards that infested the Gordon Road of my book-fed imagination.*)

I was sent to (*My 'school' was in fact*) a kindergarten (*to which I was sent*) shortly before my fifth birthday. It was run by two maiden ladies, a Miss Herring and a Miss Crisp. Having already begun reading, I had little difficulty in keeping up with the five year olds, and indeed soon overtook them. But my time at the kindergarten is memorable to me for three events: I fell in love, I discovered the atlas, and I rejected God.

The object of my love was a Miss Diana Migginson, who was about a year older than myself. (*My feelings had nothing to do with the vague stirrings induced by the nursemaids who shared my bedroom. Yet I do not think it can have been wholly platonic. I was attracted to her by something I did not try to identify then and cannot identify now. I can still see her sitting two rows in front of me, with a black and white check frock stopping short of her knees, a black bow in her hair, and, when I could get a glimpse of it, a pale piquant face. One day I followed her home and, with a tremor, saw her go into a house just up the road from 'The Crossways'.*) But I never spoke to her, then or thereafter. I soon lost all interest in girls, a phase that lasted six or seven years.

With apologies to Diana, I must confess that it was the atlas which threw around me the denser web of magic. Through some unexplained flair, the strange shapes and colours made instant sense to me, and I spent hours poring over the sinuous lines of rivers and contrasting shades of contour. The next step, of course, was to copy the maps, and my grandmother happily bought me exercise books, knowing that for a few pence she could buy hours of peace in the nursery. Later, on seeing the sketch-map in *Treasure Island*, I found that maps could be invented. This discovery resulted in a long series of imaginary countries, with complicated promontories and inlets, and improbably situated hills. When my grandmother criticised me for calling all the hills 'Spyglass Hill', I began to number them: 'Spyglass 1', 'Spyglass 2', etc. – a dodge discovered independently by Himalayan explorers and cartographers. My early absorption in maps was to develop into an appetite for travel which still endures. Perhaps it did quite a lot to loosen my roots in England.

About God. Professor Hugh Trevor-Roper has described me as a 'fossil of the past'. I hope to show that his charge is invalid, and that my views have developed with the years. But in respect to religion, I have never wavered in my rejection.* I must have been nearly six when I scandalised my grandmother by informing her that there was no God. She was a Christian in the sense that she professed belief, and went to St Michael's Church at Easter and Christmas. But she never took me with her or spoke to me of such matters. Therefore, as religion never obtruded itself at 'The Crossways', my scepticism must be referred to the kindergarten, where the miraculous element was stressed in a manner supposedly attractive to small children. In my case, the result was the opposite to that intended. I reacted in frank disbelief, repelled in particular by the wide gap between the powers attributed to Christ and the trivial use to which he put them. Why cure one leper? Why not all lepers? And so on. No argument I have since heard or read has dented my unbelief, nor can I remember the slightest twinge of religious experience. From earliest childhood to the present day, I have found the evidence of the senses far more genuinely 'miraculous' than any flight of faith.

So I had no fear of God at 'The Crossways'. Nor, I think, any fear of Man, except possibly of Mr Watson. I have no doubt that Mr Watson was an excellent fellow. But he was landlord of 'The Crossways', and was represented to me as some unspeakable menace whenever I became boisterous and threatened damage to property. His name became a hissing and a by-word. But (*like the leopards of Gordon Road, he never materialised*) I never saw him in the flesh.

Fear was almost completely eclipsed for me by my grandmother's love, which endured undiminished until, with appetite and sense of

---

* Come to think of it, the Archbishop of Canterbury has probably never wavered in a contrary view. The easiest way of explaining the Primate's lifelong commitment to a set of very dubious propositions would be to follow Trevor-Roper and dismiss him as a fossil of the past – a very distant past indeed.

fun unimpaired, she died at the age of eighty-five. She lost two sons at Ypres, one in 1914 and the other two years later. My presence must have helped to close the gap in her heart; her preference for me is otherwise inexplicable. I visited her from time to time during the Second World War, and invariably found an unopened bottle of whisky awaiting me in the sideboard; and, as I poured my first glass, she would chuckle wheezily and admonish me in a hoarse whisper: 'Mind you hide the bottle at once if you hear Aunt Kitty coming.' Her last words, spoken for the benefit of my mother who was staying with her at the time, deserve respectful mention. Standing on the stairs leading to her bedroom where she was to die a few hours later, she called down to the kitchen: 'Kate, don't forget to put out Mrs Dora's gin.'

Those were the years of the First World War. It made little impact on me. My nurses would take me to see church parade at the Royal Military College, or to admire the trenches dug on Barossa Common to simulate conditions on the Western Front for the benefit of cadets who would shortly die there. Rationing meant nothing to me. Stories of Zeppelin raids, even aeroplanes from Farnborough stunting overhead, gave me the mildest of thrills. Far more interesting were the trains passing along a high embankment within sight of the front gate; I would still rather be an engine-driver than an astronaut. Then came the armistice celebrations which baffled me to the point of irritation. I distressed my grandmother by telling her (*it was*) they were a 'lot of silly fuss'. Poor lady! They came too late for her.

Within a few months, the 'silly fuss' had an important sequel for me, by bringing back into my life two total strangers from the Middle East. They were my mother and my father.

In saying that my parents were total strangers, I am not exaggerating. I had of course 'known' them before. But my memories of earliest childhood in India are few, unrelated and blurred. Search as I may, I cannot find my parents in any of them. (*There is a scene, which I have always called Ambala, of a crescent street sweeping downhill to the left, with a continuous line of reddish terraced houses on the right, facing tree-covered rising ground. I must have seen some such sight in India, but whether it was really Ambala, I cannot say. Then there is a train journey by night, with a Mr Steen pulling my hair whenever he saw, or claimed to see, a monkey. There must be a better way of showing small boys monkeys in the dark, because I never saw one. This fades into another night journey by train, possibly the same one. I was lying on an upper bunk, whining from thirst. Somebody, I think a soldier, gave me a bar of plain chocolate to keep me quiet; but after a few nibbles the thirst grew still more desperate, and my whining louder.*)

So all my knowledge of early days in India, and of my parents in India, is hearsay, mostly from my mother. I was already 'Kim'. I am told that English was my second language; for preference I chattered Hindustani to the household servants and chuprassis. My father, who in many ways was as conventional as only an eccentric can be, would gaze at his first-born and say: 'Why, Dora, he is a regular little Kim.' And so I remained. The only other scrap of hearsay directly connecting me with my father concerned the morning weather report which he required me to give him during a holiday in Darjeeling, where our bungalow overlooked Kinchinjunga – as it was spelt in my first atlas. I was told to use one of two formulas: either 'Daddy, the mountains are wisible,' or 'Daddy, the mountains are in-wisible.' If the formula was the first, he would join me on the verandah; if the second, he would go back to sleep.

The passage from India with my mother is another series of blurs. (*I can just make out Karachi – another line of reddish buildings, and a clock tower. Then there are some strange bushes growing out of the sea, somewhere in the Mediterranean. I have never been able to place this image, or interpret it. As in India, my mother is nowhere to be seen. She told me that I was known among our fellow-passengers as Beelzebub, and I once emerged from our cabin, smeared sticky brown to the eyelashes, stoutly denying that I had stolen the chocolate.*) The one important event of the passage was an acquaintance I struck up with a boy named Guy Sells, who was a full year older than myself. He was the grandest thing I had ever seen, and the grandest thing about him was his stammer. By the end of the voyage, I had caught it, good and proper. It has since cost me some embarrassment and some fatigue, but it may also have served me well. It is easier to talk out of turn without a stammer than with one.

In the four subsequent years, my grandmother, Kate, Mr Bishop, my books and my atlas, and Camberley monopolised my vision; and it was with some concern that, one day in 1919, I allowed my grandmother to put me into my best clothes and take me to London to meet my mother. As the boat-train steamed in, a tallish woman in a black-and-white striped dress leaned out of a window, waving to us. But when she tried to gather me up, I resisted, clinging to my grand-mother's skirt. And when we returned to Camberley and my mother announced her plans, I was guilty of my first act of conscious rebellion against authority. Like most first rebellions, it was very short-lived.

My mother planned to return to London in a few days to await the arrival of my father, and to take me with her. She assured me that I would love it, staying at a hotel, the Tudor Court in Cromwell Road. I replied that I didn't want to live in a hotel and didn't want to go to London; that I wanted to stay in Camberley with my Granny. Mother must have been dreadfully hurt, though she can hardly have been sur-prised. Anyway, she paid no attention to my protest, so to London I went, to the Tudor Court, where I soon found a new interest in admir-ing the page-boys with their brass-buttoned uniforms and sophisticated manners. My mother had a shorter word for their sophistication: cheek.

Again the scene abruptly changes, to a house in St Petersburg Place, to which my mother ever afterwards looked back with nostalgia. It was a few steps from Kensington Gardens, which was convenient for my nurse and pleasant for me. Mysteriously, my father was among us; I have no memory of his arrival or of my first 'meeting' with him. But within a few days, or perhaps weeks, he took me across Kensington Gardens to the Royal Geographical Society. Here, in an upper room, he sat on a stool beside a huge table, covered with large sheets of blank paper. There were several notebooks, coloured bottles, the slimmest of pens and a lot of pencils sharpened to the finest points imaginable. My wonder grew; but when my father started what he called 'work', I was amazed. He was drawing a map, and, as far as I could see, an imaginary map at that, for he had no atlas to copy from. I remember two distinct and contradictory reactions. First, admiration at the wonderful neatness of my father's map; second, disappointment that he should describe as work an occupation I knew all about.*

For a term, I was put to school as a day-boy in Orme Square, just round the corner from St Petersburg Place. At the breakfast table on

---

* It is odd that the birth of my interest in maps coincided almost exactly in time with my father's first serious exploration, the crossing of Arabia from Uqair to Jidda.

the first day, my father remarked casually that I would be beaten once a week, as a matter of school routine. When I looked doubtfully at my mother, she confirmed it: oh, yes! I would have to learn to take my medicine like a man in this life.* I was not surprised as I had read many stories about tough school-days. So I went to Orme Square expecting to be beaten before I had done anything, and it was a week before I realised that it was a joke. It was not a very good joke, and would doubtless be considered cruel today, but I did not think so at the time. If I felt anything, it was exhilaration, even pride, that I should have to 'take my medicine' and prove that I was a boy, not a silly girl who would surely cry. At the end of term, I came out top of the bottom form, but only, I think, because my most serious rival (, *a boy named Stebbings*,) fell ill during the exams and failed to complete the course. The result confirmed my father in a resolution that he had made on the day of my birth: that I should get a scholarship to Westminster and another to Trinity, just as he had done. I have already mentioned that my father had a strong streak of orthodoxy. Meanwhile, he took me to Eastbourne to find a permanent preparatory school for me. He expected to be returning to India, though in fact he only got as far as the Middle East, where, with short breaks, he spent the rest of his life.

More important than the trip to Eastbourne, for me, was a shorter trip across London to the Oval [Cricket Club], to see Surrey play Somerset. (*The first two days of the match had been washed out, and the evening papers on the third day showed that Somerset, having gone in first, were in trouble. Expecting that they would be all out by teatime, my father*

---

* My mother's attitude to my upbringing has always puzzled me. She was incapable of conscious cruelty. Yet she never tired of telling me that life was a desperate struggle for survival and that only unremitting work and fearsome drive would pull me through. Sometimes during adolescence, she would induce panicky thoughts of early death from starvation and exposure. Where she got such ideas from, I have no idea; she must have known plenty of people in India who led comfortable lives with a minimum of work sandwiched in between polo, tennis, dancing and bridge. But in the very long run, it helped. When I found from experience that life, for a product of the British middle classes, was not so very different after all, my confidence was boosted in proportion to the groundless fears that my mother's homilies had induced. My father was much more reassuring. He had no doubt at all that his first-born would make good.

Kim Philby at the typewriter which he used to write *My Silent War*.

Philby reading *Le Monde* at the desk in his study, c. 1968.

The chair and radio where Philby sat and listened to the BBC while having his morning tea.

Kim and Rufina having a picnic on the bank of the Angara river, Siberia, 1971. G. Ageev is second from left.

Rufina and Kim during a trip to Bulgaria, 1972.

In the Crimea, near Lake Caragol, 1973.

VILLA BOSPHOR
BEYLERBEYI - AS

The house that Philby and his family lived in when he was Head of Station in Turkey, 1947–9. He and Rufina saw it once as they passed by boat.

Fishing from the launch in the Black Sea, Crimea, 1973.

With Hungarian Minister of the Interior, A. Benkay, in Budapest, 1975.

In the Memory Room, the name for the KGB/SVR museum of honour at the headquarters of the then Foreign Intelligence Directorate at Yasenevo, the day Philby delivered his speech to the assembled KGB officers, July 1977. The man on the left, the translator of Philby's speech, is designated as Gennady-X. On the right is G. Ageev, the KGB Communist Party Secretary.

In Semenovo, near Sofia,
Bulgaria, 1979.

On a rainy day in Dresden,
East Germany, 1981.

Kim Philby addressing the HVA (Hauptverwaltung Aufklarung), the GDR foreign intelligence service, East Germany, 14 August 1981. This copy was made available courtesy of Markus Wolf, who asked Philby to sign some prints for his HVA colleagues. The original, in colour, is now in the Melton Collection.

Philby with Markus Wolf during his August 1981 visit to East Germany.

At home with the family.

'Womaniser' Kim in Berlin, 1981

The entrance to Philby's apartment building.

The inside view of the main entrance to Philby's flat.

The view from a window in Philby's Moscow flat with one of Stalin's '7 sisters' in the background.

The clock presented to Kim Philby by Yuri Kobaladze and Michael Bogdanov – members of the first class of KGB officer-students he tutored prior to their assignment to an English-speaking country.

The print that arrived in the mail unannounced and unattributed in the 1970s. Philby determined that it had come from Sir Anthony Blunt (see Part 1, p. 177). It hangs in the living-room to this day.

Philby's living-room with the Burgess wing-back chair to the left in which he sat when reading and entertaining. The bookcases, sofa and chairs were provided by the KGB in 1973. The pelts and weapons on the wall were gifts, but their giver is not identified.

The entrance hallway to Philby's flat taken from the main door. The study door is open on the left to the rear of the post. The window shown is the one he mentions in *My Silent War* through which 'I can see the foundations of the future.' The bookshelves in the hallway were those Philby had before the KGB provided new ones in 1973. The top shelf contains a few of the many awards Philby received over the years.

Rufina in Kim's study. The entrance is at the rear right of the photo. Rufina bought him the desk in the foreground when the flat was redone. The old desk, where he wrote *My Silent War*, was kept for her use and can be seen in the lower left. The bookshelves shown on the right are floor to ceiling and run the length of the 22-foot room, which contains 2,500 volumes of the remaining 3,000 books in his collection.

Philby at his dacha near Moscow, c. 1985.

In Riga, during the filming of a documentary about the work of Soviet counter-intelligence in Latvia at the outbreak of the Second World War. From left to right: Lukashevich (Ret. General, former Resident in London), Kim and one of the film-makers.

Grandpa Kim with granddaughter Charlotte, her father John, and Rufina's mother, Victoria Poukhova.

The table given to Philby by former wartime SIS colleague and antique dealer, Tommy Harris. Philby had it in his Beirut apartment and the KGB saw to it that it made its way to Moscow with Philby's books. In the morning, Philby would sit in the chair on the left and listen to the BBC on the radio. The entrance doorway to the flat can be seen in the background through the doorway on the right.

Front, left to right: Genrikh Borovik, Kim, Rufina and Graham Greene
at a party in Borovik's Moscow apartment, 1987.

Rufina says goodbye to Kim at the memorial service at Kuntsevo
Cemetery, Moscow, 1988

Philby is carried in the traditional Russian fashion to his grave at Kuntsevo Cemetery.

Rufina in her husband's favourite reading chair that once belonged to his Cambridge classmate and fellow KGB agent, Guy Burgess. When Burgess died, his will gave Philby first choice over Maclean of Burgess's possessions after some specific bequests to each. Philby selected the chair. Rufina is holding one of the few signed copies of the first Russian edition of *My Silent War*.

took me to see Hobbs bat. He timed our arrival to the minute. As we bought a scorecard and settled down, Hobbs and Howell were coming out to reply to Somerset's total of 138. Then the programme went wrong. The pitch was still wet from the heavy rain and, after making only five, Hobbs cocked up an easy catch to H.D. Lyon at mid-off. Despite my father's disappointment, I sat on engrossed; and, for a small boy watching his first county match, the end was a story-book one. Early in the last over, Surrey equalled the Somerset total, then Shepherd swept the last ball of the match to the square-leg boundary, giving Surrey the first innings points.)

From that sunny afternoon dates a life-long interest in the Surrey County Cricket Club. A year later I developed a comparable addiction to the Arsenal Football Club.* Both loyalties were to give me crumbs of comfort in difficult times, Arsenal during their great period in the 30s, the years of triumphant Fascism, Surrey during theirs in the 50s, when I was in deep trouble. The comfort was ridiculously trivial compared to the disasters it mitigated, but it was there. Drowning men probably do clutch at straws.

Sport was not the only interest I acquired during my father's short stay in England. In his youth, he had collected butterflies and moths, and his interest in natural history steadily widened to include birds, animals and the whole range of insects. From his Arabian journeys he brought home specimens for the Natural History Museum, including an unknown louse, which decimated the stuffed animals stored in its neighbourhood before its identity and malicious character was established. He amused himself by naming new finds after members of the family and his friends. There is a glorious Arabian woodpecker called Dendrocopos Dorae, after my mother; and my eldest sister, Diana, felt insulted when an unattractive rodent was christened Obesus Dianae, *anglice* Miss Philby's Fat Sand Rat. But what brushed off on me in that summer of 1919 was his interest in entomology. My father's pleasure took the form of a large order to Watkins & Doncaster, which equipped me with a handsome butterfly-net, a killing bottle,

---

* I heard the BBC commentary on the 1971 Cup Final on my radio in Moscow. When Charlie George scored the winning goal, it seemed wholly fitting that Arsenal should win the double in my fiftieth, Jubilee, year as an Arsenal supporter.

store boxes, setting-boards and *South's British Butterflies and Moths* – two volumes which soon rivalled the atlas as my preferred reading matter.

So I was a different boy, and surely a very ordinary one, when my parents disappeared eastward in 1920, leaving me in the familiar home of my grandmother. I have no recollection of bad weather in Camberley; I must have spent the time reading and drawing maps. The fine weather was divided between cricket and entomology. Cricket I played alone on the lawn, with a bat, but with no ball and no opponents. I made an awful lot of runs. The butterflies and moths provided a harder challenge. The herbaceous border brought them in swarms to 'The Crossways' – blues, red and white admirals, painted ladies, peacocks and the rest. The purple plumes of a splendid buddleia would nod under the weight of struggling insects. I was made to wait until they rose and hovered before taking swipes at them, for fear of damaging the flowers. It was a happy rule, which limited the slaughter I might otherwise have inflicted. (Two years ago, in Sukhumi, I grew ungovernably angry with my Georgian host, who wantonly and messily killed the beautiful great hawk-moths that visited our evening lamp-light under the vine.)

I was taught the most efficient way of capturing moths by Ernest Green, an entomologist of high distinction who lived in Camberley; he later became President of the Royal Entomological Society. Mr Green took the kindliest interest in me, and I returned his interest with deepest respect. Once, when I was suffering from a toothache, my grandmother was inspired to invite Mr Green to tea. When he had gone, my toothache had gone too. His moth-catching technique had the added advantage of putting back my budding interest a notch or two. At dusk I would sally forth with a brush and a bowlful of treacle-and-beer mixture, and daub the pine-trees. Later, when it was quite dark, I would go out with torch and pill-boxes to gather the harvest. The treacle attracted the moths, the beer dulled their wits and they fell readily into the pill-boxes.

Meanwhile, I was going to school in Eastbourne. It was not a distinguished school for either scholarship or sports. I think that I was the first boy ever to leave it with a public school scholarship, which I won by the skin of my teeth, and my slightly better than average aptitude for games got me into the cricket, soccer and rugger teams with ease. On the academic side, I had the first experience of ups and downs in a life which has been overcrowded with both. I spent my first year in the lowest form, the fifth, but was then pushed up two forms, from the fifth to the third. But the great leap forward proved to be too great, and I was sent back to the fourth after half a term. Thereafter, I moved steadily, against moderate opposition, to the top. At the time, no doubt, prep school had its excitements, but in retrospect it seems pretty uneventful. I don't think that any of us took the slightest interest in girls.

I had two headmasters at Eastbourne, both of whom influenced me in directions of which they would have disapproved.

The first was the Rev. Harold Brown, a fifteen-stone clergyman with an uncertain temper. Poor man! He was in his sixties and, with the help of an indifferent staff, had to struggle with fifty-odd small boys. He was never cruel; just too big, too awesome and too remote. He had a spinster daughter with at least one haunch on the shelf. She once gave me an electrifying sight of her knickers, but there was no follow-up.*

The service Mr Brown did me was to reinforce my atheism by an active dislike of religious observance and a distaste for the person of Christ. He presided over the fifteen-minute tedium of daily chapel, the Sunday morning service with its long and incomprehensible sermon, the Sunday evening service held in deepening gloom with Monday looming nastily ahead. A little relief came in my last year, for it was the duty of senior boys to man the bellows for Mary Brown's organ. That meant standing in a niche hidden from the chancel, where we could suck sweets and think of knickers.

My distaste for Christ was a simple reaction to a contradiction in our upbringing. Mr Brown was fond of asserting that the object of his school was to build character – or rather Character. We were urged to be manly, brave and self-reliant. The worst disgrace was to be found in tears; a boy who cried was never allowed to forget it. Yet we were told to revere a figure who was shown to us as something quite different: as

---

* This may seem to contradict my earlier statement that we were not interested in girls. But by girls, I mean girls – females of our own age. Mary Brown was about thirty, and mysterious.

a man with long, flowing hair (more like a woman than a man), a figure drooping on the cross, a face contorted with pain. And the Bible said flatly: Jesus wept! Gazing at the cheap stained-glass window through endless, droning, empty hours of chapel, I came to the conclusion that Christ must have been a bit of a milk-sop. Later, during adolescence, many other interpretations of Christ were thrust upon me, by spoken and written word, so many and so conflicting that they had only one thing in common: a lack of serious evidence to support them. So I became neutral. The distaste left me about forty years ago, but nothing has taken its place. My picture of Christ is hardly clearer than that of Shubbililiuma.

Mr Brown died, and the school was bought by a Mr F. S. Hill, who was some thirty years younger than his predecessor. With him we had a more intimate rapport. He joined in our games, and read us Conan Doyle on Sunday evenings, sucking at a handsome pipe. As his star pupil, I was one of his favourites, and returned his liking. He was a conservative. During a General Election, he went around muttering 'cads and bounders, cads and bounders', by which he was referring, not to the socialists, but to the Liberal candidate and his friends who were challenging Tory Eastbourne; and when I asked him whether [Ramsay] MacDonald was a gentleman, he growled, 'No,' and gave me a stony glare.

Mr Hill was naturally an imperialist. He renamed our dormitories after British dominions and possessions: Canada, Australia, India and so on. And he discoursed at length on Empires, Persian, Macedonian, Roman, Mogul and British. The British Empire, he told us, was unique in one simple particular: it would last for ever. As I digested this thought, my scepticism again surfaced. Why? Why should the British Empire be different – except perhaps for the accident that Mr Hill and I were both British? I couldn't take it, any more than I could take Christ's conjuring trick at the marriage feast at Cana. I must thank the memory of Mr Hill for this early immunisation against wishful thinking.

So I was a godless little anti-imperialist before I reached my teens, a fact for which my conventional kindergarten and prep school training must take much credit.

CHAPTER 2

DECISION

As the train bore us [Philby was with his new wife Litzi – H.P.] across Germany and France towards England, my mind ranged vaguely over the future. The sequel will show that my thoughts were vain, for Fate was waiting for me in London with a carefully stuffed eelskin. But I was not to know that. My first step, as I saw it from the train, was to apply for membership of the Communist Party of Great Britain; my second, to get application papers for the Civil Service exam. I foresaw little trouble about the first, as I thought that I had won at least one spur in Vienna and Prague. But the Civil Service, and India behind it, were still blurred images. I think I had already made up my mind in Vienna that I would not pass the exam. Whatever chance I might have had must have gone down the drain as a result of my absorption in the anti-Fascist struggle in Central Europe. My studies had been both unorthodox and fitful. If somebody had approached me in the corridor and told me that I would never see India, I would have agreed. But if he had gone on to tell me that I would never join the Communist Party either, I would have been totally incredulous. I never visualised the stuffed eelskin.

Within a day or two of our arrival, we were at the King Street headquarters of the Communist Party, introducing ourselves to Willie Gallacher and Isobel Brown. I had never seen Gallacher, but had often heard Isobel Brown from the platform, swaying crowds as effectively as Harry Pollitt, which is saying a lot. There was no question of immediate enlistment. As I explained our position, and gave an account of our past activity in Austria, Gallacher took notes. He then told us, kindly, that he would have to check; there were a lot of strange types emerging from Central Europe those days. As the Austrian party was illegal, it might take some time to get a reply. He suggested that we [Philby and Litzi] should return in six weeks.

I then busied myself with my application for the Civil Service. I completed the forms, stating the subjects in which I wished to be examined and my preference for India. As references, I gave the family doctor and Dennis Robertson, the economist, who had been my tutor at Trinity. After a few days with my parents, we moved into a furnished room in East End Lane, for which, thanks to a kitchenette (more ette than kitchen), we paid as much as 17/6 a week. There I resumed my studies and renewed contact with old friends and acquaintances, mostly Communists or nearly so. We were usually hungry. On 1 May, we went to Camden Town to join the annual May Day march organised by the Communist Party. It was the last time for twenty-nine years that I openly wore my political colours.

One evening about the middle of May, we were visited by a friend whom I had seen two or three times since returning from Vienna. We had discussed with him fully our adventures there, and he knew that we had applied for membership of the British Communist Party. After a few preliminaries, he asked if I would go for a walk with him, turning to Lizy with some gallantry or other to excuse his unusual request. As we started up West End Lane, he asked me if I had received any news from King Street. When I said no, he told me that he had a proposition to make which might vitally affect my future. He had been approached by a man, a man of 'decisive importance', who was interested in me. He knew of my record in Austria, and wanted to discuss with me certain possibilities arising out of it. Would I go? My friend strongly advised me to agree, urging that it might well be in the highest interests of the cause. When I gave my consent, he said something which gave me an inkling of the truth. He asked me on no account to give Lizy any details of our talk until I had spoken to the man of 'decisive importance', to tell her it was just party business. Lizy was surprised when I returned home with sealed lips, but she was too disciplined to press her questions.

A few days later, I met my friend, as arranged, at Chalk Farm. I was disappointed to find him alone, but he laughed. 'It won't be long now.' We then began one of those journeys which were to become exasperatingly familiar: taxi, bus, underground, a few minutes on foot, then underground, bus, taxi – or in any other order. Two hours after our meeting in Chalk Farm, we were walking across Regent's Park. A man rose from the grass in front of us, and my friend stopped. 'Here we are,' he said. 'On the dot.' I shook the stranger's hand and looked around. My friend was already walking away. I never saw him again.

My stranger was a man in his middle thirties. He was rather below medium height, and the breadth of his shoulders was accentuated by his general stoutness. He had fair, curly hair and a broad, clear brow.

His blue eyes and wide mouth were highly mobile, hinting at rich possibilities of mischief. We spoke in German, in which he was completely at home. As his accent was South German, I took him at first to be Austrian, but one or two later indications, so slight that I have forgotten them, suggested that he might have been Czech. I found out later that he spoke passable English and very good French. He was an unashamed Francophile; throughout his stay in London, which he disliked, he longed for Paris.

'Otto,' he said, as we sat down on the grass. He placed himself facing one way and me the other, suggesting that I should keep an eye open for anyone paying us undue attention. Our conversation lasted less than an hour, but within a few minutes it was clear that, although Otto said nothing in so many words, I was being approached with a view to recruitment into one of the Soviet special services. Otto showed knowledge of my doings in Vienna, and applauded in general terms my intention to join the Communist Party. But, he suggested, I might do more elsewhere. If I joined the Party, I would be one of many. Any functions that I might perform in the Party would certainly be performed by someone, one way or another, whether I joined or not. But with my possibilities and my capabilities, I was qualified for a service for which recruits were few and far between.

There was flattery in this, of course, probably conspicuous flattery on Otto's part. When he spoke of my possibilities and capabilities, he meant my middle-class birth and upbringing. But he did not press it beyond the bounds of decency, knowing that nothing he said could be as flattering as the mere fact of the approach. It meant that I had been observed in quarters that were indeed of 'decisive importance', and that it had been considered in those quarters that I was worth further cultivation.

Otto passed on to politics. He spoke of the rise of Fascism in Europe, the danger of Japan in the Far East, and the equivocal attitude of the Western democracies. It was desperately important to know more of what was happening in these diverse fields. An avowed Communist could never get near the real truth. But somebody moving as a real bourgeois among bourgeois could. Without putting it in so many words, he suggested that it was my pressing duty to accept his proposition. He admitted that the proposition, as matters then stood, was vague; the details would have to be filled in later, according to circumstances of time and place. Long before he finished, I had decided to accept.

But when I told Otto that I was willing, he drew back. He would not take 'yes' for an answer at that stage. He himself, he explained, would have to report back in detail before continuing the contact. And meanwhile, he added with a touch of grimness, 'you will have some hard thinking to do'. Perhaps it will be best if I report his remaining comments in direct speech, without pretending that I can reproduce his exact words.

'In the first place,' he said, 'we know that you are not afraid of danger. But we don't like danger. We like safety. People are no use to us if they are caught. We may ask you sometimes to do something dangerous, but we will insist on your doing it the safest possible way. Our first principle is security, and security can be fearfully dull.'

He suddenly shot a question at me. 'What did you think of your roundabout trip to our meeting today?'

I replied that I had found it rather exciting.

'How long did it take?'

'About two hours.'

He grunted with satisfaction, then cocked an eye at me and smiled slyly. 'Wait until you have done it a hundred times.'

He had read me truly. Long before my hundredth rendezvous, I was sick to death of our time-consuming security routine. But as the years rolled by and I remained at large, I began to reflect that the routine might be partly responsible for my long survival.

'Our second point,' Otto continued. 'You will not join the Party. But there is more to it than that. You will drop all your Communist friends as fast as you possibly can. You cannot breathe a hint of the true reason for breaking off contact; on the contrary, you must make it clear to them that you have changed your mind, that you have renounced your former beliefs.'

He looked at me searchingly, and went on in a softer voice. 'I think', he said, 'that this will be the hardest of all for you. It is not easy to face the contempt of friends and comrades. And another thing, there is Lizy. We have made a lot of enquiries, we know that she is a devoted and tireless activist. It will be bitter for her to give up all that. Talk it over with her, see if she is willing to make the sacrifice. Tell her what I have told you. If we go on with this, I shall have to meet her myself.'

Otto went on to talk of intelligence work in general. 'Do not think that you are in for a life of high adventure. We want you to work yourself into positions where information comes to you easily and naturally, so that you can get it without endangering your subsequent usefulness. And don't think that you will ever play a big role behind the scenes. It may come to that, but probably won't. The comprehensive picture built up at home is made by piecing together hundreds of tiny snippets of information. It is we, the field-workers, who supply those snippets. The work can be as tedious as those security precautions we were talking about. It is hard, demanding work.'

He paused and, by way of a softener, added: 'Yet one day, you may get something which you know to be really important. Passing that on will be better than, than,' (he searched for the English expression) 'than making a killing on the Bourse.' He laughed happily, and the mischief spread over his face.

Otto looked at his watch and became practical. He gave me an exact time and place for another meeting a fortnight later. Before starting, I was to set my watch by a certain clock in Victoria Station and see that I arrived precisely on time. It wasn't good to be seen hanging about. Then he asked me another of his sudden questions: 'How are you going home now?'

'By bus,' I replied.

'Only by bus?' he asked, feigning great surprise. 'And what about that taxi, that underground, that other bus?'

Embarrassed, I told him that I only had a shilling on me.

'We will talk about money next time,' he said, 'if there is a next time. Meanwhile, I will give you a pound – a ten shilling note and the rest in silver. That will see you home now – by a long route, remember; and make sure you are quite clean – it will also do for our next rendezvous. Take it seriously. To you, now, it may all seem a game, but to me it is deadly earnest. And if we meet again, and things go as we hope, it will soon be deadly earnest for you, too.'

He took me to a bus stop in Great Portland Street and told me to take the first bus, whatever its destination. When he saw me on board, he would leave himself. As we shook hands, he adjured me again to think over carefully everything he had said. 'And,' he added finally, 'if I don't turn up at the rendezvous, just go ahead and join the Party!'

Lizy was quite as distressed as Otto had anticipated. The break, of course, would be far harder for her than for me. I had been brought up in middle-class England; although I had not taken to it exactly as a duck takes to water, most of it was familiar to me. There were old friendships that could be reactivated, old interests resumed. (I realised with a start that since leaving for Vienna I had not given a thought to cricket or football.) But to Lizy, middle-class England was wholly alien, and a lot of it repugnant. She was far too uncompromising to acquiesce in the smugness of London society, and she was neither happy in it nor good at it. She was later to find satisfaction during the war, working in a machine-tool factory and doing a little discreet politicking on the side. But that was still in the distant future. At the time when I told her of Otto's proposition, all she could hope for was the possibility of herself being used in due course.

Yet, for all the total upset in our prospects, I cannot remember that she said a word to dissuade me. She knew duty when she saw it. Instead, she addressed herself to the deeply painful consideration of how to break with our friends. Our conversation was long and dispirited. Within a few months, we were given brutal evidence that we had indeed made the break. By chance, Lizy ran into Hans, our staunch and gay Hungarian friend from Vienna. Forgetting the rules in her joy, she rushed into his arms and was coldly repulsed. 'Did you know in Vienna', asked Hans, 'that Kim was a police spy?' It was a cruel brush-off, but we both recognised its crazy (*perverted*) justice. We spent a very bad night. We both glimpsed some such outcome during our talk after my meeting with Otto. Anyway, as nothing had been definitely decided, we had to defer action. 'Perhaps', said Lizy, without any conviction at all, 'Moscow will turn you down.'

As I reached the rendezvous for my second meeting with Otto, a stout figure rounded the corner a few yards away. A broad smile flashed in my direction suggested that Moscow had not turned me down. After a short walk, we found an empty park bench, and Otto immediately asked after Lizy. He looked troubled and I told him how she had reacted. I felt that he had come across the problem before, perhaps even in the case of his own wife. 'I must see her, I must see her,' he kept repeating. It seemed to me also very desirable. He was ten or fifteen years older than Lizy, and came from exactly the same environment: educated, Central European and Communist. If anyone could console her, he could.

Otto's mood suddenly changed. He threw me one of his quick looks. 'From now on, you must follow instructions exactly,' he said. 'Why did you come by bus all the way instead of using the money I gave you for taxis?' How my face changed I do not know; perhaps my jaw dropped. Otto enjoyed himself hugely. 'Now tell me,' he said, patting my knee; 'how actually did you come?' I told him: bus, taxi, tube, taxi and so on. 'Very good, very good,' he said. 'And now we must get down to serious talk.' (Neither then nor thereafter did he ask me whether I stood by my earlier resolution; nor did he say a word about Moscow's response to his report on our first meeting. I took this as a sign of mutual confidence, as indeed it was.)

'We must first of all discuss your career,' Otto went on. 'We want you to get information. To get information, you must get somewhere. Not just anywhere, but somewhere useful, useful from the point of view of getting information we cannot get otherwise. You must have some ideas on the subject. Let me have them.'

In fact, my ideas were extremely vague. They were generally orientated towards India, but that was about all. I said so. 'It all depends on whether I get to India, and what happens if I get there.'

Otto reacted with disconcerting energy. 'India? INDIA?' he snarled. 'What's all this about India?' I told him about my long-standing plan for joining the Indian Civil Service, if it would have me. I made some defence of the idea. Surely the colonial movement was important? Surely it could be helped along by (*having staunch*) friends in the government? Busy with his thoughts, muttering 'India' from time to time, Otto paid little attention to my remarks. Looking back on that episode, I feel ashamed of my innocence. I was twenty-two, and had emerged from a year of hard experience. Yet it is clear to me now that my vision of helping the cause in India was woolly and romantic, deriving something perhaps from Kipling and my namesake. Many publicists have recently jumped at the coincidence of the two Kims. But I am deliberately tentative about it because, although I heard much of Kipling in my youth, it was not until the war that I actually sat down and read *Kim*.

Otto soon recovered his poise, and turned to me kindly, perhaps fearing that he was about to give me a jolt. Of course the colonial movement was important. It would certainly become more important still. But we must be practical. If I went to India, how would we keep contact? What would I do? Where would I be sent? Perhaps I would spend years in faraway spots of no interest to anyone. Anyway, the key to India lay in London, as well as the keys to many other things, including things more important than India.

He broke off and looked at me with some concern. 'How important is India to you personally? You were born in India. Do you feel you must go back?'

I replied that I was interested in the idea of India. At one time, it had seemed an obvious goal to aim at. But I was not dead set on it. If I could be more useful elsewhere, I would be willing to change my plans. Anyway, I would probably fail in the examination.

Otto had left me. 'Better not fail, better not fail,' he said absently. 'Better not take the exam than take it and fail.' Then, turning his full attention to me saying: 'Can you withdraw at this stage? Would it look odd if you backed out of it?' No, I thought, it wouldn't look particularly odd. Some of my friends might be surprised and my father would be disappointed. But people do withdraw; it could be done without fuss. Greatly relieved, Otto brought the Indian discussion to a close. 'Don't do anything yet,' he said. 'But prepare yourself for a change of plan – psychologically. I don't want you to feel broken-hearted if I tell you at our next meeting that you must forget India for ever.'

We then discussed alternatives to a career in India. My education at Westminster and Trinity had fitted me for nothing in particular, and our talk began to focus more and more distinctly on Fleet Street. A journalist can seek information and ask questions; the more people he meets, the better. And, talking of people, Otto told me that he would set me a task for (my) our next (meeting) rendezvous, 'one of those boring tasks I warned you about in our last meeting'. The task consisted of making a complete list of *all* my friends and acquaintances, with every detail, however trivial, I could remember about each. We would then have a look at them, and see what help we could expect.

I remarked that, since it was now decided what my future course should be, I should perhaps begin to break off my old contacts in the movement. 'Not just yet,' Otto replied. 'I will explain the reasons later, but for the moment you should take it easy. Try to reduce your contact with them as far as you can consistently with your old relationship. Don't give them any hint of a change of mind.' He told me not to build any false hopes on the deferment of this unpleasant duty. It would have to come soon. It was a case of choosing the right moment. I attached no special significance to this deferment at the time, beyond thinking that it would give Lizy a little more time for readjustment to the nasty inevitable. It never occurred to me that Otto's instruction contained the germ of a pretty little network which was to include, among others, Burgess and Maclean.

Before parting, we quickly disposed of the question of money. Otto evidently expected a refusal, because he raised the subject tentatively and dropped it as soon as I told him I needed no assistance. But we agreed that I should be repaid what I spent travelling to and from meetings. Each rendezvous would cost between five and ten shillings, which was much more than I could afford. Finally, Otto extracted a promise from me: that if I should ever get into financial difficulty, through folly, bad luck, ill health or any other reason, I would go to him immediately. Tactfully, he insisted that this was not for my good, but for the good of the service. I mention this promise because, eleven years later, it was to have a surprising sequel, which I shall record in due course.

I spent the next few days in trying to practise total recall on my friends and acquaintances, dividing them into Communists, sympathisers and others. Taking the more colourful first, I had lots of fun; but as the list lengthened and the characters grew duller, considerable tedium set in. I began to appreciate Otto's wisdom in warning me that much of the path ahead would be heavy going. Then an incident occurred which pleased me, because I thought it would lighten Otto's burden. It took the form of a letter from Dennis Robertson at Cambridge, whose name I had given as a reference in my Civil Service application. Robertson told me that the Civil Service authorities had referred to him, and he was afflicted by doubt. Would I really be happy in the Indian service? Would I really be able to come to terms with a system, many features of which would be repellent to me? What would I do if called upon to administer the Bengal Ordinances? He urged me to think it over. If I persisted, he said, he would be happy to recommend me in respect of character and ability, but would also feel compelled to mention my 'strong sense of social justice'.

This letter, of course, put the kybosh on India. It also relieved me of a thought which had been nagging me since my last meeting with

Otto. If he was so hostile to the idea of India, ought I not perhaps to switch my preference to the Diplomatic Service? I had dismissed it in the first place for two reasons. First, competition for the Diplomatic remained very stiff, while enthusiasm for India was waning. I might just scrape into India somewhere near the bottom of the list, but I was quite sure I had not done nearly enough academic work to satisfy the Foreign Office. Second, diplomats were still expected to have private means, and I had none. In spite of these cogent considerations, I felt, when Otto came out strongly against India, that it might be my duty to face the bigger test, however hopeless it seemed. Robertson's letter would absolve me of that duty. Though I could change my list of preferences within the Civil Service, I could hardly change my referee; and Robertson's warning would effectively bar employment anywhere in government. I did not know at the time that the stronghold could be breached through a secret backdoor.

Otto was greatly relieved. India was out; the fact that the whole Civil Service was out too did not seem to worry him. But he was very insistent that I should act soon, before Robertson could communicate with the Civil Service authorities. If Robertson's views are put into the archives, he said, there will always be a black mark against you. He also suggested that, in telling Robertson I had decided against the Civil Service, I should give some personal reason for the decision, something not directly related to my 'strong sense of social justice', our object being to bury the political aspect of the case as deeply as possible in Robertson's mind. A ready-made pretext occurred to me: my recent marriage; I could say that I had already been reconsidering the matter since my wife's health precluded long residence in hot countries. So we agreed, and so I wrote.

My list was the next item; I gave Otto a thick bundle of papers. 'Is this all?' he asked. I confessed that it was not, I hadn't had time to finish. He laughed cheerfully. 'Quite right,' he said. 'I knew you couldn't possibly manage all your contacts in a week.' He then asked me seriously to make it a regular practice, first to complete my list of past acquaintances, then to add any new ones that might come along. 'You will produce a lot of rubbish,' he said. 'But each useful page will be worth lots of waste paper.'

It was a formidable assignment which lasted thirty years and more, until well after my arrival in Moscow. I soon learnt to pick and choose of course, and to concentrate on those who might be useful as sources or dangerous as enemies. Yet it is awesome to think of the libel actions that would lie against me if the Moscow archives ever saw the light of day.

A longer time than usual elapsed before I saw Otto again. It was our system at each meeting to arrange three future dates for rendezvous, so that if either of us was unable to make the first one, we still had two reserve dates in hand. There was also an emergency arrangement, but we never had occasion to use it. Otto, I should add, had a professional horror of the telephone; he only used it once (*in our three years' acquaintance*) during our association, and then only (*at a time*) when even our emergency arrangement would not have met the urgency of the situation.

When, after about a month, Otto arrived for our meeting, he was not alone. He introduced his companion as 'Theo'. In appearance, the two were a startling contrast. Beside the short, stocky, florid Otto, Theo looked a pale giant, though he was probably not more than an inch or two above six feet. A deep hollow in each cheek and crow's feet about the eyes suggested lots of experience, even hardship, an effect enhanced by large, deep-set eyes and a melancholy smile. He was to leave with me memories of wisdom and great kindness. As he shook my hand and came out with his '*gut-en Tag. Wie geht es Ihn-en?*', I recognised the drawling German which only Hungarians can achieve.

Later, Theo was to become (*slightly*) more forthcoming about his past than Otto ever was. As a youth, he had studied for the priesthood, but had rejected that vocation in time to be conscripted into the Austrian army and sent to the eastern front. There he had been captured by the Russians. He had witnessed the February and October revolutions, and joined the Bolsheviks, fighting in the Red Army on the southern front against Denikin's Whites. How he came to join the Soviet special services, I never knew, but he had evidently been with them for some time and held a position of seniority.

Theo took the lead in our conversation, by the end of which I had been given my first serious intelligence assignment. The text of our discussion was the list of friends and acquaintances which I had laboriously compiled. Theo concentrated attention on some dozen, all of the sympathisers. 'You see,' he said with his tired smile, 'we feel that some of these might follow your example, if properly approached.' The upshot of our discussion, which lasted all afternoon and well into the evening, was the conclusion that some would, some probably would not. It will surprise no one to learn that Maclean was near the top of the list, especially since he had a good chance of getting into the Foreign Office. Burgess, owing to strong reservations I had expressed in my original character sketch, came near the bottom. My assignment for the next few weeks was to cultivate these people and assess their probabilities of successful recruitment. As some of them lived in Oxford and Cambridge, I was given money in advance for travelling expenses.

The reader does not need to be told that, in respect of Maclean, we were successful; and he will not be foolish enough to expect revelations about other names on the list. Except for Burgess – Burgess was a very special case. For weeks after Maclean and I had gone underground, Otto and I, with Theo in occasional attendance, discussed Burgess. They were (*clearly*) anxious to recruit him; his potentialities were very tempting. I felt that I had to insist on the dangers he represented. I was not so worried about discretion, since his sense of political discipline would probably look after that. His drawback was his unfailing capacity for making himself conspicuous. At the time, I thought that an ability to melt into the background was an essential qualification for our business; I had never seen (*expected*) Burgess to melt into any background, and didn't expect to. Yet I could not deny his gifts or his potentialities. Thus we went on discussing the pros and cons, meeting after meeting.

But we reckoned without Burgess himself. While we were talking, he was drawing conclusions and acting on them. He convinced himself that Maclean and I had not undergone a sudden change of views, and that he was being excluded from something esoteric and exciting. So he started to badger us, and no one could badger more effectively than Burgess. He went for Maclean and he went for me. Doubtless he went for (*badgered*) others as well, for Theo and Otto became increasingly worried. They may have doubted whether we could stand up to the pressure. They were certainly worried that, if he got nowhere with us, he might try some other tack (*means*), perhaps talk about us to people outside our circle. This consideration, which I had not envisaged, shook my resolution. (*It was blindingly obvious that*) He might well be more dangerous outside than inside. So the decision was taken to recruit him. He must have been one of the very few people to have forced themselves into the Soviet special service.

As soon as we were all underground, we were kept as far as possible apart, for solid security reasons. We met only when operational necessity dictated meeting or when, about twice a year, Burgess felt an overwhelming urge for a long talk. Even those occasional meetings were at first conspiratorial. We had a fixed meeting-place, and Burgess would call from a public telephone booth, giving just a date and a time.

Meanwhile, I had made a modest entry into journalism, as assistant editor of *The Review of Reviews*. The pay was miserable because the paper had no money; but the editor was kind enough to find me the odd freelance assignment, so I made just enough to live on. After a good week we would have a fling at Bertorelli's. The great drawback to the job, however, was that it was a dead-end. There was no prospect of advancement and it brought me into contact with very few people. Otto and I therefore cast about for ways and means of exploiting my spare time. After some prodding from me, Otto fell in with a suggestion that I should join the (*Royal*) Central Asian Society. It had a distinguished membership, and gathered regularly for dinners and lectures. I felt that my father's name would help me, and, after all, one had to start somewhere.

So I began again my laborious lists of people, this time with an orientalist flavour. Sometimes I would get a breath of inside information about British policy in, say, the Middle East or towards Japan. But I was generally depressed by my meagre pickings. Otto's main task at this time was to encourage me, and he did so earnestly and patiently. 'Think who you have already brought us,' he would say. 'You will have another turn, and another. Everyone has lean years. Hold on.' He would talk vivaciously of Moscow and Paris; sometimes he would take me to the cinema – invariably to a comedy, to see me laugh. He was very fond of *It Happened One Night* and took me to it twice.

It was Theo who came up with the next idea. One of my reports on the Central Asian Society had dealt with Sir Denison Ross, then head of the London School of Oriental Studies. He knew my father, and had taken a kindly interest in me. Theo suggested that it might be useful for me to take a course at the school, preferably one dealing with a language or a people of Soviet Central Asia. It would be interesting to know the sort of people engaged in such courses, not to mention the identity(*ies*) of anyone intending to take a permanent interest in the area. Apart from any specific interest in Soviet Asia, it was important to find out in general the purpose of the school, its areas of specialisation, its curricula.

Ross was delighted when I told him (*that I was thinking of taking a course at his school*) of my intention, but (*he*) looked doubtful when I mentioned the study of Turki. Then his face cleared. 'I know,' he said. 'I will take you myself. I have forgotten it, but we will study it together. You will learn it, and I will re-learn it.' I was disconcerted. Was I to be the only student concerned with the principal language of Soviet Central Asia? (*But*) It was too late to withdraw. Crestfallen, I reported back to Otto, but characteristically he bounced back at me. 'What do you mean a waste of time? You report that no one is studying Turki there. That itself is important. Anyway, go ahead and tell us about the other students: who they are, what they learn, what they intend to do. It is true that we do not want you to go and bury yourself in Asia for ever. But that doesn't mean that we aren't interested in Asia. Anything you get by the way, in addition to your main work, is welcome.' My main work, of course, was to get near the British Government, and I seemed as far from success as ever.

At about this time, however, I did get one small lead which was to prove useful in the long run, in quite an unexpected way. In my survey of friends and acquaintances, I had written at length about Tom Wyllie. He had been at Westminster with me, and had achieved some distinction as a classical scholar at Oxford. During our university days, I was his guest at Oxford two or three times, and he had returned my visits. Since then, he had passed into the civil service, and was working in the War Office. Otto's interest was quickened when I found out that he had become a private secretary to the Permanent Under-Secretary for War, Sir Herbert Cready. There was no question(*ing*), then, of recruiting him; but there are more ways than one of using a contact in a sensitive position.

Wyllie met me more than half-way. He was given to heavy drinking, and tried to counteract its effects by violent exercise at the weekends. To that end, he played fives regularly for the old

Westminsters. I was an obvious recruit for the team, since I had played for the school a few years earlier. So, as a regular habit, we would fore-gather on Saturdays and play any school or club that would accept our challenge. After the matches, we would settle down to convivial evenings, and I would tempt Wyllie into indiscretion. The difficulty was that he was not interested in either politics or the War Office. He was good at his job, not because he was interested, but because he combined a good mind with practical sense. Until the blue snakes got him.

The War Office information doled out by Wyllie was pretty inade-quate and Otto and I were soon discussing ways of prising more out of him. We considered blackmailing him on account of his homosexual-ity, but I advised against it; Wyllie was not a person to be pushed around and would almost certainly brazen it out rather than submit. We also discarded the idea of bribing him; he had private means and was comfortably off. Another possibility arose from the fact that Wyllie was Resident Clerk at the War Office as well as private secre-tary to the PUS. As such, he lived in a flat on the top floor of the War Office building. The furniture of the flat included a safe in the living-room. It was this that attracted our particular attention.

It was not a sophisticated safe, and I knew where Wyllie kept the key. Among other things, the safe held his whisky supply, and I had often seen him open it and toss the key back into the middle drawer of his desk. After some deliberation, we agreed on a course of action. Otto would give me a pill guaranteed to knock Wyllie out for an hour or two. When I was quite certain that he was out, I would open the safe and take a general look at its contents. I was to work quickly in case Wyllie was (*exceptionally*) resistant to sedatives. Otto suggested twenty minutes would probably be enough; I might extend it to half-an-hour if the contents of the safe seemed to warrant it. I was on no account to remove anything. On the contrary, I must put everything back, including the key, exactly where I had found it.

And so, two or three Saturdays afterwards, I met Wyllie for our weekly match, with Otto's pill, carefully wrapped in tissue paper, tucked (*away in*) into my waistcoat pocket. I need not have bothered. That afternoon we won a match that we had expected to lose, a par-ticularly satisfactory result for Wyllie as he had conceived (*an intense*) a dislike for our opposing captain. He returned to London in high spirits. Our pub crawl from the London terminus to the War Office was very thorough indeed. I dodged out of a few rounds and spilled a few others. But Wyllie dodged nothing and spilled nothing. By the time we got to Whitehall, he needed support. Safe in his flat, he announced loudly that he needed a drink. Opening the safe, he half filled two tumblers of whisky. He drained his at a gulp, tottered to his couch and was snoring within seconds. The door of the safe was wide open.

I felt cheated. Wyllie was out, without benefit of [the] knock-out drop. But now for the safe! It contained unused stationery, some bits and pieces of office equipment; also a tray on which lay a single sheet of paper. At last, I was looking at a secret document. But my first excitement was followed by bitter disappointment. The paper was a communication from the British Ambassador in Italy to the Foreign Office, reporting a talk about Soviet policy with a colleague in Rome. Like many such reports, as I was to learn later, it was of depressing unimportance. Its last sentence was such a gem of old-world diplomatic writing that it has stuck in my memory: 'The Tsarist eagle may have looked both ways, but the Soviet star points in five directions and turns with every breath of wind.' With care I replaced the paper; Wyllie was still snoring. I left him a flippant note, and despondently boarded a homeward bus.

Otto was disturbed by my report. He took unenthusiastic note of the remarks of the British Ambassador in Rome, but what preoccupied him most was the ease of the operation. Was I sure that Wyllie was really asleep? Couldn't it have been a trap? My reassurances failed to reassure him. He asked me to observe Wyllie most carefully next time I saw him, and to report in detail any change in his attitude. Most foreigners at that time exaggerated the astuteness of the British; members of the Soviet service were no exception. Otto's anxiety reminded me of an occasion on which Theo had earnestly asked me if Lawrence was really dead, and had (*previously*) been reluctant to take 'yes' for an answer.

(*By now I was getting*) I soon got bored with the Wyllie connection. We seemed to be getting very little out of it professionally, and I (*was beginning*) began to find it a personal strain. Wyllie's homosexuality never obtruded itself directly as far as I was concerned. But it meant that I often met friends of his whom I would have preferred to avoid.

It was for these personal, rather than professional, reasons that I suggested to Otto that the Wyllie affair should be transferred to Burgess. This was agreed, and I was instructed to bring them together.

But the instructions contained a reservation. I was to bring them together without Burgess knowing the purpose of the meeting. The only reason I could (*can*) surmise for this niggling restriction was that Moscow hoped to persuade each of us, at some future time, that the other was not working. It was a pretty futile exercise in security, as I told Otto at the time. The only (*real*) danger would arise if either of us had a real change of heart, and then the fat would be (*have been*) in the fire anyway. As will be seen, it nearly torpedoed the (*whole*) enterprise.

I arranged a (*small*) cocktail party, inviting both Wyllie and Burgess. I introduced them and left them to it, drifting from guest to guest as a good host should. Soon loud voices were raised in the Burgess-Wyllie corner; all was clearly not well. I caught Burgess's eye and he bounced aggressively across the room. 'Who', he asked loudly, 'is that pretentious young idiot who thinks he knows all about Proust?' I replied that I did not know anything about pretensions or Proust, but Wyllie was not an idiot. He had a very important job in the War Office. 'Ho,' said Burgess and wheeled back to Wyllie. The situation was saved. Before they left the party, they had made a date.

Although my close association with Wyllie was broken, I did not lose sight of him altogether. He belonged to the Junior Carlton Club, and among his friends there was an elderly businessman called Stafford Talbot. Talbot's family had been engaged in trade with Tsarist Russia, and had lost all in the revolution. Sometime in the 20s, he had started a journal called *The Anglo-Russian Trade Gazette*, originally designed to push the interests of British creditors of Russia. By the middle 30s, the hopes of the British creditors had become pretty shadowy, but the *Gazette* continued to report news and discuss prospects of Anglo-Russian trade. Talbot talked freely over glasses of barley water; and, although nothing that he said was exciting, it was generally acceptable to Otto. More interesting still, however, were the hints Talbot dropped about prospects he had in mind for starting a companion journal to deal with Anglo-German trade.

Meanwhile, *The Review of Reviews* was dying. In the winter of 1935/36, it was taken over by Chatto & Windus, under the editorship of Vernon Bartlett. I continued to put in a daily appearance, but it became quite apparent that I was wasting time. Otto suggested that I might try to get in with Talbot by stressing my knowledge of Germany. The timing was happy. In the spring of 1936, Talbot decided to go ahead with his German venture and offered me the editorship of the new journal – if it ever appeared. Meanwhile, he asked me to help him in his negotiations with the German authorities and with such British firms as might be interested. He said that, in view of my fluent German, I should do most of the donkey-work at the Berlin end, while he chivvied his contacts in the City. Of course we would both have to join the Anglo-German Fellowship; the firm would pay my subscription, and for all the good dinners we anticipated. Chatto & Windus released me without protest.

Otto grinned happily at the news. At last we seemed to be getting somewhere. 'See,' he said, 'you were beginning to despair. But how long have you waited? Two years! It might have been ten!'

We were indeed getting somewhere. It had been difficult to take Wyllie seriously, or the amiable orientalists of the Central Asian Society. But in the Anglo-German Fellowship and in Berlin, I was rubbing shoulders with a declared enemy and his British friends. Most important for me, personally and professionally, was the emergence of a clearly defined target: the development of unofficial relations between Britain and Germany. On the German side, the unofficial merged with the official since most Germans followed the Nazi line; that was even better.

Otto was happy to see me emerging from my early frustrations, but refused to dismiss those two years as a waste of time. 'You must regard it as a period of apprenticeship,' he said repeatedly. 'You have got security well into your system. We know that we can trust you to work without taking risks and making a fool of yourself. Above all, you have learnt that romantic gestures have no place in our work.' The last remark was a favourite of his; he would spit it out with venom.

Here sceptics will ask themselves how the prospective editor of an Anglo-German trade journal could possibly have obtained information of significance. Since the war, we have grown accustomed to spectacularly successful operators; we decry the providers of those snippets of news, those tiny essential links in the chain, about which Otto had lectured me so often. This is ignorance. It is good to sit in the middle of the web, receiving habitually more hard information than you can possibly pass on. But hard information seldom touches the most important intelligence of all, the intentions of people who take decisions for the reason that intentions often crystallise at the last moment. For instance, I did not report in 1936 how or when Hitler would swallow Austria in the following year, because Hitler himself did not know. In such areas, in the broad gap between ignorance and knowledge, the snippeteers play their role, suggesting confirmation of this or reservations about that. They help headquarters to put the whole picture together and make what Allan Dulles was fond of calling educated guesses.

But then, the sceptics will further object, nobody in the know gives information to an outsider; any information given must be trivial or deliberately planned. Passing over the fact that this is by no means true, it ignores the elementary necessity, for any intelligence operator, of learning to recognise when people are speaking their minds or talking to a brief. It is a battle of wits, the everyday stuff of diplomacy and the press; it is not a closed book to the intelligence officer. And the intelligence officer, unlike the diplomat or the journalist, starts with one advantage. He usually knows the purpose of his interlocutor, but the interlocutor seldom knows his. From my own experience, I can point to my dealings with the American CIA and FBI. But they didn't. So they covered up the wrong things.

My target on the British side, the pro-German element in British society, congregated in the Anglo-German Fellowship. There were formal dinners and informal gatherings, and the private contacts that arose from both. Three streams of opinion were discernible, though some members of indeterminate or wavering views could not be placed with certainty. There were the near-Nazis, to whom the Germans paid little attention because they were already committed to any course laid down by Hitler, short of a German attack on Britain. There was a broader, less homogeneous, stream of wishful thinkers who thought that Hitler could be bought off ('his ambitions satisfied') by concessions that would not affect the balance of power, i.e. by minor frontier rectifications in Europe with a colony or two tossed in. Their lack of homogeneity led to differences about what sacrifices should be made in Germany's favour, and by whom. Finally, there were the realists more or less, who feared that Hitler would not be satisfied by crumbs but who were prepared to string along in hopes of a change of heart, or government, in Berlin. Common to most members of all three groups was a hope that the states of Eastern Europe would make their compromise with Hitler, conceding, if essential, the free passage of German troops to the Soviet border.

Such was the picture that emerged from detailed weekly and fortnightly reports. With the benefit of hindsight, I see nothing to be particularly ashamed of in this analysis, buttressed as it was by chapter and verse. It reads like old hat now, largely because its implications were borne out by events. It was confirmed in general by the three-stage dissolution of the Anglo-German Fellowship over the next three years. The realists fell away after the rape of Austria; they were not opposed to a decently negotiated Anschluss, but regarded the brutality of the action as a calculated demonstration of power (which it was). The wishful thinkers, their stomachs soured by Munich champagne, broke up after the invasion of Czechoslovakia. The near-Nazis hung on right up to Chamberlain's trumpet-call to war, then said (*saying*), with Lord Redesdale at the eleventh hour, 'the king's enemies are my enemies'. A handful endured still longer – until they were rounded up and put inside.

On the German side, we had the Embassy in London, and the Propaganda Ministry and Ribbentrop Bureau in Berlin. In the Embassy, our three principal contacts were Bismarck, Marschall von Bieberstein and the swarthy Press Attaché, FitzRandolph, as Aryan and suave as a Persian prince. I judged that, from my point of view, Marschall would be the most promising of the three; Bismarck was busy and FitzRandolph slick. I had agreed with Otto that I should not pretend to Nazi sympathies. It would have been difficult to be convincing. So, to the Germans, I put myself forward as an Englishman who believed that an understanding with Germany, including concessions to Germany, was the best guarantee of Britain's long-term interests. It is interesting to speculate what would have happened if such a policy had been pushed through to the end. The likeliest result would have been a pretty awful world, for almost everybody except the British and the Germans. That, of course, was the whole point of the policy.

Within a few weeks, Talbot decided that he had better take me to Germany. When I reported to Otto, he looked doubtfully at my suit. It might be alright for England, he said, but in Berlin the outer shell was important. So we ended our meeting at Austin Reed's. When I emerged from the changing cubicle, in a blue suit, light grey overcoat and black Homburg hat, Otto (*he*) clapped his thigh painfully. Nobody, he decided, had ever looked a more perfect diplomat.

In Berlin, our first call was at the Propaganda Ministry. The visit caused me disappointment and some unease. Our chief contact was a certain Vogt, with whom I felt no rapport at all. He had spent some time in the United States, and spoke fluent English with an American accent. I do not think that he was a Nazi; he seemed to have no principle except perhaps self-advancement. He looked vulgar and tricky. What worried me most, however, was that Talbot seemed to be looking to Vogt for funds. I had assumed that any money we received from German sources would come from German firms with a legitimate interest in pushing Anglo-German trade. Taking money from the Propaganda Ministry meant sailing much nearer the wind. That the Propaganda Ministry should help us to make contact with German industrial and commercial circles was one thing; that Vogt should hold our purse-strings, and thus be in a position to dictate editorial policy, was another. Looking to the future, I had no wish to be branded with a Nazi, or any other, label; the cat might jump almost anywhere. As I will show, circumstances saved me in the nick of time.

Vogt arranged a small banquet that evening, in one of the Nazi Party guest-houses. My right-hand companion at dinner was an astonishingly beautiful brunette. She had been born in German East Africa, and we talked of colonial problems from cocktails to coffee. I was strongly tempted to find out if she could talk of anything else. But my time was short and my sense of duty strong. So the two dates I made that evening were both with men, of whom I now remember nothing except the date I forwent on their behalf.

The following days were divided between officials of the Propaganda Ministry and the Ribbentrop Bureau. I found the latter more rewarding. The Bureau had been created to boost Ribbentrop's stock in the field of Foreign Affairs. It regarded itself as a rival Foreign Ministry, and there was deep mutual antagonism between the orthodox and unorthodox diplomats. It was the sort of situation that Hitler encouraged; by having a lot of agencies covering the same field, he could play them off against one another, and keep the leading strings in his hands. The Bureau paid us exaggerated attention. To officials of the

Foreign Ministry, we were of little significance, though they were polite enough. But Duerckheim, Rodde, and others of the Bureau saw us as a tool which might be used to raise their prestige and harass the professionals. I cultivated them all I could professionally because it paid off in terms of intelligence, personally because it annoyed Vogt. It was not the best policy for the journal I was trying to get on its feet, because it was Vogt who counted. But I think it did something to save me from the Nazi stigma.

Such was the pattern of our activity for nearly a year. Talbot was busy trying to raise funds in the City. But he was a nice, cosy old fellow; he lacked the gift of parting men from their money. Between visits to Berlin, I kept contact with the German Embassy, and experimented with formats for our journal (provisionally entitled 'Britain and Germany'). But it was Berlin that counted, from all points of view, and the prospect gradually became sombre. As my stock with the Bureau rose, to the point of my rating visits to Ribbentrop himself, so my relations with Vogt got worse. During one set of discussions in the early winter of 1936, I got the strong impression that he was trying to force a breach; and I lacked the diplomatic resource to cope with the situation.

Back in London, I reported to Talbot that Vogt was no longer serious in his dealings with us. I hazarded the guess that he was dickering with some other group. We clung on a bit longer, but my guess proved correct. In due course, The Anglo-German Review made its appearance. Its line was Nazi, or near-Nazi, congenial to the obtuse Vogt, but useless in Britain. Though I was saddened at the time by the collapse of 'Britain and Germany', later events were to confirm my belief in a lucky star. When war broke out, most of those connected with our successful rivals fell victim to regulation 18B.

I was out of a job again, but we were not quite back to where we had started. A year of serious work had taught me something, in particular the difference between an intelligence service and a newspaper; roughly the difference between Baedeker and a travelogue. I had also gained confidence, social as well as professional. Perhaps most important of all, I had learnt to listen to abhorrent views without losing my temper, though it took the experience of a few more years to subdue it altogether.

Otto took the news of our failure serenely. He had been prepared for it, of course, but he spoke as if he and his colleagues had formed some definite plan for me. I told him I saw no future in messing about on the fringes of journalism; if I wanted to get anywhere, I had to break into a big newspaper or a news agency. He seemed to agree, but told me to do nothing until our next meeting, which Theo was expected to attend.

The meeting with Theo was a turning-point. It proved to be the first stage of the rocket that propelled me into a career. Theo commended my wish to break into daily journalism. Headquarters, so he said, thought well of my work on the Anglo-German question. But they wanted me to make more of a name for myself in London, to open us prospects of action on a more ambitious scale. Very gently, Theo outlined what was expected of me. Headquarters, he said, had marked me down for a future in the British secret service. They could do a lot to help me on my way, if such help was essential. But they would rather I got in by my own efforts, for my security and that of the others. Journalism, they knew, was a good way in.

The tired smile with which Theo dropped this decision into our conversation lessened the shock of what was surely an astonishing proposition. I can remember no definable reaction, just a whirl of remote images and a call to adventure. Wisely, Theo hurried on with practical matters. The British secret service, he said, was a long-term project. But headquarters also wanted immediate action. There was an urgent need for trustworthy people in Spain, on the Franco side. He wanted to discuss the possibility of covering all these requirements in a single operation. In other words, could I get to Franco Spain as a journalist with a threefold object in view? First, to report to the Soviet Government on the political and military situation; second, to build up a journalistic reputation for myself; third, to do this in such a way as to attract the attention of the British secret service.

Theo's mention of Spain, as an immediate possibility, did more to me than his pipe-dream talk of the British secret service. I had first visited Spain at the age of twelve, when a long holiday in Andalusia had done strange things to my imagination. In adolescence, I had read much of Spain, and dreamt more; I had been back several times. That early dilettante interest added to the emotional involvement in the civil war common to my generation; it made my involvement just that much deeper. The previous autumn, Otto had hidden photographic

241

equipment in my flat and brought Donald Maclean with brief-case full of Foreign Office documents to be read and reproduced, many of them bearing on Soviet aircraft and artillery for the Republic. So when Theo suggested Spain as a field for action, I was already wholly committed. There remained only the question of ways and means.

I doubted whether I could walk into a Fleet Street office and get myself sent to Spain, just like that. I was never good at selling myself. But Theo had another suggestion. Headquarters was willing to finance a trial trip with two aims in view: I should report on political and military subjects, and gather material for articles which would strengthen my hand in applying for a regular job. The immediate problem which faced me was how to get the required cover, needed for my visa application for Spain.

I thought that I'd fill out the application and attached letters of recommendation from friends. Further, I suggested that my visa application would be strengthened if I could coax a letter of introduction from the German Embassy to Franco's representative in London. Otto went one better, and proposed that I could ask for other letters to German contacts in Spain. We agreed on a provisional time limit of three months for the trial trip. If necessary, it could be extended, but I should not live too long without visible means of support; and if I did not get a job in Spain within three months, I probably would not get one at all.

Within a few days, I obtained several letters from editorial offices in Fleet Street, offering me no money, but expressing interest in anything I might write. It was as I expected, though less than I had hoped. At the German Embassy, I was coolly received at first; they knew that 'Britain and Germany' had failed and probably expected reproaches. But when they realised that I wanted only a letter of introduction, with perhaps a breath of fair wind, to Franco's agent in London, they turned on the charm. An hour later, I left with a quite fulsome note to the Marquis of Merry del Val, signed by Ribbentrop himself. The Marquis was not empowered to issue visas himself; he could only give me a letter to his opposite number in Lisbon, who, he assured me, would facilitate my onward journey. So there remained another hurdle to be jumped, and it was with some doubt about my prospects that I went to my next meeting with Theo and Otto.

They were disappointed that the Spanish visa was not already in my passport, but decided to go ahead. At worst, it would mean the loss of the passage money to Lisbon and back. Our talk turned to operational matters.

My only contact in Spain was to be in Seville. The time of day and place for our rendezvous was fixed; after my arrival. I was to put a cross to mark in place. We were both to display recognition and that, for our first time, was all. Its purpose was simply to show each other that we existed, that the arrangements were understood and the operation on. Contact was to be made thereafter only in exceptional circumstances: on my side, if I had news of real urgency or ran into serious danger; on his, if he had mail for me. I was to place my mark at least twenty-four hours before any rendezvous, but not at weekends, from which I supposed that the mark would lie on my contact's daily journey between his home and place of work.

Otto instructed me in the use of a simple code. It involved my carrying a small sheet of very fine paper compressed into a pellet about the size of an aspirin. As a test, I screwed up a few samples and swallowed them, no trouble at all. Then I had to memorise two cover-addresses, one in France and one in Holland, and a questionnaire, largely on military subjects. Otto was to meet me once again before my departure, to check my memory of the cover-addresses and questionnaire, and to re-examine me on the use of the code. Also to give me money, enough for the passage and three months' stay, in used fivers. Theo joined us for lunch at a Greek restaurant, where we talked of everything except business.

A few days later, having booked my passage by Nolt Line to Lisbon, I said goodbye to Lizy. We both knew it was the end. Although we still lived in the same flat, our marriage had already broken up. Undoubtedly, my secret work, the political inactivity it imposed on her, the abandonment of friendships, all hastened matters; but our marriage had crumbled for other reasons as well.

Lecture to the KGB, July 1977

*I*n July 1977, *after more than thirty years as a loyal Soviet agent and fourteen years after he defected, Kim Philby made his only visit to the headquarters of the KGB First Chief Directorate at Yasenevo just outside of Moscow. He had been invited to address an audience of more than 300 officers, including two of his students, Michael Bogdanov and Yuri Kobaladze, who had learned about Britain at Philby's safe-house seminars. Both would later serve tours in Britain. Philby spoke in English and used the occasion to discuss his motivation for choosing to become a Communist and a Soviet agent. He also devoted considerable attention to his recruitment and went on to elaborate on the problems and choices of recruitment in general. He does nothing to hide his fondness for those who were so patient during the six years it took him to penetrate the British Secret Intelligence Service (MI6). H.P.*

INTRODUCTION (IN FULL)

Thanks for kind words.

My dear Comrades

It would be an honour for me to be invited to address you at any time, but I regard as a very particular honour to be asked in the current year, 1977.

It is the year of the new Soviet Constitution. It is the year when we celebrate the 60th anniversary of the October Revolution. It is also the year when we celebrate the 100th anniversary of the birth of our greater *founder*, Felix Dzerzhinsky.

While I am speaking of anniversaries and round numbers, I must also mention a date which illustrates the extraordinarily many-sided interests of Felix Dzerzhinsky.

In the middle of all his other activities – organising the Cheka, getting the railways moving, hurrying on the harvest, speeding down to Georgia to sort out local troubles – he found time to become a noted patron of sport. So I will remind you that 1977 is also the 40th season of the Soviet football championship.

So 1977 is a year which we shall all always remember. But I have a very particular personal reason for remembering it all my life. It is the year of my first visit to Soviet intelligence headquarters.

It has taken me a long time to get here. My journey started in a London park on a sunny afternoon more than forty-three years ago. And during that long journey, I had occasion to drop in on quite a few other intelligence headquarters of rather a different colour.

I have held official passes to seven major intelligence headquarters: four British – SIS, SOE, MI5 and the Government Code & Cypher School; three American – CIA, FBI and the National Security Agency. So I can claim that this is the eighth major intelligence organisation which I have succeeded in penetrating.

Needless to say, my feelings here are rather different to those I experienced in the other headquarters. There I felt myself surrounded by wolves; here I know that I am with comrades, colleagues and friends.

Felix Dzerzhinsky once said towards the end of his all-too-short life: Yesli by mne predstoyalo nachat zhizn snova, ya nachal by tak, kak nachal [If I had the chance to do it all again, I'd do it exactly the same way].* I would like to put the same thought in slightly different words.

---

* [This quotation occurs again at the end of Philby's typewritten lecture (see page 258), but it is unknown whether Philby repeated it in the actual lecture.]

If I had [a] wish to express today, I would ask for another forty-three years of active work in our service.

Now, comrades, you are all qualified intelligence officers. Furthermore, you are familiar with intelligence and counter-intelligence techniques which were quite unknown in the days of my active work in the field. So forgive me if I do not say much about technical matters today. I would prefer to concentrate on the personal aspects of my professional career, and to endeavour to suggest certain ideas arising from it.

Motivation

I would like to say a few words about motivation.

I was enrolled in Cambridge University in the autumn of 1929, when I was seventeen. It was a few weeks before the great crash on Wall Street which heralded one of the most intense and general of all the crises of capitalism.

I cannot give you any very convincing account of my intellectual position at that time – simply because my intellectual position was unformed. But I already had a strong emotional commitment to the poor, the weak and the under-privileged against the rich, the strong and the arrogant.

You must be aware that there was plenty of arrogance in Britain in those days. It was the centre of the greatest Empire the world had ever seen, and Britain could still talk on approximately equal terms with the United States.

Where that commitment to the weak came from, I do not know. Genes perhaps? My father, though a distinguished orientalist, was pretty eccentric, and resigned from British Government service as a protest against Zionism – as early as 1924.

Personally, I think that religion may have had more to do with it. In earliest childhood – at the age of four or five – I regarded Christianity – God, Christ, the Trinity, the Resurrection and all that – as a fairy tale. While I was still at my kindergarten, I remember scandalising my grandmother by informing her that God did not exist!

As the idea of Christianity underlay the whole process of my education, my rejection of it may have contributed substantially to my general attitude of rejection towards the society in which I lived.

246

However that may be, one of my first actions on arrival in Cambridge was to join the Cambridge University Socialist Society. I was recently reminded that Dzerzhinsky also started his political life at the age of seventeen. But there, I am afraid, the comparison ends!

I naturally supported the Labour Government, which was then in power. In my ignorance and innocence, I confidently expected it to take socialist solutions to deal with the gathering problems of unemployment, lower wages and the rest.

Quite the opposite happened. The situation of the working class went from bad to worse, while the aristocracy and the bourgeoisie continued to enjoy the plunder of Empire. And, when the full fury of the financial crisis burst in the summer of 1931, the Labour leaders deserted the cause of socialism, to form an alliance with the Conservatives and Liberals in the so-called 'National Government'.

That was a great shock to me – and not only to me. It lead [sic] many of us to re-examine our whole position. The Communist fraction in the CUSS grew in numbers and activity – and I felt drawn towards them.

They introduced me to Marx, and he led in turn to Engels, Lenin and many other writers: Rosa Luxemburg, Bebel, Kautsky, Plekhanov and the rest.

It was not a sudden conversion for me. It took two years of constant study, discussion, argument and occasional political action. I do not think that those two years were wasted. Sudden conversions are liable to sudden reversals. But a conversion which results from two years of mental struggle is likely to grow deep roots.

It was quite literally in the last week of my Cambridge career that I made the final decision – to devote my life to the cause of Communism. This had an important bearing on my future, as I will now explain.

I was planning to spend a year in Austria, to perfect my German and to study Central European history, economics and contemporary politics. From a Communist friend in Cambridge – a professor of great eminence who died a few months ago – I obtained introductions to a Communist organisation in Vienna. It was there that I began my underground life – with the illegal Communist Party.

The importance of this is obvious. There is no record in England of my ever having engaged in Communist activity. If there had been such a record, my prospects of my becoming an officer in SIS at a later date would have been slim indeed.

Recruitment

I returned to England in May, 1934, and very soon I was visited by a Communist friend who told me that a 'man of decisive importance' wanted to meet me. So, as I said before, on a sunny June day, I was taken by a most roundabout route to a London park, where I was introduced to a man whom I later discovered to be the illegal resident in England. For our purposes, let's call him Arnold. He made me a certain proposition, my acceptance of which had led, after many strange twists and turns, to my addressing you today.

Another word on motivation. You may ask: why did I accept this proposition instead of declining it and working instead for the Communist Party of Great Britain?

At that time, 1934, Hitler was already in power in Germany. Japan had already invaded China. The Axis was in process of formation, and the most probable international perspective at that time seemed to be a joint Axis attack on the SU.

The SU was the first socialist state. It was the head and heart of Communism. Collapse of the SU would have put the whole world movement back for several generations.

Therefore, it seemed obvious to me that, for any true Communist with the interests of the international movement at heart, defence of the SU was the first priority, overriding the interests of any single national Communist Party.

That, comrades, was why I accepted.

Now I would like to speak at some length on the nature of my recruitment and on the man who recruited me. It seems to me an unusually instructive case of long-range penetration.

Many years later, when I was a senior officer of SIS, we talked an awful lot about the virtue of long-range penetration. But when it came to the point, all the emphasis was put on quick results. All officers of the service were under heavy pressure, from both outside and inside the service, to produce intelligence today, not tomorrow.

So let us consider the facts as they stood when I met my new friend in that London park.

I had no access to any secret information. I had no access to any information at all, outside the radio and the newspapers.

I had no job. I did not even know what sort of job I would get, except that I had a feeling that journalism would be my best hope.

Yet I was recruited. The only things which the illegal resident knew about me was that I had proved my willingness to work for the cause, illegally if necessary, and that I came from an impeccable bourgeois background, upbringing and education. In fact, he had drawn a virtually blank sheet of paper, hoping no doubt that he or someone else would one day be able to write down something useful.

So let me say a few words about that man.

I was very young at the time, in my early twenties, with little experience of human beings. I may have got him wrong in some particulars. Yet today, looking back over many years and with quite a lot of experience tucked under my belt, I still regard him as a model Chekist, a man whom Dzerzhinsky himself might have handpicked.

He was very well-informed on contemporary affairs. He absorbed a wide range of newspapers and journals, in English, French and German. We would have long discussions of current affairs in Europe, America and the Far East.

He was a really warm human being. He never forgot that everybody, however devoted to the cause, may have personal difficulties, personal problems to discuss. He was always ready to listen with attention and advise where necessary.

He had a great sense of humour. When we had despatched our professional business, we would often settle down to talk trivialities. We would sometimes laugh ourselves silly.

In a very short time, I came to regard him both as a sort of ersatz father and as a sort of elder brother. A father for guidance, advice and authority; and elder brother for fun and companionship. An ideal relationship.

But he was also very firm. He would put me through endless sermons on security. I remember once that I remonstrated with him while he was talking about security and said that I had already heard him say that ten times. 'Only ten times,' he replied. 'Don't worry. You will hear it a hundred times before I have finished with you.' Maybe his insistence has been largely responsible for my being here to address you today, instead of rotting in prison – or indeed rotting underground.

A final characteristic: patient endurance.

I have already said that I had no job when I was recruited. Later in that year, 1934, financial necessity drove me to accept a job with a most undistinguished monthly journal. For two years the results of my so-called activity were almost wholly negative. My friend might well have been excused for thinking that it might be better if I went back to the Communist Party.

But he didn't. He went on obstinately plugging away at various plans and projects for my future, all of which ended in blind alleys. It is with great sadness that I think back to the fact that at the very moment when, largely as a result of his work, I made my first big break-through into the ranks of the British establishment – with my appointment as Times correspondent to Franco Spain – at that very moment, he disappeared out of my life.

The harvest which he sowed was reaped by others. But I hope that his memory will always be held in honour. Of course – I never knew his real identity.

At this point, I would like to mention an incident which, though of a tragic nature, was to become a source of inspiration throughout my life.

It concerns not my first Soviet contact, but my second (Pavel). He was, I believe, our illegal resident for Western Europe, with headquarters in Holland, though I met him both in England and in France.

Now, we all know that in the 30s, some good people, including members of our own organisation, fell victim to cases of unfortunate disregard of socialist legality. I think that my second contact ultimately became one of them.

In the first half of 1938, I met him in France. He told me that he had been recalled to Moscow. I could sense he was in obvious distress.

But – his last words to me were truly inspirational – I humbly suggest in the tradition of Felix Dzerzhinsky himself. He said: 'Kim, we will probably never meet again. But whatever you hear about me in the future, continue on the true path.'

I never did hear of him again – but I hope that I have at least tried to be faithful to his last injunction.

I would now like to say a few words about my own personal feelings at that time – not out of egoism, but rather because it may interest you to know the psychological condition of at least one agent operating in the field [for] ideological reasons.

I said earlier that the results of my first two years were negative. That is not quite true. My very first assignment was both congenial to me and, as it happened, productive.

My friend asked [me] to revisit Cambridge – and also Oxford where I had some contacts – and make a discreet contact with former friends in, or standing somewhere near, the Communist movement. Could I bring back a detailed list of possible recruits, with full personal and political particulars, future prospects, and the rest.

I did bring back a list. I think that I am revealing no very deep secret when I tell you that two of the names on that list were Guy Burgess and Donald Maclean. The other names on the list, I am afraid, are still not for publication, or even for mention in this very restricted circle.

No sooner was that operation concluded than I received a firm instruction, inevitable in the circumstances but nevertheless of a most painful nature.

I was told to cut off absolutely all overt contact with the Communist movement. I was to cancel all my subscriptions to Marxist newspapers and periodicals, and to sell all the Marxist books in my library and never, never replace them.

Worse still, I must break with all my Communist friends – and in such a way that they would be convinced that I had been a false quantity all along. Indeed, not long afterwards, I met one of my former friends by accident in a public library. He spat at me the question: 'Were you working for the police in Vienna too?' What could I do? I just turned my back and walked away.

However, comrades, I don't want to reduce you all to tears. They say in English: 'time heals all wounds'. And in two or three years, I was able to put the pain right at the back of my mind. But it had two important consequences.

First, I was left utterly dependent, for intimate friendship, on my Soviet contacts – of whom, of course, I had many. Secondly, I began to look towards distant Moscow as my only home.

I have frequently been asked in the Soviet Union whether I am not homesick for my country. My reply has been invariable and has come from the bottom of my heart: 'I am living in my country.'

I would like particularly to stress that fact of the utter dependence of the agent in the field on the Soviet intelligence officer controlling his activity. It places on the latter a very heavy responsibility of deeply humanistic character. If you are not born with it, you must acquire it. This is, in a sense, a cry from me to you, for the sake of all our collaborators still operating in the field and who will operate in the future. It is perhaps the most important thing I have to say to you today.

Well, comrades, I am told that you know the general outline of my career, so I won't deal in any detail with the various episodes in Germany, Spain, France, England and elsewhere. But you should know that, from the very beginning, my first contact – and his two successors – impressed on me the importance of aiming at the British Secret Service as my chief aim in life.

It seemed a pretty hopeless task. Officially the secret service didn't exist; its personnel were a closely guarded secret, as were its headquarters. How to set about it?

Well, the only method I could think of was to drop discreet hints in the right quarters. My connexion with The Times had given me quite a lot of highly placed contacts, with whom I could express dissatisfaction with journalistic work and, after the outbreak of war, express the wish to do something more directly connected with the war effort.

After all, I had some qualifications for intelligence work. I knew German, French and Spanish; I had travelled extensively in Europe; and had acquired first-hand knowledge of the Fascist enemy. To suggest that I could be usefully employed in intelligence was neither suspicious nor implausible. Of course, my real qualification – the fact that I already had some experience with the cloak and dagger – was something I kept very quiet about!

Then suddenly, somehow – to this day I do not know quite how it happened – I got a foot in the door. I was summoned to the War Office and, after a short interview, directed to a London hotel for further conversations. Within a few days I was formally invited to join the secret service – by the secret service itself!

(Now I am afraid that I will try to dispose of a myth. I had always been led to believe that the British Secret Service was a ruthlessly . . .)

The point of these remarks, of course, is that the operation took six years. That is real long-range penetration! And I should add that, but for the war, it might have taken several years longer.

Well, comrades, as I said before, I am not going to take you through the long and complex story of my career in SIS. I would prefer to pick out three issues which caused me some perplexity and lay them before you for your future consideration.

When one of our agents succeeds in penetrating a hostile intelligence service, it is generally assumed that the higher the position he gets, the better it is for us.

Now, of course, there is a lot of truth in that. Officers in high position usually command a broader field than junior officers. Yet, my own experience suggests that seniority brings special problems of its own.

I did in fact achieve fairly rapid promotion. In 1944, I was put in charge of the embryonic counter-espionage section dealing with Soviet and Communist Party activities throughout the world, and a year later became head of the whole counter-intelligence department.

I should explain that SIS were so stretched by the war effort against the Axis that from 1939 onwards, there was no activity directed against the Soviet Union. Only in 1944, when the defeat of the Axis was assured, did they begin to look forward to the next enemy – namely, us.

As soon as I had taken up my new post, I was landed in situations of horrible complexity.

I could not afford to fail all along the line because I should have been sacked. Yet if I achieved too much success, I would damage our own interests.

In general, I would try to drag out decisions, to give me time to consult my Soviet friend; and, if possible, to give him time to consult Moscow. But sometimes decisions had to be taken quickly, within hours. In such cases, I had to use my own judgment.

No doubt, I made mistakes – who does not? I am simply putting the dilemma before you.

I suggest that there is no cut-and-dried solution of the dilemma; each case must be judged on its merits. High position gives you the chance to influence policy decisions, a very important point in its favour. On the other hand, a less conspicuous position has its advantages – a certain anonimity [sic], a tendency to be overlooked when something goes badly wrong.

May I put the question in this form? If you had the choice of recruiting as an agent either a major working in the Pentagon archives or the Chairman of the Joint Chiefs of Staff, which would you choose?

You may think that the answer is obvious. But I am not so sure. So I leave the problem with you. I hope that one of you will have the opportunity of making such a choice one day.

I will now turn to another problem also arising out of my personal experience – the problem of working against two or more hostile services which cooperate with one another.

Now, when I began my early studies of Marxism, the concept which most puzzled me was the concept of the dialectic – largely because it has little place in any British system of philosophy. Yet, the older I get, the more often I see the dialectic working in actual practice – more and more do situations prove to contain the seeds of their own transformation.

I began working in collaboration with the American services a few weeks after the Japanese attack on Pearl Harbour. That collaboration reached its climax in 1949, when I was posted as Chief SIS Liaison officer in Washington.

Now, clearly, both the British and the American services profited greatly by their cooperation. By pooling their information, they increased the total information of each, and facilitated the process of correct interpretation.

But, that also gave rise to a great danger. If we succeeded in penetrating deeply into one service, we automatically achieved considerable penetration of the other.

Thus, I regard the position which I held in Washington as even more advantageous than my earlier post as head of the counter-espionage section in London. The advantage derived solely from the fact that the exchange of information between the British and the Americans was very comprehensive, and there was even a certain amount of collaboration in the matter of operations.

I suggest that this intelligence and operational collaboration has immense significance for our work today.

We are now confronted by the threat of NATO. I have no intention of minimising that threat. Yet the existence of NATO – the good old dialectic at work again! – provides us with great opportunities.

NATO involves collaboration, not just between two countries, but between eleven! Penetrate one, and you get at least some access to them all.

I am not suggesting that all the information available to, say, the Americans is automatically transmitted to all the NATO partners. Quite certainly, it is not. But I have in the last few years seen papers, coming from a source unknown to me, that bear definite British, American and German markings, with more than a suggestion that the papers were available to other members of the alliance.

So I can say to you, like poor Martin Luther King, that I have a dream. It is that one day we, perhaps one of you, will recruit, say, a young Norwegian officer – perhaps even an officer-cadet. Over the years, you will nurse him into Norwegian military intelligence, and then finally into NATO headquarters in Brussels.

It may take you five, even ten years. Wouldn't that long time be well spent?

One final problem arising out of personal experience. As you all know, in the summer of 1951, Maclean and Burgess arrived in the SU, leaving me in serious trouble.

Some mistakes were made – by myself included. But the cardinal mistake was to allow Burgess to go with Maclean. Who made it, I do not know. But (*the unconcealed association of Burgess with Maclean provided the direct link between Maclean and myself*).

What to do?

I had my own emergency escape plan. Should I too bolt for cover, or should I stay and fight it out?

I knew that it was almost certain that my SIS career would be ended. But, as the English say, 'where there is life, there is hope', and I thought that if I survived the storm I might be of some further service, at a later date and in changed conditions. So I decided to stay and fight it out.

You must realise that I enjoyed three great advantages.

Many senior officers of SIS – from the Chief downwards – would be greatly embarrassed if it were proved that I was working for the Soviet Union. They would certainly want to give me the benefit of any doubt.

Second, I knew the SIS and MI5 archives in great detail. I knew the sort of evidence they could bring against me. (*I had recognised myself in several scattered references in the files.*

For instance, Krivitsky had said that the Soviet Intelligence had sent a young British journalist to Spain; Volkov had said that a Soviet agent was

255

working as head of a counter-espionage section in London.) So I had time to prepare my answers.

Third, I knew British security procedures inside out, having been involved in many cases involving German, Italian and Soviet agents. I knew that much of the information in the possession of the security authorities cannot be made the basis of a charge in the courts, as it either cannot be corroborated or comes from sources too delicate to be revealed.

In such cases, the security service interrogate suspects with the object of extracting a confession. And, as soon as they started on me, I knew that the information in their possession was not enough to start a court action against me.

So I knew that, provided I stuck to stout denial of any connexion with the Soviet Intelligence, I would be all right. It was a long battle of nerve and wits, lasting – on and off – for five years.

Then, after an incident in Parliament, I was informed by SIS that they had finally decided in my favour – they actually offered me a job as SIS agent in the Middle East operating under journalistic cover. I accepted.

There is a lesson of general application to be drawn from this.

In my experience, and that of others with whom I have been in contact, there seems to be a general reluctance on the part of our intelligence officers to discuss with agents what they should do in the event of arrest.

No doubt our officers feel that discussion of such problems might undermine the agent's morale. With respect, I suggest that this attitude is wrong. Any agent must at least occasionally consider the possibility of arrest; and if the agent actually asks his controlling officer what to do in the event of arrest, he has already – by definition – considered the possibility.

(*I once met an agent who had been arrested, confessed and was sent to prison. I chanced to meet him when he came out and asked him why he had confessed.*

He told me that he had repeatedly asked his controlling officer what to do in the event of arrest and had simply been told: 'If we do our work properly, the occasion will not arise.' So, when arrested, he thought it didn't matter what he did. So he confessed because it was easier.

Again, many agents may confess in the belief that, if they cooperate, they

*will get a more lenient sentence. What they do not realise – not knowing any
of the limitations placed on Western security services – is that if they do not
confess, they stand a very good chance of getting off altogether.*

So I suggest that you should all consider the following proposition.

*Certainly any agent who asks what to do in case of arrest – and proba-
bly even agents who do not specifically ask – should be given a clear-cut
instruction in the matter.)*

They should be told that on no account should they admit dealings
with Soviet – or any other – intelligence. They should refuse to concede the validity of any evidence brought against them – much of it
may well be faked anyway. They should on no account sign any document implicating themselves.

If all agents followed this procedure resolutely, probably half would
never be brought to trial – let alone convicted.

We must always remember that bourgeois law is designed primarily
to safeguard the possession and acquisition of property. It therefore
involves elaborate safeguards for all sorts of individual skullduggery. It
is up to us to take every opportunity of using bourgeois law, and turning it against itself.

One final point. Any confession involves giving information to
the enemy. It is therefore – by definition – wrong.

Well, as I have said earlier, I went to the Middle East, arriving in
Beirut in 1956. Contact with our service was re-established, and all
went happily along until January, 1963. Then the final blow fell.

An SIS officer came out specially from London to tell me that they
at last had definite evidence that I had worked for Soviet intelligence
up to 1949. They assumed that I had then had a change of heart, so
they offered me a deal. They would not take action against me – provided I told them all I knew.

Some deal!

Only one course of action was possible – escape. And I would like
to thank all the comrades involved from the bottom of my heart, and
to congratulate them on the brilliant efficiency of the operation.

And so, comrades, at last I came home to Moscow.

I regret to say that one of my first actions was to disobey the instructions which I had received in the summer of 1934 – about keeping
away from Marxist literature. I subscribed to Pravda, and began to
replace my lost Marxist library.

I need hardly tell you of the warmth and comradeship that I found here.

There was indeed a period in the late 60s when I felt that I was not being used to the limit of my capacity – I felt a sense of loss. But some years ago business picked up again and I am kept very satisfactorily occupied.

I have no regrets about the past – except for the mistakes I committed in both personal and professional life. I comfort myself with the reflection that a human life passed without mistakes must be a very extraordinary life indeed.

Meanwhile, I think not about the past, but about the future, which, so far as can be seen, will impose on our service duties no less compelling than in the past.

Our founder, Felix Dzerzhinsky, said towards the end of his all-too-short life: Yesli by mne predstoyalo nachat zhizn snova, ya nachal by tak, kak nachal.

I would like to express the same idea in rather different words. If I had a wish to express, I would wish for another forty-three years of active work in the service of the KGB.

So I will extend to you all my best wishes for the success in your important and responsible labours, and I hope to continue playing my small part in any capacity that our leadership may judge useful. Thank you all very much.

3

Should Agents Confess?

*I*t is not clear whether Philby's article on confession (originally untitled and
undated), reproduced below, was requested by his KGB masters or volunteered based on his experience. In any case, he leaves no doubt as to his
own view on the matter. 'Confession is wrong,' he argues, whether the
agent is motivated by ideology or greed – the modern agent's vitamin – especially when one is caught by a Western service. He then explains how one
may take advantage of the evidentiary requirements of the Western legal
system with its insistence on demonstrating guilt beyond a reasonable doubt.
As examples of his views, Philby discusses the cases of atom spies Allan
Nunn May and Klaus Fuchs, suggesting that they would not have been convicted had they remained silent. The article ends without comment on his
own confession to SIS just before his defection in 1963. H.P.

This article supplies answers to certain questions arising from the possibility of an intelligence operative being arrested on a charge of
espionage. It is based on the facts of life in England and the United

States, known to me from personal experience. But the answers may have a wider application to other Western nations, and even to certain third world countries adhering to legal systems based on Western models.

The various questions may be subsumed under two general questions:

[i] If an operative is charged with espionage, should he confess or deny the charge?

[ii] Should our intelligence officers instruct operatives in their conduct under interrogation or arrest:

[a.] if the operative asks;

[b.] even if he does not ask?

I should begin by saying that I never had any doubts in the matter, basing myself on the simplest of logical constructions, the syllogism:

Major premise: Giving information to the enemy is wrong.

Minor premise: Confession is giving information to the enemy.

Conclusion: Therefore confession is wrong.

The trouble with this syllogism is that it applies only to operatives working for ideological reasons. Operatives working for non-ideological reasons, e.g., money, do not regard the opposing counterintelligence services as 'enemies' with any strong moral commitment. On the contrary, they may hope that a full confession will bring lighter punishment, and cooperate accordingly. Furthermore, even the ideological operative may not realize the true strength of the syllogism. On being charged, they may assume that the counterintelligence service know everything, in which case confession would not add to their knowledge and (again) might bring them a lighter sentence.

(*When I joined*) During my work in the counterintelligence section of SIS, (*and started my*) involving close collaboration with MI5 (and with the corresponding services in the US), I became increasingly aware that there is a further consideration to be taken into account and, equally important, that (*this consideration*) it applies [to] all agents alike, ideological and non-ideological. This consideration (*involves*) rests on the fact that it is not sufficient that the counterintelligence services have evidence that convinces them that an individual is guilty of breaches of the Official Secrets Act. In order to prosecute the suspected offender, it must have evidence that will convince a jury that the suspect is in fact guilty 'beyond a reasonable doubt'.

This gives rise to many difficulties. Sometimes the evidence comes from such delicate sources that it cannot be produced in court at all. Sometimes it comes from agents who cannot give evidence in court without jeopardizing their subsequent usefulness, or even endangering them or their associates. On yet other occasions, it may be evidence which is inadmissible at law, e.g., wireless intercepts. Finally there is always the doubt whether the jury will accept the word of a prosecution witness as truthful and accurate. In short, the course of the prosecution is plagued [with] doubts and difficulties. The best possible way of overcoming them is to induce the suspect to confess. This immediately removes the case from legal argument, the security of sources and the unpredictability of juries. And it ensures conviction.

Equally, refusal of the suspect to confess leaves the doubts and difficulties to the prosecution. They may decide not to act at all, if [they] are too delicate or the evidence too (*insubstantial*) unconvincing without independent corroboration. Even if they prosecute, a competent Defence Counsel can raise enough doubts about the credibility of the evidence and witnesses to secure an acquittal. In the worst case, that of a successful prosecution, the authorities will at least have had a very long battle – which is better than giving them victory on a plate.

My answer to the first question is therefore an unhesitating recommendation that no operative should ever, under any circumstances, whatever evidence is laid before him, confess. Provided he denies everything, he stands a chance of never being prosecuted at all, and, even if prosecuted, he stands a chance of acquittal.

I come to the second (*general*) general question: Should one [sic] intelligence officers instruct operatives in their conduct under investigation or arrest?

I know of two cases in which operatives asked their officers this very question, and each of them received an evasive reply. I can quote from memory the exact words of one reply: 'If we do our work properly, the question will not arise.'

Now, I am aware that these evasions were based on psychological considerations concerning morale (*of an operative*). It is not good for operatives to think too much about the possibilities of discovery. But are these psychological considerations valid? I suggest that they are not.

The post-war years have seen a flood of newspaper reports and [coming?] of serious books and spy-fiction, on the subject of espionage and counter-espionage. Any operative who supplies secret information to unauthorized recipients must give occasional thought to the possibility of discovery unless he is totally devoid of imagination. And, of course, if he actually asks, it is obvious that the problem is already on his mind. It is a sensible question, which deserves a sensible answer.

I am also inclined to think that, even if an agent does not ask, he should nevertheless be instructed. Here we are on less well-charted ground, since much must depend on the character of the operative, [and] his relations with our intelligence operative.

Allan Nun MAY

In September, 1945, Igor GOUZENKO, a cypher clerk in [the] office of the Soviet Military Attaché in Ottawa, defected to the Canadians. To establish his bona fides and prove his right to asylum, he took with him a number of confidential and secret documents. Among them were two telegrams of recent date: one from Ottawa to Moscow, another from Moscow to Ottawa.

The first telegram informed Moscow that a certain ALEK was being transferred from Canada to England, and gave details of a proposed rendezvous in London. The second telegram, from Moscow to Ottawa, rejected the suggested rendezvous and proposed another, to take place in a public-house near the British Museum at a specific time after dark, at a date soon after ALEK's scheduled arrival in England.

According to a statement made by GOUZENKO to the Royal Canadian Mounted Police (Security Division), ALEK was a pseudonym for Allan Nunn MAY, a British physicist working at the nuclear research centre at Chalk River, Ontario.

This information was telegraphed by the RCMP, through British Security Coordination, New York, to London (SIS). As head of R5, the SIS section responsible for anti-Soviet and anti-Communist activity, I was responsible for handling the information. As MAY was of British nationality, my first duty was to pass the news to Roger HOLLIS, my opposite number in M.I.5.

I telephoned the essential details to HOLLIS, and made an appointment with him for later in the morning. Before I arrived, HOLLIS had already checked (with HARWELL, the British nuclear research headquarters?) that MAY had indeed been transferred from Canada to England. To the best of my recollection, he was already on the high seas.

It seemed obvious to HOLLIS and myself that GOUZENKO was speaking the truth. There was no plausible reason why he should have equated ALEK with MAY unless he was a spy. It seemed unlikely that a Soviet cypher clerk would have even heard of MAY unless he had had some connection with the Soviet Embassy. The similarity between his pseudonym, ALEK, and MAY's first name, ALLAN, was suggestive. The fact that MAY had been transferred to England from Canada squared with the facts in the telegram.

HOLLIS then invited the head of the legal section to join our conference. The latter agreed that the information looked conclusive, but firmly maintained that it was not sufficient to support legal action. A successful legal action would have to prove:

a. the telegrams were genuine. (GOUZENKO had access to Embassy stationery, type-writers and stamps, seals, etc., and [could] have concocted the telegram himself. His object? To enhance the cash value of his defection.)

b. that ALEK was in fact MAY. (The fact of his transfer, though suggestive, was by no means conclusive. GOUZENKO could have learnt of his impending move and used it to fabricate evidence.)

In short, the whole case would rest on the unsupported evidence of GOUZENKO. Supposing, said the legal advisor, MAY denied the allegations, which would the jury believe: a distinguished British physicist or a Soviet cypher clerk of dubious origin? He was certain that the Director of Public Prosecution would refuse to act solely on the evidence available.

It was therefore necessary to obtain more evidence. The first obvious step was to cover the rendezvous in the hope of catching MAY red-handed with his Soviet contact. That same afternoon, HOLLIS and I had a further meeting, this time attended by Leonard BURT. BURT was a professional CID officer, seconded to MI5, where his specialisations were (a) liaison with Scotland Yard, and (b) interrogation of suspects. It was agreed that BURT should arrange with CID for their coverage, by plain-clothesmen, of the public-house on the date given for the rendezvous. MAY himself was also to be placed under full-time surveillance, and his telephone tapped. (Needless to say, I took the first opportunity of informing my Soviet contact, but cannot remember [the] exact time-lag involved.)

The day of the rendezvous arrived. BURT's plain-clothesmen took up position. Nothing happened. No Soviet contact appeared; MAY spent all day in his flat, apparently, according to the telephone record, talking to himself. No words were distinguishable. The non-appearance of the Soviet contact was understandable; my warning had been delivered. But why did MAY not appear? Had he decided to give up work? Had we been able to warn him in spite of the surveillance? I don't know.

The British now were in an awkward position. MAY's failure to keep the appointment could be interpreted to mean that GOUZENKO's information was spurious; or that he had made a genuine mistake. After another round of talks, it was decided that BURT should make a direct approach to MAY in order to attempt to force a confession. On a given day, BURT went to MAY's flat.

I revisited HOLLIS's office to hear BURT's report. The first attempt was a failure; MAY had denied all allegations. But BURT was an experienced and shrewd operator. He said that he would give MAY twenty-four hours 'to stew' and return to the attack the next day.

At the second attempt, BURT was successful. MAY had signed a confession. It was an extremely limited confession, saying merely that he had passed certain (unspecified) information to a Soviet contact (unnamed) and had also supplied a small amount of enriched uranium 235. But it was enough for prosecution.

There was yet one more snag for the British. In allowing the confession, BURT had not given the statutory warning legally required in all police investigations, viz. 'Anything you say will be taken down, and may be used in evidence against you.' Therefore, a matter of strict legal technicality, MAY's confession had been illegally attested and was therefore inadmissible as evidence in a court of law. A strong Defence lawyer might have succeeded in having the proceedings quashed on this technicality. Unhappily, MAY did not have the means to pay for a strong Defence. His solicitor acted for him at his trial, which I attended together with HOLLIS and BURT. The solicitor actually mentioned 'the apparently irregular manner' in which the confession had been attested. 'But', he immediately added, 'I do not propose to labour this point.' As he said this, I saw BURT's face; he was grinning happily. MAY's last possible line of Defence had been surrendered without a fight.

Now, let us suppose that MAY had denied the allegations. I have already indicated that there would probably have been no prosecution. But, to clarify the legal position, let us also suppose that the authorities did decide to prosecute. How would the case have gone?

The prosecution, having charged MAY with espionage and having been met with a denial, would have had to introduce as evidence two telegrams exchanged between Ottawa and Moscow. They would also have had to produce GOUZENKO in person as a witness. GOUZENKO would have sworn on oath: (a) that the telegrams were in fact telegrams exchanged between Ottawa and Moscow, and (2), that the ALEK of the telegrams was in fact MAY. ALEK would have denied, on oath, that he had any knowledge of the affair.

There is no doubt that a competent Defence Counsel would have had little difficulty in destroying the prosecution's case. (As British law, the prosecution must prove the case 'beyond a reasonable doubt'.) The Defence would have emphasized that GOUZENKO had double-crossed his own side; his character was therefore suspect. Knowing Soviet procedures, he could have faked the telegrams to boost his own standing with the Canadian authorities. Even if the telegrams were genuine, GOUZENKO could have decided unilaterally to equate ALEK with ALLAN; or he could have been misinformed; or he could have made a genuine mistake. In short, the whole prosecution case was beset by abundant cause for doubt.

The only possibility for success in (*withstanding the prosecution's case*) obtaining a jury's verdict of guilty would have been offered in one or both of two events: (a) that MAY made a very bad impression on the jury; (b) that the Defence Counsel bungled his presentation of the defence.

In view of the above conclusion, I have no doubt that the M.I.5 legal advisor was correct in saying that the Director of Public Prosecutions would have refused to act.

KLAUS FUCHS (1949–50)

If the MAY case had presented legal difficulties for the British authorities, the case of FUCHS presented two greater ones, from the viewpoint of both law and intelligence procedures.

Here there were no Soviet telegrams; there were no witnesses to give evidence on oath. In this case, the only evidence consisted of the interpretation put on certain telegrams allegedly between New York and Moscow between mid 1944 and mid 1945. These telegrams had been intercepted and deciphered by appropriate Anglo-American services. There were comparatively few in number. (*some were faultily intercepted and were therefore partially unreadable; some, even if correctly interpreted, were partially indecipherable with the knowledge existing at the time.*) Of those few, some were partially unreadable, owing to faulty interception or inadequate cryptographic knowledge.

Nevertheless, the telegrams showed that the Soviet services in New York had been receiving information from a source in the nuclear research station at LOS ALAMOS. Minute comparison of the contents of the telegram with the traceable movements of LOS ALAMOS personnel led to the virtual certainty that the source had been FUCHS. This conclusion was the result of about a year of research and analysis, and was conducted on a generally negative basis: by eliminating all those who did not fit the evidence of the telegrams, leaving [FUCHS] as the only possible suspect.

(*The first legal difficulty*) Now, this position presented an insurmountable legal difficulty. Intercepted (*telegrams*) wireless signals are not, on their own, admissible as evidence in a British court of law: (a) there are too many possibilities of error, such as faulty interception, cryptographic mistakes, etc; (2) there is no proof that they were sent by the organization to which the intelligence community attributed them. Confirmation would have been required from a Soviet official prepared to state on oath that the (*telegrams were from*) intercepts corresponded to telegrams actually sent by the M.G.B. and that they applied to FUCHS. In this case there was no such official, and the intercepts were therefore inadmissible as evidence. (*In any*) (Even if there had been such an official, the case would have presented the same difficulties as that of GOUZENKO: the unsupported word of a Soviet defector against a distinguished scientist.)

That was the legal difficulty. There was also an insurmountable obstacle from the point of view of intelligence procedures. Wireless interception has the highest of all security classifications in the UK and the USA. It is the agreed policy of all UK and US security organizations that (*intercepts are*) the fact of interception, let alone an actual intercept, are never revealed to unauthorised persons. (Of course, there have been numerous leaks, since hundreds of people engaged in wartime interception & cryptography returned to civilian life. But the principle still holds good. In general, the authorities are reluctant to prosecute those guilty of leakage, for fear of attracting further public attention to the issue.) Therefore, even if the intercept had been legally admissible as evidence, it is quite certain that SIS and MI5 would have vetoed their use.

It may be said that the case would have been heard *in camera*. But that means only excluding the public, the press, & a few minor court officials. True. (*But*) Even when sitting *in camera* the court must be attended by an unacceptable number of people. There is the judge and the clerk of the court; the prosecutor (*his assistant*) and the Defence Counsel (*and*) with their assistants; twelve members of the jury; *and* the accused himself. It would be quite impossible to guarantee lasting secrecy from such a mixed gathering. The accused alone, if (*imprisoned*) convicted and imprisoned, could spread the information among literally hundreds of fellow prisoners who would return, after serving their time, to society. Therefore, even a hearing *in camera* would have been ruled out.

As soon as suspicions against FUCHS crystallized (he was working at the time at HARWELL), MI5 put him under surveillance. Nothing came of it. Had he broken off contact? Had he means of contact which surveillance could not uncover? For fear of the latter eventuality, MI5 soon decided that prolonged, possibly unproductive, surveillance was too risky, since FUCHS might still be passing vital information. They decided to try to force a confession from him – and succeeded.

As in the case of MAY, the prosecution was based solely on his own confession. Without it, no action could have been taken.

As an additional note to the FUCHS case, I should add that evidence obtained from the same source was a few months later to show that MACLEAN also had contact with us. Again, & for the same reasons, no prosecution could have been brought without a confession, and it was decided to interrogate him on May 28, 1951. I need not enlarge on this case, since MACLEAN left England on May 25.

Part 3

A Martyr to Dogma

by Mikhail Lyubimov
Translated by Geoffrey Elliott

*R*etired KGB Colonel Mikhail Petrovich Lyubimov, now a successful Moscow author, was serving in the KGB Foreign Intelligence Directorate in Moscow when he met Kim Philby in 1975. The initiative for the meeting came from his own Third Department that was responsible for operations in the United Kingdom, Australia, New Zealand and Scandinavia. In the broad sense it was part of the on-going KGB efforts to improve relationships with defectors from the West then in Russia, thereby making the Soviet Union more attractive to potential defectors. Kim Philby was to be the exemplar and Colonel Lyubimov was to work with him.

One outcome of their association was a series of safe-house seminars aimed at providing young KGB officers with insights into life in Britain and other English-speaking countries before being assigned there. The article that follows tells the story of how the course developed and the friendship that evolved between the KGB Anglophile and the retired KGB agent. Lyubimov was assigned once again overseas. Lyubimov includes a startling account of how My Silent War came to be published in the West and he explains why its publication in the Soviet Union was delayed until 1980. In the process, he gives his personal assessment of Philby, the incipient Soviet dissident, who in the end remained an Englishman to the core, never quite coming to grips with Soviet reality. H.P.

'What is to be done?', the famous Lenin question was the first that leaped to my mind that day in 1974 when I was appointed Deputy Chief of our Anglo-Scandinavian Department to be tasked with breathing some semblance of a spark into the cold ashes of the London Residency, which had been destroyed in 1971 when 105 Soviet diplomats were expelled.

The Residency had a glorious past. Like a banquet table laden with caviar, sturgeon and bottles of vodka, it was overflowing with valuable agents, who had, at various times, permeated every pore of the British Establishment.

What, I wondered, was the secret of the little gold key which had opened the door to such spectacular successes? It was now up to me to be the moving spirit, the Moscow organiser of espionage against Britain.

Could I glean anything from talking to the Englishmen who were now living in Moscow and who might be able to offer wise counsel, based on practical experience? My career had given me the tools to find out.

As a self-important schoolboy, I used to read (or used to create the impression I read) Shakespeare in the original English, complete with the Glossary. Later, at the Moscow Institute of International Relations – the elite blacksmiths' shop where the careers of future leaders of the diplomatic and intelligence services were forged – we used to dissect the 'embodiment of capitalist evil' in the minutest detail. The Institute's holdings of non-Communist literature were tucked away on special shelves in the Library (books with any markedly anti-Soviet flavour were banished completely), and if the few Western newspapers to which the Institute subscribed (such as *The Times*) ever carried reports on Soviet espionage, these were diligently snipped out by the censor's scissors. Until Stalin's death in 1953, students had to get special permission even to read the Communist *Daily Worker*. The Institute presented Britain to its students in a series of heart-rending vignettes of poverty, a country lorded over by terrible men like Charlotte Brontë's Mr Rochester, the shameless deceiver of Jane Eyre.

Strange as it may sound, the first I heard about Soviet espionage, and also about Philby, was in 1958, when I was posted to Finland for the Ministry of Foreign Affairs. Once there, I quickly realised that diplomatic work was about as bland and boring as chicken broth. As a militant Bolshevik, I was far more attracted to the concept of secret work aimed at the overthrow of capitalism. I began to work so actively with our intelligence people that they invited me to join them, and by 1959 I found myself in the Intelligence Training School near Moscow. There I discovered an amazing library of English-language books on Soviet espionage, from which I reckon I got far more value than I ever did from the tedious, soporific lectures of the Service's old-timers.

I trained first for Finland, but out of the blue – as always happened in our planning-based state – I was switched to the British target. I can only think that this was because, at twenty-six, I looked a bit like Byron might have if he had been to the barber's for a short back and sides. Perhaps of more relevance, I did quite a bit of bookshop browsing (with side trips to restaurants thrown in) with my Section Head, Evgeny Tarabin, and it was he who pushed me into the front line of 'the battle against capitalism' by steering me away from the musty ex-province of the Russian Empire that was Finland towards decadent England.

I arrived ready for action in the island home of what Heine described as 'The Carthaginians of the North Sea' in 1961 and plunged off the deep end into my espionage work. I kept at it until I was declared persona non grata in 1964. Ironically, although I fought staunchly against the Conservatives, it was the newly elected Labour Government who kicked me out, adding insult to injury.

It is interesting that even after Kim fled Beirut in 1963, neither he nor the 'Five' were ever mentioned in general conversation in the Third Section of the KGB's First Chief Directorate, on whose staff I had been since 1959. The KGB's obsession with secrecy, the principles of 'need to know' (or, as we like to say in Russia, 'The cobbler should stick to his last'), were so overwhelming that even asking personal questions was reckoned to be out of order.

In 1967, the Soviet 'man in the street' learned from an article in *Izvestiya*, 'Hello, Comrade Philby', that there still existed in good old England men of honour who loathed man's inhumanity to man, dirty bourgeois morality and bogus democracy. It was for these profound reasons of principle – at least according to *Izvestiya* – that Kim had been driven to seek political asylum in the USSR.

But to go back to 1975. How could I get the phoenix to rise from the ashes? With the agreement of my senior colleagues, I began a series of meetings with our burnt-out cases. Donald Maclean and George Blake had both immersed themselves in academic research and had neither the time, nor, in my view, the inclination, to get involved in an issue as unpromising as this was likely to prove.

The only British agent who hadn't embarked on a thesis, and who wasn't daydreaming about becoming an Academician, was Kim Philby. I was introduced to him on 1 January 1975 at a birthday party for him in a private room at the very upmarket Prague restaurant.

Even now, my mouth waters when I think of the goodies on offer at the lunch. The guests were less appealing. Most were ex-Party bigwigs of the kind who are constantly being drafted in to 'beef-up' the upper echelons of the KGB. They spoke no English, so could do little more than proffer lengthy, banal toasts in poor Russian to Kim's health, his professional successes and the like. What 'profession', one might well have asked? Even I knew that up to that point he had been employed only sporadically in the 'active measures' area; i.e. for drafting phoney letters in English or larding NATO secret documents we had purloined with phrases which would reinforce our use of them to cast NATO in the worst possible light and to stir up anti-American sentiment.

When I read in the Western press from time to time how Philby's unseen hand lay behind most Soviet intelligence operations against the UK, that he had Andropov's ear, that he was one of his advisers, etc., I had to laugh. Sadly, Philby was a run-of-the mill, semi-unemployed pensioner, who was dying to get stuck into some real work and passed his days hoping against hope that at long last the KGB would involve him in something serious.

There were toasts, more toasts, and still more toasts. Even I delivered a few dinner-table platitudes, albeit in English, something which seemed to leave my bosses – by now making heavy inroads into the booze – rather cold. No doubt they felt a bit let-down, having to listen to their junior officer's painstaking Oxford aspirates. It was heavy going, all the more since Kim, a true Englishman who felt learning foreign languages rather beneath him, said less and less as time went on, simply standing up with the rest of us for each toast, clinking glasses and smiling politely. Those around us were of course men of a far lesser intellectual calibre than those with whom it had been Kim's good fortune to work in the past. 'Some are far distant, some are dead,

as Sadi sang in years gone by . . .' There had been a time when he had
worked alongside such exceptional Comintern officers as Arnold
Deutsch of the OGPU/NKVD, who had died in the war, and
Theodore Mally, the Hungarian ex-priest whom he had worked with
in the 1930s and who was stupid enough to return to Moscow, where
he was swiftly shot. Or General Alexander Orlov, who proved rather
more perspicacious than Maly and who escaped to the USA, where he
remained until his death in 1973 without ever naming Philby or other
agents whose identities he knew.

While I was still a trainee, I had taken a British Young Communist
to see the well-known Soviet columnist Ernest Genri (S. Rostovsky).
The latter lived on the outskirts of Moscow, in a tiny book-lined room
in a three-roomed communal flat, one family per room. I did not know
at the time that Genri had been connected to Philby, but I was struck
by his utter indifference to his surroundings or the way he lived. How
right Marx was when he remarked, 'The more you have, the less you
exist.' At least that's what I thought then as a romantic Bolshevik.

In today's era of savage neo-Russian capitalism, it strikes me again
that old man Karl may have got that right!

It has always surprised me when the Western press accuses Philby of
treachery. Kim Philby was a spy, and thus liable to punishment under
English Law. But whom did he betray? How is he different from other
British Communists who sought to follow the logic of their beliefs? If,
of course, you take the position that all Communists are traitors, then
Philby too is a traitor. The word can be applied to the CIA's Aldrich
Ames, or the Admiralty clerk John Vassall, both of whom switched
sides. But Philby's situation was totally different. He never switched
anything; he was a Communist in his heart of hearts from the very
beginning. He penetrated SIS on orders from Soviet intelligence.

Did the Bolsheviks really have a country they could call the
Fatherland? Proletarians have no fatherland, they said. After all, Lenin
collaborated with the Germans for the sake of the Russian Revolution
and already in 1918 had no scruples to instigate German workers
against the Kaiser.

It always annoyed Philby, incidentally, when people referred to him
as 'a double agent'. 'How stupid these journalists are,' he would
exclaim. 'All my life I've worked for only one intelligence service – the
Soviet service!'

The only way to make sense of Philby is in the context of the 1930s: a world crisis, the menace of Fascism, Chamberlain's Munich policy, lines of unemployed at soup kitchens, bankrupt businessmen committing suicide. Didn't geniuses like H. G. Wells and George Bernard Shaw feel some sympathy (albeit with reservations) for the 'country of workers and peasants'? So did distinguished authors like André Gide and André Malraux. Well-known wordsmiths such as Leon Feuchtwanger and Henri Barbusse sang Stalin's praises. How many great scientists like Nils Bohr or Robert Oppenheimer regarded the Soviets in a rather favourable light?

The list of those that fell in, and then out of, love with Communism is long – virtually endless and sad. It includes George Orwell, Arthur Koestler and even Dennis Healey (who, in the dim and distant past, was a Young Communist), and one of the Labour leaders, Dick Crossman.

Intellectuals, God bless them, are forever being seduced by the good intentions with which the road to Hell is paved. But even the renowned British spy Sidney Reilly wrote heatedly in a personal letter to his colleague and friend Robert Bruce Lockhart, a former representative of the British Government in Russia: 'I reckon that as long as this system offers practical and constructive ideas for greater social fairness, it must gradually win over the whole world.'

The Cold War is over. It is time to discard its stupid stereotypes, which portrayed the people on one side of the barricade as schizophrenics, homosexuals, alcoholics, chiselers and scoundrels, and their opponents as pure saints, committed to moral values. This applies, by the way, as much to the KGB as to the Western services.

If we don't put this behind us, we shall never be able to make sense of the greatest confrontation of the twentieth century: the war between two ideological systems, a war which brought so many misfortunes.

I do not go so far as to propose replacing Nelson's statue in Trafalgar Square with an effigy of Philby. I am simply urging that it is time to rise above the propaganda. Philby has been depicted as a roué (though he was far from being a Casanova, and even clean-living members of the Tory Party have been known, as he did with Melinda Maclean, to seduce their friends' wives), as an alcoholic (there were indeed years when that was true), and as a villain (did he not betray Volkov and many other agents?) . . . But that was precisely what his job was! An intelligence service is not a Charity.

Someone recently put forward a theory that Kim's spying was hereditary; after all, they pointed out, his father had also been a spy. This is a magnificent discovery, and the officers of the CIA and MI6 should be lined up immediately for blood tests.

Even the Soviet poet Voznesensky, very far removed from the world of spydom, portrayed him in a poem called *Kim Philby's Return*. 'Kim', he wrote, evidently visualising Philby as Adam after he had taken a bite of the famous apple, 'rides towards Eve like a Kamikadze . . .'

The Nobel Prize winner Joseph Brodsky wrote a huge essay on Philby, an essay so convoluted you would need the finest minds in the British and Russian codebreaking services to crack its meaning.

It is of interest that there were different views inside the KGB on Philby and The Five. In the first place, many career intelligence officers (and not only in the KGB) like to think of themselves as 'the salt of the earth', and they consider the agents who work for them as second-raters, traitors to their country (a view they naturally keep to themselves). This leads to condescension, if not lurking suspicion.

Secondly, Philby's persona made it difficult to fit him into the idealised image of a positive Chekist hero. He did not have working-class or peasant roots, but was the son of a scientist from an upper middle-class family, a Cambridge graduate, and a bosom pal of all those Comintern types whom Stalin had so successfully put up against the wall and shot. In and around the Communist Party Central Committee I very often heard people say, 'Don't trust the Western Communists. They are not like us.' And Philby too was 'not one of us'. The differences were only sharpened by his fondness for Scotch, rare steaks and those exotic spices he had learned to love in India. He wasn't a crack shot. He had never made a parachute jump. He hadn't the slightest interest in anything but spectator sports, and he had never learned karate. Wimps like that were just not KGB material!

Last, but by no means least, Philby never quite managed to smother that damnable, quintessentially English love of independence. He did his best to keep it hidden, to be careful what he said, but it was still there behind the façade of his politeness, and it was something that simply did not fit in the framework of a totalitarian system. He even indulged in a little joke in English when he made the first major speech of his life at the Soviet Intelligence Centre in Yasenevo in 1977 [see pp. 244–58].

He had, he said, been inside the HQ's of almost all the world's major intelligence services. At long last he had now managed to penetrate another one. There was a terrible silence. The brighter sparks in the audience permitted themselves a discreet private smile, but the humourless blockheads whispered angrily. After an artistic pause, deft as always, Philby saved the day by adding that formerly he was surrounded by wolves, but now he was in the company of friends. There was wild applause.

In 1948, Madame Modrzhinskaya, then head of the MGB British Department, who later enjoyed considerable success as a member of the Academy of Sciences, wrote a memorandum analysing Philby and his Cambridge colleagues, which I came across while leafing through his case file in the secret archives. After a meticulous, if biased, analysis, she delivered the verdict that all five were no more than British plants, deception agents and provocateurs. It is true that the then ruling Politburo member, Lavrenty Beria, who was responsible for security matters, declined for some unknown reason to give the green light for the case to be pursued. We remained in contact with our agents and, unlike the glorious 1930s, no hitmen were dispatched to Britain to 'wipe the traitors off the face of the Earth'.

But Modrzhinskaya's view persisted. Indeed I remember, even as recently as the Perestroika years, I was strolling – like Faust with Mephistopheles – along the tree-lined paths of a Moscow park with General Leonid Raikhman, former Deputy Head of Counter-Intelligence. Raikhman, who had spent time in jail under both Stalin and Khrushchev, and who was an old chum of my Chekist father, was always wary about having a conversation inside a building. He told me flat out: 'Philby and that whole crew – it was all a fiendishly clever plant by British intelligence. I'll tell you why I think so. It's because most of the wartime intelligence they provided turned out to be unreliable.' (Based on my own practical experience, I might add here that, by and large, a lot of the information reaching an intelligence service is either not secret, or does not match the real facts.)

I pressed him. 'Why? Is that really why you think so?'

Raikhman replied, 'You obviously don't realise what the (British Secret) Intelligence Service is like. They are truly bent. Amazingly skilled at double-dealing. Past masters at playing the long game.'

This mythical portrait of SIS is just as exaggerated as that of the omnipotent KGB. It is nonetheless a fact that the British Service has always been regarded in Russia as its most dangerous adversary.

Before the Revolution, it fought against a Russia it saw as poised to meddle in India, Afghanistan, Turkey and the countries in its sphere of influence. In 1918, there was a plot – or, more accurately, a link – between the British envoy Robert Bruce Lockhart and the Social Revolutionary Boris Savinkov, which led to the anti-Bolshevik rebellion in Yaroslavl and a plan to arrest Lenin and co. The British worked closely with the White Guards, supplied them with arms and ammunition, and even sent their own forces to Russia.

Despite Stalin's twists and turns, Hitler did not manage to invade the British Isles but attacked the USSR instead in 1941 – another triumph for British diplomacy and intelligence. What about the war itself? The delay in opening the Second Front? How can you even begin to compare the British losses with those suffered by the Russians?

Devilishy cunning, these British, with an amazing knack for getting others to do their dirty work for them.

Even today, there are those who still believe in this 'super-capacity' of British intelligence. V. Trubnikov, the present Head of the SVR, quite recently stated in public that he thought the most powerful intelligence service (naturally, after the Russian) was the British.

It is therefore hardly surprising that in their dealings with their British agents, the KGB were always particularly suspicious, perhaps not without some justification.

As the years passed, Kim's views clearly evolved from the 1930s. It was relatively easy for him to justify the bloodshed of the Civil War in Russia as the price that had to be paid for revolution. But Stalin's purges in the late 1930s left him with a choice. Philby himself wrote that to renounce the cause, as Malcolm Muggeridge and Arthur Koestler had done, was totally alien to his nature. But I suspect the reasons are more deeply hidden.

First, as Philby saw it on the moral scale of things, the Spanish Civil War and the Nazi threat outweighed the Stalinist purges.

Second, in marked contrast to the politicians and the intellectuals, Philby was already up to his ears in espionage. He understood all too clearly that to break with Soviet intelligence, and retrace his steps, would lead either to a British jail, or to a bullet in the head from a Cheka hitman – the fate of Soviet agents G. Agabekov and Ignace Reiss among others.

All his life Philby walked a tightrope. In 1951, he had been suspected of being the Third Man, who had tipped off Burgess and Maclean. The extraordinary stress he suffered, the scandal, being fired from MI6. And yet, at the time, he preferred to move no further than Beirut, rather than to his 'Second Homeland'; life in that particular paradise seems to have held few attractions for him.

But en route to Moscow in January 1963, still glowing from the whisky in Beirut's Normandie Bar, he possibly had no idea of the grim hands that would be laying out the welcome mat for him.

It is an enormous problem for any intelligence service to have to resettle a burned-out agent forced to seek refuge in a foreign country.

Hardly surprising, therefore, that so few defectors manage to find their feet. Most have problems adjusting, drink too much, lose interest in life and yearn for home. Philby was given a hero's welcome. After being allowed to rest and recover (having vast facilities at its disposal in every resort in the country, the KGB rose splendidly to the occasion), it was time for debriefing. Kim often complained to me that this had been the most idiotic period of his life. What more could he tell them? He had long since passed over to his handlers every scrap of significant intelligence that came his way. To go over it again was an exercise in futility. He understood better than most that whatever he told them now was valueless and would simply end up in the wastepaper basket (as indeed it did).

Philby had anticipated that he would immediately be brought into the operations being run against the USA and Great Britain. He was full of energy and at that stage was still very much in touch with current affairs. He told me he had hoped to be given his own office, to work regular hours, and to take part in meetings as an equal member of the team. *Sancta simplicitas!* How naive, especially coming from a professional intelligence officer. One has to wonder whether any country in the world would permit defectors access to agents' files and to be 100 per cent involved in operational matters.

Philby could not grasp that he was no longer a valued agent, but a problem, especially given the KGB's obsession with secrecy. This dictates that they have to keep an agent under very tight control. His flat and telephones are bugged, in some cases he is tailed, and a meticulous log kept of every single contact. 'Trust, but verify', as a Russian proverb runs.

The possibility that Philby was a British plant could not be excluded. Short of that, no one could predict whether he might do something stupid. The KGB still had painful memories of a drink-sodden Guy Burgess buttonholing British visitors to Moscow to boast about his exploits.

Until the day he died, the KGB lived in terror that Philby would one day go too far in talking to the British press, or, God help us, would suddenly announce that he wanted to return to Britain; what a blow that would have been to Soviet prestige. All Kim's correspondence was constantly monitored, and if any hints of possible 'negative' acts were spotted, they were immediately reported to the most senior levels. I ought to note that in actual fact the KGB never had the slightest problem with Philby on the secrecy front; he was a man of discipline, steeped in tradecraft, and he understood the rules of the game. He went like clockwork to the main Post Office to pick up *The Times* and other British papers, and made no contacts with foreigners without the knowledge of the KGB. In a nutshell, he tried very hard to obey his orders.

But doing so used to drive him crazy! When he talked about the veil of secrecy in which he had been wrapped in those early Moscow years, his stutter became more noticeable, and his eyes burned with rage.

In explaining to Kim the necessity to isolate him, the KGB naturally sugar-coated the pill. It was concern for his safety, they declared; the perfidious and vengeful British intelligence service might make an attempt on his life, or try to spirit him out of the country. Why not indeed?

But enough of the past, 1975 again. Soon after his birthday lunch, I met Kim at the Aragvi restaurant – one of his favourites – whose authentic Georgian cuisine was unrivalled.

It was clear to me from the beginning that it was of course totally unrealistic to think of involving Philby on a regular basis for analysing specific agent operations, though his views on particular operational issues would be worth having. In fact, however, issues falling under that heading were few and far between.

Philby's counsel on restoring the Residency to its former glory was not particularly original: finding reliable recruiters to target civil servants; stepping up operations against the British around the world, especially in Third countries where people tended to drop their guard and where surveillance was lax; employing local residents working in British Embassies; and finally cultivating young people (as with Philby himself) who could be fed into the higher levels of the Establishment. Perhaps he thought we hadn't considered all those things ourselves when drawing up our own strategic plans.

We nevertheless used some of Kim's ideas to validate our own proposals. In presenting them to Kryuchkov, we would sound far more convincing if we were in a position to say we had consulted Philby. One example was when we were authorised to organise operations against Britain in the same way as against our main enemy, the USA, i.e. on a global scale. Directives on British-targeted tasks winged their way to Residencies in Africa and Asia. We then took the Residencies' own plans to formulate a global strategy for undermining the UK. An innovation on this scale was a 'first' in the history of our service.

In reality, 'The mountain has brought forth a mouse', as Horace wrote long before the Cold War. But at least we were able to create the impression that we had stepped up our operations against Britain. This pleased Kryuchkov and especially pleased me.

Soon after our first meeting, I visited the Philbys' apartment in Trekhprudny Lane, where I met Rufina. I was enchanted by her intelligence and tactfulness – qualities not much in evidence among the wives of our KGB colleagues. The apartment itself was also unusual by KGB standards. All too often the apartments in which our people lived reminded you of a furniture store: a wall unit, armchairs, not a book or picture to be seen, parquet-strip floors, pine-panelled walls along the corridor and, of course, the crowning glory, a garishly tiled loo and bathroom combined.

Upon visiting the Philbys' flat, I found myself in an old Moscow building with a quiet courtyard. It was clear that the furniture had been chosen with taste. His old bookcases were stuffed to overflowing with books. Even though I prided myself on being well read, there were many authors of whom I had never heard. Some were attractively bound in morocco – they were the sort of books which, at the turn of the century, if you admitted you had not read them, it would have been as grave a faux-pas as picking up the wrong knife at dinner to cut your fish!

Macauley, Boswell on Johnson, Gibbon, Thomas Carlyle, Renan, Herodotus, Plutarch and Tacitus were there, along with long-forgotten nineteenth-century novelists like Trollope, Kingsley and Hope. Among Russian authors, Tolstoy and Dostoyevsky were represented, but there were none of the Soviet 'classics'. Philby tend to be sniffy about contemporary authors. It is true, though, that he gave his friend and former colleague Graham Greene high marks.

I had naturally brought with me a bottle of good Scotch. Rufina laid on for us a splendid assortment of hors d'oeuvres and Kim turned out to be a dab hand at cooking various dishes with spices I had never heard of. We discussed – in English – a range of top-secret topics, but I think that even if Rufina had been a British spy, she would have had a hard time figuring out what we were talking about, since we were using so much operational slang.

I became a frequent visitor. I don't now remember after which particular bottle of Scotch it was that the Trekhprudny apartment became the birthplace of our idea to set up what we jokingly called the 'courses for illiterates', for young spies who were to be posted to Britain. It is hard to describe Philby's delight when he realised he now had something to get his teeth into. He later gave me a photograph of himself inscribed 'To Michael Petrovich, inspirer of a new course'. I was now on a par with Franklin Delano Roosevelt [who inspired the New Deal]! It all sounded quite straightforward. Young men with inquiring minds would gather at a safe-house, wearing either tweed jackets or pinstriped suits, with a glimpse of an old Etonian tie. There would be a few measly snacks on the sideboard in the English style, and just a finger of whisky, a relaxed atmosphere, and the bluish haze of smoke from the cigars that the young lions would soon be rolling expertly between finger and thumb like true aficionados at the Oxford & Cambridge or the Army & Navy Clubs!

Things did eventually develop along these lines, but not straightaway. As readers now know, Kim was being 'run' by the Counter-Intelligence Directorate, then headed by the young and upwardly mobile General Kalugin.

When I began to review the idea at the level of Philby's case officers, and went as far as to suggest that the Directorate should send a
couple of its own officers on the course, I ran straight into a brick wall.
What about secrecy and our security, they demanded? Why put officers
at risk; Philby would know their faces, and there could be no guarantee that he would not leave the country one day. And as a matter of
general principle, was it right to bring a group of spies together under
one roof?

Fortunately, I knew Kalugin quite well and brought him into the
discussion. It was soon all straightened out. A memorandum was
drafted and we secured the agreement of Kryuchkov, who reported this
'great initiative' to Andropov himself. Everyone was happy.

I felt I ought to attend the first few sessions myself (to make sure the
young chaps did not drink too much and start pestering Kim with
stupid questions) and did so. But everything went fine. The chaps, and
more important Kim himself, were satisfied. A new course was set in
train.

I knew Kim well by the time the Russian edition of his book My
Silent War was finally due to see the light of day in 1980. The book's
genesis is an amazing story.

From 1963 on, several Western houses made offers to publish
Philby's memoirs. The idea struck the KGB like a bolt from the blue;
it was totally unprecedented. No one had ever written a word about
the peacetime operations of our intelligence service. There was no way
Kim would have been given permission to write, had not the young
lions at the KGB (they did exist) decide to convert the idea into an
'active measure'! Philby was given carte blanche (subject to the KGB's
right to censor what he eventually produced, but he had more than
enough self-censorship skills anyway). It was however put to him that,
without stretching the truth too far, he might delicately play up in his
narrative any instances where there had been differences between the
CIA and the SIS, and also inside the SIS (these differences always
existed), so as to pour a little fuel on the flames in the noble cause of
undermining the hostile services. Andropov had no difficulty getting
the agreement of the Party's Central Committee to the 'active measure', as it was in any case wholly within the KGB's remit.

By the standards of the time, the English version of the book was
published quite rapidly. Appearing in London in 1968 with an

introduction by the eminent Graham Greene, it caused a sensation and has been reprinted many times since. In fact, the book came under attack in 1968 not from the odious bourgeois press (well known to be a bunch of reptiles who enjoy nothing better than vilifying splendid Soviet spies!), but from our own side. At a visit to Mikhail Suslov, the Party's leading ideologue and Brezhnev's right-hand man, the General Secretary of the British Communist Party complained that the book had damaged the Communist movement in Britain. This was because Philby had said he sympathised with Communists and had mixed with them socially, comments which could not help but create the impression among the book's readers that the Party was a source of recruits for Soviet espionage! Interesting that in his time [former General Secretary, the late] Harry Pollitt used to report regularly to the heads of the NKVD on his ideas for stepping-up intelligence operations in Britain.

Suslov detested Andropov, but the Central Committee had endorsed the 'active measure', Brezhnev knew about it, and so he had to sulk in silence. He did however have the power to take revenge by putting the Russian translation on indefinite hold: it was difficult to counterclaim that this version fell within the 'active measure' as originally defined.

I have never been able to comprehend the tunnel vision of the Soviet propaganda machine. One would have thought that anyone whose job it was to promote Communist ideals would have had the book translated into Russian at the outset (it was hardly worthwhile targeting a British audience), so that Soviet citizens could see for themselves the kind of hero who toiled for the cause in foreign parts, and so that they could swell with pride at this manifestation of Soviet power!

It was more than ten years before the book appeared in Russian. It was produced by Voenizdat, the Military Publishing House, on dreadful newsprint-quality paper, and without Greene's introduction, in which he was felt to have expressed himself too freely. Getting this translation through the eye of the bureaucratic needle took enormous effort and nervous energy.

My Silent War never, of course, got as far as the Soviet bookstore shelves. The laws of supply and demand governed not only caviar and sausages, but also books on espionage. All the copies were snapped up by the most senior Departments of State – the Central Committee, the

KGB, the Ministry of Defence, and so on. Nor were there any reviews or press comments. It was a forbidden topic and the book simply vanished into thin air.

It is easy to imagine the anger of someone like Solzhenitsyn. When he wrote, he had the enemy clearly in his sights; when they silenced him, he clenched his fists, but at least he knew why they were against him. It is far more difficult for us to comprehend the impotent fury of a man who had been a devoted Communist from his youth, who had written a pro-Soviet book, and who expected it to be greeted with paeans of praise. Instead, the powers-that-be put every spanner they could in the works, dragged their feet and simply refused to discuss the matter. For God's sake! Kim's anger when he got on to the subject was deeply felt. He simply could not understand why the System had behaved that way.

In fact, no normal human being could possibly envy Kim's life, a bird in a gilded cage. Virtually isolated from the outside world (though, thank Heaven, Rufina to some extent made up for this), conscious, as a sensitive man would be, of the latent suspicion of the KGB, he was constantly required to grit his teeth and sound off about 'loyalty to the common cause' and to put on the bogus façade of a 'Builder of Communism'.

It interested me that Kim preferred to avoid talking about the Chekists with whom he had worked; he often professed to have forgotten their surnames and to remember only their first names. He never bragged about his past, and although I would have been very interested to know more about his work as a newspaper correspondent on Franco's side in the Spanish Civil War, he said very little about it and never gave me any interesting titbits.

This, I think, is explained by his professional caution. Almost all the case officers who had run him since the beginning had either been purged or driven out of the intelligence service. A recent example was Anatoly Gorsky, who had apparently concealed the fact that he was the son of a gendarme (how a Jew could have served in the Tsarist Secret Political Police must remain a mystery!).

As professionals, we both assumed his apartment was bugged, though sometimes we got carried away and would tell stories about Brezhnev, or indulge in 'constructive' criticism of the regime. Once, when we were discussing Solzhenitsyn, I tried to sugar the pill by putting the blame for his expulsion on the narrow-minded secret police, the KGB's Fifth Directorate, which dealt with dissidents. 'That's not true,' Kim yelled angrily. 'You're responsible too. So am I. We are all responsible!'

Over the years, Kim became 'Russified'; he learned our word '*blat*' (the essence of which was that what mattered was whom you knew, not what you knew). He knew what could be said aloud and what was best left unsaid. He even came to like our cheap and nasty Dymok cigarettes, which for some reason – perhaps their sheer strength – reminded him of his favourites, Gauloises.

But he still hated his golden cage, ending up as an agent run by a case officer – however intelligent that case officer might be. In our conversations, we naturally talked as equals, and we always stressed the word 'we' ('in our interests', 'our intelligence service'). I made every effort to keep on emphasising tactfully how much we appreciated everything he said and to stress that he was indeed 'one of us'. However, he once snapped at me, 'Aren't you just being a bit too polite? Do you think I don't know I'm an agent with whom you are in operational contact? Just an agent . . .'

We spent a lot of time talking about Britain and the British. I had spent two whole years on my candidate's dissertation: Special Features of the British National Character and their Utilisation in Operational Work. I have always been in love with Britain, notwithstanding the fact that the British had declared me persona non grata (in the same way, I suppose, as one goes on loving one's wife even after she has whacked you over the head with an iron!). I had read most of what there was to read on the British and their national character. I had poured over Marx's essays on Lord Palmerston and Gladstone, ploughed manfully through Ruth Benedict's psychological studies, revelled in Dr I. Bloch's *Sexual Life in England* and read from beginning to end the memoirs of Lloyd-George and Churchill. I had even read Oliver Goldsmith's *The Citizen of the World*, in which he describes the British through the eyes of a Chinese philosopher living in London.

I had used my readings in Russian as well as English (including, by the way, a most interesting book written by Guy Burgess as a secret training manual for Soviet intelligence officers) to compile a table of what I saw as the principal features of the British character. There were quite a few: aggression (Engels had much to say on this in writing about the British infantry), self-control, hypocrisy, understatement, etc. I then related these features to our British operations, and concluded with a series of sage and pragmatic recommendations, which I hope no one ever followed. I don't want the reader to think I was obsessed by the notion of constructing some universally applicable methodology for recruiting the entire population of the British Isles, including the royal family. Happily, the British character is just as incomprehensible as the Russian. The real reason I wanted to become a Candidate of Sciences was that it would boost my standing and also bring me a ten per cent salary increase!

To give the whole game a serious scientific flavour, I even composed a questionnaire and asked my fellow officers for their views on the British. I could hardly avoid asking Philby, too.

When I first spoke to him about the British national character, he thought I was having him on. He then quizzed me at length about the essence of my dissertation and expressed surprise that the KGB bothered itself with such rubbish. He questioned whether there was any such thing as a national character. Wasn't it one of those concepts dreamed up by wise men in order to make money out of simpletons? I explained patiently that 'national character' was a very broad scientific concept, and that if indeed aggression was one of its components, it did not follow that every Englishman was aggressive.

'Now I inderstand,' he said; 'they're only aggressive when they've had a bit too much down at the pub.' Chuckling to himself, he went through the rest of my questionnaire in the same style. He obviously enjoyed it. My memory tells mc that in our delight we drank more whisky than usual that evening and brought our scientific work to an early end. But of course I referred to Philby's assistance in the dissertation!

Much nonsense has been written in the West about 'General' Philby, as a member of the Soviet elite. He never had any rank, his pension, which was 500 roubles a month at the outset and later raised to 800, was perfectly adequate. It was the same as a KGB general's salary. But by Western standards there were still many things he just couldn't have or get. I don't know what love for one's homeland means, but it very likely also includes being homesick for Russian salted herring, or, mutatis mutandis, Stilton. I am convinced that Kim missed England, even though he was at pains to hide this even from those close to him. He was an Englishman to his fingertips, and he needed those now-vanished relics of his former life.

In 1976, when I was getting ready to leave for Denmark as KGB Resident, I suggested we set up a sort of 'shop' for Philby. A memorandum duly went to the Head of the Service, and I was authorised to spend US$1,000 a year, though prices were lower then. We had decided not to ask for more. As Brezhnev said around that time, 'An economy must be economical' – a great aphorism!

I recently wrote elsewhere that Soviet Intelligence always sought to be economical in the way it spent money, a comment hotly refuted by Oleg Gordievsky (who has now virtually transformed himself into the Ideological Section of MI6). He highlighted the millions paid to Ames and others. Of course there are exceptions to every rule; for instance, the big money we laid out to acquire Western military technology, and on scientific and technical intelligence. But as Resident in Denmark, I got about $500 a month and my deputy there, Gordievsky, around $400 (needless to say this was not of great consequence for him, since he was being rather more richly rewarded by SIS). We also had strict limits on spending money on contacts and agents. Then there was the $1,000 for Philby. It was, incidentally, not that easy at first to spend the $1,000. Whenever I asked what to send him, Philby would tell me there was nothing he needed. Couldn't I just spend the whole $1,000 on his favourite sauce?

When I went home on leave, I had to have a heart-to-heart talk with him, telling him that the KGB had allocated the money as a modest top-up to his pension; it was not a favour from me, or a present. With this 'civil service' reasoning, plus a little help from Rufina, I eventually persuaded him to give us a list of some everyday things he needed.

For the next four years we supplied Philby with his favourite foods, from Oxford marmalade to curry powder, as well as more material items such as corduroy trousers and Jaeger pullovers. If on top of that you add the Danish lager I used to ship periodically to Kryuchkov and Andropov, you can well understand the enormous contribution our Residency made to Soviet intelligence.

From time to time Kim and I would correspond via the diplomatic bag, in a sort of jokey jargon that makes the extracts below read like a dialogue from a drawing-room comedy.

Kim wrote:

My dear Michael, A very fine sight greeted us the other day: Victor appearing on our doorstep with a very heavy parcel. It contained a splendid supply of marmalade, self-raising flour, not to mention saffron, moutarde Maille and the very elegant notepaper on which I am now writing for the first time. I only wonder what the monogram 'K' stands for: Kennedy? King Kong? Or could it be . . . We are most grateful, as always, for these magnificent gifts, and the lemon pickle will remind me of the spice of our conversation.

I responded:

We're quite quiet here. No one has decapitated our boring Little Mermaid, no terrorist acts, no expulsions, no arrests. Our Ruritania [which as Kim suggested we used as the cover name for Denmark] has had the chairmanship of the EEC for six months, and has thus been the center of Europe. You may rest assured that Ruritania is now bemoaning a shortage of marmalade. Did poor Muggeridge [a colleague of Philby's but later an enemy] know of your disarming penchant for marmalade? It would have made a good novel!

In another letter, I wrote:

Your silver-framed portrait hangs directly above our office counter near the portraits of the Gods. If my office were raided it would be evidence enough to have me declared persona non grata. [I had hung Philby's picture, with the inscription wishing the Residency good luck, in my Resident's office. Uninitiated visitors who sometimes came to see me used to be a bit nonplussed to see a picture of someone so evidently a foreigner. They usually assumed he was a foreign Bolshevik, a Danish Communist or a Comintern official.]

Kim:

The Rowlandson [a book of erotic etchings by the famous painter and caricaturist] I have not yet seen. Our friend, Victor, with discretion wholly appropriate to our profession, delivered it in a sealed brown envelope, explaining to me its contents. Unfortunately, my mother-in law is inside . . . and I don't know how she would respond to erotica. You can be sure of one thing – I won't burn it or return it to you. On the contrary, I will cherish it as my very own; or, if the worst comes to the worst and inflation erodes the value of my pension, I shall sell it to one of those black-marketeers who lurk in the corners of our Central Post Office, at a very high price!

Michael:

Don't sell Rowlandson en bloc, but as individual prints. If you can manage to have them framed and put on a little exhibition, you'll pull in enough money not just for us, but to restore every Rowlandson-related site in Britain.

Kim:

. . . You have at last solved the problem, which has baffled the arithmeticians over the past year or two. All Rufa needs now is to lose another of the few kilos, which she put on during trips to Bulgaria and Hungary, and the jeans will be perfect . . . You say you want me to keep the earlier ones for your secretary. Okay – provided you produce her so that I can persuade myself that they really do fit her. No doubt I shall fumble a bit, but then I fumble most jobs.

Michael:

I'm delighted you are pleased with our service! It reached its high point, of course, when we ordered your wife's glasses. Thanks for the good jokes. I'm now rounding out my Hope collection, and I now no longer have to wonder where the name Rupert of Hentzau or Rudolf Rassendyll came from,

though I have still to track down the book about Ruritania and
Black Michael.

Kim:

Unless my memory is playing me tricks (which it often does
these days), you will find Black Michael in the Prisoner of
Zenda – the first of the Rassendyll books . . .

The Tuborg brought back memories of mornings spent (or
misspent) at the Normandy bar at Beirut. You may also have
heard a few rumours about the kapitalny remont (major repairs
to the flat) which we endured for the last four months of 1979.
As one mutters when suffering from a severe hangover: Never
again!

We heard a hint or two of the good news that you would be
returning. You will have to get used to seeing girls walking
around with clothes on. I don't know whether you read Anatole
France's 'Penguin Island'; if you have, you will remember that
the boy penguins were exclusively interested in the one girl
penguin who was shameless enough to wear clothes.

Michael:

I have a small favour to ask. I am proud indeed that you have
dubbed me a Knight, with the title of Black Michael of
Ruritania. Would you however please ask Oleg [Kalugin] to use
this splendidly piratical codename in place of my boring old
007 designation! I'm sure you know how sick we all are with
these numbers!

In one letter [see p. 144] Kim, when writing about his case officers,
exclaimed that 'every big organisation must have its share of bloody
fools'. This was a real cry from the heart. Kim became quite fond of
some of his case officers, but to others he took an instant dislike.

He was well aware that the Communist system was in ferment,
with an as yet invisible conflict going on between the liberals (who
later came together around Gorbachev) and the reactionaries, who
belonged in Verkhoyansk.

But like the rest of us (including the omniscient CIA), he could not conceive that the process would lead to *Perestroika*, with all its unforeseen after-effects. Kim supported *Perestroika*, but I am convinced that had he not died in 1988, he would not have hesitated to speak out against the senseless destruction of the Soviet state and the impoverishment of a significant part of its people.

After I retired in 1980, my only contacts with Kim were by phone, since I knew that our relationship was frowned upon; I was thought to have 'personal aims'. We often agreed that we would meet when we had time, but we never managed it.

I had known he was ill, but his death came as a shock. I read the short obituary in the army paper *Red Star*. There was not even a photograph. It was just signed by 'a Group of Comrades'. Again a secrecy about his life and deeds – those invisible comrades were masters at that.

Isn't it odd that the KGB made no professional documentary with its hero? No Russian book was written about him when he was alive, only translations after he passed away. No wonder. It was the style of the organisation, which could love only dead heroes.

Novokuntsevo cemetery: a modest headstone. As Hamlet said: 'The rest is silence.'

Philby was less interesting to me as a spy than as an individual, an outstanding representative of a generation which has left a considerable, often blood-clotted, mark on the twentieth century. What an unusual, puzzling generation, those old Bolsheviks, the old Chekists (of whom Philby was one in spirit). They marched towards the sound of gunfire, yet were terrified of speaking out of line, even when talking to their closest friend. They would give a friend the shirt off their back, yet denounce him in an instant for daring to doubt the wisdom of Stalin or the Party. They flocked to Spain to defend Spanish peasants, yet mowed down the peasants in their own country without compunction. They sang '*The International*' with tears in their eyes and promptly repaired to their Lubyanka HQ to interrogate and torture their colleagues. Almost all of them ended up in prison or camps themselves. Only a few survived.

Kim Philby belonged to this cruel and magnificent generation, though life of course shielded him from the viciousness of Soviet reality. But I feel closer to him than I do to one of those former Central

Committee bigshots who has deftly privatised some of our national assets and turned on a dime from being a Communist stalwart into something akin to the Statue of Liberty, or a bastion of democracy. I feel closer to him because along with my own generation, along with me, he lost his way, though we were already far more cynical and materialistic. Alas, but a new way for Russia has not yet been discovered. Had Philby stayed on to become a pillar of the Establishment, he might have got his 'K', headed SIS or become an MP, and avoided the foul-smelling Dymok cigarettes in a modest Trekhprudny apartment, wolfing hard-to-get salami from the KGB canteen. Instead, it would have been Churchill cigars, lolling in a Chippendale armchair in a Georgian house down by the Thames, weekend shooting parties in Scotland, or in Montmartre sipping onion soup. (I have to concede that I don't believe for a moment such crazy thoughts ever entered his head.)

This was a generation of fanatics and idealists, whose blood was sucked by the Idea itself.

As Boris Pasternak, the Nobel Prize winner, wrote: 'You probably won't flinch as you sweep Man out of your path. Well, martyrs to Dogma, you are also victims of the Century.'

Part 4

The Philby Literature

by Hayden Peake

PREFACE

In June 1997, a group of American, Canadian, British and Russian authors and retired intelligence officers gathered in Moscow for a dinner. At some point during the evening the conversation turned to the late Kim Philby, known to the Westerners present from books and to the Russians from personal contact. We marvelled at the sustained interest in this spy over the years. So much has been written about him it is hard to tell the truth from the fiction. Would his legacy ever be sorted out, someone asked rhetorically? Public enlightenment about Philby's career, according to the cynical conventional wisdom of the evening, awaited only the opening of his KGB files to Western authors.

Then, two of those present, Nigel West and Oleg Tsarev, announced that they were co-authoring a book on Philby based, in part, on those very files. They had been given access to the reports Philby sent to his KGB masters during the years he served in the British Secret Intelligence Service (SIS). This work, eventually published as *The Crown Jewels*, would reproduce selected examples of material to show how valuable an agent Philby had been, if one viewed the issue from the KGB side, or how much damage he had done, if the reader was from the West. It was not total access, but it was more than anyone had expected.

And that was not all, said Yuri Kobaladze, then head of the Public Affairs Office of the Russian Foreign Intelligence Service. Philby's wife, Rufina, planned a book about her life with Kim that would fill another gap in his otherwise well-chronicled life.

At this point it occurred to me that it might be useful to have a look at what had been published about Philby, to identify the facts, the persistent errors, the myths and the contradictions that I knew existed in the literature. It might also be of interest to identify those works that best documented the actual impact Philby had had and those given more to rich, anecdotal gossip. In pursuit of this goal, I could seek the help of some of his former KGB colleagues and those in the West who knew him at various stages of his career, in order to help establish the truth. In the event, the task was greater than I had anticipated, but so was the co-operation from both sides, and I undertook a survey of the major works and where possible used first-hand testimony to help resolve the contentious issues. The fruits of my research have been combined with Rufina Philby's memoirs to provide a comprehensive account of a truly extraordinary individual.

When apparent errors and conflicting stories were encountered, I have turned to those with first-hand knowledge wherever possible to resolve the point. Where that was not possible, I have so indicated. Thanks to Rufina Philby I have been able to use her husband's correspondence to give an idea of his opinions on various matters. In other cases, the FBI files were helpful.

The degree to which some measure of success has been achieved is dependent on the help I received from three groups of friends and colleagues. By any measure, I am forever indebted to Rufina Philby, who granted me hours of her time and access to Kim Philby's library. She patiently explained whatever obscure point I was trying to understand with great patience, wit and kindness. She has my deepest appreciation and thanks.

I thank too all those who sat still for interviews and questions. Most are identified in the footnotes, but also deserve recognition here. Those from the West who knew Philby personally include: Richard Beeston, Robin Brooks, Cleveland Cram, Lord Dacre of Glanton,

Richard Helms, William Hood, Phillip Knightley, Robert Lamphere, James McCargar, I. I. Milne, Yuri Modin, Hugh Montgomery, Patrick Seale, Richard Thompson and John Waller.

Philby's Russian and former KGB colleagues who knew him in Moscow and in some cases before he arrived, include: Michael Bogdanov, Genrikh Borovik, Vassilli Dozhdalev, Gennady-X, Oleg Kalugin, Vadim Kirpichenko, Yuri Kobaladze, Sergei Kondrashev, Lev Koshliakov, Mikhail Lyubimov, Oleg Tsarev and Markus Wolf.

Those in the final group helped in many different ways. They include: Christopher Andrew, Jim and Inge Atwood, T. H. Bagley, Tom Bower, Gervase Cowell, Geoffrey Elliott, Oleg Gordievsky, Samuel Halpern, David C. Martin, H. Keith Melton, Terry Message, Chris Moorhouse, Scotty Miler, Dan Mulvenna, David Murphy, Verne W. Newton, Walter Pforzheimer, John Ranelagh, Herbert Romerstein, Emma Sullivan, Helmut Trotnow, Bronson Tweedy, Nigel West and William J. West.

My grateful thanks to all of the above. And while their help was indispensable, I alone must bear the burden for any valuable works overlooked and, as always, any errors.

INTRODUCTION

Books about espionage have been published with increasing frequency since Matthew Smith's *Memoirs of Secret Service* (London: 1699), and 1968 proved to be a benchmark year. For the first time, five books by different authors were published about the same spy – Harold Adrian Russell (Kim) Philby – in the same year. First on the shelves was *Kim Philby, The Spy I Loved* by Philby's third wife, Eleanor.[1] The next two, *Philby: The Spy Who Betrayed a Generation* by Bruce Page, David Leitch and Phillip Knightley, and *The Third Man* by E. H. Cookridge,[2] appeared in quick succession in February. In April, Hugh Trevor-Roper's essay *The Philby Affair* was published in *Encounter* and subsequently in a book, with minor changes, by the same name.[3] The

---

[1] Reviewed by Hugh Trevor-Roper, *Sunday Times*, 14 January 1968.
[2] Both reviewed by Graham Greene, *Observer*, 18 February 1968.
[3] Complete citations for these books and those subsequently mentioned may be found in the bibliography.

quintet was complete when Philby's memoir, My Silent War, came out in April in America and in September in Britain.[4]

At the time Philby was often called 'the spy of the century' and thirty years later was still described in the West as 'the most remarkable spy in the history of espionage'.[5] Are these assessments accurate? What did the KGB think of him? One of its former leaders, Lt-Gen. Vadim Kirpichenko, now editor of the six-volume KGB history – a work in progress – judged Philby, in retrospect, from a strictly professional point of view. 'Philby', he said, 'was the most important counterespionage agent the KGB had in the West during the early Cold War, but Donald Maclean was an equally important source of political intelligence, including atomic policy.'[6] Retired KGB Colonel Yuri Modin, the man who received, translated and evaluated much of the material Philby sent to Moscow Centre in the 1940s, echoes this conclusion.[7] If any doubt remained, it was eliminated when another former KGB officer, Oleg Tsarev, working with British author Nigel West, published selected wartime reports, provided by Philby and transmitted to Moscow, that described MI6 personnel, organisation and operations in extraordinary detail.[8] No mole had better served his master.

But the KGB view does not explain why the public's fascination with what Philby did, or is thought to have done, has the persistence of nuclear waste. Some of the tales about him are fantasy and can be easily refuted. There are other questions of players, motives, and espionage operations, that may never be completely resolved. A clue to

---

[4] With the exception of typographical errors, the two versions are essentially identical in narrative content. However, the American edition does not have the list of abbreviations or Graham Greene's introduction, both found in the British version. The latter does not have the organisation chart present in the Grove Press version. Both have chronologies, but they differ in several respects as discussed in the chronology herein.

[5] Phillip Knightley, PHILBY: K.G.B. Masterspy, dust-jacket blurb.

[6] Author interview with Vadim Kirpichenko, Moscow, 10 September 1998.

[7] Author interview with Yuri Modin, Moscow, 19 November 1997.

[8] Author interview with Oleg Tsarev, 4 June 1997. These documents eventually appeared as Appendix II, 'The Philby Reports', in Nigel West and Oleg Tsarev, The Crown Jewels: The British Secrets at the Heart of the KGB Archives, pp. 294–344.

the answers, however, may be found in the extensive literature – books, articles and letters – his case has spawned. And that is what will be examined here.

THE MISSING DIPLOMATS

The first five Philby books did not appear out of the blue. They were in part a journalistically inevitable consequence following the defections of British diplomats Guy Burgess and Donald Maclean to the Soviet Union in 1951, about which five books had also been written between 1952 and 1963. The first one, by Maclean's friend Cyril Connolly, did not name Philby; neither did the last, by Burgess's friend Tom Driberg.[9] The others were careful to mention only what the Government had made public in 1955 when the Foreign Secretary, Harold Macmillan, stated in the House of Commons that Philby was not, as one member had alleged, the third man – the one who had tipped off Burgess that Maclean was about to be interrogated by MI5, thus allowing them to escape. Constrained by the libel laws and the silence of the Security Service on Philby's role in the Burgess-Maclean affair, the matter rested until Philby defected in January 1963 and he became fair game on both sides of the Atlantic. Then British journalists focused on where Philby was, the Americans on what he had done.

The American magazine *Newsweek*, unconcerned about British libel laws, stated flatly in a June 1963 article that Philby had been a Communist since Cambridge, that he *was* the third man, and that he had most likely defected to the Soviet Union. The British Government issued a statement indirectly confirming the basics of the

---

[9] Cyril Connolly, *The Missing Diplomats*; Geoffrey Hoare, *The Missing Macleans*; John Mather (ed.), *The Great Spy Scandal: The Inside Story of Burgess and Maclean* (London: *Daily Express*, December 1955); Tom Driberg, *Guy Burgess: A Portrait with Background*; Anthony Purdy and Douglas Sutherland, *Burgess and Maclean*. Purdy and Sutherland was published after Philby defected but too late to revise the book. Thus they note on page 78 that Philby is 'now the correspondent for *The Observer* in Beirut'. The Driberg account contains one lie after another from Burgess when it comes to being a Soviet agent, and Driberg adds almost as an afterthought, 'Nor do I believe that he was ever a Soviet agent' (p. 109).

story, but said little else for four years. The Soviet Government confirmed Philby's whereabouts on 30 July 1963 when it announced in *Izvestia* that he had been granted citizenship.

In the 15 February 1964 issue of the *Saturday Evening Post*, Edward R. F. Sheehan, the press attaché at the American Embassy and Philby's friend when they served in Beirut, wrote in some detail about Philby's role as a KGB agent and his activities in Lebanon just before his disappearance. In the epilogue to his memoirs, *My Silent War*, Philby cited the article, without mentioning the author by name, as an 'illustration of the bland invention which characterizes so much of the current writing on secret service matters'. Philby was correct. Sheehan did make a considerable number of unforced errors. For example, he stated that Philby entered Cambridge in 1931 instead of 1929; that he joined the Communist Party there, though he never did join; that Burgess left Washington without Embassy approval, whereas he was sent home by the ambassador; and that Philby divorced his first wife in 1938, rather than 1946. Sheehan was also one of the first to state that the British placed Philby under constant surveillance before he escaped, something Philby denied, but others who were there also asserted.[10]

Authors David Wise and Thomas Ross avoided these errors in the brief summary of the Philby case in their 1967 book, *The Espionage Establishment*, but Vernon Hinchley did not and he managed to include some new ones in his book, *The Defectors*, the same year.[11]

Whether these mistakes in the 'current writing', as Philby put it, were a proximate cause of his memoirs, written 'at intervals since my arrival in Moscow', is not clear. And although completed in typescript form by the summer of 1967, the desire to set the record straight was not sufficient motive for prompt publication. Philby tells us that after 'consulting a few friends', the consensus was that the book 'should be shelved indefinitely' to avoid, as he put it without elaboration, causing 'a rumpus with international complications the nature of

---

[10] See Richard Beeston, *Looking for Trouble*, p. 31.

[11] See Hinchley, *The Defectors*, p. 116, where he claims that Kim got his nickname at Westminster rather than from his family, and began Cambridge in 1931 instead of 1929. On page 117 Hinchley writes that Kim 'married a Polish girl', which of course he never did. There are more in kind.

which it was difficult to foresee'. All this changed, wrote Philby, when in October 1967 a series of articles appeared in the *Sunday Times* and the *Observer* that, 'in spite of a number of factual inaccuracies', presented 'a substantially true picture of my career'.[12] What had suddenly energised the British press?

A CAMBRIDGE COINCIDENCE?

According to Harold Evans, in 1967 the recently appointed editor of the *Sunday Times*, the articles were the consequence of an observation made to him by Jeremy Isaacs, then with Thames Television and later producer of the CNN Cold War television series. '"How interesting it was", said Isaacs, "that Guy Burgess and Donald Maclean, who spied for the Soviet Union, and that other man Philby, who defected," were all educated at Cambridge University in the 1930s.'[13] Evans agreed and assigned his full-time investigative Insight team of four reporters to determine whether there was anything worth pursuing. By the end of the project, the staff had grown to thirty-eight and one result was *Philby: The Spy Who Betrayed a Generation*. This book is a fine exemplar of investigative journalism, notwithstanding the grade of 'beta minus', awarded by that wizard of semantic terrorism, Malcolm Muggeridge.[14]

The quest started with a few clippings from the newspaper archives, and after learning the right questions gradually gained the co-operation of the right people: many former Foreign Office and SIS (Secret Intelligence Service/MI6) officers who knew Philby. The amount of new material discovered was staggering from the Government's point of view and it was about to become public. Until that time, Philby's role in the Foreign Office was unknown publicly and his position in SIS unsuspected. *The Spy Who Betrayed a Generation* changed all that. Throughout it provided unheard of historical and political context with regard to the SIS while concentrating on Philby's role and personal

---

12 Philby, *My Silent War*, p. xiii.
13 Harold Evans, *Good Times Bad Times*, p. 41.
14 Malcolm Muggeridge, 'Refractions in the Character of Kim Philby', *Esquire*, September 1968.

characteristics that have become so familiar. In the process it discusses details of Philby's SIS service including the Volkov Operation, how important he was, his education and political background, how long he had served as a Soviet agent, and something of his life in Beirut and Russia. It also makes reasonable estimates of what he did after he was fired from SIS in 1951, what damage he had caused, and how he managed to escape.[15] One omission is worth noting: there is little about Philby's relationship with the FBI, a topic he discussed at some length. There is also an admittedly speculative chapter suggesting that Philby worked in Cyprus for SIS after formally leaving the service. With the exception of the Cyprus issue, each of these topics would be explored in greater depth in books to come, including one by Phillip Knightley.

The Spy Who Betrayed a Generation was not without errors, an enemy no author has defeated. In its internal review of the book, the FBI noted the statement that one of its agents sent to Britain in 1943–4 was 'Melvin Purvis, the man who killed John Dillinger', was 'not correct since Purvis was not in the Bureau' at the time. The

---

[15] There are three sources that provide first-hand details about how the book was created: Harold Evans's memoirs, Phillip Knightley's memoirs, and the second, revised edition of the Page *et al.* book (Penguin, 1969, paperback; Signet in America). All include material that emerged after the first edition was published. A Sphere Books issue, 1977, was the same as the 1969 edition. The Ballantine issue that was published in 1981 was the same as the first edition. A word of caution. Page *et al.* make an inscrutable, gratuitous and unexplained comment: 'ex-denizens of the secret world lie whether they are telling the truth or not'. It contradicts the entire book; disregard.

The revised edition (1969) also adds more source material and makes some corrections, the most notable concerns the content of chapters 13 and 14 that had been switched in the first British edition. The American Doubleday first edition had the chapter titles and narrative correct, but switched the two chapters in sequence creating a discontinuity in the narrative. Philby's copies of both British editions (now in the author's possession) indicate he read them. He annotated the first edition with 'Xs' and exclamation points, but only where it commented on his family and early years, nothing operational. Although Melinda Maclean was more expressive by adding a few words, her annotations too were on parts dealing with her husband and family. Philby did not annotate the revised edition, but he did place several bookmarks in its pages and there are other signs of it being read.

review goes on to characterise as 'completely fictional' the story that a 'muscular pistol-toting Agent strode into the British Embassy and demanded to question Philby about the whereabouts of Burgess'.[16] Other factual errors were minor: Claude Dansey died in 1947, not 1944 (p. 123); Dick White attended the University of California, Berkeley, not the University of Southern California; OSS was not 'closed down in 1946', but in 1945; and Guy Burgess was not a First Secretary (that was Philby's rank) when assigned to the British Embassy in Washington – he was at most a second, some say third.

And here too the authors established a precedent and a theory that would persist in many of the writings to follow. The precedent recognised that to write about Philby was to write about Burgess and Maclean; the links were inseparable. What the authors didn't mention was the possibility of more than three *Cambridge spies*. The theory they introduced suggested that Philby was confronted in Beirut and intentionally frightened into defecting to avoid embarrassing revelations all around. This too would be explored by other authors. Philby told Markus Wolf, former Head of the East German Foreign Intelligence Service (HVA), that he believed it too.[17]

THE DEVOTED WIFE

When the Insight team began its work on the series of articles that would precede the book, it was already aware that Patrick Seale of the *Observer* was ghosting the memoirs of Eleanor Philby (Philby's third wife) and that they would probably serialise first. As it turned out, both published on 30 September 1967. The *Sunday Times* concentrated on exposing what Philby had done, while the *Observer*, which beat its

---

[16] Memorandum To: W. C. Sullivan, From: W. A. Branigan, Subject: Book Review, 'The Philby Conspiracy', by Bruce Page, David Leitch and Phillip Knightley, 28 June 1968, page 2 of 2 pages. As indicated in a 23 February 1968 memo. involving Philby, to and from the same individuals, Subject: HAROLD ADRIAN RUSSELL PHILBY . . ., the FBI routinely reviewed books on intelligence and espionage with emphasis on 'criticisms and remarks made concerning the Director and the Bureau'.

[17] Author conversation with Markus Wolf, 12 December 1997.

competitor to the streets by a few hours, focused on why Philby had been a Soviet agent with particular emphasis on his marriage to Eleanor. Her memoirs, published the following January, left the 'why' for Seale to deal with in his book eventually published in 1973 and to be discussed below. The central theme of Eleanor's book was life with Kim.

Eleanor Brewer, wife of the *New York Times* correspondent in Beirut, met Philby in 1956, married him in January 1959, joined him in Moscow in September 1963, left him for good in May 1965 and returned to California, where she died in 1968 shortly after her book was published. *The Spy I Loved* gives a unique first-hand account of Philby's life first in Beirut as a lover, husband, father and journalist, and then of his first two years in Moscow as her husband, Soviet agent and adulterer. No one who reads both this book and Rufina Philby's memoirs will have any doubt that they write about the same man. Eleanor describes the 'painful Christmas of 1964' with Philby 'in a haze of alcohol'; the excessive smoking with unkept promises to cut down; his affection for cricket, the London newspapers and the BBC; the same favourite Moscow restaurants; their troubled travels; KGB concern about assassination attempts; their trips to the Central Post Office; their problems with housekeepers; the day-to-day vicissitudes of life in Moscow; and the often 'sordid life controlled by the KGB'. We learn too that in the early years in the Soviet Union, Philby had an office somewhere in Moscow while he worked on Gordon Lonsdale's memoirs,[18] that he was treated with deference by the KGB and was 'pathetically pleased by Soviet compliments', and that Philby had a 'self-inflicted wrist accident'.[19]

And then she tells of their experiences with the Macleans. The latter took two forms. The first was social: time spent together eating, drinking and reading. She comments that Melinda Maclean read the

---

[18] Many authors have commented on Philby's helping Lonsdale with his memoirs. Philby admitted to Murray Sayle that he had polished the prose. O. F. Snelling, who knew Lonsdale well, writes in his *Rare Books and Rarer People*, p. 238, that whatever help Philby provided, the style of the result was pure Lonsdale. He adds, 'although I did my best to change his mind, David Leitch remained unconvinced'.

[19] There is no indication whether the 'wrist accident' refers to Philby's suicide attempt mentioned by Rufina Philby, but from the timing, it is more likely that this referred to another incident.

Purdy and Sutherland book to them out loud; Philby liked it, Donald Maclean 'hated it'. And it was during these sessions that Eleanor heard Donald accuse Philby of being 'a double agent' still with links to the SIS. The second form was Philby's affair with Melinda. Although Rufina tells of Kim's comment that he never had more than one woman at a time, if Eleanor is to be believed, this was not true. The affair was carried on for months while Eleanor suspected, for more months after she was told, and finally was the cause of her departure.[20]

The Spy I Loved is the source of some well-known Philby quotes and puzzling remarks. Notable in the quote category is his response to Eleanor's query, 'What is more important to your life, me and the children or the Communist Party?' He answered 'without a moment's hesitation: "The Party of course."' In the puzzling remarks category is her comment that 'Kim was not permitted' to attend Burgess's funeral, 'but I found out later he saw Burgess very briefly, as he lay dying in the hospital'.[21] This contradicts the conventional wisdom as will be pointed out below.

Eleanor was not bitter. She ended her book noting that Kim 'betrayed many people, me among them. But men are not always masters of their fates. Kim had the guts, or the weakness, to stand by a decision made thirty years ago, whatever the cost to those who loved him most . . .' What she did not say, and perhaps did not suspect, is that once a serving agent, he had little choice.

The Third Man

According to E. H. Cookridge, an Austrian by birth, he 'knew Kim Philby over a period of thirty-three years', but the only meeting mentioned in his book, *The Third Man*, occurred in Vienna in 1934. At the time Cookridge was living under his true name, Edward Spiro, working both as a freelance journalist for several British newspapers and as an agent for the British Secret Intelligence Service. Arrested by the

---

[20] Author conversation with Rufina Philby, 24 November 1997. The affair was over when Rufina and Kim decided to get married, but there were lingering details to be resolved. Melinda's things were still in Philby's flat and she owed Kim $5,000.00. She never paid back the debt, and he had to return her things by taxi to the Maclean flat near Smolensky Square.

[21] Eleanor Philby, *The Spy I Loved*, p. 74.

Gestapo and imprisoned in Dachau, the British brought diplomatic pressures to bear for their *journalist*. He was released and went to England, where he was both a journalist and an MI5 informer. After the war he began writing books on espionage under his new name.[22] Although he claims to provide the 'first complete dossier on Philby's fantastic double life', he falls short of the goal.

The book's overall unreliability follows from too many unsupported assertions and errors. In the latter category, he gives Philby's birthday as 31 December 1911 (it was 1 January 1912), states that Gerhard Eisler was once the KGB *rezident* in New York, and that Philby's only English wife Aileen, was American. The former include claims that the FBI determined that Donald Maclean had been handled by KGB agent Arthur Adams (the Bureau made no such claim and Adams was GRU),[23] that Philby had met with Colonel Rudolf Abel in New York and Willie Müzenberg in Germany and Paris, and that Philby's house in Washington on Nebraska Avenue was a few blocks from the White House.

There are also too many 'must haves' as in the case of GRU defector, Ismail Akhmedov, who 'must have discovered Philby's double role' after Philby debriefed him in Istanbul in 1948. This knowledge was valuable to the CIA, notes Cookridge, when Akhmedov informed the Agency in 1953. He does not explain why it made much difference then, two years after Philby had returned to London, or why the CIA was not told in Istanbul in 1949 when they debriefed Akhmedov.

Cookridge's first-hand account of Philby as a courier in Vienna for the Republican Defence League partially fills the gap left in his unpublished memoirs (see page 219 above) which largely avoids this topic. Only when Philby mentions returning from Vienna, does he refer to the time period and events described by Cookridge. It is doubtful however that Philby went to Vienna already working for the Communists, as Cookridge claims. Still, as Hugh Trevor-Roper concluded, this 'otherwise shaky book seems to me worth reading for this episode alone'.[24]

---

22 Nigel West (ed.), *The Faber Book of Espionage*, p. 372.

23 FBI Memorandum To: W. C. Sullivan, From: W. A. Branigan, Subject: BOOK REVIEW, 'THE THIRD MAN', by E. H. Cookridge, 4 March 1968.

24 H. R. Trevor-Roper, 'The Ideal Husband', *New York Review of Books*, 9 May 1968.

The Philby Affair

When Hugh Trevor-Roper met Kim Philby for the last time, in Baghdad as it turned out, he had been told by Sir Dick White, then head of MI5, that Philby was a Soviet agent. He never mentioned it to Philby and it does not seem to have influenced *The Philby Affair*, written after that event. The essay is a thoughtful contribution from a former colleague that comments on each of the other Philby books published in 1968, but is most valuable for his insights into the SIS context of the times and to Philby himself during the war. He knew that Philby had been a Communist – his MI6 colleague and Philby's friend, Tim Milne, had told him so years before Philby's assignment to Section V. He knew too that MI6 and MI5 were 'fanatically anti-Communist' and viewed all Communists as 'potential Philbies'. Consequently, at the time Trevor-Roper assumed that they too were aware and that Philby's political views had changed or he would not have been hired. The Establishment, on the other hand, assumed that, whatever one's politics, 'there were no Philbies'. Either way he was safe.[25]

From *The Philby Affair* we learn too of Philby's considerable managerial and bureaucratic skills, his genuine concern and understanding of others' problems, the competency with which he performed his wartime work and the high regard in which he was held. Philby is described as calm, caring and charming, adjectives that follow him throughout the literature – with one exception to be discussed later – but have a special significance coming from a colleague and friend. Likewise, we get a feel for his personality, although, as will be seen, the aspect of his personality varies with the writer.[26] Only in hindsight does Trevor-Roper recognise occasions where Philby acted in the Soviet interest without explanation and reflects that it was amazing he had acquired sufficient power to get away with it.

---

[25] Author interview with Lord Dacre, 28 November 1997.

[26] The Philby seen by Cookridge and Trevor-Roper differs on at least one issue: the nature of his conversations. Cookridge notes that Philby, while reserved when it came to personal questions, 'was always ready to discuss politics, books, art, or other intellectual subjects' (p. 246). Trevor-Roper, on the other hand, 'never had a serious conversation with him'. He wrote that Philby 'never discussed an intellectual subject' and that he always kept the conversation casual, 'tending to be flippant, even cynical'. *Ibid.*, Lord Dacre interview.

In the book, Trevor-Roper deals too with what was to become a persistent assertion: that by the end of the war, Philby was destined to be Chief of the Service. 'I never doubted . . . what his future would be,' he writes, or 'that he was being groomed to head the service: that he would have been in the 1950s, the new "C".' In a recent interview, Lord Dacre mentioned that only later did he learn that even before the defection of Burgess and Maclean, it had been concluded that it was 'impossible for Philby to head the service'. This conclusion was the outcome of an informal MI6 selection process carried out in anticipation of Sir Stewart's departure. Philby was indeed one of several possible successors considered for the post, eventually, if not right away. The Foreign Office requested that Patrick Riley interview Philby, which he did. In a letter to Lord Dacre after Menzies retired, Riley said that he had noticed such a difference in Philby since they met during the war, 'in particular his shifty eyes and sinister manner, that he must not be "C"'.[27]

In *The Philby Affair*, Trevor-Roper confronts the questions that are even now not fully answered, but are central to the Philby saga and more generally to the Soviet espionage successes of the period: How did he ever get in? How was it possible that Philby was a traitor? What harm or even good did he do? What difference does it all make? What should SIS have done after Philby confessed in Beirut?[28] Author John le Carré argued that if the Government 'had wanted him back in England, I am persuaded that SIS could have got him . . . if they had wanted him. Did they, in a sporting way, allow Kim to run for it?'[29] This theme will surface again in later books. Trevor-Roper responds that this kind of 'rich flatulent puff' cannot be considered practical; his other comments on le Carré are equally insightful. He is equally harsh with Philby's 'chief English apologist, Mr Graham Greene,' and his 'historical fantasy' in his introduction to the British 'expurgated edition' of *My Silent War* that attempts to justify Philby's devotion to Communism.

Lord Dacre found Kim Philby something of a paradox. He recalls

---

[27] *Ibid.*, Lord Dacre interview.
[28] *Ibid.*; see also, *The Philby Affair*, p. 16ff.
[29] John le Carré, in his Introduction to Page, Leitch and Knightley, *Philby: The Spy Who Betrayed a Generation*, p. 20.

that in nearly five years, despite genuine intellect, they never had a serious conversation. Still, Philby wrote stingingly accurate, often cynical, even flippant, assessments of people and events. His unmistakable style was evident in *My Silent War*. There was no doubt in Lord Dacre's mind that it was Philby's work. Philby wrote his old friend 'a jolly letter' from Moscow expressing a desire to remain friends; Lord Dacre never answered.

My Silent War

Of all the contributions to the Philby literature, *My Silent War* was the most controversial at the time of publication and it remains so today. In 1968, Graham Greene wrote that 'we were told to expect a lot of propaganda; but it contains none, unless a dignified statement of his beliefs and motives can be called propaganda'.[30] The *Sunday Times* found it to be 'an indictment of Western secret operations against the Soviet Union'.[31] Twenty-six years later, E. D. R. Harrison called it 'a striking example of KGB propaganda'.[32] In between, Hugh Trevor-Roper wrote that even 'if Philby's memoirs are primarily propaganda, that does not mean they are necessarily untrue'. As to the portions about his war service, Trevor-Roper added, 'I can say with confidence that, as far as they go, his memoirs . . . are factual.' In her review of the book, Rebecca West unfairly nettled Trevor-Roper for this comment by failing to mention that he restricted the time frame to the war years. And though she went on to assert that Philby made 'mistake after mistake', she didn't identify the errors.[33]

The Harrison article precipitated an exchange of views with Robert Cecil, in the journal, *Intelligence and National Security*. Cecil, who from 1943 to 1945 was personal assistant to 'C', the chief of SIS, was

---

[30] Greene, 'Reflections on the Character of Kim Philby', *Esquire*, September 1968.

[31] 'I'll swap my book for the Krogers', *Sunday Times*, 17 December 1968.

[32] E. D. R. Harrison, 'Some reflections on Kim Philby's *My Silent War* as a Historical Source', in Richard J. Aldrich and Michael F. Hopkins (eds), *Intelligence, Defence and Diplomacy: British Policy in the Post-War World* (London: Frank Cass, 1994), p. 205.

[33] Quoted in Robert Cecil, 'Philby's Spurious War', *Intelligence and National Security*, Vol. 9, October 1994, Number 4, p. 764.

concerned that Harrison and others should realise that Philby's memoirs were not 'a round, unvarnished tale', as Philby claimed, but an expression of his long cultivated 'cover personality'.

On the charge of propaganda – the use of selected truths, exaggerations and even lies in the systematic propagation of a doctrine – Cecil was not pleased that one of Philby's principal themes, 'the shabby failure' of MI6 and MI5 in the Second World War, showed, according to Harrison, a 'surprising degree of reliability'.

Other elements of Cecil's article enumerate the principal errors and distortions in *My Silent War*, providing in the process a most valuable critique of its defects. The distortions include details surrounding the ousting of Philby's superior Felix Cowgill, his own appointment as head of Section IX, and the escape of Burgess and Maclean. The omissions named are equally important, as for example his assignment to assassinate Franco. On the other hand, the official KGB history, *Essays on the History of Russian Foreign Intelligence*,[34] did not mention it either. Similarly, Philby omitted any mention of his interview with the GRU defector, Akhmedov, in Turkey.[35] A curious omission that Cecil did not mention was that Philby made no reference to his family or even to the fact that he had ever been married.

And then there are some plain untruths in the book. In the former category Cecil dismisses Philby's statement, made three times in *My Silent War*, and in an interview with Murray Sayle,[36] that he had been a KGB staff officer for thirty years. The truth is that Philby was always

---

[34] Vadim Kirpichenko (ed.), OCHERKI ISTORII ROSSIYSKOY VNESHNEY RAZVEDKI, Tom 3, 1933–41, Moskva, 'MEZHDUNARODNYYE OTNOSHENIYA', 1997 (*Essays on the History of Russian Foreign Intelligence*, Vol. 3, 1933–41, Moscow, International Relations, 1997).

[35] *Ibid.* Cecil knew four of the so-called Cambridge Comintern – Philby, Blunt, Burgess and Maclean – and at one point he worked for Maclean in the Foreign Office. In his article, 'The Cambridge Comintern' and his biography of Donald Maclean, *A Life Divided*, Cecil provides additional detail about Philby; he acknowledges his high marks during the war, discusses his motivations, and points out that the arrest of atomic spy, Alan Nunn May, exposed by Igor Gouzenko, was cause for concern since May had been Maclean's classmate at Trinity Hall, Cambridge.

[36] Murray Sayle, 'I am a K.G.B. officer', *Sunday Times*, 17 December 1967.

just *agent Tom*, a fact, his KGB colleagues said, that bothered him throughout his Moscow years.[37]

Ironically, as Mikhail Lyubimov has related (see page 284 above), *My Silent War* was even more controversial among the Communist Party elite who held up publication of the Russian edition until 1980. Two more editions were eventually printed, one in 1983 and the last in 1989; only the latter contained some photographs. Graham Greene's flattering Introduction was not included in any of the Russian editions. An alternative Preface was supplied by O. Kedrov – actually Oleg Kalugin. Similarly, the East German edition omitted the Greene Introduction, included the Kedrov version, and added a new Preface by Philby.[38]

According to several of Philby's KGB contacts, the reason for the publication delay was not properly explained to Philby at the time and he was greatly disturbed. This, coupled with his break-up with Melinda Maclean in late 1968, the noticeable reduction in work assigned and a growing awareness that he was not fully trusted by the KGB,[39] led to

---

[37] A related rumour, not mentioned by Cecil, was that Philby was a KGB general. Although technically untrue, he had many general officer perquisites. Moreover, after Yuri Andropov became KGB Chairman, Oleg Kalugin attempted to persuade Andropov to award Philby the rank of general; but it was not approved. Nevertheless, writes Kalugin, 'we instructed Philby to tell Western reporters he had been made a general, which he did, and I assured him, "With what you have accomplished you're more than justified in feeling that you are a general."' To which Philby replied, 'I know I'm a general.' See Oleg Kalugin, *SpyMaster: My 32 Years in Intelligence and Espionage against the West*, p. 141. Whatever his titular rank, for most of his time in the Soviet Union Philby received the perquisites and retirement benefits – apartment, pension, travel, medical care, possession of Western books – of at least a senior colonel. This result comes from interviews with several of Philby's former KGB colleagues: Lt-Gen. Vadim Kirpichenko, Colonel Michael Bogdanov, Colonel Mikhail Lyubimov and Maj.-Gen. Yuri Kobaladze, Moscow, the week of 3 September 1998.

[38] There were also West German, French, Mongolian, Czech and Bulgarian editions of *My Silent War*, but copies were not available for this study.

[39] Genrikh Borovik, *The Philby Files*, p. 365. Modin, West and Tsarev, Andrew and Gordievsky, are among others who have commented on various periods of distrust that Philby endured.

despondency that manifested itself in what Kalugin called 'legendary bouts of drinking and womanising'. Yuri Modin wrote of this period that Philby 'lived an empty bored existence' and was 'drinking with a vengeance . . . drowning his sorrows in wine or whisky if he could get it'. It was sometime between late 1968 and early 1970 that Philby is said to have attempted suicide.[40]

Just when Philby decided to write his memoirs is unknown, though

---

[40] Kalugin, *op. cit.*, p. 135. Retired KGB colonel Yuri Modin worked with Maclean, Blunt, Burgess and Cairncross in London during parts of the late 1940s and early 1950s. Modin writes in his memoirs, *My Five Cambridge Friends* (p. 257), that, although he saw Philby once in London, he did not meet him until 1964 when he was assigned to help him write what came to be *My Silent War*. In his book *The Philby Files* (p. 278), Genrikh Borovik wrote that Modin 'never saw him [Philby] abroad'. When asked about the apparent discrepancy, Borovik checked and said his notes reflected what he wrote during the interview with Modin. Modin, on the other hand, was sure of his experience since he had been told by his superiors not to meet with Philby, who had been brought to a meeting by Blunt (on Blunt's initiative) and sat some distance away. Modin added that he may have misunderstood Borovik's question.

After a few months' work with Philby in 1964, Modin was assigned overseas and left Philby's monitoring to others. Modin writes that he met Philby and Rufina after they were married, but she is certain she never met him until her husband's funeral.

Rufina Philby was the first publicly to acknowledge Philby's attempted suicide (see page 59), but she is unable to add details in terms of time or seriousness of the act; Philby refused to discuss it. Based on the interviews with her, and the writings of and interviews with Cecil, Knightley, Kalugin, and Borovik, the most probable time is the last half of 1968 to late 1969. Although Modin puts Philby's depression as beginning in '1966 when Melinda Maclean returned to her husband', this date cannot be correct. Phillip Knightley sent a copy of the Insight Team book to Philby with a covering letter dated 15 February 1968. Both Philby and Melinda read and annotated the book (now in the author's collection) thus indicating the break was in the future. By sometime in 1969 Melinda was back with her husband, according to Robin Denniston who visited them in Moscow (see Robert Cecil, *A Divided Life*, p. 177). The separation was apparently gradual since some of Melinda's clothes were still in the apartment when Rufina moved there in 1970. Author conversation with Rufina Philby, Moscow, 25 November 1997.

Modin wrote that he began in 1964.[41] Philby appeared to support this view when he wrote in the Foreword that 'This short book has been written at intervals since my arrival in Moscow nearly five years ago . . .',[42] while noting that he had accepted some suggested changes from trusted friends and rejected others. In the Epilogue, he indicates he was writing in the 'Summer, 1967'.

The decision to publish, according to Phillip Knightley, came after

> the appearance of the *Sunday Times* series on Philby in November 1967, the KGB decided it would be a good idea for Philby's own version of these events to be published. Since Philby had written an extensive account of his life as part of his debriefing, it was not difficult to convert part of this into a manuscript.[43]

The Foreword to *My Silent War* provides a clue that Philby did indeed draw on his KGB debriefing autobiography. On page xvi, he writes that 'I did beat Gordon Lonsdale to the London School of Oriental Studies by ten years.' Neither before nor after those words does he provide any explanation of what this meant. Until this point, there was no indication in his career that he had ever attended any college except Cambridge. The reference becomes clear when his unpublished works are consulted (page 232 above). It is there that he explains why he took a course at the School at the suggestion of 'Theo' (Arnold Deutsch), his NKVD case officer. Whether Philby left this short reference in *My Silent War* intentionally, or whether the editor just didn't pick up on the discontinuity, or both, is not known. But it does suggest that what little he said about his recruitment by the KGB in *My Silent War* came from a more complete narrative that, because it mentions operational detail, was not written as part of his memoirs.

---

[41] Modin, *My Five Cambridge Friends*, p. 257.

[42] Philby, *My Silent War*, p. xiii.

[43] Knightley, *Philby: K.G.B. Masterspy*, p. 230. Since Philby had told *The Times* reporter, Murray Sayle, in early December 1967 that he was willing to 'withdraw my book' if the Krogers (two Americans convicted in Britain in connection with the Lonsdale case) were released – it didn't happen – some form of manuscript presumably existed then.

After devoting only a few pages to his life before joining the British Secret Intelligence Service in 1940, the final three pages cover what he cares to say about the period from 1956 to 1963 and his arrival in Moscow. The 151 pages in between summarise his quick rise in MI6 and his assignments in Turkey and the United States. While much has been written about these portions of his career, as will be seen below, there are several topics worth attention here. The first concerns the confession of atom spy Klaus Fuchs which, Philby writes (p. 125), 'led inexorably to the Rosenbergs who were duly executed'. This startling admission of guilt, in a book passed by the KGB censors, was overlooked by analysts of the Rosenberg case (though it did not escape the attention of the FBI) until Verne Newton mentioned it in his 1991 book *The Cambridge Spies*.[44]

Another topic which may have upset his former SIS colleagues was the comment that during the Second World War, 'Dilly Knox . . . had succeeded in penetrating the secrets of the cypher machine used by the Abwehr . . . It was not long before we had a very full picture of the Abwehr in the peninsula.' This was six years before publication of *The ULTRA Secret*.

Finally, although Philby doesn't disclose that while based in Lebanon he was the British representative for the *Observer* and the *Economist*, the chronology makes that explicit. What is peculiar is that no mention is made – there or anywhere else – of his work for the American magazine, *The New Republic* (*TNR*), which published eleven articles by H. A. R. Philby from April 1957 to May 1958 (see bibliography). The *TNR* Editor-At-Large throughout this period was

---

[44] FBI Memorandum, Subject: *My Silent War*, dated 29 April 1968, 2 pages, unsigned. Newton, *The Cambridge Spies*, p. 402, fn. 26; he cites the US edition of *My Silent War*, p. 170. Newton's book focuses on the activities of Maclean, Burgess and Philby in the United States. He wrote to Philby on 11 April 1985 and asked him some questions after outlining the book. To demonstrate the extent of his research, he related how he had tracked down the name of the restaurant (The Peking on Connecticut Avenue) where he and James Angleton had their last meal together. Newton had asked Angleton first without response. Angleton confirmed the restaurant only after Newton located a witness. Philby never answered the letter, though he did note parenthetically on page two 'unknown to me'.

a 1937 Cambridge graduate and one-time NKVD agent, Michael Straight. In 1983, when asked about the circumstances leading to the Philby articles, Straight said that he had forgotten about them and didn't know the details. He added that he had not known Philby, who appeared at Cambridge only once after returning from Vienna in 1934.[45]

With all the attention *My Silent War* received on publication, it was only the beginning. As authors, journalists and scholars sought to understand and document Cold War espionage, its causes, its products and its by-products, Kim Philby would become for one side the model ideological agent and for the other, a symbol of shameless treachery. As a consequence, in the more than thirty years since 1968, his memoirs have become one of the most quoted books on counter-intelligence.

AN ESPIONAGE ICON EMERGES

In the decades following the initial outburst of Philby books, interest in the case did not diminish. By the late 1990s, it had been mentioned in varying degrees of detail in more than 100 books and articles (see bibliography) making Kim Philby the best known, if not the most important, spy since the Second World War. Despite the large number, the question of where to start learning about the case – what to read and in what order – is manageable.

The approach adopted here is based on the assumption that, in general, the books fall into one of three categories: brief case summaries; biographies and books devoted primarily to Philby; and portions of memoirs or intelligence service histories that discuss the case. The basis for choosing between the first two alternatives is self evident, although the choices among the entries may be less so, and the comments on each are intended to aid that decision. Similarly, the third category offers information on particular aspects of the Philby case – for example, motivation, recruitment, the third man issue, the materials he gave the KGB, how he worked with his

---

[45] Author conversation with Michael Straight, 7 April 1983.

Cambridge colleagues, the circumstances of and reasons for his defection – and they will be emphasised herein.

Characteristic of books in the first category are short narrative descriptions, usually including his Cambridge spy colleagues Burgess and Maclean, and sometimes Anthony Blunt and John Cairncross, the other members of the so-called Cambridge Five. They are useful for gaining a broad overview of the case, but often err when it comes to detail. Sorting out the correct answer is not always easy and sometimes impossible. Nevertheless, comments on reliability are included in titles discussed below and those in the bibliography.

Typical errors include: details of Philby's recruitment; claims that he joined the Communist Party at Cambridge; the statement that Philby was a KGB officer (the rank varies); the comment that his second wife worked at Bletchley Park; and, the most frequent, that he was himself a double agent. Representative of this group are the Electronic Encyclopaedia Britannica – it makes them all – Richard Deacon's *Spyclopaedia*; Jay Robert Nash's *SPIES*, Ronald Seth's *Encyclopedia of Espionage*; George O'Toole's *Encyclopedia of American Intelligence and Espionage*; Mark Lloyd's *The Guinness Book of Espionage*; and the most recent and the best of the lot, Polmar and Allen's *SPY Book*. See the bibliography for a list of titles in this group.[46]

---

[46] The errors found in these volumes are the result of basing the summaries on secondary sources. Some entries cite sources used at the end, without giving a page number. Others include a bibliography. The most unreliable do neither. Other examples in this category include Janusz Piekalkiewicz's *Secret Agents, Spies, and Saboteurs*, an encyclopedia-like collection of espionage cases; Michael Burn's *The Debatable Land*, with Philby on the cover, but barely mentioned inside; Ronald Seth's *SPIES: Their Trade and their Tricks* (NY: Hawthorn Books, 1969); and Bernard Newman's *Spy and Counterspy* (London: Robert Hale, 1970). Piekalkiewicz published an updated edition in German, *Weltgeschichte der SPIONAGE: Agenten, Systeme, Aktionen*, in 1988, that contains a large section on the case. A limited English edition, translated by William M. Henhoeffer and Gerald L. Liebenau, was published in 1998 as the *World History of Espionage: Agents, Systems, Operations*, by Südwest Publishers GmBH & Co., KG, Munich. The *Encyclopædia Britannica Online* lists 170 articles having to do with Philby (http://www.eb.com:195/bol/topic?eu=61146&sctn=1).

THE PHILBY BIOGRAPHIES

This category contains only six entries and one, Morris Riley's *PHILBY: The Hidden Years*, doesn't deserve serious consideration from an overall point of view. It does quote an interesting 1971 interview with Philby (pp. 122–5) in *Kodummaa* (13 October 1971, No. 41) in reaction to the expulsion from Britain of 105 Soviet intelligence officers. In the article Philby names SIS officers and agents in the Middle East. But otherwise Riley's efforts resemble counter-espionage according to Inspector Clouseau. He would have us believe that Philby was 'a recruited Soviet agent before he left Cambridge', and later not only a KGB agent but 'also an agent for the CIA, which he helped to form'; that Philby was once an agent of Walter Krivitsky and in 1962 was controlled by 'Yuri Modin'; that there was a 'deadly collaboration between Philby and George Blake' while both were SIS officers; that Philby didn't live in Moscow and had to be brought there when needed; that Philby was a 'chief recruiter' of Nazi war criminals for British Intelligence and later a KGB officer 'based in Moscow' before being appointed 'head of the Department of Western Propaganda for Novosti'.[47] A note in the revised edition explains its prior problems. Biographical data, Patrick Seale's name and the index have been deleted, and there is some additional material. Both editions remain shameless examples of exaggeration, inaccuracy and sloppy reliance on secondary sources.

---

[47] None of these assertions is documented and they are only a few of the appalling mistakes in this short book. Krivitsky never met Philby, nor did Modin until after Philby defected. Both Blake and his former case officer, Lt-Gen. Sergei Kondrashev, maintained in interviews with the author that neither Philby nor Blake knew of the other's KGB connection before Blake's arrest and Philby's defection. Author interviews with other retired KGB officers including Oleg Kalugin, Yuri Modin, Lev Koshliakov, Vassilli Dozhdalev, Gennady-X, Yuri Kobaladze and Vadim Kirpichenko, and Phillip Knightley, all of whom knew him at various times during his Moscow years, leave no doubt that Philby always lived in Moscow after his defection, was not involved with recruiting Nazis and never headed any Soviet Department, however much he might have wished otherwise.

The other five books, in order of publication, are: the 1969 revised edition of Page, Leitch and Knightley, *Philby: The Spy Who Betrayed a Generation*; Patrick Seale and Maureen McConville, *PHILBY: The Long Road to Moscow* (1973); Phillip Knightley, *PHILBY: K.G.B. Masterspy* (1988), Anthony Cave Brown, *Treason in the Blood* (1994) and Genrikh Borovik, *The Philby Files* (1994). While each has its own viewpoint, there is a rough consensus on the question of Philby's motivation. His conversion to Marxism in 1933, followed by his decision to work secretly for the Soviet Union in 1934, allowed him to do something about Fascism in a manner agreeable to him. It is well put by a former colleague, 'Philby adopted both with the tenacity of a priest taking vows.' But, he went on, 'Philby's conversion was intellectual, not humanitarian, whatever he may have said subsequently . . . the sufferings of the working class meant nothing to him. He never endured them himself.'[48]

Philby: The Spy Who Betrayed a Generation

The 1969 Penguin revision of Page *et al.* has a new twenty-five page Author's Preface that discusses the points of coincidence and differences with Philby's memoirs which they had not seen when the first edition went to press. They also mention some sources omitted from the first edition, comment on what some of the reviewers said about their book, and explain why, despite official pressure not to publish, they went ahead. There is nothing new on the FBI, but the chapter that mentions the Elvis-like Philby sighting along the Turkish-Soviet border, sometime after he left SIS in 1951, expresses less confidence in that tale than was indicated in the first edition.[49] The comment about FBI special agent Melvin Purvis was not corrected and Philby's activities in the United States get only a brief

---

[48] Unpublished comments from a former SIS colleague who prefers to remain anonymous. He also described Philby 'as a man of great pride and to have gone back on either of his decisions would have been personally traumatic'.

[49] The authors did add some sources at the end of the chapter who are 'almost sure – but not quite – that Philby was in Cyprus in the early fifties', but they also deleted a sentence that said 'on balance, we are inclined to think that this was a genuine glimpse . . .' Page *et al.*, *Philby*, 1969, p. 291.

comment. With these limitations, the book remains an exemplar of investigative reporting about an organisation that, at the time, did not officially exist.[50]

Philby: The Long Road to Moscow

Seale and McConville's 1973 book is one of the major Philby biographies and still has much to recommend it as a good overview of the case. It is a story well told, well documented and not given to the tooth-fairy speculation of some later authors. Seale knew Philby in Beirut – eventually succeeding him there – and had ghosted Eleanor Philby's memoirs. The insight and understanding gained as a consequence is evident throughout.

While the account of Philby's recruitment and his years in Moscow is incomplete – and they recognised the fact – in view of what is now known, many details about his family background, education, personal life and his tour of duty in Washington had not been covered before and provide a genuine sense of the man. It is here, for example, that one learns that Philby's scholarship earned at Westminster was to Oxford, not Cambridge. Only after his father intervened was the destination changed. We learn too that after his resignation from SIS in 1951, he had an affair with 'Connie', a British civil servant,[51] by whom he had a son while married to Aileen, his second wife.[52]

One of the grey areas of Philby's career concerns what he did after

---

[50] The 1977 Sphere issue of the book included the new preface, but the 1969 Signet and the 1981 Ballantine editions, published in America under the title *The Philby Conspiracy*, did not. All editions included the Introduction by John le Carré.

[51] Seale and McConville, p. 220 passim, are the only writers to mention 'Connie', a name thought to be a pseudonym. Nicholas Elliott is the only other author to mention this affair; see his book, *Never Judge a Man by his Umbrella*, p. 186.

[52] According to *The Times* (13 March 1984), the boy, then forty-four, 'was rejected by his parents'. This led to 'a life of drunkenness, drug taking, and crime'. He lives under the name of Alan Young, is a former soldier, has '12 convictions for offenses of dishonesty', and was a 'market trader of Selbourne House', before serving two and one half years 'after admitting to blackmail and burglary'.

leaving SIS in 1951 and going off to Beirut in 1956. The authors were the first to fill in part of the gap when they mentioned that Philby had gone to Ireland in January 1956 for six months to help a Foreign Office friend (and later a Member of Parliament) from his Istanbul days, W. E. D. Allen, write a family history. The introduction to his book mentions only that certain portions were written by a friend of the author 'who wishes to remain anonymous'. Allen reassures the reader that his friend is 'an experienced journalist and social historian' who provided 'a fair and objective account'. Many years later, Tim Milne confirmed that his boyhood friend, classmate and MI6 colleague, Kim Philby, had indeed been the anonymous friend mentioned by Allen.[53]

Seale and McConville also raise crucial and even now not completely answered questions: why did he do it and, once started, did he have any choice other than to continue? Their explanations give the reader, unfamiliar with the times, a better grasp of the social and political conditions that operated on Philby in his formative years from which he seemingly never deviated. The short final chapter on Philby the pensioner in Moscow shows how little was known about him there even ten years after his defection. It would be another fifteen years before Phillip Knightley changed the situation.

PHILBY: K.G.B. Masterspy
In early 1988, Phillip Knightley travelled to Moscow and became the first Western journalist to interview Philby at length – some six days – about his life and career. They had corresponded since 1968 and Knightley had tried to arrange an interview before. Whether it was finally granted because of *glasnost*, ill health, some secret KGB motive, or all three, can't be known, but the result was worth the effort. He began writing this book on his return to London and was planning a second visit to Moscow when Philby died in May 1988.

It had been twenty years since he co-authored one of the first Philby biographies with Page and Leitch, and Knightley begins with the story of how that book originated. He then describes each of the

---

[53] W.E.D. Allens, *David Allens: The History of a Family Firm 1857–1957*. Author conversation with Tim Milne, 12 November 1997.

principal phases of Philby's life, but this time, based on Philby's own input from the interviews and their long correspondence. The results tell much that was new about Philby and his Moscow existence – and something about Knightley, who does not hold the practice of espionage in high regard – with pictures of his oft-mentioned flat, including the library of something over 3,000 volumes.[54] Knightley summarises the kinds of books found in the eclectic Philby collection and the photographs on the walls, before going on to describe the living- and dining-rooms of the flat.

The Philby that emerges from the Knightley interviews is no cheerleader of Communism – he found the 'Brezhnev period stultifying'. When in the early 1980s things changed, he told Knightley that he 'never did discover what went wrong with his relationship with the KGB' (p. 234). The work just stopped coming. Still, it appeared that he had accepted the Soviet class distinctions – hypocritical or no – and admitted to enjoying the privileges of a general – 'strictly speaking, I have no military rank' (p. 256) – while acknowledging such privileges should be, but are not, available to all.

---

[54] Knightley gives a figure of 12,000 books on page 16 of the book. In September 1998, I made a count of the books still in the library and the figure was 2,952. Most were in the study, some were in the hallway, and a few remained in the living-room (see photo section above). Approximately 100 volumes had been sold at the Sotheby's auction in July 1994, and a few had been given away or sold privately. But one unalterable fact argues against the 10,000 or 12,000 figure: there is just not enough room for that many books on the existing shelves in the flat, and they are all that have ever been there, according to Rufina Philby. When questioned about the large figure, Knightley recalled that the one he used came from Philby during their 1988 conversations. To confirm this he kindly checked his notes and found that they reflected the 10,000 figure. He may have recorded the lower of the range of Philby's estimate. Why Philby had such a large figure in mind is impossible to tell, but my experience with casual, visual estimations of the number of volumes in a given area is that it is usually off by two times. I doubt that Philby even counted his volumes; there was no need since they were not inventoried for insurance purposes. Author conversation with Phillip Knightley, 5 December 1997; phone conversation, 21 December 1998; e-mail from Knightley, 25 December 1998.

Not all of Knightley's questions were answered. The areas of Philby's recruitment and espionage activities for the KGB were still off limits.

Masterspy concludes with reflections on the question of why Philby remains something of an obsession with the British – and to some extent the American – public, thirty years after he defected. He is less surprised than some of his journalist colleagues about this situation and even envisages positive outcomes from it all. As he sees it, Philby's case has more to do with betrayal of class than betrayal of country; 'he did it for his ideals'. For Knightley, Philby is 'the most remarkable spy in the history of espionage'. For the reader, this book is essential to understanding Philby's case.

Treason in the Blood

After reading Anthony Cave Brown's book, *Bodyguard of Lies*, 'with enjoyment', Philby wrote to Phillip Knightley about the 'monster book' problem:

> Such books are: 70% true and much of that important; 15% dead wrong and the rest distracting decoration which is becoming regrettably fashionable these days, 'what-Monty's-batman-had-for-breakfast-on-D-Day [sic] sort of thing'.[55]

While the numbers may vary, the admonition also applies to Brown's 678-page *Treason in the Blood*. That said, it must also be acknowledged as the most comprehensive treatment of the Philby story, providing, as it does, a dual biography of Kim and his father, the famous Arabist, author and explorer, St John. And though the focus here is on the son, it is worth pointing out that the thesis implicit in the title – that both were guilty of treason that was somehow in their genes – is intriguing but not proved. St John may have been viewed as the radical Professor Moriarty of the Colonial Office, but when their differences could not be reconciled, he resigned, renounced his citizenship and became an Arab. His son chose another form of rebellion.

---

[55] Philby letter to Phillip Knightley, 30 October 1977.

Brown has taken full advantage of the Philby literature and added other valuable sources to produce a singular work that tracks the Philbys from birth to death. The book makes use of Philby's unpublished papers and materials declassified by the CIA, as well as interviews with Philby's former FBI and CIA acquaintances and his KGB colleagues. More on the latter to follow.

There are a number of facts and anecdotes that appear here for the first time. One of the most interesting and important is the role of Madame Modrzhinskaya, the NKGB analyst who, according to Mikhail Lyubimov, suspected Philby and his Cambridge colleagues of being provocations. Brown does not, unfortunately, discuss the impact of the suspicion; that would come later in West and Tsarev, *The Crown Jewels* (see below). Brown is also the only one to mention Philby's equivalent British rank of major during the war and to identify his secretary in Istanbul, Miss Whitfield, who travelled with him there and accompanied him to Washington. As to what Philby actually did in Moscow for the KGB, Brown quotes a former KGB comrade, identified only as Gennady-X, who was a specialist in Active Measures (often disinformation operations designed to influence, if not distort, the opponent's opinions). Gennady-X worked with Philby for many years and he tells in general terms how Philby was often asked to help with operations involving English-speaking adversaries.[56]

In another intriguing first-time revelation, Brown tells of the CIA Black Band Boxes, so named because of the black tape around the boxes that contained them in the CIA archives. One of the folders in the Black Files dealt with Philby and, according to Brown, contained evidence that William K. Harvey, the man in charge of CIA counterintelligence while Philby was in Washington, 'suspected Philby was a traitor' from the time Philby arrived in Washington in 1949. Brown

---

[56] Brown, *Treason in the Blood*, p. 599. Brown was prohibited from using Gennady-X's surname, but in a mischievous gesture, he noted that Gennady-X had accompanied Oleg Kalugin to Columbia University in the late 1950s. Kalugin acknowledges him in his book, *The First Directorate*, and uses the surname in the narrative. He also includes his picture without naming him in the caption. See Kalugin, p. 341.

documents his position with first-hand comments from John Mapother, who, along with several of his colleagues, read the Philby folder in the Black Band Files.[57] The assertion is further reinforced with quotes from Hugh Montgomery, Harvey's assistant and confidant at the time, and later a UN Ambassador. In a recent discussion Montgomery confirmed that Brown was correct about Harvey's suspicions prior to the Maclean-Burgess defections, but was unsure when they began. He added that he had discussed the Philby case with Harvey often and at great length; Harvey convinced him that he had suspected Philby's true role for some time prior to the defection of Burgess and Maclean.[58] Unfortunately, the record is blank as to what, if any, action was taken by Harvey before Burgess and Maclean defected.

There are a number of things to keep in mind when reading *Treason in the Blood*. First, while there are many endnotes, there are also numerous instances where a source citation was needed but not provided. In either case, the book is prone to small factual errors and

---

[57] Brown, *ibid.*, pp. 421–2. Brown calls them the 'Black Files', but according to Mapother and former CIA officer Samuel Halpern, the correct term is the Black Band Files or Boxes. Brown also writes that he was told by Robert Joyce, a State Department employee, that Frank Wisner had suspected that Philby was a Soviet agent in 1950 when the Albanian operations were compromised, well before Burgess and Maclean defected. He adds that confirmation that Wisner told anyone 'is nowhere evident'. What he doesn't discuss is why Wisner and the CIA went ahead with the Albanian operations if he suspected Philby then, and especially after Burgess and Maclean defected and Philby was recalled and dismissed.

[58] *Ibid.*, p. 422. Mapother does not now recall the date of Harvey's memos in the Black Band Boxes, nor does he remember saying that Harvey's suspicions went back as far as 1949, but it is possible that he did. But there is no doubt, he said, that the files indicated that Harvey was suspicious of Philby. Phone conversation with Mapother, 9 March 1999. Author conversation with Ambassador Montgomery, 16 March 1999. Author David C. Martin tells a version of the Harvey story to the effect that Harvey told friends that the truth about Philby 'had come to him as he sat stalled in traffic one morning on his way to work'. No indication is given as to when this flash occurred, but it could have happened anytime before Philby was recalled. Martin, *Wilderness of Mirrors*, p. 54.

ambiguities presented as fact. This is probably inevitable in a work of this size, but a few examples should alert the reader. In this regard, Arnold Deutsch, the man who recruited Philby after his return from Vienna in 1934, did not die in South America in 1942 as Brown indicates (p. 194); he was lost at sea when his ship, the *Donbass*, was sunk on its way to the United States.[59] And, former Westminster classmate I. I. Milne was not withdrawn as Head of Station in Hong Kong after Philby defected; he was not even in Hong Kong. Similarly, he was not a witness at Philby's wedding with Aileen as Brown claims.[60]

On page 219 Brown asserts that Colonel Claude Dansey, the MI6 assistant chief of staff, ran 'the Rote Drei, the Soviet intelligence service in Switzerland'. Although Brown is not the only author to make the claim in the literature, the others cite no evidence in support, and none is given here.[61] Then there is Brown's claim that Yuri Modin had 'had contact with Philby since 1944'; Modin says and wrote that he

---

[59] Although Brown doesn't mention it, the Russians are divided on where Deutsch was headed when he died. Volume 3 of the KGB History says that Deutsch's eventual destination was Latin America. Weinstein and Vasilliev, on the other hand, write in *Haunted Wood* that Deutsch was headed for the New York Residency to expand its recruiting operations. Neither Brown nor Nazhestkin, *The KGB History*, cite a source. *Haunted Wood* cites KGB file #35112, Vol. 1, p. 38.

[60] Brown, *Treason in the Blood*, p. 531. Conversation with I. I. (Tim) Milne (nephew of A. A. Milne), 3 December 1997, Red Willows, England. Milne said that Philby did not like Westminster and 'did not mince words about it'. Milne rode in Philby's sidecar on their first of several trips to Europe as college students and worked with him in SIS Section V during the war. Milne said that although Philby sometimes fought to get out a word, his stammer was hardly apparent if one knew him well. And to set the record straight, Milne did not, as Brown (and others) claimed, live in the same staircase at Oxford as Hugh Trevor-Roper, who was two years junior.

[61] Neither the CIA nor the SIS studies of the Rote Kapelle/Rote Drei give any hint whatsoever that Dansey was linked to the Rote Drei network, let alone directed it. See *The Rote Kapelle: The CIA's History of Soviet Intelligence and Espionage Networks in Western Europe, 1936–1945* (Frederick, MD, University Publications of America, Inc., 1986); SERPELL/HEMBLYS-SCALES Report, *The Rote Kapelle*, National Archives, College Park, MD.

didn't meet Philby until after his arrival in the Soviet Union in 1963.[62] Brown also writes that DCI Turner brought KGB defector Yuri Nosenko 'into the bosom of the CIA as a top analyst' and was turned 'loose on the most secret of American secrets' (pp. 561–2); it just didn't happen.[63]

Finally, Mikhail Lyubimov first met Philby in 1974, not 1964 (p. 587); Philby was fifty-eight when he met Rufina, not sixty-eight, and her father was Russian not Polish while her mother was Polish not Russian (p. 595). And Rufina strenuously objects to Brown's statement that she 'moved in KGB circles' before she married Kim, because people have told her it implies she was a KGB asset. This is not so, she said, despite Brown's citations of interviews with her implying she provided the information.[64] On this point Oleg Kalugin and Rufina agree. He states emphatically that she 'was not a KGB informant, nor did she socialize with KGB officers, and might even be considered a dissident'. The phrase *'moved in KGB circles'*, he said, should be read as being acceptable to the KGB after background inquiries were made.[65]

Of much greater importance as far as Philby's espionage career is concerned, are several propositions advanced by Brown that at first glance suggest new explanations for and/or reinforcement of old Philby questions, but, when sources are examined, amount to little more than speculation. While the arguments are not presented as analytical cul-de-sacs, the critical points are not always self-evident; Brown makes one think.

---

[62] Interview with the author, National Hotel, Moscow, 8 June 1987. Brown also cites interviews with Modin in Washington and Moscow as the basis for his statement. I asked Col. Modin about this and he replied that Brown had misunderstood him when he spoke of meeting with the other Cambridge agents in London. I asked five other retired KGB officers and two serving SVR officers about the disparity. Their responses were unanimous; Modin was under orders not to meet Philby in London. Rufina Philby says Kim never met Modin in London or in Moscow, while she was married to him.

[63] Personal knowledge.

[64] Author interviews with Oleg Kalugin, Moscow, 11 June 1997, and Washington DC, 14 March 1999; and with Rufina Philby, Moscow, 24, 26 November 1997, 10, 11 September 1998.

[65] Author discussion with Oleg Kalugin, Washington DC, 14 March 1999.

The first proposition has to do with an issue raised in some detail by Andrew Boyle in his *Climate of Treason* (1979). Boyle stated that James Angleton, head of CIA Israeli accounts, was aware, through Israeli intelligence, that Philby, Burgess, and Maclean were Soviet agents long before the latter two defected, and moreover that he used them for disinformation purposes against the KGB. Boyle's treatment will be dealt with later in a discussion of that work.

Brown summarises Boyle's version and then adds two additional sources that tend to support it. The first is William Corson, who in his book, *The Armies of Ignorance*, published two years before Boyle, makes the same accusations. Brown does not mention that Corson's allegations were not documented. The second new source is Major-General Edwin L. Sibert, former G-2 of 12th Army Group and later an Assistant Director of the CIA, who, in an interview with Brown, said that Philby was 'used as a conduit of disinformation about the effectiveness of SAC [the Strategic Air Command] and the size of the US atomic arsenal "at the time of the Korean war"' (pp. 401–3). Brown does not conclude that Sibert was correct, but does say that Philby was a good candidate for such a 'stratagem'. The reader is left to sort out reality.

The second proposition is linked to the first and implies that Philby was really a British mole recruited, if not doubled, and controlled by 'C' to penetrate or feed disinformation to the KGB, and perhaps be a source even after he defected. This is a favourite theme of Brown's; he attempted to develop it more in an earlier biography of Sir Stewart Menzies, the 'C' involved.[66] Brown suggests that Philby was indeed used in this manner, with the blessing of 'C', and in support of this argument he quotes a book edited by Allen Dulles:

> His [Philby's] particular task was to mastermind British double agents, to penetrate [German] intelligence and – ironically – *to feed false information to the Soviets*. He soon established a reputation for brilliance in the work . . . Since one of his official duties was maintaining liaison with Soviet intelligence . . .

---

[66] Brown, *The Secret Servant*, pp. 742–51.

The source for this quote is Allen Dulles's *Great True Spy Stories* (NY: Harper & Row, 1968), pp. 54–5. Brown thus concludes that:

'C', initially at least, recruited Philby as a deception agent for work against both the Soviet Union and the Third Reich. Dulles's high authority in world espionage, his trustworthy mien, lend his statement a rare credibility. Dulles was there, he knew about Philby. And it was a view to which Philby could never admit. [p. 265]

How Dulles knew all this is not stated. Neither is the fact that the author of the quote is Edward Sheehan, not Allen Dulles. Brown provides no basis for accepting the conjecture that Philby was a British KGB mole.

The third proposition concerns Brown's description of Philby's wartime activities. While other writers have concluded that Philby dealt with British operations against the Nazis in Spain and later the Mediterranean, Brown asserts that Philby was 'inextricably interwoven' with 'four wartime Soviet institutions in the underground of Europe' in geographic areas outside his nominal responsibility, specifically:

'An unspecified component of the French resistance movement' (p. 246).
'The German communist resistance movement, known as the Rote Kapelle (Red Orchestra)' (p. 245).
'A German operation against the Dutch resistance movement, code-named North Pole' (p. 246).
'The Soviet point for operations inside Germany. The main Soviet network there was code-named the Rote Drei, the Red Three' (p. 246).

The first item is not worth commenting on without documented specifics; Brown does not provide them, though he does speculate at length (pp. 566–7).

For the other three items Brown cites the following source: 'CIA: *Review of Intelligence*, declassified 1985; "Intelligence in the recent Public Literature", on the subject of classic Soviet nets.' Since the CIA does not publish a *Review of Intelligence*, he clearly meant the quarterly journal, *Studies in Intelligence*, that does have a section called Intelligence in the recent Public Literature, which contains book reviews. The first review in the Fall 1968 issue is titled *Classic Soviet Nets* and discusses Philby's memoirs, *The Philby Conspiracy* (Page *et al.*), Cookridge's *Third Man* and Eleanor Philby's, *The Spy I Married*.[67]

In its comments on *The Philby Conspiracy*, the review criticises the authors for ignoring Philby's 'role in Operation North Pole and his connection with Communist resistance in France and the Rote Kapelle'. None of the other Philby books or articles had made this claim before and no source is given by the review author in this instance, nor does he describe the nature of Philby's role. Had this been an official CIA assessment, specifics would have been required, but a book review is just opinion.[68] Beyond this reference to the Red Orchestra, Brown never mentions it again with respect to Philby.

Operation North Pole is a different matter and here Brown identifies another source. The late CIA analyst William Henhoeffer, writes Brown, 'looked more closely into Philby's "inextricable involvement" . . . and concluded that Philby . . . passed [North Pole] intelligence to his Soviet contact in London' (p. 248). Brown admits that Henhoeffer's evidence 'was entirely circumstantial', but he doesn't say, and he may not have known, that Henhoeffer based his conclusion on the book review comment quoted above.[69] Brown does point out that if Philby was the source of the intelligence that

---

[67] This review, whose author is not given, is listed in the index of *Studies* articles published by the Center for the Study of Intelligence in 1992. Copies are available at the National Archives.

[68] North Pole involved sending Dutch agents, trained by the British SOE, into Holland to help the resistance; over fifty were caught, most of whom were executed after helping the Germans fool the British. The story from the German Abwehr and Gestapo side is told in H. J. Giskes, *London Calling North Pole* (London: William Kimber, 1953). Philby taught at Beaulieu, the SOE base where the first group of agents was trained, and he met them there, if you accept his statement to that effect in his memoirs. Thus he could have told the Soviets about the Operation as he would do after the war when he reported CIA and SIS attempts to put agents in Albania, with the same results.

[69] Author conversation with Bill Henhoeffer, October 1991.

compromised North Pole, the Germans had to get it from the Soviets, and this was possible before June 1941 under the terms of the 1939 Hitler-Stalin Pact. The reason for their doing so, he suggests, is that the Soviets didn't want non-Communist resistance movements in Western Europe. Although Brown cites other sources for his Philby-North Pole argument, they are indirect and do not mention him specifically. In the end, if Philby played a role in the giving up of North Pole, the details remain a secret and Brown's assertion remains just that.

Despite the 'inextricably interwoven' comment above about Philby and the Rote Drei, Brown makes only one oblique reference to Philby in that regard:

> The CIA's *Review of Intelligence* [sic] asserted that the 'lines and personalities of the Philby case [were] inextricably interwoven' with the Rote Drei (the Red Three), the Soviet intelligence system in Switzerland, which was controlled by C. [p. 268]

It was not, of course, the CIA's *Review of Intelligence* taking an official position any more than the writer of a review in *The New York Times* speaks for the paper. Just what the 'lines of the Philby case' are or mean is not discussed in the review or by Brown. But the assertion that the British controlled the Rote Drei network is preposterous and must have enraged the GRU since it was one of their best organisations. The sources cited for this claim are the same *Review of Intelligence* and the CIA *Rote Kapelle Survey Report, Swiss Section, Swiss Personalities*, but neither mentions the issue. Moreover, the latter citation is incorrect. The CIA produced no such survey report. It did release a document called *The Rote Kapelle: The CIA's History of Soviet Intelligence and Espionage Networks in Western Europe, 1936–1945*, but it does not mention the British Secret Intelligence Service (MI6) or its Chief, Stewart Menzies. This study does make clear that the Rote Drei furnished intelligence to the British, the OSS, the Swiss and the Soviets, but Philby is not named as playing a role. Philby is mentioned twice, but not in connection with the Rote Drei.[70]

---

[70] See *The Rote Kapelle* report, pp. 212–17.

In sum, all of the above is presented to suggest that the reader approach the many interesting stories in *Treason in the Blood* with care.

The Philby Files

The memorial service for Kim Philby was held in the KGB club, just to the rear of the old headquarters building known to the world as the Lubyanka. At the direction of KGB Chairman, Vladimir Kryuchkov, the first of the many guests to walk by the open casket was Major-General Oleg Kalugin. The second was the novelist, playwright, journalist and TV commentator – the Dan Rather or Jeremy Paxman of the Soviet Union – Genrikh Borovik.[71] This distinction came to Borovik in part because he had earned the respect and friendship of Kim Philby, and the KGB, during a series of taped conversations lasting fifty hours beginning in the summer of 1985.[72] He had also arranged a series of Moscow meetings for Philby with his old friend, Graham Greene, that earned him the lasting gratitude of the old KGB agent.

Borovik had originally intended to do a movie based on the interviews, but after Philby's death he decided against it. For various reasons having to do with his busy TV schedule and other interests,

---

[71] Author conversation with Oleg Kalugin, 3 February 1995.

[72] In a conversation with Genrikh Borovik, 20 November 1997, he explained that the Philby interviews grew out of a request to the KGB in 1985 to allow him to interview a spy, any spy, since many of his competitors had published stories of various agents or operations. He said he was owed such an opportunity because the KGB had prevented publication of his espionage novel in the 1960s. In the new *glasnost* atmosphere, he decided to try again. To his surprise he was offered the opportunity to interview Philby, if Philby agreed; he did. To some in the West, this form of KGB debt-paying will seem unusual. But Oleg Kalugin confirms that Borovik had a good reputation with the KGB for at least two reasons. First, he would write articles about KGB operations based on KGB briefings when asked to do so. Second, when so asked, he always demanded to know if the story was true and would not write it unless he received assurances that it was. Unfortunately, as Kalugin admits in his book (p. 158), Borovik was given the assurances, in one case by Kalugin himself, when the story was not true; but those were the rules of the day.

nothing at all was done until he mentioned the interviews to Graham Greene on his last visit to Moscow. Greene suggested doing a book contrasting Philby's view of his career as told in the interviews with Philby's KGB files, an idea that would never have occurred to Borovik. But he followed through with a letter to the KGB and to his surprise was granted unprecedented access to the Philby case file No. 5581. *The Philby Files* was the result.[73]

The book begins with Philby in Beirut when he is interviewed by his old SIS friend, Nicholas Elliott, who convinces him that his former Service had acquired convincing evidence of his years as a Soviet agent. The story jumps to Philby's days at Cambridge, his activities in Vienna, his subsequent recruitment – a topic he wouldn't discuss with Phillip Knightley or anyone else – and continues through each of the familiar stages of his career until his death, on 11 May 1988. What makes it worthwhile reading the story again is the material Borovik obtained from Philby's case file, juxtaposed to Philby's own recollections and views. Here we learn facts that, in some instances, not even Philby knew. One of the most interesting examples tells why the Soviets came to distrust Philby, Burgess and Cairncross – though not Maclean – before the war. Here we learn details of why KGB analyst Yelena Modrzhinskaya, mentioned briefly by Anthony Cave Brown in *Treason in the Blood*, concluded that Philby and his colleagues were really British provocations, and how he continued his work and regained their trust, with some exceptions, without ever realising his predicament.

After many hours of interviews, Philby finally reveals that the person who introduced him to his recruiter in London was Edith Tudor-Hart, a connection MI5 long suspected but never proved. He also gives a slight variation on the story behind the defection of Burgess and Maclean. Borovik then contrasts this with information from Burgess's case officer in London, Yuri Modin. Borovik concludes that Burgess had not planned to defect, and went to Moscow only on the promise that he would be allowed to return. The KGB then refused to let him leave. This, of course, put Philby in jeopardy. But no explanation is offered as to why the KGB did what it did. As Modin said when asked why, 'It just happened.'

---

[73] *Ibid.*

In his insightful and candid introduction to *The Philby Files*, Phillip Knightley, the author of his own valuable Philby biography, writes that 'The reader should be prepared to have his views about the KGB and Philby shattered for ever. I know that some of mine have been.' For this reason alone Genrikh Borovik deserves praise for his efforts. That the book is stimulating reading is an added benefit.

None of the biographies discussed above cover precisely the same events and, where there is overlap, most offer pertinent differences in detail. For these reasons, no one book is recommended as *the* one to read. Given the time and the desire to acquire a sense of the Philby case with all its nuances and controversies, a sensible approach would be to start – though the sequence is not crucial – with Seale and McConville's *PHILBY: The Long Road to Moscow*, followed by Knightley's *PHILBY: K.G.B. Masterspy*, Borovik's *The Philby Files*, and finally Anthony Cave Brown's *Treason in the Blood*. Even this approach will leave the serious reader with questions. Fortunately, many of them can be answered by consulting one or more of the following books that make important but narrower contributions to the case.

SUPPLEMENTARY PHILBY SOURCES

In most cases, the books in this section add details or discuss facts about the Philby case that are either not covered at all, or in sufficient depth, in the biographies and early studies discussed above. Also included are comments from Philby, on various books about intelligence-related subjects, found in his correspondence.

The Mosley Connection
In 1978, Leonard Mosley, an author not distinguished for accuracy or modesty, wrote about Philby in his biography of the Dulles family.[74] Mosley was able to establish contact with Philby through British friends and the subsequent correspondence is quoted in the book. It was also the subject of an article in *Esquire* magazine (28 March 1978)

---

[74] The first chapter of *Dulles* describes a party attended by a number of CIA officials at the home of Allen Dulles in Georgetown that never took place.

that began by telling the reader how well he (Mosley) knew Philby, an assertion conspicuously absent in the book. Nevertheless, Mosley sent Philby two sets of questions, the first addressed to 'Colonel Philby', the other simply to 'Mr Philby'. In due course, Philby answered them in some depth, criticising Dulles, Wisner and Eisenhower in the process, while complimenting Kim Roosevelt, the grandson of Teddy Roosevelt and the CIA officer in charge of US interests during the 1953 coup in Tehran, and DCI Walter Bedell Smith. Others about whom Mosley asked included 'members of Allen Dulles' circle – Bob Amory, Cord Meyer, Walter Pforzheimer, Lawrence Houston, etc . . . and Colonel Schwarzkopf [Gen. Norman Schwarzkopf's father]'. With regard to this group, Philby replied that if he had ever met them it had 'slipped his memory'. In response to a question about British General Kenneth Strong, Eisenhower's wartime intelligence officer, and the possibility that DCI Smith wanted Strong to be Deputy Director of Intelligence, Philby replied that 'I find it impossible to believe . . . except in jest.'[75]

Whatever Mosley's failings, lack of candour was not among them. In a letter of 24 April 1977, Mosley, who had read Philby's articles in the *Observer*, wrote that 'I had forgotten how well you write . . . *My Silent War*, though fascinating and amusing, seems to me to have been written by you with only half your mind on it, as though your thoughts were strongly engaged elsewhere.' Mosley went on to say that Philby would probably consider this a 'most impertinent' remark and apologised in advance. 'On the contrary,' replied Philby on 25 May 1977:

I know very well that it is highly pertinent, an awful lot had to be omitted, not only for reasons of state. I have been writing pretty assiduously to fill the gaps. But when, or even if, the material will ever be published is another matter, depending on a lot of things happening on both sides of the fence.[76]

The papers found in Philby's files after his death do not indicate that he wrote anything during the period covered by the letter, though

---

[75] Letter to Leonard Mosley from Kim Philby, 6 April 1977.

[76] A year later, in a 13 April 1978 letter to Philby, Mosley commented on the reception of his Dulles biography by the Dulles family. 'Eleanor', the sister, 'accuses me of writing fiction about her family, but came up with no specifics.'

such material could have been among that collected by the KGB when it went through his things, reclaiming, inter alia, his typewriter.[77]

Then in a letter written on 13 April 1978, Mosley tells Philby that the response to the publication of Philby's portion of their correspondence had been very positive. In fact, he notes, Professor Richard H. Ullman in his *New York Times* review of the Dulles book wrote that 'Philby's letters, written from Moscow . . . contain, in fact, the best writing in it.' Finally Mosley wrote, 'The Agency appears to be annoyed at my picture of Allen, and extremely irritated by the quotations from your letters.' There is no Philby response in his files, nor do they contain any reason why he chose to carry on the correspondence. Mosley's contribution remains the elicitation of Philby's views as expressed in the letters.

The Fourth, Fifth, Man Controversies

After Kim Philby defected, it was finally acknowledged that he was 'the third man' of the Burgess-Maclean defection operation and a member of what later came to be called the Cambridge Ring of Five. It was not long before suggestions that the count need not stop at three began to be heard. One of the first mentions of a *'hypothetical fourth man'* in a book is found in T .E. B. Howarth's *Cambridge between Two Wars* (p. iii), but it was a qualified comment suggesting that the *fourth man* was the one who recruited Philby, Burgess and Maclean. Howarth ignored Goronwy Rees's suggestion in his *Chapter of Accidents* that, if the defectors Burgess and Maclean were Soviet agents, 'others remained . . . in the ranks of the security services themselves'. Rees knew what he was talking about. In 1951, after Burgess and Maclean escaped, Rees went to MI5 and named a number of former and serving Soviet agents in MI5. He delicately excluded himself, but included Anthony Blunt. Apparently he had no suspicions about Philby and left him off the list.[78]

At the end of the 1970s Phillip Knightley wrote to Philby about

---

[77] Conversation with Rufina Philby, Moscow, 8 June 1997.

[78] Rees, *Chapter of Accidents* (London: Chatto & Windus, 1972), p. 221. Rees, a life-long friend of Burgess, had himself been a Soviet agent maintaining contact until the mid-1960s. After the defection of Burgess and Maclean, Rees volunteered names to MI5 of other possible Soviet agents, excluding himself. For more on his role in the affair, see West's *Molehunt*.

two new books: Richard Deacon's 'The British Connection . . . full of the Fourth-Fifth-Sixth Man stuff' and the soon-to-be-published Andrew Boyle's Climate of Treason, 'said to be about to name the Seventh-Eighth-and Ninth Man'.[79] Deacon, a former Sunday Times journalist, had discovered that Sir Anthony Blunt, a Cambridge colleague of Burgess and Maclean, had also been a Soviet agent and intended to name him as the fourth man in the book. After making his intentions known, Blunt promptly threatened – bluffed – legal action and Deacon's publisher was forced to back-off. He settled for an indirect description of Blunt's links to his fellow Cambridge agents, while suggesting that rather than search for an omnipotent agent recruiter, 'what one should be looking for is not a Fourth or a Fifth Man, but for the sixth, seventh or eighth, etc.,' as agents not recruiters. Unfortunately for Deacon, one of his candidates for the agent queue was Sir Rudolf Peierls, whom he identified as dead. When questioned by the press, Sir Rudolf replied that 'The allegation that I have been a Russian spy is as inaccurate as the claim that I am dead.' The British Connection was withdrawn from the bookstalls never to return.[80] The irony in all this is that Deacon was right about Peierls too, as Nigel West was to show in his book, Venona: The Greatest Secret of the Cold War.

In his reply to Knightley, Philby did not comment on Deacon, but he applied a new version of his dictum on 'monster books' to Boyle's Climate, as he called it. 'I have read the Climate,' he wrote, and

---

[79] Letter from Phillip Knightley to Kim Philby, dated 15 June 1979, in Rufina Philby's possession. Like Deacon, Boyle had identified Blunt as the fourth man but, without hard evidence, could not risk naming him for legal reasons; Sir Anthony was after all Keeper of the Queen's Pictures. Boyle circumvented the issue by describing a Blunt-like fourth man identified only as Maurice. The correlation was so close that Blunt was soon named in the magazine Private Eye (8 November 1979).

[80] Deacon accepted the circumstance with grace. Asked why the book was not corrected and republished, he said by the time that could be accomplished, Boyle's Climate of Treason was out and made the effort moot. Author conversation with Deacon, Beckenham, Kent, 8 May 1988. See also West, Molehunt, pp. 79–80.

such books are dangerous. Give or take a few points, they are 25% important truth, 25% unimportant truth, 25% unimportant untruth, and 25% important untruth. The trouble is that unless the reader knows the subject better than the author, he cannot tell which is which. I will not go into the important untruths. But for a work which, according to the blurb, was based on 'detailed researches' and claims to be 'the general reader's definitive account', I was amazed by the amount of unimportant untruth (in other words trivial mistakes).[81]

After enumerating and, with characteristic humour, correcting eleven trivial errors,[82] Philby notes that these occurred at the rate of two per page and suggests that if that rate is typical, the book contains over one thousand trivial mistakes. What does this say then, he asks rhetorically, 'about the serious ones'? Answering his own question, he concludes, 'No, for a definitive work based on detailed researches, I am afraid it just won't do.' Then he confesses an error of his own: 'I admit that my own book contains at least *one bad mistake: the arrest of Fuchs, my account was quite wrong. Inexplicably, I mixed it up with a totally different incident.* But I was writing from memory' (emphasis added). Just what was that 'one bad mistake'?

---

[81] Letter to Phillip Knightley, signed Kim Philby, dated 15 June 1980.

[82] The corrections are: 'There never was any University Labour Club [p. 87]. It was the Cambridge University Socialist Society. Acol Road [p. 89] is in West Hampstead, not Maida Vale. I never played football at Cambridge [p. 91]. Lady Lindsay-Hogg is Frances [p. 162] and Patricia [p. 232]. She was never Lady Frances Lindsay-Hogg. Her maiden name was not Dobie [pp. 162, 482], but Doble. Denniston is Brigadier [p. 226] and Commander [p. 240]. I did not meet Aileen [p. 232] in 1940, but on September 3, 1939, a date well remembered . . . Her only West Country connection was the marriage of her eldest sister to a Somersetshire farmer. She was blonde, not brunette. She never worked at Bletchley . . . Most oddly of all, in the group-photograph of the Apostles Anthony Blunt is carefully and wrongly identified as "centre wearing an open necked shirt". Actually, he is behind open-neck, wearing a tie.' The error in the photo caption and the name Dobie were the only ones corrected in the paperback edition. The American edition, *The Fourth Man*, did not have photos and all the other errors remain.

The index in *My Silent War* indicates that Fuchs is mentioned on eight pages, but his name appears on only six and one of those is in the Introduction by Graham Greene. While Fuchs is indeed mentioned on the five remaining pages written by Philby, the word 'arrest' is not used at all and there is no lengthy discussion of the Fuchs case or incident. Page 123, however, contains a paragraph that may provide a clue to what Philby meant. In it Philby berates the FBI generally, and J. Edgar Hoover in particular, for being

> more conspicuous for failure than for success. *Hoover did not catch Maclean or Burgess; he did not catch Fuchs, and he would not have caught the rest if the British had not caught Fuchs and worked brilliantly on his tangled emotions*; he did not catch Lonsdale, he did not catch Abel for years . . . he did not catch me. [emphasis added]

Now Philby knew, because he was apprised of the Venona progress, that Venona and the FBI had precipitated the defection of Burgess and Maclean, although MI5 played a role. He also knew that the FBI, not the British, using Venona had identified Fuchs's espionage. The FBI would also have caught the rest since they too were named in the Venona traffic. Whether the others – Harry Gold, David Greenglass and the Rosenbergs, to name a few – would have been prosecuted without Fuchs's confession and identification of Harry Gold, that made this possible, is unlikely. Philby's comment on Lonsdale is a gratuitous falsehood since he knew full well that the illegal Lonsdale never worked in the United States. His comments then reflect more his unrelenting animosity to Hoover and his men than an expression of black-letter history.

If the Fuchs portion of Philby's comment above is what he meant by his errant account of the 'arrest of Fuchs', it is unlikely that his reference to a 'totally different incident' referred to Fuchs since everything Philby said about Fuchs was germane to the case; he just didn't explain it properly. The solution of this conundrum may be found in the two pages after Fuchs's name in the index on which, in fact, he is not mentioned. Here we do find a 'totally different incident' explained in much greater detail than was afforded in Philby's comments on Fuchs. Although no names are used, the incident described is that of Fritz

Kolbe (aka: George Wood), a German walk-in who offered his services to the British in Berne, Switzerland. After he was promptly rejected by the British as a provocation, he contacted Allen Dulles and OSS, who accepted him and his Foreign Ministry material as genuine – which turned out to be the case. OSS shared the take with the British in London and that is where Philby became involved. When he cross-checked the Wood material with the ULTRA decrypts, Philby realised that Dulles was correct. Philby tells how, despite working in a climate of parochial spite and animosity, he managed to convince his superiors of their value while at the same time hiding the OSS role, thereby leaving the impression that it was a successful MI6 operation and enhancing his own career in the process.

Whether either or both of these explanations are correct, can't be known with certainty. Nor can we know whether Philby became confused by looking up what he thought to be his treatment of the Fuchs case in his own book only to find the Wood case. Thus we are left with a Philby fortune-cookie dilemma – what he said is clear; what he meant is not.

The final comment in the letter to Knightley of interest here is Philby's statement that he would not go into 'important untruths'. His implication that *Climate of Treason*[83] contains some is quite correct. In the one involving Philby, Boyle alleged that CIA officer James Angleton was the first to determine that Maclean and Burgess were Soviet agents, and the first to suspect Philby after he got to the United States. Moreover, still according to Boyle, Angleton, with the help of the Mossad, identified *the fifth man* of the Cambridge ring, codenamed *Basil*, whom he used as double agent to feed information to the Soviets through Maclean. It isn't over yet. In order to protect this CIA operation and acquire evidence against Philby, Boyle asserts that Angleton did not tell the British about their traitorous colleagues. The secret was so closely held, he says, that only Angleton, DCI Smith, 'Scotty Miler and Jim [sic] Rocca were aware of the full game' (p. 309). Boyle is mixed up here and casts doubt on his own story. Scotty Miler was in

---

[83] Boyle's book, as with Deacon's *British Connection*, intended to name Anthony Blunt as the fourth man. For legal reasons, Boyle called him *Maurice*, but left it clear whom he meant.

Korea when Angleton was allegedly running the operation and didn't join Angleton's staff until 1964. That it was Ray, not Jim, Rocca raises other questions.[84]

With his knowledge of the CIA, the FBI, the British and later the KGB roles, Philby had good reason to doubt this *fifth man* concoction. And there was another reason: he knew the identity of the actual fifth man, John Cairncross, who would be exposed publicly in 1990 by Christopher Andrew and Oleg Gordievsky.[85] The press, of course, did not share Philby's knowledge and made their best guess contribution when they identified Dr Wilfred Basil Mann as the fifth man, based on Boyle's description in *Climate*, shortly after the book appeared. Mann, a British-born now American scientist then working at the National Bureau of Standards, was so upset at the allegations that he enlisted the help of American historian Allen Weinstein to examine the evidence. Weinstein, using Mann's passport and other evidence, determined that Mann had not even been in Washington when the alleged meetings between *Basil* and Maclean took place. In 1982, Mann published a book refuting the charges in detail.[86] Philby wrote to Knightley that 'for a view of Boyle's reliability as a witness . . . I refer to Allen Weinstein's comments on the *Climate* in the *New York Times Book Review* of January 6, 1980. Poor Wilfred! I was very fond of him.'

In the end, *Climate of Treason*, so far as the Philby case goes, merely muddied the waters; Philby must have had a chuckle over that.

Wilderness of Mirrors

In a post-retirement interview on Thames Television, James Angleton, the former Chief of the CIA Counterintelligence Staff, characterised *Soviet* disinformation and intelligence operations as a 'wilderness of

---

84 Some of Boyle's critics have asked that since Angleton was not head of the CI/Staff when Philby was in Washington – he assumed that role in 1954, more than two years after Philby returned to England – why was he of concern to Philby? Part of the answer is that Angleton ran the Israeli desk and was aware of, if not involved in, other clandestine operations in his role as assistant to the head of the Office of Special Operations (OSO).

85 Andrew and Gordievsky, *KGB*, pp. 406, 441.

86 Wilfred Basil Mann, *Was There A Fifth Man?: Quintessential Recollections*.

mirrors'.[87] Author David C. Martin used the phrase as the title of his book, and it became a popular epithet for counter-intelligence. In *Wilderness*, Martin dealt with the careers of Angleton and one of his predecessors as the head of the CIA counterintelligence staff, William K. Harvey.

Among other topics, Martin is concerned with a number of controversial issues involving Angleton and Philby. The most important follows from the fact that though both men had known Philby, the details of the acquaintance varied with the teller. Martin learned that not everyone at the CIA agreed with Andrew Boyle, whose *Climate of Treason* argued that Angleton had been aware of Philby's spying – and Burgess and Maclean as well – long before the latter defected. If, as Boyle alleged, Angleton had in fact used Philby against the Soviets, this mitigated, if not reversed, an apparent failure. On the other hand, if Angleton had not known, Philby had deceived him just as he wrote in *My Silent War*. Who was right and had Harvey been fooled too? Reputations were at stake.

Martin and Boyle agreed that the defection of Burgess and Maclean cast suspicion on Philby, who was promptly recalled to London for consultations, never to return. But Martin adds facts to the equation that Boyle did not have.[88] DCI Smith had asked Angleton and Harvey to prepare memos giving their assessment of Philby's role in the episode, if any; both did so. Martin, the first to quote from the memos,[89] also pointed out that Harvey – a former FBI special agent – had the advantage of knowing about the Venona material – the CIA (and Angleton) had not been officially informed and would not be until 1952. Using this knowledge, what he had learned of Philby's role in the Volkov case and the Albanian operations, coupled with Philby's friendship with Burgess, Harvey submitted a five-page well-reasoned and documented memo concluding that Philby was also a

---

[87] See Robin Winks, *Cloak and Gown Scholars . . .*, pp. 327, 536 fn. 1.

[88] Neither author makes clear whether or not either Harvey or Angleton were aware that Krivitsky had provided a clue to Philby in 1940 to the British, although Krivitsky is mentioned in connection with MI5 by both; nor did either author mention Philby's Communist background.

[89] Tom Mangold quotes even more of the memos in his *Cold Warrior*, pp. 65–7.

Soviet agent. Angleton's memo, submitted four days later, suggested that Burgess had duped Philby and cautioned the DCI against accusing Philby of being a Soviet agent. When viewed in light of Ambassador Montgomery's comments mentioned above, and those of other players at the time who did not make their views known until later, Martin was correct in concluding the honour went to Harvey.[90]

A few other points are worth noting. Martin also states that the DCI forwarded both memos to 'C' at MI6, making it clear in the covering letter that Philby was no longer welcome in the United States. In a later treatment of these events in *Cold Warrior* (a biography of Angleton), author Tom Mangold agrees that Harvey's 'suspicions were immediately passed on to MI6', but that Angleton's 'warning went unheeded'. The consensus view of Martin, Mangold, Montgomery and the other CIA officers mentioned, is that prior to Philby's departure, contrary to Boyle's judgment in *Climate*, Angleton had not given 'the slightest indication that he suspected' Philby;[91] but, equally curious and still not explained, apparently Harvey hadn't either.[92]

Finally, Martin quotes a CIA officer on the nature of the Philby-Angleton professional relationship, another point of contention in the literature. 'Philby was Angleton's prime tutor in counterintelligence,' says the unidentified officer. Mangold, on the other hand, writes that 'Angleton and Philby met briefly in London during the war. But according to Philby, their relationship initially amounted to little more

---

[90] In conversations with the author, former CIA operations officers William Hood and Samuel Halpern (both of whom knew Angleton and Harvey) confirm that Harvey knew about the Venona material from his FBI days, that he never, to the best of their recollection, mentioned it to Angleton until officially allowed to do so in 1952, and that Harvey was the first at the CIA to suspect that Philby was a Soviet agent.

[91] Martin, *Wilderness of Mirrors*, pp. 36–58; Tom Mangold, *Cold Warrior*, p. 66.

[92] Although Martin interviewed Harvey for his book, he did not ask him what action, if any, he had taken after becoming suspicious. Author phone conversation with David C. Martin, 21 March 1999. According to the late Richard Deacon, British Major Donald Darling suspected that Philby was a Soviet agent during the Second World War. When he expressed his views after the war, his life was made a misery for his efforts. See Deacon, *The Greatest Treason*, p. 174.

than an occasional meeting. The acquaintanceship was renewed and grew much closer' in Washington. William Hood, who was in OSS London with Angleton, agrees with Mangold on this point.[93]

The Second Oldest Profession

In this book, author Phillip Knightley reveals his cynical views on the need for and utility of espionage. The portions of the book that deal with Philby, Burgess and Maclean reflect the current thinking as the author attempts to put their contribution into his overall perspective.

Over the years in his writings about Philby, Knightley has not hesitated to revise his views on the case when he thought it appropriate. In this work, Knightley modifies his beliefs concerning how Philby was recruited. While he was wrong again – as compared with his book with Page and Leitch – and would go on to make additional corrections (see his introduction to the Borovik book), it was not for want of seeking assistance from the best living primary source on the subject.

When the ideas for *The Second Oldest Profession* were still fermenting in his mind, Knightley wrote to Philby explaining what he had in mind and asking for his thoughts on the matter. Philby's candid response did not mention his recruitment, but did identify some authors that might be of value, others that would not, and suggested some ideas:

> What to say about your new project? Another 10-year job? There has been a spate of good books about the large ultra family recent: Winterbotham, Beesley, Lewin. R. V. Jones is also to be highly commended . . . But what an appalling mess of bad books: Cookridge, Copeland, Stevenson, Fitzgibbon ad infinitum. Perhaps the best of the bad ones is *Bodyguard* [Brown], which illustrates the difficulty . . . Stateside, I recommend Ray Cline [former CIA Deputy Director of

---

[93] Mangold, *Cold Warrior*, p. 64. Author phone conversation with William Hood, 15 March 1999. Former Philby SIS colleague and Westminster classmate I. I. Milne was at Ryder Street at the time and remembers Angleton being there only a few months. Author conversation with I. I. Milne, Red Willows, England, 3 December 1997.

Intelligence], who disguised a good book under a terrible title.
People like Helms [former DCI], Angleton [former CIA/Chief,
counterintelligence staff], Bissell [former CIA Director of
clandestine service] probably feel too embattled to be of much
use. Kim Roosevelt is urbane and quite talkative. David Wise
writes good books, but I doubt his devotion to accuracy. Frank
Lindsay, alias Christopher Felix, might be helpful, a nice
fellow.[94]

Christopher Felix, of course, was the pseudonym of James McCargar,
not Frank Lindsay; Philby had worked with both when he was in
Washington. After the advice on books, Philby commented on the
question of 'how the pre-Dulles CIA . . . turned into the raving beast.
The answer requires a book – yours – so here are only a few ideas:

Dulles, through JFD [his brother John Foster, Secretary of
State] had far too much power, which Ike couldn't curb and
JFD wouldn't. (Ike probably knew very little about it). AD, for
his part, was the genial chairman who could never get his
mouth around the essential 'No'. So side by side with a lot of
very sensible chaps, a lot of maniacs were allowed to go off
every-which-way and do more or less what they liked. The

---

[94] Letter to Phillip Knightley from Philby, 30 October 1978, 3 pages, signed 'K.
Ph.' Since this letter was written, Richard Bissell and Roosevelt published
their memoirs; Richard Helms is writing his; James Angleton died without
writing his. The Frederick Winterbotham book referred to was either *The
Ultra Secret* (NY: Harper and Row, 1974) or *The Nazi Connection* (NY: Harper
and Row, 1978), or both; the Patrick Beesley book mentioned is *Very Special
Intelligence* (NY: Doubleday, 1978); the Ronald Lewin book is *Ultra Goes to
War* (NY: McGraw-Hill, 1978); and the R. V. Jones book is *Most Secret War*
(London: Hamish Hamilton, 1978). The Cookridge book mentioned is *The
Third Man* (see bibliography); the Miles Copeland book is *The Real Spy World*;
the William Stevenson book is *The Man Called Intrepid* (NY: Harcourt, Brace,
Jovanovich, 1976); and the Constantine Fitzgibbon book is *Through the
Minefield* (NY: W. W. Norton, 1967). The Cline book mentioned is *Secrets,
Spies and Scholars: Blueprint of the Essential CIA* (Washington, DC: Acropolis
Books, 1976).

dirty tricks multiplied of their own momentum. Naturally, if you think of the global struggle, dirty tricks are inevitable; but without control or purpose, they become incredibly wasteful and too often counterproductive.[95]

Knightley uses this quote in *The Second Oldest Profession* in his chapter on the CIA (p. 257). For those interested in intelligence and Philby, this book will prove a provocative read.

Deadly Illusions and *The Crown Jewels*

Authors John Costello and Oleg Tsarev surprised the world in 1993 with their book, *Deadly Illusions*, about former NKVD general Alexander Orlov. Until then, Orlov was known as the one-time NKVD officer who had defected to the United States in 1938 and then disappeared until 1953, when he surfaced after Stalin died. *Deadly Illusions* reveals that Orlov was one of the men involved in the recruitment of Philby, Burgess and Maclean in the mid-1930s, a secret he took to his grave in 1973. The FBI and CIA case officers that knew him for the last twenty years of his life were aware he had not revealed everything he knew but were shocked when they learned of his role with the Cambridge spies.[96]

---

[95] *Ibid.*

[96] Raymond Rocca, Orlov's CIA contact, told the author in 1992, when he learned that Orlov's role with the Cambridge agents was to be exposed in *Deadly Illusions*, that he regretted not asking Orlov specifically about visiting London; he said it just never came up. Similarly, Ed Gazur, Orlov's FBI contact the last two years of his life and his literary executor, told the author in April 1998 that he had not suspected Orlov's role even after hours and hours of conversation. Nevertheless, there is one indication in the literature that someone suspected that Orlov had been in England. In a chapter on Orlov in Gordon Brook-Shepherd's milestone study of Soviet defectors, *The Storm Petrels* (London: Collins, 1977), pp. 203–4, he discusses Orlov's creation of illegal networks in Europe during the 1930s. After noting that it was the most sensitive part of Orlov's work, Brook-Shepherd added that:

it was a part he never fully disclosed in his later years to his Western interrogators. England lies at the centre of this nebulous maze. That he

347

Orlov was not loyal only to his former British agents, but to his former NKVD colleagues as well. In 1957, when the FBI arrested KGB Colonel Rudolf Abel, Orlov was shown his picture and asked if he knew him. Orlov replied that he did and it was definitely Rudolf Abel. What he did not say was that he knew very well that the man in the picture was not Rudolf Abel, but Willi Fisher, Orlov's radio operator in London in 1936 when Philby was recruited.[97]

Costello and Tsarev, using documents from the KGB archives, explain how all this happened, why Orlov kept his secret, and why the KGB decided in the last months of the Soviet Union to make it public. It is this book that first reveals the names of those involved in Philby's recruitment, the nature of his first assignments, his codenames, and when it all occurred. To some extent, *Deadly Illusions* corrects, confirms

---

had read many top secret British documents . . . became, eventually, all too clear. *Yet, sometimes, his detailed knowledge, not only of this material but also the exact location and appearance of various buildings in Britain, seemed to surpass what even the most privileged official, gifted with the most prodigious memory, could have retained just by perusing papers at a Moscow desk. Was it therefore firsthand experience? Did Orlov ever come to London himself during this darkest undercover period of his career, and help to set up and develop that famous top-level Soviet spy network which was to become the espionage sensation of the fifties and the sixties?* That riddle belonged to the future. [emphasis added]

In a discussion of this quotation in London, 12 October 1998, Brook-Shepherd said that he could not recall the source of this information, but it was most probably a CIA officer close to Orlov, perhaps Rocca, to whom the book is dedicated. It was not Gazur; Brook-Shepherd didn't meet him until 1996. And it was not Orlov; he was dead by the time Brook-Shepherd began the book. Whether Orlov made the comments before or after the Burgess-Maclean defection is not known. It is not likely, however, that having kept the secret and protected his Cambridge agents for so long after he arrived in 1938, that he ever put them in jeopardy. For details of Orlov's Soviet and American lives, see *Deadly Illusions*.

[97] Costello and Tsarev, *Deadly Illusions*, pp. 371–2. Author conversation with Oleg Tsarev, 10 September 1998. The radio man story was not included in *Deadly Illusions*.

or extends what is speculation in earlier books as far as the Philby case goes. Philby's recruitment into the Soviet intelligence service is one example. Another concerns the NKVD plan to 'use [Philby] to set up the assassination of Franco', although 'it was not clear from the files whether he was to commit the act or help others do so'.[98] In the event, for reasons not explained, neither happened. This story was first reported by Andrew and Gordievsky in their 1990 book, *KGB*, based on Gordievsky's recollections. Thus the surprise in *Deadly Illusions* is that the KGB confirmed Gordievsky's (he was a KGB defector under death sentence) memory allowing KGB files to be cited as the source. Borovik added more important detail when he wrote that Philby had mentioned to him that GRU/NKVD defector Walter Krivitsky had told MI5 'in 1940 about a young British journalist that the GPU/NKVD had sent to kill Franco', but he didn't know his name.[99] While Philby was one of several young British journalists in Franco's Spain during the war at various times, the pattern of his career suggests that Krivitsky's threat did not cause him to be suspected before Burgess and Maclean defected, although in retrospect many think it should have.

Since the focus of *Deadly Illusions* is on Orlov, and he defected in 1938, the book contains little about Philby after that time and this is where *The Crown Jewels* takes over. There is some overlap. *The Crown Jewels* is based almost entirely on KGB documents and adds confirmation to previous speculation – as for example his recruitment – while providing new detail about Philby's early days working as a Soviet agent. It is here we learn the story of how Philby recruited his first agent, Peter Smollett. He had not been authorised to do so and received a reprimand for his efforts, though Smollett was kept on the books.[100]

Although missed entirely by that well-known gadfly of intelligence history Donald Cameron Watt in his review of the book,[101] the

---

[98] *Ibid.*, p. 165.

[99] Borovik, *The Philby Files*, p. 83.

[100] Andrew and Gordievsky, *KGB*, pp. 334–7, were the first to confirm that Smollett was a Soviet agent, but they did not name Philby as his recruiter.

[101] *Electronic Telegraph*, Issue 1037, 28 March 1998.

collection of documents provided by Philby to his Soviet masters shocked professional intelligence historians in terms of quality and quantity. Likewise, intelligence officers and readers who have long wondered just what Philby gave the Soviets during the Second World War will be astounded at the extent and level of detail, hand-written and typed, that he managed to produce while working full time for SIS and advancing steadily within its ranks. It was this output – officers' and agents' names and code designations, places, organisational details and policies, personal characteristics – in fact, that raised suspicions in the mind of NKGB analyst Yelena Modrzhinskaya and caused her to conclude in 1942 that SIS had found out about Philby and the other Cambridge agents and used them as a sources of disinformation. They were too junior, their access too great, and their product so apparently genuine, she reasoned, to be true.[102] About this Philby knew nothing and his output continued without interruption throughout the war. Here we learn that Philby reported on the British *Tube Alloy* or atomic bomb programme, the details of D-Day, Churchill's Polish policy, intelligence operations in Yugoslavia, the Balkans, OSS activities in Italy, SIS operations in Istanbul, and the activities of First United States Army Group (FUSAG), to name a few. Since Philby had not been briefed that FUSAG was a fictitious deception in connection with FORTITUDE, his reports treated it as a legitimate military operation.

There is other non-operational fallout from the analysis of Philby's documentary legacy in the KGB archives. Philby had an unmistakable style that shows up quickly in his pronouncements on others. In *My Silent War*, he wrote about the Deputy Chief of Service, Colonel Valentine Vivian, 'But Vivian was long past his best – if, indeed, he ever had one. He had a reedy figure, carefully dressed crinkles in his hair, and wet eyes.' About John Boyd, Assistant Director of the FBI, Philby wrote, 'He was one of Hoover's original gunmen in Chicago – and looked the part. He was short and immensely stocky, and must have been as hard as nails before he developed a paunch, jowls, and the complexion that suggests a stroke in the offing.' Graham Greene wrote in his introduction that

---

[102] West and Tsarev, *The Crown Jewels*, pp. 159–62.

'His character studies are admirable if unkind. Don't talk to me of ghost writers: only Philby could have been responsible for these' (p. viii). There were occasional charges that the KGB ghosted *My Silent War*, but like Greene, and for the same reasons, most accepted Kim as the author. *The Philby Reports* in *The Crown Jewels* puts a full stop to the dialogue. About a colleague whom he visited in Spain after the war, he wrote: 'DESMOND BRISTOW, 24, 5'10", fair hair, long and narrow face, grey eyes . . . Speaks perfect Spanish. Good athlete and mechanically minded. BRISTOW is the weak link in section VD owing to immaturity and inferior brain.' There are many other examples.

Philby continued to apply his ability to assess others with crisp semantic vividness. From 1976 to 1986 he produced an evaluation of each student in his KGB social-tradecraft seminars. Both parties were told that the comments would be attached to the officer's personnel file. After Philby's death, one of Philby's favourite students, Colonel Michael Bogdanov, recently returned from England after being burned in the fire when Gordievsky identified his former colleagues to SIS, discovered a file marked for destruction with all of Philby's student evaluations; he saved his own. Apparently the virus of suspicion persisted in some quarters.[103]

Reading *The Crown Jewels*, which is constrained to pre-war and wartime events, quickly raises the question of Philby's production in the post-war era. The authors too were aware of this interest and are preparing a companion book, tentatively titled, *TRIPLEX*, that will include documents that address this question.

---

[103] Author conversations in Moscow with former Philby students Colonel Michael Bogdanov (KGB, Ret.), 9 September 1998; Colonel Lev Koshliakov (KGB, Ret.), 24 November 1997; and student seminar supervisor, Colonel Mikhail Lyubimov (KGB, Ret.), 8 September 1998. Interview in Alexandria, VA, with former KGB Colonel Oleg Gordievsky, 10 August 1998. While a British agent and a KGB officer, Gordievsky had translated some of Philby's student assessments into Russian. While working for the British, he gave up the names of the KGB officers he knew in London. Bogdanov was among them forcing him to return short of tour to the Centre.

BRIEF FIRST-HAND ACCOUNTS

Spycatcher

Almost without exception, authors have described Kim Philby as charming, engaging, destined for a knighthood and possibly even Chief of Service. Peter Wright, author of *Spycatcher*, met Philby once and liked him immediately. He 'had charm and style', said Wright, 'and we both shared the same affliction – a chronic stutter'. Philby appears from time to time throughout *Spycatcher* from a different point of view than that provided by most authors. Wright, scientific and technical adviser to MI5, tells of bugging the safe-house where Philby was 'interrogated near Sloane Square' in London. He also describes the devices used and how the transcriptions were made with the help of the Post Office. He tells us that Philby did not sound convincing to the surreptitious listeners. Wright suggests that Philby was helped over the rough spots by his MI6 colleagues doing the questioning, implying that they wanted him cleared of the charges. Nevertheless, the immediate outcome was the Foreign Secretary's comments in Parliament, to the effect that there was no evidence against Philby. He was free to go to Beirut.

There was more bugging in connection with the Philby case. When Flora Solomon, a one-time friend of Philby's who knew about his Communist connections and had kept quiet, finally revealed what she knew to MI5, Wright bugged Victor Rothschild's apartment where she was interviewed. Wright was also involved with Philby in Beirut, though indirectly. It was Wright's task to improve the poor recordings made of Philby's confession to Nicholas Elliott. On these tapes, he writes (p. 194), Philby admitted spying since 1934 and never asked Elliott how MI6 had learned the truth.

Spycatcher encounters Philby again in the damage assessment investigation of penetrations of MI5 and MI6 done by a joint group – codenamed the FLUENCY Committee – that revisited known and suspected moles. Here the reader gets an idea of the bureaucratic and to some extent operational damage Philby and the other Cambridge agents caused.

Even with his first-hand experience, Wright gets some things wrong in his account. He was convinced that Modin was Philby's controller in London, which is now known to be false (see Modin's book plus West and Tsarev for details). Wright also has Modin handling Philby's escape from Beirut. This too is now known to be incorrect (see Borovik, and Rufina Philby, p. 197 above). And Wright gets some dates wrong; Philby was dismissed in 1951, not 1955. But overall, it is an interesting and valuable contribution to the Philby lore.

FBI-KGB War: A Special Agent's Story

Not everyone was charmed by Kim Philby. One important exception is former FBI special agent Robert Lamphere, the principal Philby contact at the Bureau between 1949 and 1951, when Philby was Head of Station in Washington. In his memoirs, *The FBI-KGB War*, Lamphere, who had met Philby's boss, 'C', Sir Stewart Menzies, was unimpressed with the 'seedy', stuttering, lazy, even boring, shabbily dressed potential successor. 'I'd never liked Philby,' he wrote. But neither had he suspected that Philby was a Soviet agent until Burgess and Maclean defected, and even then didn't think he was still 'active'. The chapter on Philby in his memoirs deals mainly with the reasons Philby finally came under suspicion at the FBI and MI5, the damage done and what was done about it. Lamphere's unique position makes his comments on the case, and on the propaganda content in *My Silent War*, particularly valuable.

SpyMaster: My 32 Years in Intelligence and Espionage against the West

Although mentioned elsewhere in this survey, Oleg Kalugin's book has more to contribute. He tells about his role in Philby's rehabilitation in the early 1970s and explains the reason that it happened as a consequence of the defection in London of KGB officer Oleg Lyalin. There had been other defections to the West and Andropov wanted to reverse the direction by making life in the Soviet Union more attractive to potential defectors – Philby was to be one of the role models and Kalugin was to make it happen.

His telling of his part of the Philby story is challenged emphatically on several points by Rufina Philby (see pp. 41–3 above). In particular, she disputes Kalugin's version of his first visit to the Philby flat and the circumstances surrounding the acquisition of, and Philby's reaction to, the new furniture provided by the KGB; especially the episode where Kim is said to have got up in the middle of the night to admire his new furnishings. These different recollections cannot be resolved; both adhere passionately to their versions. What can be concluded, however, is that the overall impressions each conveys of Kim Philby's years in Moscow is remarkably consistent.[104]

Kalugin describes the programme of seminars he approved to be given by Philby for selected students from the KGB Higher School (graduate level) who were to be assigned to English-speaking countries. These proved valuable to all concerned as Rufina Philby indicated (see pp. 87–9 above). His favourite student Michael Bogdanov (identified only as Michael by Rufina) became a friend and correspondent. Presumably, it was this close relationship, the KGB teachings on the case, and a lack of familiarity with the Western literature on Philby, that allows for his comment in the Foreword to Rufina's book (see p. 11 above) to the effect that Philby 'put not a single British life at risk', a statement even Philby would have not have made.

Kalugin learned that after his transfer to Leningrad, KGB operational contacts with Philby diminished without explanation,[105] although the seminars continued into 1988. In short, Philby was retired, left without defining activity. Here too Kalugin agrees with Rufina about Philby's dissatisfaction with the Soviet handling of things.

Man without a Face
'The only Communist country he steadfastly refused to visit was East Germany; [Philby] never was able to forgive the German people

---

104 Author interviews with former KGB officers Colonels Michael Bogdanov and Mikail Lyubimov, June 1997, and Lt.-Gen. Vadim Kirpichenko, Colonel Lev Koshliakov, September 1998, failed to reconcile the differences in the stories of Rufina Philby and Kalugin. But they affirm the accuracy of their overall impressions.

105 Gennady-X substantiates this assessment. For reasons never explained to him, he was given other duties and told not to have further contacts with Philby. Conversation with the author, Moscow, 25 November 1997.

for supporting Hitler and Nazi fascism,' wrote Oleg Kalugin in his memoirs.[106] Markus Wolf did not challenge the point directly in his book, *Man without a Face*,[107] but he did include a picture of Philby with him at HVA (the East German foreign intelligence service) headquarters the day Philby addressed the officers there in 1981 (after Kalugin had gone to Leningrad). Wolf later provided the signed photo of Philby addressing his officers included in this volume.[108]

Asked what Philby spoke about, Wolf said his talk, which he gave in English with an interpreter and no sign of a stammer, lasted about one hour. He spoke from notes and told his life story as an agent, 'what was in his memoirs, nothing about life in Moscow', because few in the audience knew anything about him. There were no questions after Philby's talk. Privately, speaking German, Wolf asked Philby about the circumstances of his defection. Philby replied that he thought the British had wanted him to defect in Beirut and that it was a very difficult decision which the KGB left entirely up to him.[109]

---

[106] Kalugin, *SpyMaster*, p. 138.

[107] The title of Wolf's memoirs refers to the legend that arose around him that no one in the West knew what he looked like. What he didn't know was that the CIA Station in Berlin had collected photos of all attendees at the Nuremberg War Crimes trials, where Wolf was an accredited Soviet journalist and had met William J. Donovan in the course of his duties. In 1951, the photos were shown to an East German agent that knew Wolf. The agent picked out Wolf's photo. For details of this story see David Murphy, 'They Call Him MISHA', *International Journal of Intelligence and Counterintelligence*, Vol. 11, Number 1, Spring 1998, p. 93. Wolf mentioned the meeting with Donovan in a conversation with the author, 12 December 1997, in Berlin.

[108] In a 12 December 1997 discussion with the author in Berlin, Wolf said that he had had several copies made up during the visit and Philby agreed to sign them for later distribution to his officers and others interested. The original in this case is now in the Melton Museum of Intelligence in Boca Raton, FL. Wolf referred to Philby as a genuine *kundshafter*, or agent of conviction, in the mould of Richard Sorge.

[109] Author conversation with Markus Wolf, Berlin, 12 December 1997. Philby's talk was recorded and should have been in the Gauck Archives, but could not be located. The author thanks Dr Helmut Trotnow, Director of the Alliierten Museum e.V, for his efforts in trying to locate them.

In his book, Wolf compares Philby with George Blake. He finds Philby, whom he 'admired immensely', the more outgoing and suave, a judgment he developed during his several visits to East Germany. As with Kalugin, Wolf detects that Philby was not pleased with the direction things were going in the Soviet Union. They also talked about 'books, ideas and cooking'. Wolf adds that 'I do not agree with Western accounts that [Philby] was miserable in Moscow. The truth is he had no other option, but Philby was able to manage better than other spies.'

After one of his visits, Philby sent Wolf a copy of the West German edition of his memoirs, My Silent War, with the inscription, 'the FRG translation leaves much to be desired. K.P.' Wolf commented in his book that the remark 'amused me', as an 'indication of Philby's pedantic concern for accuracy'.[110] Asked later how the West German edition compared to the East German version, Wolf said that the former was essentially a translation of the English, while the latter was more selective. Even the introduction Philby had written for the GDR version was edited to about half its original length. Although Wolf hasn't read all the books on Philby, he said that Phillip Knightley's 'understood Philby the man very well'.

Looking for Trouble

Richard Beeston, a correspondent for the Daily Telegraph, knew Philby in Beirut and later met him in Moscow. His memoirs, Looking for Trouble, tell what he and other correspondents knew and heard about Philby while they were working in the Middle East. At the time, Beeston didn't believe that Philby had been 'a Soviet spy', though he was sure SIS Beirut was suspicious of him and kept him under surveillance. At a party, Beeston's wife Moyra asked Kim 'directly if he were the Third Man. He grasped her ferociously by the wrist and replied, "You know, Moyra, I always believe that loyalty to your friends is more important than anything else"' (p. 32). Richard Beeston once asked Philby whether he knew George Blake, who had just been arrested as a Soviet spy. Philby replied, 'Never met Blake, never even heard of the chap until his arrest' (p. 33). Rufina Philby has told about meeting the

---

[110] Wolf, Man without a Face, p. 93.

Beestons by accident in Moscow, where Kim greeted them warmly and helped them find a decent apartment (see pp. 100–1 above).

After Beeston returned to London, he wrote to Philby in November 1979, thanking him again for his help in Moscow and requesting a comment on the recent exposure of Anthony Blunt as one of the Cambridge spies. Philby replied that he was 'sincerely sorry . . . the answer must be "no."' Then after some small talk, Philby wrote, 'Nina sends her regards.' 'Nina', it turns out, was the name used by Philby to refer to Rufina in letters to the West, a cover of sorts to reduce the likelihood of getting to him through his wife.[111]

These and other stories about Philby's personal life add dimension to this complex man and make this volume a valuable source.

Never Judge a Man by his Umbrella and With My Little Eye

At the opposite end of the spectrum of Philby associates from Robert Lamphere was a long-time friend and SIS colleague, Nicholas Elliott. In his memoirs, Elliott devotes a chapter to the man he had known since 1941 who:

> had the ability to inspire loyalty and even affection in his staff . . . had an impressive clarity of mind and also, despite his stammer, of speech; his writing was a model of economy and lucidity . . . outwardly a kindly man. Inwardly he must have been cold, calculating and cruel – traits he cleverly concealed from his friends and colleagues . . . Beneath his veneer of charm lay an emotional but ruthless personality.

Elliott is the only author and close friend to confirm that Philby had a mistress in London after he was dismissed from SIS – a fact mentioned in the literature by Patrick Seale and Maureen McConville in *PHILBY: The Long Road to Moscow* – though he does not mention the illegitimate issue of the relationship.[112]

---

[111] Letter from Dick Beeston to Kim Philby, 17 November 1979. Letter from Kim Philby to Dick Beeston, 29 November 1979. From time to time, books and articles about Philby refer to his wife as 'Nina' for that reason. She began using her real name in the late 1980s shortly before Kim's death.

[112] Elliott, p. 186.

The chapter looks at Philby the man, his family, his wives – Aileen and Eleanor – and a few comments about his friends. Elliott tells of their contacts over the years, of Aileen's hospitalisation in Switzerland, their contacts in Turkey and Beirut. There is not great detail, but the experiences are first-hand and shouldn't be overlooked.

Towards the end, Elliott makes a puzzling comment about Guy Burgess. After noting that Philby's third wife, Eleanor, had told him that Burgess's death had been a 'grievous blow . . . [to Philby] though the legacy of his library had been a great solace', Elliott adds his own observation:

> Curiously enough, unlike the death of his [pet] fox [in Beirut] and his father, Philby seemed totally unmoved by news of the death of his fellow traitor and *expressed to me some annoyance at this legacy*. [emphasis added]

Since Burgess died after Philby arrived in Moscow, one is left to wonder how he could have expressed anything on the subject to Elliott whom he never met again after his defection.

The only clue he gives to the answer comes in his second volume of memoirs, *With My Little Eye*, in a section titled 'Philby: Some Final Reflections'. Here he tells of a letter he received from Philby from Moscow suggesting that they meet in Berlin or Helsinki, without the knowledge of MI6 or Elliott's wife. Elliott never answered, but he did tell MI6. Although he doesn't say what else was in the letter, it may have contained the comment on Burgess.

With My Little Eye contains a curious comment of its own on another subject: the KGB suspicion of Philby. Citing 'an impeccable private source', Elliott summarises the distrust discussed above in *The Crown Jewels*, but he identifies the lady KGB analyst involved as Zoya Nikolayevna Ryskina. Since West and Tsarev have copies of the documents signed by Yelena Modrzhinskaya, one must conclude that Elliott's source got it wrong.

Elliott returns briefly to the subject of *My Silent War*, noting that it was certainly Philby's unmistakable style and puzzling over why it stopped where it did. He also notes that Graham Greene wrote a 'shameful preface', which was replaced in the Russian edition by one written by Oleg Kalugin. Sadly, while acknowledging his confrontation with Philby that produced his putative confession, he adds nothing more about it.

Elliott concludes the Philby chapter in *Never Judge a Man by his Umbrella*, with a very personal comment about his old friend who had become part of the detritus of espionage. The 'world is well rid of him. But the Russians are sure to keep alive memories of their "master spy" for many years to come.'

Forthcoming Contributions to the Philby Literature

While *The Private Life of Kim Philby: The Moscow Years* and *TRIPLEX* may seem to fulfil Elliott's prophecy, Western writers will make a contribution also. The year 2000 will see the first biography of Guy Burgess – Andrew Lownie's *Stalin's Englishman: The Double Life of Guy Burgess* – which will include material about the Cambridge agents as their paths crossed.

Norman Sherry's forthcoming *The Life of Graham Greene, Volume Three* will evaluate the post-war correspondence between Greene and Philby, conducted, Sherry believes, under the guidance of 'SIS and the CIA'. Sherry is quoted as saying, 'I am convinced [Greene] was hoping to make Philby a treble agent,' although he admits that the theory is pure supposition.[113] The second volume of his Greene biography is primarily concerned with the Philby-Greene relationship during the war years, but it does mention Greene's rationale for writing his introduction to *My Silent War*, and suggests that in keeping up his correspondence with Philby, Greene was 'helping his country's intelligence services'. Sherry also hints at the treble agent theory – are we seeing Anthony Cave Brown's influence here? He quotes Yuri Modin asking, 'I wonder whether Kim cheated us like he cheated everyone else?' If Philby did cheat Moscow, writes Sherry, 'it must have been with Greene's help'. Perhaps volume three will clarify this murky conjecture.

Three books on the Venona project will be published in 1999. *Venona: Decoding Soviet Espionage in America* by John Haynes and Harvey Klehr is due out in April. It will be followed in June by *Venona: The Greatest Secret of the Cold War* by Nigel West, and in the

---

[113] Sam Allis, 'Tinker, tailor, soldier, spy', *Boston Globe*, 21 March 1999, p. E1.

autumn, Eric Breindel and Herbert Romersrtein's *The Venona Secrets* will complete the trio. Although the Philby case will be mentioned in each one, they will add little new regarding case detail, but they will provide chapter and verse documentation for much of what other authors have been forced to report based on interviews and unnamed sources.

A Work in Progress

Mind Your Own Business is the autobiography of Richard Thompson, Oxford graduate, linguist, jazz musician, teacher, amateur actor, international scientific instrument representative, author, one-time asset of Britain's Secret Intelligence Service in the tradition of Greville Wynne, and friend of Kim Philby.

The Philby connection began on a day in 1959 when student Thompson visited his father Sir Harold (Tommy) Thompson in his St John's College office. Professor Thompson was out, his new secretary, Josephine Philby, explained. The name meant nothing to young Richard, but Josephine's pretty face and abundant silhouette stirred his interest – they became friends. In today's terms, a relationship developed and before they went their own ways – he to international business, she to Beirut – Richard met her father when he visited London with his third wife, Eleanor.

By 1968, having acquired fluent Russian, Richard was representing various companies at international trade fairs, which meant in his case being a frequent visitor to the Soviet Union. This access led to contacts with SIS, and he began servicing dead drops in various Soviet cities, including Moscow. A signal that a prearranged drop in Moscow had been filled, Thompson explains, came from a

> musical code issued by a trumpeter in the Bolshoi Theatre orchestra, during the warm-up before a performance. He would signal me where to go the following day by playing different musical phrases. For example, the first few bars of 'A Tree in the Park' meant that there was something waiting for me in a certain tree in Sokolniki Park.

And it was in Sokolniki Park, one day in 1970, as Thompson was hoping to service a dead drop, that a man on a nearby bench said to him, 'I wouldn't bother old boy, it is empty.' It was Philby, of course, to Thompson's great surprise. This was one of 15–20 meetings in various places – including Philby's flat where Thompson met his wife – in Moscow during the next couple of years. Thompson didn't notice any surveillance. 'Philby just wanted to talk about Josephine, cricket and England,' he writes, 'it was nostalgic for both of us.' Thompson added that, overall, Philby seemed 'miserable and unhappy'. Naturally he told his SIS contacts, and while they were 'interested, they never gave me any instructions' about the meetings and he was not asked to serve as a British conduit to Philby.

In 1975, during his last trip to Moscow, Thompson was arrested by the KGB 'on a spurious charge of drunkenness . . . and was interrogated at the Lubyanka the next morning'. Among other things, he was shown a photo of Kim Philby whom he acknowledged he had met. Spending his nights in a cell, he was interrogated each day and even taken to the place in Sokolniki Park where he had first met Philby. After about two weeks, Thompson went to trial and Philby appeared to give evidence in his defence. The trial was adjourned without a formal verdict, and Thompson was confined in various prisons for another month before being flown to East Germany. There he was accompanied across a bridge 'into the hands of SIS and CIA officers whom I didn't know'.[114]

To followers of the Philby case, Richard Thompson's story comes as a shock and the first response is disbelief; so is the second. Could it really be true? The unsatisfactory answer to that question is, some parts can be verified, some shown to be in error, and some remain unproven.

British sources, who wish to remain anonymous, have confirmed that the Thompson manuscript was reviewed by SIS and approved for publication. They hasten to add that that does not mean that its contents are endorsed as truth. It does mean that some relationship with

---

[114] The quotations in the Thompson story are from his draft manuscript. As of this writing, April 1999, no publisher has been found. The factual comments not in quotes come from a phone conversation between Professor Thompson and this author on 4 February 1998, and from an interview at his home in Oxford on 12 November 1998.

SIS existed and that no security problems will result from publication. Professor Thompson can also verify a relationship with Josephine Philby through copies of their correspondence and pictures of them together. And Mikhail Lyubimov has confirmed that Philby enjoyed going to Sokolniki Park.

From there a mist of ambiguity engulfs the facts. Professor Thompson was shown photos of the flat where Philby lived when they met in Moscow, and he admitted it was not where they met; a safe-house is a reasonable explanation, but can't be confirmed.[115] Rufina Philby is adamant that she never saw Thompson, that Kim never spoke of him, brought him to their flat, or spoke to Josephine about him during one of her visits – at least not in Rufina's presence.

She is equally insistent about Kim attending a trial without telling her and adds that he would not have gone to the Park alone.[116] Oleg Kalugin, Chief of KGB Foreign Counter-Intelligence at the time, agrees; 'impossible,' he says, 'they couldn't have met without our knowing about it and I am positive no such meetings were reported or authorised. We would have known about the trial too.' Mikhail Lyubimov agrees that the likelihood of any meetings is small.[117]

When looked at from the intelligence services involved, if one assumes that the KGB knew the meetings were taking place, they also knew that the SIS were aware of them and that the dead drops that Thompson had been servicing were all blown. Why then would the British allow Thompson to continue functioning for them? Did they assume that Philby was meeting without KGB knowledge, or didn't they care because they just wanted to communicate with Philby?

These are some of the issues Professor Thompson will have to resolve in his book, a task that may be possible today under the new conditions in Russia. In the event, if he is successful, there will be one more new Philby story after all.

---

[115] *Ibid.*, interview, 12 November 1999.
[116] Conversations with Rufina Philby, Moscow, 8 September 1998. Discussion with Oleg Kalugin, Washington, DC, 23 February 1999.
[117] Author phone conversation with Mikhail Lyubimov, 21 February 1999.

DENOUEMENT

For all its volume and diversity, the Philby literature does not compel a single view of the man or the reasons he lived his life as he did. The reality, indeed, is that it does much the opposite. There is consensus that he originally betrayed his country for his ideals, but multiple reasonable views on why he stayed the course under Stalinism. It is clear, too, that his defection in 1963 was, on the one hand, more of a shock to his wife and journalist colleagues than to his former service; it had long since adjusted to the costly impact of his treachery. On the other hand, its consequence was a shock to Philby himself. Moscow was not a Communist theme park. And he was not taken on board the KGB staff but left after his debriefing and writing of his memoir in solitary obscurity until 1971. To the occasional old friend who saw him, he remained the happy, even helpful, congenial rogue with his seedy charm intact. To many in the West he was now the KGB's foremost dissembling peddler of disinformation. Rufina Philby's memoirs give a different picture. In his later years, which she did so much to make happy, Kim Philby remained a lonely eminence sustained by many very British traditions he had once sought to demolish.

Will the questions and incongruities remaining in the story of Philby's life ever be answered? Retired KGB Lt-Gen. Vadim Kirpichenko tells us that the forthcoming volumes of the official history of the Russian foreign intelligence service will add more detail about Philby's career as an agent, but little concerning his private life. In the absence of finding an unknown autobiography, it is likely then that Kim Philby, so often aggravated by the inaccuracies circulated about him in his lifetime, has assured that many will continue after his death.

Bibliography

SELECTED BOOKS AND ARTICLES

The books and articles reviewed in the preparation of this survey are listed alphabetically below. Those discussed in the narrative are not further annotated, but the complete citation is given. Those books not mentioned, or mentioned only briefly in the narrative, are annotated here to give some indication of their contribution to the Philby story. Where both British and American editions were published, the bibliographic details for each are included.

1. AARONS, Mark, LOFTUS, John, *Ratlines: How the Vatican's Nazi Networks Betrayed Western Intelligence to the Soviets* (London: Heinemann, 1991); *Unholy Alliance: The Vatican, The Nazis, and Soviet Intelligence* (NY: St Martin's Press, 1991).

The chapter titled 'The Philby Connection' draws on a mix of primary and secondary sources from which the authors reach dubious conclusions. The comments regarding Philby's links to White Russian Prince Turkul and SIS officer Dick Ellis are unsupported as are his putative links to the Windsors, whom they allege were both Nazi spies.

Without evidence they claim that Philby 'personally trained a Baltic agent' in Stockholm, and that he 'launched his own Vatican operation'. The conclusion that Guy Liddell was a Soviet agent is likewise undocumented and not taken seriously by those with first-hand knowledge of the cases like Robert Cecil. Moreover, *Father* [*sic*] Mally was not a priest, nor did he recruit Philby. On the latter point, the authors cite Costello's *Mask of Treachery* as their source while overlooking Christopher Andrew and Oleg Gordievsky. The analysis of the Gouzenko case is confused, as is the treatment of Venona (Lamphere was not consulted). The assertion that Philby 'merged all of the Vatican Nazi groups . . . into one giant Soviet sewer' is inexplicable and undocumented. In short, this is an unreliable chapter on Philby.

2.   ———, *The Secret War against the Jews: How Western Espionage Betrayed the Jewish People* (NY: St Martin's Press, 1994).

The undocumented and erroneous claims that Kim Philby was known to be 'a secret homosexual and communist' (p. 27), and that 'his father's espionage career outlasted his son's' (p. 37), are illustrative of this book's unreliability. With regard to Kim Philby, it draws on material from the book above repeating the same errors.

3.   AKHMEDOV, Ismail, *In and Out of Stalin's GRU: A Tatar's Escape from Red Army Intelligence* (Frederick, MD: University Publications of America, 1984).

In 1948, six years after he defected, former GRU officer Ismail Akhmedov was finally interrogated in Turkey for a few hours by a 'tall, slim, fair-complected' member of the British Secret Intelligence Service, whose name he was not told. Sometime later the contact was continued in Istanbul and there Akhmedov learned that his inquisitor was Kim Philby, about whom he felt 'vague misgivings', but he said nothing at the time. The chapter on 'Kim Philby' in these memoirs tells the rest of the story.

4.   ALDRICH, Richard J., 'More on Stalin's Men: Some Recent Western Studies of Soviet Intelligence', *Intelligence and National Security*, Vol. 11, No. 3 (July 1996), pp. 601–5.

This is a review article and includes Anthony Cave Brown's *Treason In The Blood*.

5.   ALLEN, W.E.D., *David Allens: The History of a Family Firm 1857–1957* (London: John Murray, 1957).

Philby wrote part of this book. To read a portion of what he wrote, see the entry for Nigel West's *Faber Book of Espionage*, below.

6.   ANDREW, Christopher, and GORDIEVSKY, Oleg, *KGB: The Inside Story of its Foreign Operations from Lenin to Gorbachev* (Sceptre edn, 1991), p. 233.

Although the photos were not included in this edition, it does contain essential corrections. The Philby case is presented as part of the Cambridge Five story, based largely on information supplied by KGB defector Oleg Gordievsky. It is a good source to become familiar with the case.

7.   BEESTON, Richard, *Looking for Trouble: The Life and Times of a Foreign Correspondent* (London: Brassey's, 1997), 178 pp., bibliography, photos, index.

8.   BLAKE, George, *No Other Choice: An Autobiography* (NY: Simon & Schuster, 1990; London: Jonathan Cape, 1990), no index.

Blake argues that he was imprisoned for spying against Britain for the KGB while Philby was warned 'not to return to England' by his SIS colleagues and thus allowed to escape to the Soviet Union. He tells of their meeting in Moscow in 1970, how his Russian wife Ida introduced Kim to Rufina, and why their friendship soured. The story is consistent with that told by Rufina, but does add a few details about Kim.

9.   BOROVIK, Genrikh, *The Philby Files: The Secret Life of the Master Spy – KGB Archives Revealed*, edited with an introduction by Phillip Knightley (London: Little Brown, 1994).

10. BOWER, Tom, *The Red Web: MI6 and the KGB Master Coup* (London: Aurum Press Ltd, 1989).

This is the story of how the KGB compromised the Baltic operations of MI6 with the help of Philby, who reported them to Moscow from the beginning until 1947. Bower argues that Philby's implication in *My Silent War* not to have 'caused the arrests of British agents' was an attempt by his KGB masters 'to obfuscate his true role'.

11. ———, *The Perfect English Spy: Sir Dick White and the Secret War 1935–90* (London: Heinemann, 1995; NY: St Martin's Press, 1995).

A fascinating book in itself, the portions about Philby are of particular interest because they are based in part on interviews with Sir Dick White, one of the MI5 and later MI6 officers that thought Philby guilty after his first interrogation in 1951. The story of Philby's *limited confession* to Nicholas Elliott differs from what Philby later told Borovik. Bower has Philby stating that he broke contact with the NKGB in 1949, while Borovik quotes Philby saying that it was Elliott who took this inexplicable position. Since the White version is supported by the then Head of Station in Beirut, Peter Lunn, it is more credible.

12. BOYLE, Andrew, *The Climate of Treason: Five Who Spied for Russia* (London: Hutchinson, 1979).

13. BREINDEL, Eric, and ROMERSTEIN, Herbert, *The Venona Secret: The Soviet Union's World War II Espionage Campaign against the United States and How America Fought Back* (NY: HarperCollins, 1999).

14. BRISTOW, Desmond, *A Game of Moles: The Deceptions of an MI6 Officer* (London: Little, Brown, 1993).

Desmond Bristow was recruited into SIS in September 1941; his first boss was Kim Philby. They became friends and Bristow's memoirs provide a rare, first-hand glimpse of what life was like during the early days of Philby's career as head of the Iberian element of Section V. Bristow recalls Philby wearing a leather jacket from his Spanish Civil War days; clicking his fingers to 'fight his stammer'; smoking a pipe; drinking, but not heavily; that Kim's sister was also in SIS; and that thanks to Kim's long-time friend, Tim Milne, the ULTRA decrypts were used effectively to neutralise Nazi agents. Bristow befriended Kim in Spain after Philby resigned, although he had been instructed not to. He found it hard to accept that Philby was a Soviet agent and is one of those convinced that Philby 'was allowed to escape'. It is anecdotal and good reading.

15. BRODSKY, Joseph, 'A Philby Fantasy', *The New Republic*, 20 April 1995, pp. 19ff.

This strange article, stimulated by the issuing of a Philby stamp by the Soviet Union, is largely what its title suggests. The author himself states that 'several of the assertions I am going to make are, in their turn, quite loony . . .' Contrary to the title, the story is as much about Alexander Orlov (one of Philby's recruiters in 1934) as about Philby. But he does argue that 'for all its industry, cunning, human toil, and investment of time and currency, the Philby enterprise was a bust. Were he actually a British double-agent, he couldn't inflict a greater damage on the system whose fortunes he was actually trying to advance.'

16. BROWN, Anthony Cave, *Bodyguard of Lies* (London: W.H. Allen, 1976).

In his chapter on the so-called Schwarze Kapelle (a group of German officers headed by Admiral Canaris who conspired to overthrow Hitler), Brown has Philby doing whatever he could to prevent Allied co-operation with the Canaris group. In the correspondence reviewed for this survey, Philby did not comment on this aspect of the book.

17. ———, *The Secret Servant: The Life of Sir Stewart Menzies, Churchill's Spymaster* (London: Michael Joseph, 1988); *'C': The Secret Life of Sir Stewart Menzies Spymaster to Winston Churchill* (NY: Macmillan, 1987).

18.   ———, *Treason in the Blood: H. St John Philby, Kim Philby and the Spy Case of the Century* (Boston: Houghton Mifflin, 1994; London: Hale, 1995), pp. 678, 23 illus., bibliography, index.

19.   ———, *Oil, God, and Gold: The Story of ARAMCO and the Saudi Kings* (Boston: Houghton Mifflin, 1999).

Although the principal Philby involved in this story is Kim's father, Brown makes an intriguing comment (p. 123) about the son during his 1947 visit to his father. Brown writes that 'Widely regarded as Britain's ablest intelligence officer during World War II, [Kim] was also an important Soviet agent, *a fact that was just then becoming clear in high British and American intelligence*' (emphasis added). No source is provided and the point is not further discussed. Since the earliest candidate date of Kim's coming under suspicion – 1949 in the United States by Bill Harvey – occurs in his own book, *Treason In The Blood*, students of the Philby case are provided with another conundrum to investigate.

20.   ———, and MacDONALD, Charles B., *On a Field of Red: The Communist International and the Coming of World War II* (NY: G. P. Putnam's Sons, 1981).

The treatment of Philby's recruitment and subsequent handling is inaccurate as to the names and other details of those involved. He does make a comment worth noting on p. 460. Here Brown states that 'Both Burgess and Philby quickly joined the Communist cell at Cambridge. Kim Philby was ready-made for conversion: *it was in his blood* [emphasis added]. His father before him had experienced a mystical transformation upon arrival at Trinity . . .' Aside from the fact that Philby did not join the Communist cell at Cambridge, the statement suggests that the theme of Brown's 1994 book on Philby and his father had been thought of much earlier.

21.   BURANELLI, Vincent and Nan, *SPY/COUNTERSPY: An Encyclopedia of Espionage* (NY: McGraw-Hill, 1982).

22.   BURKE, Michael, *Outrageous Good Fortune: A Memoir* (Boston: Little, Brown and Company, 1984).

Burke was a CIA officer involved with the covert action operations in Albania. He tells of dining with the 'charming' Philby once in London in 1950 and meeting his father, the famous St John, afterwards. Burke was impressed that such a senior man could show him such attention. He was later shocked to learn that Philby had betrayed the Albanian operation to the Soviets.

23. BURN, Michael, *The Debatable Land: A Study of the Motives of Spies in Two Ages* (London: Hamish Hamilton, 1970).

The picture of Philby on the dust jacket of this book is misleading. Burn is concerned with the reasons some Englishmen spy for foreign powers, and most of the book is a history of spying beginning in the later part of the sixteenth century. Towards the end of the book he devotes a few pages to Philby and his motivations for his treachery explained in *My Silent War*.

24. CAIRNCROSS, John, *The Enigma Spy: The Story of the Man Who Changed the Course of World War II* (London: Century, 1997).

The memoirs of the so-called *fifth man* reveal a former Soviet agent resentful that when discovered by MI5 he was not accorded an offer of immunity as offered to Anthony Blunt and Philby. He was proud of his work and told MI5 as much, before being allowed to leave the country and eventually settle in France. Cairncross is justifiably critical of Peter Wright's molehunt, but much of what he says about his own role contradicts his previous admissions, the facts released by the KGB, and those revealed by Yuri Modin, his case officer, in his book, *My Five Cambridge Friends*.

25. CARLTON, Eric, *TREASON: Meanings and Motives* (Hants., UK: Ashgate Publishing Ltd, 1998).

In the chapter on 'Treason and Ideology', Carlton compares the problems faced by agents living two lives, one under a cover. He compares Philby and Richard Sorge, but gives insufficient detail on the former. Carlton's comparison of the Cambridge spies' background is superficial.

26. CAVENDISH, Anthony, *Inside Intelligence: The Revelations of an MI6 Officer* (London: HarperCollins, 1997), with Introduction by Nigel West.

Anthony Cavendish had only one conversation with Kim Philby while both were in SIS. He writes that 'most of the remarks made by Kim deprecated the way in which the [CIA] was run'. They met again in Beirut. By then Cavendish had left the Service considering himself badly treated. He knew of the suspicions against his former colleague, but gave him the benefit of the doubt treating him as any other one-time SIS officer. Kim, he wrote, 'always wanted to talk about SIS matters'. It was inconceivable that someone as important as 'Philby could have been a traitor'.

27. CECIL, Robert, 'The Cambridge Comintern', in Christopher Andrew and David Dilks (eds), *The Missing Dimension: Governments and Intelligence Communities in the Twentieth Century* (London: Macmillan, 1984).

A benchmark article giving background on the Cambridge spies, although at this time the fifth man, John Cairncross, had not been identified as one of that quintet.

28. ———, *A Divided Life: A Biography of Donald Maclean* (London: The Bodley Head, 1988).

This biography of Donald Maclean is essential reading for an understanding of the Philby case. Of particular concern is Cecil's explanation of how the British handled the hunt for Maclean and Philby's role. Cecil does not agree with Lamphere's charges that the British deliberately delayed their investigation, but his argument doesn't convince most readers.

29. CONNOLLY, Cyril, *The Missing Diplomats*, with an Introduction by Peter QUENNELL (London: The Queen Anne Press, 1952).

30. COOKRIDGE, E. H., *The Third Man* (NY: G. P. Putnam's Sons, 1968).

31. COOPER, H. H. A., and REDLINGER, Lawrence J., *Catching Spies: Principles and Practices of Counterespionage* (Boulder, CO: Paladin Press, 1988).

This book is an unreliable source that uses its own exotic espionage vocabulary. Starting with calling Volkov a defector, and going on to date the recruitment of Philby and Maclean as occurring in 1933, it steadily challenges readers' and scholars' confidence. The one thing that can be said in its favour is that the footnotes are indexed.

32. COPELAND, Miles, *The Real Spy World* (London: Weidenfeld and Nicolson, 1974).

One-time CIA officer Miles Copeland, a friend of Philby's in the Middle East in the late 1950s, writes that he 'was told by both CIA and SIS officers that Philby was still suspect . . . and that I would be doing a great service to my country were I to keep an eye on him'. And he did, though he admits, 'I didn't have the slightest suspicion that he was a Soviet agent.' Much of the material is anecdotal and unverifiable. Although Copeland and Philby corresponded after he defected, it didn't stop Philby from calling this 'an appallingly bad book'.

33. ———, *The Game Player: Confessions of the CIA's Original Political Operative* (London: Aurum Press, 1989).

Copeland expands on his claim of being asked to keep an eye on Philby in Beirut, made in the book above. Here he names CIA's James Angleton as the player with the rank and money who financed the surveillance and required the reporting. Copeland's first book, *Game of Nations*, received good reviews. This one and his subsequent efforts did not enjoy that advantage.

34. CORSON, William R., *The Armies of Ignorance: The Rise of the American Intelligence Empire* (NY: The Dial Press, 1977).

A conspiracy theorist when it comes to his treatment of the Philby-Angleton relationship. It is poorly documented and unreliable.

35. COSTELLO, John, *Mask of Treachery* (London: Collins, 1988; NY: William Morrow and Company, Inc., 1988).

A controversial biography of Anthony Blunt that necessarily includes much on Philby. Had the author lived, he would have published a revised edition based on the materials released after the collapse of the Soviet Union. Most of what is written about Philby is accurate, though the portions about his recruitment are not. When concerned with a particular point, validation with another later source is recommended.

36. ———, *Ten Days that Saved the West* (London: Bantam Press, 1991).

Another controversial book, but it does reveal that Philby's work for Soviet Intelligence began much earlier than heretofore suspected. He spied on his college friends and obtained material on the Hess case among others. All this was verified by KGB documents Costello was able to get released for this book, a first for a Western author of intelligence books.

37. ———, and TSAREV, Oleg, *Deadly Illusions* (NY: Crown Publishers, 1993).

Another controversial book, but with Spanish Civil War buffs more than on the treatment of Philby. This is the book that identified Alexander Orlov's role in the Cambridge spy story, including his contacts with Philby when he was a journalist in Spain. It is based largely on KGB documents that its co-author, Tsarev, was given access to when he was permitted to join forces with Costello in a groundbreaking relationship.

38. CUNNINGHAM, Cyril, *Beaulieu: The Finishing School for Secret Agents* (London: Leo Cooper, 1998).

Beaulieu (pronounced Bewlee by the British) was Kim Philby's first assignment after he joined Section D (later SOE) of SIS. Cunningham tells something of his days there, suggests the Soviets were responsible for at least part of his tradecraft training, and acknowledges that he 'taught brilliantly' the propaganda and political warfare course that he designed.

39. DEACON, Richard, *A History of the British Secret Service* (London: Frederick Muller, 1969).

Deacon hints at links between Sidney Reilly and Walter Krivitsky, and he relies on Philby's own account of his recruitment. He is also one of those who suggest that Philby was sent to Beirut as an unknowing double agent to serve as a conduit for disinformation to the Soviets. Later events proved these judgments to be incorrect. His sketchy summary of Philby's service with SIS is accurate.

40. ———, *SPYCLOPAEDIA: The Comprehensive Handbook of Espionage* (London: Macdonald, 1988).

A chronological list comprised of descriptions of famous spies and intelligence organisations prone to error and not well documented. Should not be relied on without corroboration.

41. ———, *The Greatest Treason: The Bizarre Story of Hollis, Liddell and Mountbatten* (London: Century, 1989, revised edn).

The first printing of this book was withdrawn when Lady Avon got an injunction because of statements Deacon made that reflected adversely on her reputation. The revised edition avoided the subject. Both versions suggest that MI5 officer, Guy Liddell, was the fifth man, later judged by most authorities to be in error. Deacon's comments about a close Philby friend, Tommy Harris, the antique lover and former MI5 officer, who gave Philby what became the dining-table in his Moscow flat, are of interest. So is his undocumented assertion that an SIS officer, Donald Darling, suspected that Philby was a Soviet agent during the war. Deacon also states, without identifying a source, that Philby suggested to his interrogator in Beirut that his old friend Ian Innes Milne was a Soviet agent. Others reported the same charge; all agree with Deacon and SIS that it was 'outrageous and untrue'.

42. DOBSON, Christoper, and PAYNE, Ronald, *The Dictionary of Espionage* (London: Harrap Ltd, 1984).

As with most summaries at that time (1984), Philby's recruitment details are wrong. The discussion of Philby in America states that Angleton 'kept him at arm's length', but provides no support for this controversial assertion. And the authors make the claim that Philby was a KGB general. While they also say that Philby became a member of the KGB inner circle, they attribute this to defector Vladimir Sakharov, without comment.

43. DOWNTON, Eric, *Wars without End* (Toronto: Stoddart Publishing Co., 1987).

Journalist and war correspondent Eric Downton knew Richard Sorge in China and Kim Philby in Beirut. He travelled with Philby throughout the Middle East and assumed that Philby still had MI6 connections. Philby and his wife Eleanor attended a dinner party at the Downtons two days before he defected to Moscow. Philby, writes Downton, was showing stress, drinking heavily and stammering more than usual – 'a troubled man'. Downton tells of the much written about the incident that evening when Philby 'stunned his wife with a karate chop' (p. 322), and gives his own reasons as to Philby's motivations generally and why he left Beirut just when he did. As with many who knew Philby at the time, Downton is 'convinced MI6 made it possible for him to escape'. Downton sees Philby first as the 'ruthless double agent [*sic*] who sent people to violent deaths and hideous tortures' (p. 331). And while he was also the 'most publicized spy of the day', Sorge was the more valuable.

44. DRIBERG, Tom, *Guy Burgess: A Portrait with Background* (London: Weidenfeld and Nicolson, 1956).

An apologia for Burgess, Philby's close friend and Cambridge colleague. Driberg concludes that Burgess was never a Soviet agent. The book is of interest here because it discusses events that involved Philby without ever mentioning him.

45. DULLES, Allen, *The Craft of Intelligence* (NY: Harper & Row, 1963).

Dulles covers the Burgess-Maclean-Philby case in one paragraph, calling the three 'communist sympathizers'. Philby had just defected at the time of writing and he is identified as the 'third man' without qualification. Dulles adds that their value was enhanced because 'each served a tour of duty in Washington in the early 1950s'; partly true for Philby and Burgess, but Maclean left in 1948.

46. DURAN, Leopoldo, *Graham Greene: An intimate portrait by his closest friend and confidant* (London: HarperCollins, 1994).

Little of Philby interest here except for a Greene quote. Father Duran asked Greene how Philby was regarded in Russia? Greene replied, 'People said that Andropov wanted to convince the members of the Politburo that the Russian Service should be organized on British lines, and that Philby should be put in charge. I don't know whether there is any truth in that.'

47. ELLIOTT, Nicholas, *Never Judge a Man by his Umbrella* (Wiltshire: Michael Russell, 1991).

48. ———, *With My Little Eye* (Norwich: Michael Russell, 1993).

49. EPSTEIN, Edward Jay, *Deception: The Invisible War between the KGB and the CIA* (London: W. H. Allen, 1989; NY: Simon & Schuster, 1989).

Author Ed Epstein's principal source for this book was James Angleton. Thus when in the chapter 'Kim and Jim' Epstein states that James Angleton 'had fleetingly known Philby during his counterintelligence training in London', it casts doubt on those who argue for a long intimate relationship there. The Epstein version of the Venona decrypts and their links to the Cambridge spies is inaccurate. His conclusion that Angleton was 'temporarily stunned' by Philby's recall after Burgess and Maclean defected, counters those, as for example Andrew Boyle and Anthony Cave Brown, who suggest that

Angleton was aware of Philby's agent role long before the defection. The commentary on Angleton's reaction to the defection is of value.

50. EVANS, Harold, *Good Times, Bad Times* (London: Weidenfeld and Nicolson, 1983).

51. EVELAND, Wilbur Crane, *Ropes of Sand* (NY: W. W. Norton, 1980).

When Eleanor Philby left her husband for the first time in Moscow and returned to America, she stayed much of the time in California with friends she had known in Beirut, Bill and Mimi Eveland. In his memoirs Eveland, who worked for the CIA in the mid to late 1950s, tells how he met Philby, what Dulles said to him about Philby, and hints that had the CIA been interested, he might have found out about Philby's true role before disaster struck. Eveland corresponded with Philby in Moscow, but never saw him after Beirut.

52. FISHER, John, *Burgess and Maclean: A New Look at the Foreign Office Spies* (London: Robert Hale, 1977).

Of value mainly because it gives a view of the Cambridge Comintern controversy at the time. Fisher is one of the first to mention that Philby had married for the fourth time in Moscow and he identifies his new wife as 'Nina'. This was the name Philby and the KGB used to help protect Rufina from unwanted contacts until sometime in the 1980s. Rufina reports that Fisher was correct when he wrote that Philby gave his new 'bride a full length Mink coat' as a wedding gift (p. 229). Fisher's comparison of the motives and situations of Burgess, Maclean and Philby are of interest.

53. FOOT, M. R. D., *SOE: The Special Operations Executive 1940–46* (London: BBC, 1984).

Some interesting comments about Philby's days in SOE. Foot, an authority on the Dutch resistance, discusses Operation North Pole but does not, for good reason, link Philby to it, as Brown and others have done.

54. GARDINER, Muriel, *Code Name 'Mary': Memoirs of an American in the Austrian Underground* (New Haven: Yale University Press, 1983).

The author tells of meeting Philby, her 'secret visitor', in Vienna in 1934. At the time she did not know his name and only learned it years later by chance when she saw a copy of Cookridge's *The Third Man*. In her discussion of the Philby meeting, she notes a number of errors in the Cookridge treatment.

55. GLEES, Anthony, *The Secrets of the Service: British Intelligence and Communist Subversion 1939–1951* (London: Jonathan Cape, 1987).

This book deals with the controversies surrounding the British mole-hunt about which Chapman Pincher and Peter Wright have written at length. The comments on Philby offer little new, but in some cases are disturbing, as for example the undocumented statement that KGB defector Anatoli Golitsyn confirmed that Philby was a Soviet agent. This credits more to Golitsyn than is anywhere justified. The Philby portion of the book concentrates on the period of his British service and adds some valuable input to the conditions of Philby's Parliamentary exoneration in 1955. It is also illustrative of the public controversy over the case one year before Philby's death.

56. GORDIEVSKY, Oleg, *Next Stop Execution: The Autobiography of Oleg Gordievsky* (London: Macmillan, 1995).

From time to time Philby was tasked to analyse cases for the KGB. In 1978, he reviewed the so-called Haavik affair. Philby's conclusion was that the KGB had a leak. He was right. It was Oleg Gordievsky, but suspicion would not fall on him until Ames began his espionage in 1985. In the meantime, Gordievsky was involved with the translation of some of the evaluation reports Philby wrote about the students that attended his seminars from the late 1970s to the mid-1980s. His comments on Philby's style and KGB role at the time, although brief, are interesting and insightful. Though they never met, Philby inscribed a copy of a Danish book about him with the comment, 'To My Dear Friend Oleg – Don't believe everything you see in print! Kim Philby.'

57. HAYNES, John Earl, and KLEHR, Harvey, *Venona: Decoding Soviet Espionage in America* (New Haven, CT: Yale University Press, 1999).

58. HERSH, Burton, *The Old Boys: The American Elite and the Origins of the CIA* (NY: Charles Scribner's, Sons, 1992).

Philby is not a major player in Hersh's incessant hectoring of the CIA, but *Old Boys* does include some attention-grabbing comments about the man by some of those in the CIA with whom he had contact. For example, Hersh writes that Carmel Offie, 'Washington's most unembarrassed social climber by 1950 . . . seems to have made it a point *never* to appear in public with Philby, just then the intelligence crowd's greatest lion. Juxtaposition could invite sparkouts' (p. 271). The reader is left without elucidation or a citation. He does add a quote from Gratian Yatsevich, one of Philby's contacts on the Albanian operation, that the latter 'always maintained a certain level of reserve' with Philby, but then notes that Yatsevich had invited Philby to Maine for a visit; Philby was recalled before the event.

59. HINCHLEY, Colonel Vernon, *The Defectors* (London: George G. Harrap & Co. Ltd, 1967), no index.

The dust-jacket blurb says that this book is 'unlikely to bore'. Perhaps this is because Hinchley's treatment of Philby and his Cambridge spy colleagues is packed with fantasy and errors. Not recommended for anything but an example of the myths surrounding the case.

60. HOARE, Geoffrey, *The Missing Macleans* (London: Cassell & Co. Ltd, 1955; NY: The Viking Press, 1955).

61. HOOD, William, NOLAN, James, and HALPERN, Samuel, *Myths Surrounding James Angleton: Lessons for American Intelligence* (Washington, DC: Consortium for the Study of Intelligence, 1994).

Writing from first-hand knowledge, Hood states that 'the perceived wisdom that Angleton was tutored in counterintelligence by Kim Philby . . . is not true'. His reasoning makes sense, as do Hood's further comments that cast doubt on the commonly held view that Angleton 'gave away the store' when he knew Philby in Washington.

62. HOOPER, David, *Official Secrets: The Use and Abuse of the Act* (London: Secker & Warburg, 1987).

Argues, with examples, that 'objections raised to books on security matters disappear when a proposed book records a triumph of British intelligence'. The problems encountered by Page, Leitch and Knightley with their book are discussed.

63. HOWARTH, Patrick, *Intelligence Chief Extraordinary: The Life of the Ninth Duke of Portland* (London: The Bodley Head, 1986).

The Duke of Portland was Chairman of Britain's high level Joint Intelligence Committee (JIC). Here he provides very brief but interesting comments on the attendance, at different times, of Philby, Burgess, Maclean and Blunt at JIC meetings and the reaction of some present. He rates the SIS as 'wholly ineffectual. It was given no information of importance and could learn little else.' The author suggests, contrary to conventional wisdom, that Philby was not 'privy to the secret of ULTRA' and speculates on what might have happened if it had been otherwise.

64. HOWARTH, T.E.B., *Cambridge between Two Wars* (London: Collins, 1978).

65. KALUGIN, Oleg, *The First Directorate: My 32 Years in Intelligence and Espionage against the West* (NY: St Martin's Press, 1994).

66. KERR, Sheila, 'British Cold War Defectors: the versatile, durable toys of propagandists', in *British Intelligence, Strategy and the Cold War 1945–51*, edited by Richard ALDRICH (London: Routledge, 1992), pp. 111–40.

A thoughtful article that analyses the careers of Philby, Burgess and

Maclean in terms of the Cold War propaganda they have disseminated at the behest of the Soviet Union. In Philby's case, among many examples, are his boasts about the superiority of the KGB, and KGB attempts to build his image as a super spy. Dr Kerr also claims that the CIA participated in the battle by spreading 'two rumours to make life difficult for Philby'. The British were players too. Before his defection, 'MI6 deliberately fed Philby information hoping to disinform the Soviets'. In both cases the sources she cites are less confident than she. Several British writers are accused of expressing 'the themes of KGB propaganda that became Philby's "Western serenade"'. But the Soviets get and deserve most of the attention as she documents how they used their new subjects' writings, medals, meetings with Westerners, and even obituaries, to further their image-building.

67.   KNIGHTLEY, Phillip, *The Second Oldest Profession: The Spy as Bureaucrat, Patriot, Fantasist and Whore* (London: André Deutsch, 1986).

68.   ———, *PHILBY: K.G.B. Masterspy* (London: André Deutsch, 1988).

69.   ———, *A Hack's Progress* (London: Jonathan Cape, 1997), no index.

In this memoir, Knightley reviews, inter alia, some of the changes he has made in his thinking about the Philby case over the years as new material about him surfaced after the collapse of the Soviet Union. Of particular interest are the reasons he concludes that a 'splinter of suspicion' remained in the KGB 'for the rest of Philby's active life'.

70.   KOCH, Stephen, *Double Lives: Spies and Writers in the Soviet War of Ideas Against the West* (NY: The Free Press, 1994).

Professor Koch deals with the question of what Communist organisation Philby was affiliated with when he went to Vienna after graduation. Koch cites Costello to support his 'inference that Kim Philby began his secret service work in Europe through Gibarti's *World Committee for Relief of the Victims of German Fascism* and was thus linked to Willi Münzenberg. But Costello and his co-author also state that Philby's classified (and still not made public) KGB memoirs identify the organisation as MOPR (translated in Borovik, *International Organization for Aid to Revolutionaries*). The Official KGB History, Volume No. 3 (see below) also states that Philby worked for MOPR in Vienna. Since MOPR was an organisation run out of Moscow and having nothing to do with Gibarti, the putative link with Münzenberg asserted by Koch, initially by Costello, and others, is incorrect.

71. LAMPHERE, Robert J., and SHACHTMAN, Tom, *The FBI-KGB War: A Special Agent's Story* (Macon, Georgia: Mercer University Press, 1995).

There is a chapter on Philby in which Lamphere makes clear the relationship they shared. He also discusses Philby's role in the Venona project, how the FBI reacted to the defection of Burgess and Maclean, and how they viewed Philby from then on.

72. LEIGH, David, *The Wilson Plot: How the Spycatchers and their American Allies Tried to Overthrow the British Government* (NY: Pantheon Books, 1988).

Some interesting comments on the Philby-Angleton relationship and on Philby's memoirs.

73. LLOYD, Mark, *The Guinness Book of Espionage* (NY: Da Capo Press, 1994).

74. LONSDALE, Gordon, *SPY: Twenty Years in the Soviet Secret Service, The Memoirs of Gordon Lonsdale* (NY: Hawthorn Books, Inc., 1965; London: Neville Spearman Ltd, 1965).

The book that some say Philby ghosted; Philby says he polished. Snelling says it is Lonsdale's work, his unmistakable style.

75. MACDONALD, Bill, *The True 'INTREPID': Sir William Stephenson and the Unknown Agents* (Surrey, British Columbia, Canada: Timberholme Books, Ltd, 1998).

There are many surprises about Stephenson in this book, but none about Philby. The author does quote the Dick Ellis comment that Montgomery Hyde's book, *The Quiet Canadian*, was 'related to the defection of Soviet double agent [*sic*] Kim Philby'. He then quotes author William Stevenson stating that *The Quiet Canadian* had nothing to do with Philby. Stevenson was right, but he gave no reason. Thus Macdonald goes on to say that 'indirectly it is possible the release of *The Quiet Canadian* might have had something to do with the defection of Kim Philby and boosting the morale of the Western security services' (pp. 136–7). But that cannot be. As Nigel West pointed out in *Counterfeit Spies* (p. 95), the Hyde book was published before, not after, Philby defected.

76. MACLEAN, Fitzroy, *Take Nine Spies* (London: Weidenfeld and Nicolson, 1978; NY: Atheneum, 1978).

A good summary of the Cambridge spies for its time. Unsourced, but it includes first-hand observations of the author when he too served in the Foreign Office.

77. MAHONEY, Harry Thayer and Marjorie Locke, *Biographic Dictionary of Espionage* (Bethesda, MD: Austin & Winfield, Publishers, 1998).

This summary of the Philby case while hitting the main points is original in many respects. Mahoney sees Philby, Burgess and Maclean as a 'classic Comintern espionage organization' when most other scholars take the view that their espionage links didn't begin at Cambridge and were less than formal afterwards. While Mahoney states that Philby knew Münzenberg, the evidence does not support this view. It is also unusual to say that 'there was at first no suspicion Philby was involved in the disappearance' of Burgess and Maclean when the evidence that he was the prime suspect from that moment on is substantial. Similarly, Mahoney's description of Philby's days in Beirut and the details of his defection deserve close attention and comparison with other, including KGB, depictions. When he arrived in the Soviet Union, Philby did not go to Kuybishev as Mahoney suggests, but remained in Moscow, and it was Eleanor not Aileen who joined him there. He was buried in the same cemetery as Ramon Mercader (*sic*) but Konon Molody (Lonsdale) and Rudolf Abel rest elsewhere. Mahoney is careful to note that Cookridge's *The Third Man* has 'many inaccuracies, but is pleasant reading'.

78. MANCHESTER, William, *American Caesar: Douglas MacArthur 1880–1964* (Boston: Little, Brown & Company, 1978).

The question of whether Philby, Burgess and Maclean informed the Soviets about American and British policy with regard to Korea has often been raised and Manchester analyses the possibilities here. He wrote to Philby 'through a mutual acquaintance', later revealed by Rufina Philby as Leonard Mosley, and asked him directly. Philby replied that he didn't know the answer and probably couldn't tell if he did. He added that there were many others who could have accomplished the act, though he didn't identify them. Manchester notes that 'it is absurd to conclude . . . that the Philby apparatus bore no responsibility in the matter'.

79. MANGOLD, Tom, *Cold Warrior: James Jesus Angleton: The CIA's Master Spy Hunter* (London/NY: Simon & Schuster, 1991).

80. MANN, Wilfred Basil, *Was There a Fifth Man?: Quintessential Recollections* (Oxford: Pergamon Press, 1982).

81. MARTIN, C. David, *Wilderness of Mirrors* (NY: Harper & Row, 1980).

This book was the first to mention Maclean's Venona cryptonym, HOMER; he didn't mention Philby's or Burgess's.

82. MINNICK, Wendell, *Spies and Provocateurs: A Worldwide Encyclopedia of Persons Conducting Espionage and Covert Action, 1946–1991* (Jefferson, NC: McFarland & Company Inc., Publishers, 1992).

A brief but accurate account until the portion on Philby's 'confession to Elliott'. Minnick adds questionable detail. And Philby's presence in Moscow was confirmed in 1963 by the Soviets, not in 1965 by a journalist.

83. MODIN, Yuri, *My Five Cambridge Friends* (London: Headline Book Publishing, 1994).

84. MONROE, Elizabeth, *Philby of Arabia* (NY: Pitman Publishing Corporation, 1973).

A valuable biography of Kim Philby's father.

85. MOSLEY, Leonard, *Dulles: A Biography of Eleanor, Allen, and John Foster Dulles and their Family Network* (NY: The Dial Press, 1978).

86. ———, *The Druid: The Nazi Spy Who Double-Crossed the Double-Cross System* (NY: Atheneum, 1981).

As with most fiction, this book has no index, nor does it cite any sources. A number of SIS and MI5 officers are correctly identified in *The Druid*, including Philby, but the conversations quoted and operations described are the product of Mosley's creative imagination. For details, see the chapter of the same name in Nigel West's *Counterfeit Spies*.

87. MUGGERIDGE, Malcolm, *The Infernal Grove: Chronicles of Wasted Time: Number 2* (NY: William Morrow & Company Inc., 1974).

The colourful Muggeridge served with Philby during the Second World War and describes him here as 'a sort of espionage Raffles' (p. 127). His first-hand account of the experiences they shared in England, and later in Paris, make good reading and add valuable insights to his motivation.

88. NASH, Jay Robert, *SPIES: A Narrative Encyclopedia of Dirty Deeds & Double Dealing from Biblical Times to Today* (NY: M. Evans & Company Inc., 1997).

Nash paints a picture of a 'vain, arrogant, cynical, double agent [sic] oozing with confidence', who helped 'Willi Münzenberg set up the World Peace Congress'. Nash doesn't say that this organisation was formed in 1949, nine years after Müzenberg's death. While the broad events are depicted accurately, Nash gets too many other details wrong, including Philby's recruitment. He also claims that Philby was involved with Sandor Rado of the Rote Drei network, and the Tyler Kent case, and has him conferring with Allen Dulles in London during the Second Word War. He closes with a comment that Philby had a desk at KGB headquarters and the rank of general. No detail should be accepted without independent validation.

89. NAZHESTKIN, O. I., 'Philby Makes His Choice', chapter 2, in Primakov, Academician Ye. M., and Kirpichenko, V. A. (eds), *Essays on the History of Russian Foreign Intelligence*, Vol. 3, 1933–41 (Moscow: International Relations, 1997) (in Russian).

Philby's career is discussed from the Russian point of view in chapter 1, 'The Man Who Started the Cambridge Five', and chapter 2, 'Philby Makes His Choice'. The details of his wartime service will be included in the two-part Volume 4 of the series due to be published in 1999.

90. NEWTON, Verne W., *The Cambridge Spies: The Untold Story of Maclean, Philby, and Burgess in America* (Lanham, MD: Madison Books, 1991).

91. O'TOOLE, G. A. J., *The Encyclopedia of American Intelligence and Espionage: From the Revolutionary War to the Present* (NY: Facts On File, 1988).

A brief but informative summary of Philby's career, although some details are incorrect: Philby did not join a Communist cell at Cambridge (or anywhere else), nor was he recruited there. Similarly, he didn't continue to work for SIS after Burgess and Maclean defected, nor did he serve in an administrative role with the KGB in Moscow.

92. PAGE, Bruce, LEITCH, David, and KNIGHTLEY, Phillip, *The Philby Conspiracy* (NY: Doubleday & Company, 1968); *PHILBY: The Spy Who Betrayed a Generation* (London: André Deutsch, 1968; Penguin Books, 1969, revised edn), both with an introduction by John le Carré.

93. PARRISH, Thomas, *The Cold War Encyclopedia* (NY: Henry Holt, 1996).

A concise summary of Philby's career until the defection of Burgess and Maclean. Following that event, writes Parrish, Angleton's suspicions forced his dismissal from SIS; when Harvey was the primary force in this case. The suggestion that the British allowed Philby to defect is again put forth, but with no documentation, as is the claim that he was made a KGB general after he defected.

94. PENROSE, Barry, and FREEMAN, Simon, *Conspiracy of Silence: The Secret Life of Anthony Blunt* (London: Grafton Books, 1986).

While the focus of the book is squarely on Anthony Blunt, the authors develop his relationship with Philby and Burgess, for whom he had great affection, and with Maclean, for whom he did not. It was Blunt who was used by the KGB to contact Philby again after nearly three years and to give him a substantial sum of money – some say £5,000 – to help in those years without steady income. The reader will not find a collection of the Cambridge spy myths here. Moreover, the authors are careful to identify speculation as when they report that MI6 had used Philby to pass misinformation to the Soviets. Philby drops from the narrative after his defection.

95. PERRY, Roland, *The Fifth Man* (London: Sidgwick & Jackson, 1994).

Four years after Andrew and Gordievsky had satisfied most of the espionage glitterati that John Cairncross was the fifth man – as he himself later admitted – Perry concluded that they were wrong: it was Victor Rothschild all along. He based his conclusion on the work of

Peter Wright of *Spycatcher* fame, a series of unidentified KGB colonels and CIA operatives, plus Yuri Modin. The result is a narrative that contains excessive errors of fact: James Angleton was never Director of CIA, *OTTO* was not Theodore Mally, Venona was not a Russian code name, and Philby's flat was hardly modest 'even by Moscow standards' (p. 290). And much of what he attributes to Modin was in fact accomplished by others. Modin was to tell this author that he does not understand how this happened. Although Perry was the first to state that Philby slashed his wrists in a suicide attempt, he implies that Modin knew of it and that it occurred before Philby wrote his memoirs, something Modin denies. The section on Philby's student seminars is short but informative. Approach with caution.

96. PHILBY, Eleanor, *The Spy I Loved* (London: Hamish Hamilton, 1967); *The Spy I Married* (NY: Ballantine,1968).

97. PHILBY, H. A. R. (Kim), 'Saudi Arabia – A Correspondent's Report', *The New Republic*, V136, 1 April 1957, pp. 7–8.

This article and the ten which follow were written by Philby when he was in Beirut nominally working for the *Observer* and the *Economist*. At the time, the editor-at-large of *The New Republic* was Michael Straight, one-time Soviet agent, recruited by Anthony Blunt at Cambridge. For reasons unknown, they have not previously been mentioned in the Philby literature.

98. ———, 'Arab Unity Is Not Breaking Apart', *The New Republic*, V136, 15 April 1957, p. 6.

99. ———, 'How Successful Is Our Diplomacy In the Middle East?', *The New Republic*, V137, 9 September 1957, pp. 14–15.

100. ———, 'What Obsesses the Arabs?', *The New Republic*, V137, 7 October 1957, pp. 8–9.

101. ———, 'Some Western Illusions About King Saud', *The New Republic*, V137, 21 October 1957, p. 7.

102. ———, 'Mr Philby Replies', *The New Republic*, V137, 28 October 1957, pp. 3, 22.

103. ———, 'Jordan's Survival', *The New Republic*, V137, 16 December 1957, p. 6.

104. ———, 'What Comes After Union of Egypt and Syria?', *The New Republic*, V138, 24 February 1958, p. 12.

105. ———, 'Iraq and Jordan – Union of Unequals', *The New Republic*, V138, 12 May 1958, p. 11.

106. ———, 'What Nasser Wants From Moscow?', *The New Republic*, V138, 21 April 1958, p. 7.

107. ———, 'Is the Middle East Now Beyond Hope?', *The New Republic*, V138, 19 May 1958, pp. 9–10.

108. PHILBY, Kim, *My Silent War* (London: MacGibbon & Kee Ltd, 1968).

109. PINCHER, Chapman, *Inside Story: A Documentary of the Pursuit of Power* (Briarcliff Manor, NY: Stein & Day, 1978).

In his first book commenting on the Philby case, Pincher adds no new facts. After dealing with the interesting question of why Philby was not left to drown in alcohol in Beirut, he gives his reasons for believing that MI6 encouraged Philby to defect. His claim that Philby married Melinda Maclean in Moscow is incorrect, as is his use of the oxymoron *defector-in-place*. Pincher's subsequent books are more accurate and more informative.

110. ———, *Their Trade Is Treachery* (London: Sidgwick & Jackson, 1981).

In retrospect, there is little to be learned about the Philby case from this book because much of what appears here is repeated in later treatments. The theme of the book is the search for a high-level mole in the Security Service (MI5) which generated an investigation by The Fluency Committee. Philby figures prominently at the outset because it was his defection in 1963 that convinced some senior MI5 officers that their service was penetrated and that the mole was either the Deputy Director General or the DG himself! After several investigations, it was finally concluded that neither was guilty, although this book ends before the issues had been resolved. Pincher identified the Venona cryptonyms for Burgess (HICKS) and Philby (STANLEY) in this book, apparently for the first time.

111. ———, *Too Secret Too Long: The great betrayal of Britain's crucial secrets and the cover-up* (London: Sidgwick & Jackson, 1984).

This is an expanded successor to *Their Trade is Treachery*. Although nearly three times as long, there is little new about Philby. Pincher does suggest that Philby played a role in the case of alleged atom spy Bruno Pontecorvo, but cites an anonymous source. The chapter assessing the damage Philby did is largely a summary of his career. More sources are cited here than in *Their Trade . . .*, including his main one, molehunter Peter Wright. Pincher uses Philby and the other cases to argue for Parliamentary oversight. This is a good source to view British Intelligence in the early 1980s, but it reveals the problems experienced rather than the solutions later implemented.

112. POLMAR, Norman, and ALLEN, Thomas B., *SPY BOOK: The Encyclopedia of Espionage* (NY: Random House, 1998, updated and revised quality paperback edn).

113. PORTER, Bernard, *Plots and Paranoia: A history of political espionage in Britain 1790–1988* (London: Unwin Hyman, 1989).

Philby and his Cambridge colleagues figure obliquely here as the discussion considers their impact on British Intelligence and security. Porter assumes the reader knows the case details and concentrates on the broader problems.

114. POWERS, Thomas, *The Man Who Kept the Secrets: Richard Helms and the CIA* (NY: Alfred A. Knopf, 1979).

While confined to Philby in America, Powers gives a good assessment of his impact on the CIA, adding at the same time genuine insight into the fundamental issues facing counter-intelligence officers. A pleasure to read.

115. PURDY, Anthony, and SUTHERLAND, Douglas, *Burgess and Maclean* (Garden City, NY: Doubleday & Company, 1963).

Philby's third wife wrote that Maclean 'hated' this book. She didn't say why, but it could have been because it told the truth about Maclean's espionage and traitorous behaviour. Philby is incorrectly identified as working for MI5 during the war but otherwise seldom mentioned; he had not yet defected when the book was printed.

116. RANELAGH, John, *The Agency: The Rise and Decline of the CIA* (NY: Simon & Schuster, Touchstone Edition, revised and updated, 1987).

Although, as with Powers, Ranelagh concentrates on Philby's relationship with the CIA, there is less overlap than might be expected. The differences are worth pondering, especially the comments on Philby's impact on the CIA. On the 'who suspected Philby first' issue, Ranelagh makes the surprising claim that 'the British were the first to suspect Philby early in 1951 . . . in all likelihood they hoped to use him as a disinformation agent' (p. 151). These assertions have yet to be proved by anyone. Ranelagh also implies that both Bill Harvey and James Angleton had their own suspicions before Burgess and Maclean defected, while most observers credit Harvey alone with this accomplishment.

117. RICHELSON, Jeffrey T., *A Century of Spies: Intelligence in the Twentieth Century* (NY: Oxford University Press, 1995).

This survey of modern intelligence has a good summary of espionage activities of Philby and the other Cambridge spies from their recruitment to their exposure. Maclean is seen as the 'most potentially valuable' member of the Ring of Five.

118. RIEBLING, Mark, *WEDGE: The Secret War between the FBI and CIA* (NY: Alfred A. Knopf, 1994).

Nothing new on Philby, but Riebling looks at the case in terms of the FBI-CIA relationship, which he finds less than loving and operationally harmful. Based on interviews with the players, *Wedge* shows how bureaucratic battles can impact counter-intelligence.

119. RILEY, Morris, *PHILBY: The Hidden Years* (Cornwall: United Writers Publications Ltd, 1990; London: Janus Publications, 1999, paperback edn).

120. ROSITZKE, Harry, *CIA's Secret Operations: espionage, counter-espionage and covert action* (NY: Reader's Digest Press, 1977).

Harry Rositzke knew Kim Philby in London and Washington. He gives a characteristically candid assessment of the man – competent, precise, careful – noting his rare talent for the sustained double life. Rositzke challenges the conventional wisdom that Philby knew all that the CIA knew about Soviet operations.

121. ————, *The KGB: The Eyes of Russia* (Garden City, NY: Doubleday & Company Inc., 1981).

This book contains a very good summary of the Philby case from his university days until his departure from SIS. Of equal or greater importance are the thoughtful comments of a professional on agent motivation in context, and more broadly on whether or not espionage really matters.

122. SAWATSKY, John, *For Services Rendered: Leslie James Bennett and the RCMP Security Service* (Toronto: Doubleday Canada Ltd, 1982).

The RCMP Security Service, not to be outdone, had a molehunt of its own with the prime suspect being the head of its counter-espionage element, James Bennett – he proved to be innocent. Sawatsky tells this story here. Philby had liaison duties with the Canadians while he served in America. In telling his story, Sawatsky gives the Canadian perspective to the Philby case and shows how it influenced the molehunt and helped ruin Bennett's career. There are no source notes, but the book has stood the test of time and professional analysis well, even though it did make Philby's father a Knight, something the Queen never did.

123. SEALE, Patrick, and McCONVILLE, Maureen, *PHILBY: The Long Road to Moscow* (London: Hamish Hamilton, 1973).

124. SETH, Ronald, *Encyclopedia of Espionage: The Spy's Who's Who* (London: New English Library, 1972).

Seth earned his reputation for producing many undocumented, carelessly written books on espionage. But in the case of his Philby summary here, there are no glaring errors. Based entirely on *Philby: The Spy Who Betrayed A Generation*, it summarises Philby's life from birth to defection.

125. SHELDON, Michael, *Graham Greene: The Man Within* (London: Heinemann, 1994).

Sheldon covers more of the Philby-Greene relationship than other Greene biographers to date, but excludes their Moscow meetings. He also claims that SIS told him officially that Greene gave them his help in exchange for expenses when travelling to various countries, including Russia where he met Philby several times. Whether, as Sheldon suggests, Greene wrote *The Third Man* with Philby in mind as Harry Lime is debatable. The links to *The Human Factor* are closer, as Sheldon points out.

126. SHERRY, Norman, *The Life of Graham Greene: Volume Two: 1939–1955* (London: Jonathan Cape, 1994).

127. SILVERSTEIN, Herma, *Spies among Us: The Truth about Modern Espionage* (NY: Franklin Watts, 1988).

Poor case summary; chronological gaps, too many errors in what is left.

128. SINCLAIR, Andrew, *The Red and The Blue: Intelligence, Treason and the Universities* (London: Weidenfeld and Nicolson, 1986).

Unreliable on important espionage issues involving Philby, but it does provide interesting commentary on the Communists at Cambridge in the 1930s and in the Government afterwards.

129. SMITH, Michael, *New Cloak, Old Dagger: How Britain's Spies Came in from the Cold* (London: Victor Gollancz, 1996).

The chapter on the Ring-of-Five gives a good summary of the Philby case and its links to the other Cambridge spies.

130. SNELLING, O. F., *Rare Books and Rarer People: Some Personal Reminiscences of the Trade* (London: Werner Shaw, 1982).

131. SOLOMON, Flora, and LITVINOFF, Barnet, *Baku to Baker Street: The Memoirs of Flora Solomon* (London: Collins, 1984); *A Woman's Way* (NY: Simon and Schuster, 1984).

Flora Solomon's account of her contacts with Philby and what caused her to report him officially to MI5 as a Soviet agent.

132. STEVENSON, William, *INTREPID's Last Case* (NY: Villard Books, 1983).

Stevenson writes here of Philby, the KGB general, and that Philby planned to have GRU defector Gouzenko killed. These errors, the other unsourced comments about Philby, and the author's track record in his previous book, *A Man Called INTREPID*, will depress the conscientious reader. Treat as unreliable unless independent corroboration is found.

133. SUTHERLAND, Douglas, *The Great Betrayal: The Definitive Story of Blunt, Philby, Burgess, and Maclean* (NY: Times Books, 1980), published in the UK with the more accurate title, *The Fourth Man: The Story of Blunt, Philby, Burgess, and Maclean* (London: Secker & Warburg, 1980).

The British edition of Sutherland's book, with every justification, omitted the word *Definitive* from the title. It reveals something of what was thought of the case at the time, but subsequent books have come closer to the goal set out here.

134. THOMAS, Rosamund, *Espionage and Secrecy: The Official Secrets Acts 1911–1989 of the United Kingdom* (London: Routledge, 1991).

In a chapter discussing 'Problems of Evidence', Thomas cites the Philby case at several points, though she provides no new detail. What is of interest is the way she uses the open intelligence literature, cited in detail, to make her legal points.

135. TREVOR-ROPER, Hugh, *The Philby Affair* (London: William Kimber, 1968)

136. VERRIER, Anthony, *Through the Looking Glass: British Foreign Policy in an Age of Illusions* (NY: W. W. Norton, 1983).

The theme of this book is that Britain has, or had, a clandestine foreign office (MI6) making and implementing policy. While there is nothing new about Philby, the author's views of his role, and to a lesser extent that of Burgess and Maclean, in several foreign policy crises is interesting.

137. VOLKMAN, Ernest, *Spies: The Secret Agents Who Changed the Course of History* (NY: John Wiley & Sons Inc., 1994).

Rehash with new errors: Modin was not Philby's London control, nor did he arrange for Philby's defection to Moscow from Beirut; and Philby learned of the Venona operation before, not after, he arrived in Washington; Theodore Mally was never a priest, nor did he recruit Philby, etc., etc.

138. ———, *Espionage: The Greatest Spy Operations of the 20th Century* (NY: John Wiley & Sons Inc., 1995).

More unreliable, undocumented rehash.

139. WALLER, John H., *The Unseen War in Europe: Espionage and Conspiracy in the Second World War* (NY: Random House, 1996).

Wilhelm Canaris, the central character of this book, was head of the German Abwehr, or military intelligence, and he collaborated secretly with the resistance to Hitler. Although they never met, the paths of Canaris and Philby crossed several times – Philby wanted to have Canaris assassinated – and John Waller gives the details in this book.

140. WEINSTEIN, Allen, and VASSILIEV, Alexander, *The Haunted Wood: Soviet Espionage in America, The Stalin Era* (NY: Random House, 1999).

This book is based on material from the KGB archives. In the discussion of the Elizabeth Bentley case (the NKGB agent who defected to the FBI in 1945), the authors cite a cable that names Philby as the one who informed the NKGB centre in Moscow, on 20 November 1945, of her defection. At that time she had not even completed her debriefing. His role in her case had not been known previously. The other references to Philby provide no new data.

141. WEST, Nigel, *Unreliable Witness: Espionage Myths of the Second World War* (London: Weidenfeld and Nicolson, 1984); *A Thread of Deceit* (NY: Random House, 1985).

142. ——, *Molehunt: The Full Story of the Soviet Spy in MI5* (London: Weidenfeld and Nicolson, 1987; NY: William Morrow and Company, 1989).

143. ——, *The Friends: Britain's Post-War Secret Intelligence Operations* (London: Weidenfeld and Nicolson, 1988).

This study of Britain's Secret Intelligence Service (MI6) in the post-war era includes a chapter on Philby that provides a succinct summary of the case from his birth to the end of his MI6 service. Although West states that Philby spent three years at Cambridge (actually four) and that he did not know Maclean, something shown by Philby's unpublished chapters, included herein, to be incorrect, it is otherwise valuable.

144. ———, *Counterfeit Spies: Genuine or Bogus? An Astonishing Investigation into Secret Agents of the Second World War* (London: St Ermin's Press, 1998).

This fascinating book dispels a number of espionage myths and claims to spy glory. In one, *The Druid*, a fictional account of an agent in Britain during the Second World War, author Leonard Mosley involves Philby. West tells why and how Mosley knew he got it wrong.

145. ———, *Venona: The Greatest Secret of the Cold War* (London: HarperCollins, 1999).

146. ——— (ed.), *The Faber Book of Espionage* (London: Faber & Faber, 1993).

West has assembled herein samples of writings by former SIS (MI6) and Security Service (MI5) officers, adding to each a brief anecdotal description of their intelligence roles. Philby's contribution is from the privately published W. E. D. Allen family history (see above), and reproduced here for the first time outside that volume. Philby's *My Silent War* is mentioned elsewhere in the book, but no excerpt is included because it has been so widely quoted. Similarly, Philby himself is mentioned in many of the entries because he crossed paths with so many of the authors. The bibliographic essay on intelligence books in general in the introduction is particularly valuable.

147. ——— (ed.), *The Faber Book of Treachery* (London: Faber & Faber, 1995).

While Philby is often characterised as a traitor, none of his written work appears in this volume, but he is mentioned on many pages because those writing include their Philby experiences. The format followed is the same as that used in West's espionage volume mentioned above. Not all the authors included are traitors, some, as for example Desmond Bristow, just write about them, in his case, Philby. As with West's companion volume on espionage, the bibliographic essay at the beginning is thorough and good reading.

148. WEST, Nigel, and TSAREV, Oleg, *The Crown Jewels: The British Secrets at the Heart of the KGB Archives* (London: HarperCollins, 1998; New Haven: Yale University Press, 1999).

149. WEST, Rebecca, *The New Meaning of Treason* (NY: The Viking Press, 1964).

In her argument against excessive government secrecy, West cites various incidents in the Philby case and takes the Government to task for allowing Philby his freedom after 1955, and thus the opportunity to defect in 1963 (her date of March is incorrect). She speculates that Philby was kept on as an unqualified leftover from the Second World War, but this theory is not supported by the facts.

150. WEST, W. J., *The Truth about Hollis: An Investigation* (London: Gerald Duckworth & Co., 1989)

151. ———, *SPYMASTER: The Betrayal of MI5* (NY: Wynwood Press, 1990).

SPYMASTER is a revised edition of *The Truth about Hollis*. Philby is mentioned frequently in both. In his case, the content is the same and reveals nothing new. The books focus on the MI5 molehunt and attempt to show that its one-time Director General, Roger Hollis, was indeed a Soviet mole. A difficult job is made harder for the reader since no sources are cited.

152. ———, *The Quest for Graham Greene* (London: Weidenfeld and Nicolson, 1997).

West provides some interesting insights into the Philby-Greene relationship based in part on their correspondence, which he quotes. He too analyses Greene's *Human Factor* in terms of Philby's career, but does not do the same for *The Third Man*.

153. WINKS, Robin, *Cloak and Gown Scholars in America's Secret War* (London: Collins Harvill, 1987), p. 263.

This is a wonderful book about Yale graduates who served in OSS during the Second World War. Philby knew many of them and some harboured 'mild suspicions' about him during the war, but said nothing to their subsequent regret. There are no new details about Philby the man, but his links to OSS are described, as are the errors he made in assessing some of the OSS personnel.

154. WISE, David, and ROSS, Thomas, *The Espionage Establishment* (NY: Random House, 1967).

The authors present a good summary of the Philby case from his birth to his defection, with emphasis on how the British Government dealt with it – not very well. The book, and the serialisation that preceded it, created a ruckus in Britain when it printed the address of 'C' at 21 Queen Anne's Gate for the first time.

155. WOLF, Markus, *Man without a Face: The Memoirs of a Spymaster* (London: Jonathan Cape, 1997).

156. WORTHINGTON, Peter, *Looking for Trouble: A journalist's life . . . and then some* (Toronto: Key Porter Books, 1984).

A brief account of meeting a drunken Philby in Beirut; also claims Gouzenko provided a lead to Philby that was ignored at the time.

157. WRIGHT, Peter, *Spycatcher: The Candid Autobiography of a Senior Intelligence Officer* (NY: Viking, 1987).

Philby Chronology

N.B. Regarding the entries in the Source column, the number to the left of the slash indicates the number of the book or article listed at the end of this chronology; the number to the right indicates the page reference of the book cited.

Date(s)	Event	Source(s)	Comment(s)
1 Jan. 1912	Birth of Harold Adrian Russell Philby, Ambala, Punjab, India, to Harry St John Bridger Philby and his wife Dora Johnston Philby.	1/3	Oldest of 4 children; the others were girls (Diana, Patricia and Helena).
1919	Sent to Aldro, a Prep school in Eastbourne, England.	1/8	'With a slightly better than average aptitude for games - cricket, soccer, rugger', he got on the teams 'with ease'. (3/pt1.13)
June 1924	Philby becomes a King's Scholar at Westminster.	13/27	Kim was the first student to 'leave the school with a public school scholarship'. (3/pt1.13)
Summer 1924	Tours Spain with father.	1/9	
18 Sept. 1924	St John Philby takes his son to Westminster School on his first day.	1/10; 13/27	There were only 40 King's Scholars and they were the elite of the school.

Date(s)	Event	Source(s)	Comment(s)
Spring 1929	Philby wins a scholarship to Trinity College, Cambridge University.	1/12	The original scholarship was to Oxford, but his father had it changed to his alma mater, Cambridge.
October 1929	Enters Trinity College, Cambridge, to read history.	1/20 2/156	*My Silent War* (*MSW*) chronology states he joined the CUSS in 1929, but Seale (1/27) notes that the CUSS didn't exist until 1931. Kim wrote that he never joined its predecessor, the Labour Club.
1930	Meets student Harry Dawes, former coal miner, who gives Philby his first view of Marxist reality.	1/24	Dawes read economics and told his colleagues about the reality of working in the mines.
October 1930	Guy Burgess enters Trinity College, Cambridge, from Eton, on a history scholarship.	1/43; 2/126; 15/82–4	Burgess first went to Eton in January 1924 because he was too young to enter the Royal Naval College at Dartmouth. In 1927, he entered Dartmouth for 33 months, after which he was forced to withdraw because he failed the eyesight examination. He then returned to Eton.
Summer 1931	CUSS founded; Philby joins.	1/27	

Date	Event	Ref	Notes
October 1931	Switches to economics after a third in Part I of the History Tripos.	1/24	Brown gives the date as 1930, but the Tripos Part 1 is only given after two years.
	Works for socialist candidates in national election, one of the few times Philby acted publicly on political matters.	1/29	One of Philby's Cambridge colleagues, D.W. Ewer, who worked with him for the socialist candidates, was the son of a fellow-travelling Communist, William Norman 'Trilby' Ewer of the *Daily Herald*, who, unbeknownst to Kim Philby and the son, was an active Soviet agent, though he later turned anti-Communist.
	James Klugmann and Donald Maclean start Cambridge from Gresham's; both soon become Communists. Joins CUSS.	1/39;10/30 1/27	
27 Oct. 1931	Labour Party annihilated in a general election; Philby becomes more ardent socialist.	1/29; 2/xviii	
Summer 1932	Philby and Tim Milne, his Westminster classmate and now Oxford student, tour Europe.	1/49; HBP conversation with Milne	Experienced Nazism in action. Hugh Trevor-Roper recalls Milne mentioning his *Communist* travelling companion, Kim Philby. (1/50)
1932	(Sir) Dennis Robertson introduces Philby to Guy Burgess at Cambridge	1/43	Sir Dennis was a friend of St John Philby.
October 1932	Philby becomes treasurer of CUSS	1/41; 2/156	Maclean at 20 was at least a salon Marxist; Philby had still not made up his mind.

403

Date(s)	Event	Source(s)	Comment(s)
1932–3	Philby meets Maclean casually and infrequently.	1/45	
Spring 1933	Communists take over CUSS just before Philby graduates and decides to commit himself to the cause.	1/51; 2/xviii	
Spring 1933	Philby wins Trinity prize of £14.00; spends on works of Marx.	1/53	Philby was drinking by this time. The evening before final exams in June 1993, he had doubles with his Communist mentor Jim Lees. (1/53)
Summer 1933	Philby fills out Foreign Service application; does not submit when his reference, Sir Dennis Robertson, says he can't recommend him, 'unfit . . . too far left'.	1/52	Philby was now a Communist without a card.
Summer 1933	Philby graduates with second-class degree in economics.	1/54	The chrono. in MSW says Philby left Cambridge 'with only a pass degree' (2/156).
Autumn 1933	Philby given £50.00 by his father for editing his book, The Empty Quarter. Kim uses the funds to buy a motor-bike and go to Vienna.	1/54	Kim is not mentioned in the book's acknowledgments.

404

Autumn 1933	In Vienna, Philby meets Litzi Friedman; becomes active in Communist underground MOPR work against the Dollfuss Government. 'Philby becomes a Soviet agent.'	1/58ff 2/156	MOPR or IOAR (see Borovik, 7/14) depending on the translation; a Communist group controlled from Moscow, not Berlin as Koch claims (see bibliography entry for Koch). The MSW chronology does not say what kind of agent. The new portions of his memoirs published herein suggest that he was more an asset.
24 Feb. 1934	Philby marries Litzi in the Vienna Town Hall; she gets British passport.	1/64; 2/156 22/160, 420	According to Brown, Teddy Kollek, the future Mayor of Jerusalem, 'was present at the wedding'. Years later Kollek would tell Angleton of Philby's political background.
April 1934	Philby and Litzi, who is in danger because she is a Jew, leave for England via Paris by train.	1/67; 3/219	
April 1934	Philby goes to CPGB HQ in King Street, London, and inquires about joining the Party. Is told to wait.	3/219	Philby notes that he and Litzi did this within a day or two of their arrival in London.
Early May 1934	Philby addresses the CUSS about his Vienna experiences; meets Communists John Cornford (close friend of Michael Straight) and Burgess.	1/70	At the time Cornford was described as 'the dominant figure in Cambridge communism'. He was killed in Spain during the Civil War. (1/70)

Date(s)	Event	Source(s)	Comment(s)
Mid-May 1934	Visited by Edith Tudor-Hart, a friend from Vienna; asked about meeting with a man of 'decisive importance'. When Philby agrees to meet him, his recruitment begins. Meets 'Otto' in Regent's Park a few days later. Otto becomes one of several case officers to handle Philby; Alexander Orlov is another. He is recruited at the second meeting with Otto 2 weeks later and tasked to produce a list of other candidates.	3/220 3/224–7	Philby told the same story to Borovik in the 1980s. Philby referred to Hart as 'he'.
22 June 1934	One of Philby's initial assigned tasks is to spy on his father, whom the Soviets suspect is a British spy. He goes through his father's papers in his London residence.	7/39	Based on Borovik interview with Philby.
Mid-July 1934	Otto introduces Philby to 'Theo', true name Theodore Mally. They review the list of candidates, placing Maclean near the top. Ultimately Centre decides to recruit Burgess since he knows about his friends and can be controlled if he is a player.	3/229 10/117–19	Philby's memory may be off here; Mally was based in France at the time, but he did visit England occasionally in 1935.

Late Autumn 1934	Philby takes job as a sub-editor and contributor to the *Review of Reviews*, at £4.0 a week.	1/72 3/231
1934–5	Joins Central Asian Society; prepares summaries of its members for Otto. Takes course in Turkish at the London School of Oriental Studies. *Review of Reviews* near death; Philby looks for other work.	3/231 3/232 3/235–6	The WYLIE (spying on a friend in the War Department) case occurs during this period and Philby gets some practical tradecraft experience. (22/172)
Spring 1935	Philby's father visits London; Philby is again tasked to go through documents and photograph most interesting ones of the 'famous Anglo spy'.	7/52
Autumn 1935	Philby tasked with reporting on various British individuals selected by Centre; on-the-job espionage training.	7/54
Spring 1936	Philby offered editorial job on a planned Anglo-German trade journal; Otto approves. Philby joins Anglo-German Fellowship and travels frequently to Germany; meets Goebbels. Journal never published.	1/78; 3/236	Based on Borovik's review of Philby's KGB file; Philby is identified by his cryptonym SÖHNCHEN (SONNY).

Date(s)	Event	Source(s)	Comment(s)
December 1936	London Residence suggests sending Philby to Spain as freelance journalist; Centre approves; gets letters of intent to publish from British newspapers.	7/63	
January 1937	Philby goes to Paris, where he receives 2 weeks' training in codes, contact addresses, targets and Nationalist operations. NKVD provides the funds.	7/63	Seale uses autumn as departure date (1/86–9); Borovik says January 1937 and cites cables from Centre.
3 Feb. 1937	Philby leaves for Spain; overt mission as freelance reporter; clandestine mission to arrange Franco assassination.	4/233; 1/87 7/68	Costello and Tsarev confirm this date in *Deadly Illusions*, p. 166.
5 May 1937	Several of Philby's articles supporting Franco are published in Britain. Sends information on troop movements to letter drop in Paris in secret writing.	1/90 7/69	Seale credits Philby with an article on Guernica, but it was written by Philby's predecessor. (7/108) The secret address Philby learns later was the Soviet Embassy.
24 May 1937	Philby returns to London on NKVD instructions. With his father's help, he sends unsolicited article to *The Times*. It is published and he is hired to return to Spain as its correspondent to Franco.	1/90 7/87–91	

10 June 1937	Philby leaves for Spain via Paris.	7/93	Tsarev reports that Alexander Orlov, Philby's contact in Spain, told him never to contact him by phone because of his stammer.
Summer 1937	Philby becomes lover of actress Francis Doble; affair lasts 2 years.	7/111	He later tells Borovik that Litzi was aware of the affair.
31 Dec. 1937	Philby wounded by Soviet artillery while covering battle; 3 of his companions are killed.	1/96–8 7/97–9	
2 March 1938	Franco awards Philby Red Cross of Military Merit for exposing himself to the dangers of war.	1/98	
August 1939	Philby returns to England on 3 weeks' holiday.	1/103	Cookridge (6/61) has Philby being assigned to Berlin after returning from Spain.
3 Sept. 1939	Philby meets Aileen Furse, who was to become his second wife, at the home of Flora Solomon while he was on leave.	5/172; 1/112	Others (see references) have put this date in 1937 and 1940. But Philby wrote to Phillip Knightley on 28 March 1980 correcting the 1940 date in Boyle's *Climate of Treason*, adding that it 'was a date well remembered'.

Date(s)	Event	Source(s)	Comment(s)
September 1939	Philby sent to France to cover the BEF for *The Times*. Soviet case-officer reminds Philby his long-term mission is to penetrate British Intelligence.	1/105 7/155	
December 1939	Philby is disillusioned by Hitler-Stalin Pact and Soviet purges of his case officers; asks himself if he is aiding the Fascists. Misses meetings with NKVD.	7/xii	For more, see Knightley's Introduction to Borovik.
Early 1940	GRU/NKVD defector Walter Krivitsky debriefed by MI5. He tells of British journalist in Spain during the Civil War who was a Soviet agent assigned to kill Franco.	7/122 4/233	Some authors have written that Krivitsky named the correspondent for *The Times*, but Philby told Borovik that Krivitsky didn't know the newspaper involved.
23 Feb. 1940	After several missed scheduled meetings, Centre breaks contact with Philby.	7/146–9	
21 May 1940	Philby returns to England from France.	1/110	
1 June 1940	Philby attempts to re-establish contact with NKVD in a letter passed through Maclean.	7/150	

Date	Event	Ref	Note
4 June 1940	NKVD (Sudoplatov) orders no contact.	7/151	Philby is left to wonder why.
11 June 1940	Philby returns to France, but things fall apart too quickly to remain.	1/110; 7/142	
13 June 1940	Philby goes back to England, this time to stay. On the return trip he meets *Daily Express* correspondent Esther Marsdon-Smedley, who, Philby believes, nominated him to SIS.	1/111 7/156–7	This contradicts the conventional wisdom that Burgess was responsible for Philby's entry into MI6.
Summer 1940	Applies for a job at GC&CS; is rejected as over-qualified.	1/117	Seale says at NKVD urging; Borovik says on his own, according to KGB Philby file.
End June 1940	Leslie Sheridan meets Philby at the War Ministry regarding *special work*.	7/158	Captain Sheridan was a British army officer seconded to MI6.
July 1940	Philby joins SIS Section D; assigned to work for Burgess.	1/127	Page *et al.* put the date at August 1940 (8/109).
19 July 1940	SOE created; Section D abolished.	9/20–1	Burgess was fired; Philby retained.
December 1940	Philby assigned to SOE London and subsequently to the training centre at Beaulieu to instruct in underground propaganda; his slogan: 'Germany is the main enemy.'	2/12–15 1/132	Cunningham, *Beaulieu*, p. 53.

Date(s)	Event	Source(s)	Comment(s)
December 1940	NKVD, learning of Philby's employment by SIS, re-establishes contact and he reports on MI6 organisation and operations throughout war.	7/153–4	For samples of the extraordinarily detailed reports Philby filed, see West and Tsarev, *The Crown Jewels*, pp. 294–345.
September 1941	Philby assigned to MI6, Section V (D), counter-espionage, then at St Albans; responsible for Iberia and Atlantic Islands.	1/134 10/312–13	
Spring 1942–June 1944	NKVD CI analyst, Yelena Modrzchinskaya, questions Philby reports that there are no MI6 agents in the Soviet Union; he remains under suspicion of being an MI6 plant until June 1944.	7/196 7/232 10/159	Modrzchinskaya suspected all the Cambridge agents. In general, their material was just too good for such inexperienced agents she reasoned; they must be provocations.
Autumn 1942	Section V (D) area responsibilities increased to include North Africa and Italy. Philby gets his sister a job in MI6/CI as filing clerk.	2/157 7/207	
April 1943	OSS X-2 element arrives in UK to establish liaison with MI6; by June	2/157 11/263	OSS X-2 sets up and trains; begins work on 15 June 1943, not 1942 as in the

412

Date	Event	Citation	Notes
1943	it is functional.		*MSW* chronology (p.260, US edn; p. 157, UK edn). The latter states Philby married Aileen in 1942; also incorrect.
Winter 1943–4	Philby's section moves to Ryder Street, London, where he first meets James Angleton, then very junior to Philby.	2/157; 8/181	The US edition chronology does not mention the move. The level of contact with Angleton varies with the source. Philby told Borovik it was short and casual.
June–July 1944	When Philby selected to head a new section IX responsible for Soviet CE, his reputation is completely rehabilitated at NKVD Centre.	2/157; 12/437 7/233–4	The chronology in the US edition of *MSW* puts this event in 1945.
7 Aug. 1945	Philby nominated for the Order of the Red Banner, but it is not approved at this time.	7/249	
August 1945	KGB Colonel K. Volkov offers to defect in Istanbul and reveal Soviet penetrations of MI6; Philby sent to meet him; Volkov gone by time Philby arrives.	1/179–80 7/238	Philby later comments that this and the Krivitsky case were two close calls.
September 1945	Philby sends names of GRU agents revealed by defector Igor Gouzenko to Moscow.	7/239	Weinstein, *Haunted Wood*, p. 104.

Date(s)	Event	Source(s)	Comment(s)
20 Nov. 1945	Philby reports to his NKGB contact that Soviet agent Elizabeth Bentley has defected to the FBI.	24/104	Bentley's first debriefing did not end until 30 November 1945.
1 Jan. 46	Philby awarded OBE.	1/174	
Summer 1946	Philby gets MI6 permission to contact his wife Litzi, now a known Communist, and get a formal divorce. Final decree granted 17 Sept. 1946.	1/181–2	
25 Sept. 1946	Philby marries Aileen.	1/173	Aileen was pregnant at the time.
Oct.–Dec. 1946	Philby undergoes SIS espionage training.	7/251	In preparation for assignment as Head of Station, Turkey.
February 1947	Philby posted to Istanbul as Head of Station.	13/142; 1/184	
August 1949	Philby told of posting to Washington. In London, he is briefed in what would become known as the VENONA decrypts and realises Maclean is in danger; also briefed on joint USA/UK Albanian operations.	7/255–6	He also worked with James McCargar

414

September 1949	Philby arrives in Washington DC as liaison officer to CIA and FBI.	2/110–15; 1/194–6
	on the Albanian covert action.	
	Aileen was not pleased with this development.	
August 1950	Burgess posted to Washington; lives with the Philbys.	1/208
17 April 1951	Maclean under MI5 surveillance in London; Philby's Soviet control tells him to alert Maclean through Burgess.	12/546–7 12/549 2/128ff.
	Philby tells Burgess to help Maclean defect to the Soviets, but warns Burgess, 'Don't you go too,' since that would throw suspicion on Philby.	
1 May 1951	Burgess sails for London on the *Queen Mary*.	12/550
	Meets his old friend Maclean in London; plans defection.	
25 May 1951	Burgess and Maclean defect to the Soviet Union.	14/327
10 June 1951	Philby recalled by SIS; told he can't return because of a letter from DCI stating he is a suspect too.	14/336
Mid-July 1951	Philby questioned by Dick White (MI5), who concludes he is guilty, but Philby won't confess and there is no proof.	15/393
	Philby then asked to resign by 'C'. Given £4,000.00, part in installments, to cushion departure. Seale writes that former deputy to 'C', V. Vivian, said Philby told Menzies, 'I think you had better let me go' (1/218). Macmillan's statement says Philby was asked to resign. (15/417) See also Bower, pp. 132–4.	

Date(s)	Event	Source(s)	Comment(s)
Nov. 1951– Feb. 1952	Philby undergoes a series of MI5 interrogations by H.J.P. Milmo and William Skardon (Arthur Martin attends), at the request of 'C'.	2/142–4; 1/223	
Feb.- June 1952	Philby searches for a job in Madrid; then applies to several London firms; has an affair with a senior civil servant in London.	1/224	See also Bristow, p. 265, who saw Philby when he made a trip to Madrid for the *Observer*. She had a son by him that he never recognised.
June 1952–mid-1953	Finds position with London trading firm. Aileen writes to Foreign Office that Philby is the third man, but is not believed; she becomes an alcoholic.	1/224–6	
2–3 April 1954	KGB Colonel Vladimir Petrov and wife Evdokia defect in Canberra; name Burgess and Maclean as Soviet agents; information not made public for a while.	15/405	
mid-1953–March 1955	Philby agrees with André Deutsch to write memoirs, but never does; advance repaid by Tommy Harris.	1/224	Harris was an MI5 friend Philby had known during the war; some say his closest friend. Harris was suspected as a Soviet agent too, but died in a car crash in the 1960s.

August 1954	Philby works briefly for *Fleet Street Letter* writing diplomatic stories for £15.00 per week.	1/224
Summer 1955	KGB sends £5,000.00 to Philby through Anthony Blunt.	16/231–2
18 Sept. 1955	Petrov's evidence naming Burgess and Maclean as KGB agents is made public in UK; Philby not mentioned by name; rumours circulate.	15/408
	Brown and other authors write that FBI director Hoover precipitated the question.	
25 Oct. 1955	MP Marcus Lipton asks the PM whether he has decided to cover up Philby's dubious third-man activities.	15/412
7 Nov. 1955	The Parliamentary response to Lipton's question by Foreign Secretary Macmillan clears Philby.	15/417
8 Nov. 1955	Philby holds victory news conference in his mother's flat; challenges Lipton to repeat his comments in public; Lipton apologises.	15/419
Jan.-July 1956	Philby invited to Ireland to ghostwrite portions of the W.E.D. Allen family history; he had served with Allen in Turkey.	15/419–20; 1/233
	See West (ed.), *The Faber Book of Espionage*, pp. 557–61, for a selection written by Philby.	

Date(s)	Event	Source(s)	Comment(s)
August 1956	Philby arrives in Beirut as stringer for the *Economist* and the *Observer*, an arrangement engineered by his former colleagues in SIS. Lives at first with his father.	1/235; 1/240	
September 1956	Philby meets Eleanor Pope Brewer, wife of the *New York Times* correspondent in the Middle East; they quickly become lovers.	1/241	
1 April 1957–19 May 1958	Philby publishes 11 articles on Arab matters in the *New Republic*.	RGPL	See bibliography, pp. 389–90.
1957–63	Philby uses pseudonym of Charles Garner for 'trivial' stories that might reflect negatively on his reputation as a serious journalist.	1/238	
December 1957	Aileen dies in London. Eleanor goes home to get a divorce.	1/243	Philby leaves his children in England in school; they visit during vacations.
24 Jan. 1959	Philby and Eleanor are married while he is on leave in London; I.I. (Tim) Milne attends.	1/243	Milne was a classmate of Philby's at Westminster, had travelled with him in Europe on vacations and served with him in MI6 during the war. Their married life appeared happy to

Date	Event	Ref	Note
30 Sep. 1960	Philby's father dies during a visit with his son and his new wife in Beirut.	1/249	journalist friends, though both drank heavily. (See Bristow and Downton entries in biblio.)
April 1961	SIS officer George Blake arrested in London as KGB agent.	1/251	He was convicted and sentenced to 42 years, a judgment he thought harsh since the atomic spy Fuchs had received only 15. After six years Blake escaped and made his way to Moscow, where he still lives.
May 1961–Aug. 1962	Philby travels as journalist throughout Middle East.	1/253–4	
August 1962	Flora Solomon tells MI5 about Philby's attempt to recruit her in the 1930s for Soviet work.	19/293–4; 18/172	See Solomon's account in her memoirs (bibliography, p. 395).
September 1962	Philby learns of KGB officer Golitsyn's defection in December 1961.	1/254	Wright states (18/184) that Golitsyn used the name STANLEY; Bower (19/290) says he did not; Wright's assertions to the contrary are an invention.
Oct.-Nov. 1962	Philby travels to Sanaa, Yemen, after ruler is overthrown; takes revolutionaries' side in his reporting.	1/256	See Elliott account in *Never Judge a*

Date(s)	Event	Source(s)	Comment(s)
December 1962	New evidence necessitates that Nicholas Elliott go to Beirut to interrogate Philby about his service as a KGB agent and get confession.	1/257	*Man by his Umbrella.*
12 Jan. 1963	In a Beirut safe-house, Nicholas Elliott accuses Philby of being a Soviet agent; offers immunity. Philby asks for time to think about it.	19/297	Philby's and Elliott's versions of their conversations differ. Philby insisted he did not spy after 1949. See Bower, 19/299. Borovik (7/3) writes that Philby was surprised when Elliott insisted that he had only spied for the Soviets until 1949; Bower writes (19/299) that Philby insisted to Elliott that he spied only until 1949.
13 Jan. 1963	Philby meets Elliott, accepts immunity and hands him a 2-page written confession of early years as agent; says he stopped in 1949. Provides 2 more pages the next day.	19/299–300	
16 Jan. 1963	Elliott returns to London with the confession. Philby arranges meeting with his KGB contact, does not tell him he has confessed, tells of future interrogations; the Centre decides to exfiltrate Philby; the final decision is his.	19/300–1 20/97	
19 Jan. 1963	Philby files last story from Beirut to the *Observer*.	1/261	Fails to appear at a dinner party after

23 Jan. 1963	Philby goes missing in Beirut.	19/302 telling Eleanor he would be late.
27 Jan. 1963	Philby arrives in Soviet Union on the freighter *Dolmatova*. Gets a physical in Moscow. Begins 3-year debriefing.	13/219 Philby told Phillip Knightley, in their 1988 Moscow discussions, that the 13/226 information he provided the KGB with in 1963 was not out of date even then.
1 March 1963	Eleanor receives a cable from Cairo signed H. Philby, saying Philby is on assignment. The first contact she has had.	1/265
3 March 1963	The *Observer* acknowledges it doesn't know where Philby is.	1/265
29 March 1963	PM Heath announces that Philby is missing.	19/305
3 June 1963	*Izvestiya* announces that Philby is in Yemen.	1/265
June 1963	*Newsweek* announces that Philby was 'The Third Man' and is now in Russia'.	1/266
1 July 1963	PM Heath concedes to Parliament that Philby was indeed the third man and a KGB agent.	1/305

Date(s)	Event	Source(s)	Comment(s)
30 July 1963	Philby granted Soviet citizenship and political asylum; given passport and awarded a lifetime pension.	1/305 7/360	
19 Aug. 1963	Burgess dies; leaves Philby library and £2,000.00.	13/222	Knightley says Burgess's library contained 4,000 volumes. If so, less than 2,500 made it to Philby's flat; some of those were sold at the Sotheby's auction.
26 Sept. 1963	Eleanor arrives in Moscow. Writes (for KGB) a detailed account of her contacts since Philby left in January.	13/221, 228	
Summer–November 1964	Eleanor returns to the USA to visit her daughter. State Department seizes her passport for 5 months. Philby begins 5-year affair with Melinda Maclean.	13/227	Philby wrote to her to demand her passport be returned. She did, it was.
1964	Yuri Modin assigned to help Philby write the official KGB version of his autobiography.	16/257	Modin writes that Philby lived three flights up; it was six. He said he did not want to give the real location away.
1965	Philby 'polishes' Gordon Lonsdale's memoirs, SPY.	1/269	Brown says she left on 18 May 1964;

18 May 1965	Eleanor leaves Moscow forever with Philby in hospital. Writes *The Spy I Loved*, and dies in 1968 just after its publication.	13/229	Knightley is correct, according to Eleanor's memoirs.
10 Aug. 1965	Philby receives Order of the Red Banner.	1/269	Brown dates the award in April 1964; Philby told Knightley he only received one; Rufina Philby said it was 1965 after his OBE was withdrawn.
Autumn 1965–Spring 1967	KGB suggests he write his memoirs using his debriefing as a starting point.	13/230	
Spring 1967	Philby begins work on his book, *My Silent War*.	16/259	The start date varies with different authors.
November 1967	The *Sunday Times* publishes first in a series of articles on Philby by Insight Team.	19/230	The *Observer* starts a Philby series on the same day.
17 Dec. 1967	*Times* journalist Murray Sayle publishes a story of his recent meeting with Philby in Moscow at the Minsk Hotel to discuss Philby's proposal not to publish *My Silent War* if the Cohens are released from British jail; offer rejected by Foreign Office.	13/231 *Sunday Times*, 17 Dec. 1967	

Date(s)	Event	Source(s)	Comment(s)
18 Dec. 1967	*Izvestiya* publishes first story in the Soviet press about Philby, 'Hello, Comrade Philby'. *New York Times* publishes English version, 19 Dec. 1967.	*Izvestiya*, 18 Dec. 1967	
January 1968	*The Spy I Loved* by Eleanor Philby published in London.	*Sunday Times*, 14 Jan. 1968	Review by Hugh Trevor-Roper.
February 1968	*PHILBY: The Spy Who Betrayed a Generation*, by Bruce Page, David Leitch and Phillip Knightley, published in London.	*Observer*, 18 Feb. 1968	Review by Graham Greene.
April 1968	*My Silent War* published in New York.	*New York Review of Books*, 9 May 1968	Review by Hugh Trevor-Roper.
September 1968	*My Silent War* published in London and Paris.	*Esquire*, Sep. 1968	Review by Graham Greene.
1969–Autumn 1970	KGB neglects Philby without explanation; he becomes despondent, starts heavy drinking and attempts suicide during this period.	13/236–7 23/290	Confirmed in interviews with Modin, Kalugin, Kirpichenko, Kondrashev and Lyubimov. Perry puts the suicide attempt two years earlier, but it doesn't fit the facts as told by Philby's case officers then and later; those

Date	Event	Reference	Notes
Autumn 1970	George Blake and his wife Ida introduce Philby to Rufina. With her help, he begins to turn his personal life around.	13/236; Rufina's memoirs	interviewed above.
October-November 1971	Andropov initiates programme to attract defectors and make current defectors the envy of Western KGB agents.	21/132	This effort was in reaction to the Lyalin defection in London that caused 105 Soviet intelligence officers to become *persona non grata*.
19 Dec. 1971	Philby marries Rufina.	13/237; Rufina's memoirs	
Early 1972	KGB General Oleg Kalugin ordered to re-establish working contact with Philby, give him work, increase his pay and rehabilitate him. Flat renovated.	21/135–7	
1972–80	Philby consults on various active measures operations by Gennady-X and Mikhail Lyubimov.	21/136 Lyubimov chapter above	These sessions were generally in the

Date(s)	Event	Source(s)	Comment(s)
1972–88	Philby and Rufina travel within Soviet Union and one country outside Soviet Union each year, e.g. Bulgaria, Hungary and East Germany. Philby holds periodic orientation sessions with KGB officers being assigned to English-speaking countries.	21/137–8	latter part of the year and involved a few English-speaking officers, who were to be assigned to English-speaking countries.
1976	KGB establishes $1,000.00 per year fund for Lyubimov to purchase Western goods for Philby.	Lyubimov chapter above	
July 1977	Philby gives first and only lecture at KGB Foreign Intelligence Directorate headquarters (the Centre) at Yasenevo.	Interviews with Kobaladze, Kirpichenko	Kalugin's book puts the date at July 1976, but in his talk Philby refers to 'the current year, 1977'. Borovik has the lecture taking place at the KGB Officers' Club in Moscow, but General Kobaladze confirmed to this author that it was Yasenevo. Philby only went to the KGB Club after he died.
1978	Philby becomes motivational adviser to Soviet national hockey team.	13/238	
Autumn 1978	Philby and Rufina travel to Cuba.	Rufina's memoirs	

426

Date	Event	Reference	Notes
1980	*My Silent War* published in Russian. Philby awarded Order of Friendship of Peoples by Andropov.	13/238 21/252	
14 Aug. 1981	Philby addresses East German foreign intelligence service (HVA) in East Berlin; guest of Markus Wolf.	Interview with Markus Wolf	
1982	Philby receives the Order of Lenin.	22/610	Brown notes the Order is the 4th highest Soviet decoration. Philby told Knightley that it was 'equivalent to a knighthood'.
6 March 1983	Maclean dies in Moscow.	13/242; 23/362	
June 1985	Borovik begins 3 years of tape-recorded conversations with Philby.	7/ix	
September 1986	Graham Greene visits Philby in Moscow for the first time.	13/246	The meeting with Greene was arranged by Borovik (7/370–2).
September 1987	Greene visits the Philbys for a second time.	Rufina's memoirs	
October 1987	Philby and Rufina travel to Riga, Latvia, where he participates in a TV documentary.	Rufina's memoirs	They stayed 6 days and the material was

Date(s)	Event	Source(s)	Comment(s)
18 Jan. 1988	Phillip Knightley and his wife arrive to interview and visit Philby in Moscow.	13/14	used in Knightley's book, *PHILBY: K.G.B. Masterspy*.
February 1988	Greene visits Philby for the last time.	Rufina's memoirs	
11 May 1988	Philby dies.	13/259	Only Yuri Kobaladze and Michael Bogdanov, both former seminar students, visited Rufina to console her the day Philby died.
12–13 May 1988	Philby lies in state in the KGB Officers' Club behind the Lubyanka; a memorial service is held there with Chairman Kryuchkov and other senior dignitaries in attendance.	21/146	
13 May 1988	Philby buried in Kuntsevo Cemetery	13/259	The press was allowed to attend.

428

Unless otherwise stated, see bibliography for publishing details.

1 Patrick Seale and Maureen McConville, *PHILBY: The Long Road to Moscow*.

2 Kim Philby, *My Silent War*.

3 Philby's unpublished memoirs, part 2, pages 206–43. While *MSW* puts his return to London in May (1/156), in his unpublished memoirs Philby makes it late April and mentions attending the May Day parade in Camden Town.

4 Christopher Andrew and Oleg Gordievsky, *KGB: The Inside Story of its Foreign Operations from Lenin to Gorbachev*, p. 233.

5 E. H. Cookridge, *The Third Man*.

6 Flora Solomon and Barnet Litvinoff, *Baku to Baker Street: The Memoirs of Flora Solomon*.

7 Genrikh Borovik, *The Philby Files: The Secret Life of the Master Spy – KGB Archives Revealed*, edited with an introduction by Phillip Knightley.

8 Bruce Page, David Leitch and Phillip Knightley, *PHILBY: The Spy Who Betrayed a Generation* (London: Penguin Books, 1969, revised edn).

9 Nigel West, *Secret War: The Story of SOE* (London: Hodder & Stoughton, 1992).

10 Nigel West and Oleg Tsarev, *The Crown Jewels: The British Secrets at the Heart of the KGB Archives*.

11 Robin Winks, *Cloak and Gown Scholars in America's Secret War*, p. 263.

12 John Costello, *Mask of Treachery*.

13 Phillip Knightley, *PHILBY: K.G.B. Masterspy*.

14 Verne W. Newton, *The Cambridge Spies: The Untold Story of Maclean, Philby, and Burgess in America*.

15 Andrew Boyle, *The Climate of Treason: Five Who Spied for Russia*.

16 Yuri Modin, *My Five Cambridge Friends*.

17 W.E.D. Allen, *David Allens: The History of a Family Firm 1857–1957/ Reader's Guide to Periodical Literature, 1957–8*.

18 Peter Wright, *Spycatcher: The Candid Autobiography of a Senior Intelligence Officer*.

19 Tom Bower, *The Perfect English Spy: Sir Dick White and the Secret War 1935–90*.

20 Nicholas Elliott, *With My Little Eye*.

21 Oleg Kalugin, *The First Directorate: My 32 Years in Intelligence and Espionage against the West*.

22 Anthony Cave Brown, *Treason in the Blood: H. St John Philby, Kim Philby and the Spy Case of the Century*.

23 Roland Perry, *The Fifth Man*.

Index

430

Index

Index